Sol LeWitt

The Writer Within

Lary Bloom's Connecticut Notebook

Something Personal

Alone Together

Letters from Nuremberg (with Christopher J. Dodd)

The Test of Our Times (with Tom Ridge)

The Ignorant Maestro (with Itay Talgam)

When the Game is on the Line (with Rick Horrow)

Twain's World (editor and contributor)

A Still, Small Voice (contributor)

Conversations with Yusef Komunyakaa (contributor)

The Book That Changed My Life (contributor)

This New England (contributor)

Miles Ahead (with Bill Andresen)

Ensign-Bickford 1936–2011

A

DRIFTLESS CONNECTICUT

SERIES BOOK

This book is a 2019 selection in the

Driftless Connecticut Series, for an

outstanding book in any field on a

Connecticut topic or written by a

Connecticut author.

Sol LeWitt

A LIFE OF IDEAS

LARY BLOOM

WESLEYAN UNIVERSITY PRESS

Middletown, Connecticut

Wesleyan University Press
Middletown CT 06459
www.wesleyan.edu/wespress
© 2019 Lary Bloom
All rights reserved
Manufactured in the United States of America
Designed by Rich Hendel
Typeset in Utopia and Owen fonts by
Passumpsic Publishing

The Driftless Connecticut Series is funded by the
Beatrice Fox Auerbach Foundation Fund
at the Hartford Foundation for Public Giving.

Library of Congress Cataloging-in-Publication Data available upon request
Hardcover ISBN: 978-0-8195-7868-6
Ebook ISBN: 978-0-8195-7870-9

5 4 3 2 1

TO SUZANNE

CONTENTS

Illustrations follow page 138

INTRODUCTION

In June 2011, four years after Sol LeWitt's death, *Vanity Fair* published
a short piece that became a call to biographical action. A photograph
showed LeWitt in 1961 in his studio, a rundown heap of a place on Manhattan's Lower East Side — the neighborhood where he and his circle of
rebellious peers tore art down to its basics and started over again. The
text beneath the picture was written by Ingrid Sischy, the former editor
of Andy Warhol's *Interview Magazine*:[1]

> Ask any artist who his or her secretly favorite artist is. Chances are
> the answer will be Sol LeWitt, a pioneer of both minimalism and
> conceptual art, whose wall drawings, photographs, and sculptures
> . . . have a commonsense beauty. When LeWitt died . . . there was
> a recognition among art-world insiders that one of the greats had
> gone, but the commendations were all very quiet — like the man
> himself. Prediction: Time will bring LeWitt the broader accolades
> that are his due . . . LeWitt was everything we expect of an artist
> but all too rarely get these days: stubborn, generous, iconoclastic,
> uninterested in money — other than giving it away to help other
> artists — suspicious of power, and as visionary as anyone who ever
> made art.[2]

Paradox is at work here. Reflecting its title, *Vanity Fair* lavishes attention on those who seek it, not on people such as LeWitt who avoid the
limelight. In this case, though, limelight avoidance is what landed the
artist on the magazine's pages. Indeed, LeWitt himself created the primary obstacle to the level of recognition that Sischy argues he deserves.

The Connecticut native left us at least two contradictory legacies: a
radiant body of work and a faint self-portrait. The latter — his refusal to
participate in the culture of celebrity — is the source of Sischy's premise. The market for contemporary art benefits from public awareness of
artists' personalities and intimacies. In the case of LeWitt, though most

fans know of his revolutionary campaign to change the definition of art, few know anything about his private life (or how it influenced his work) or could have picked him out in a crowded gallery in New York, São Paulo, Sydney, Venice, Düsseldorf, Tokyo, or London.

When the artist attended exhibition openings, he was the quiet and burly fellow in the corner who wore a sport coat with no tie. By choice he was the wallflower, the man with the bald pate whose pleasantly round visage, circular eyeglasses, and tolerant smile hid his distaste for party chatter and art speak. Even at the height of his long career, he never fit the image of the ego-driven artist in need of constant adulation. On party nights, he preferred to stay at home to watch a televised baseball game; read a book of history or philosophy; or listen to one of his more than 4,000 tapes of classical music, jazz, and opera with the volume turned up because of his partial hearing loss. All of that was more attractive than making small talk. As his wife, Carol, once said in regard to his tolerance for public events, "Sol doesn't *do* fun."[3]

He also didn't do the rituals of self-aggrandizement. He frustrated photographers and interviewers intent on prying into his life, arguing that it had nothing to do with his art. In the early 1970s, when an Italian magazine asked for a photograph, LeWitt sent a picture of his dog.[4] When in his later years he had an opening in Perugia, Italy, and balked at going, one of his assistants took his pooch instead.[5] Patrons wanted to know the man behind a reinvention of art making — the *Los Angeles Times* referred to him as the figure "who changed art internationally"[6] —but this reinventor, according to the *New Yorker*'s art critic Peter Schjeldahl, was an artist of "militant anti-personality."[7]

LeWitt's primary impact on contemporary art was his insistence that the role of the artist is that of a thinker instead of a craft master, and that the product of the mind is more significant than that of the hand. The artist's task, LeWitt argued, is to develop the scope, purpose, and site-specific impact of the work rather than focus on its execution, which he considered "perfunctory."[8] For centuries, it had been the practice of artists, with rare exceptions, to make compositional decisions as they worked. For his major pieces, LeWitt made all decisions before a drop of acrylic paint or an element of sculpture was ever applied. And even then, it was other artists who applied them, not LeWitt. "The idea," he wrote, "becomes the machine that makes the art."[9] Until his ideas took hold, critics assessed art primarily by examining art as a physical object, not the idea that produced it.[10]

LeWitt created in the same manner as an architect or composer does, in effect providing only blueprints or scores and hiring multitudes of young artists to finish and install what he had conceived. His oeuvre was vast, consisting of more than 1,250 wall drawings, many of them measured in yards and boldly colored; hundreds of sculptures that he referred to as structures, as a way to demystify art; photography that turned ordinary images into theme-driven statements; an uncountable number of gouaches (because he gave so many away); and books published to promote and distribute the work of colleagues to the general public. In a subjective field like art, there is no reliable way to measure one artist's output versus another, but the curator Gary Garrels tried in 2000: "LeWitt's fecundity is staggering. Perhaps not since Picasso has an artist worked with such relentlessness and range."[11]

At the same time that he created opportunities and challenges for young artists, he did the same for viewers of contemporary art. For example, through his work on variations on open cubes, he let viewers note the elements that were missing and complete the work in their heads. Cubism had introduced the idea,[12] but only in painting and, notably, not using cube shapes.

LeWitt came into his own when the art market began to rival other forms of investment and many artists, particularly the later abstract expressionists and pop art innovators, became media darlings. Some also prospered by branding themselves—doing work over and over again once they had discovered a way to earn money in a competitive art market. LeWitt considered reliance on formula to be lethal to the creative soul. On the effect of market-driven pressures, LeWitt said, "The artist is seen like a producer of commodities, like a factory that turns out refrigerators."[13] Yet by doing things his own way and ceaselessly pushing himself to come up with new ideas that by their nature undermined the idea of branding, he managed to earn millions—and gave a good deal of that fortune away to younger artists and to causes in which he believed.

Following his death from the effects of colon cancer in April 2007, the media focused on his professional achievements and made only sketchy references to anything personal. The obituary in the *New York Times* called him "a lodestar of American art."[14] *Pravda* quoted Joanna Marsh, the Wadsworth Atheneum Museum of Art's curator of contemporary art, who referred to LeWitt as "one of the most influential artists of the 20th century."[15] The *Guardian* said, "He left in his wake a gaggle of the world's most ponderous art critics disputing over whether he was a conceptualist or a minimalist or both, while he himself bent his own rules with wiggly lines, irregular geometrical shapes, and even splotches of paint."[16]

LeWitt contributed to the confusion. Among his contradictory (and often wry) views was the belief that "it's not too important what art looks like."[17] He also said that he preferred the kind of art that is "smart enough to be dumb."[18] When given credit for the innovation of wall drawings, he responded, "I think the cave men came first."[19] (The cave men, however, valued permanence, and LeWitt did not.) His sense of humor and highly personal use of words were examples of demystification and the art of the twist: "The wall drawing is a permanent installation, until destroyed," he said, and "irrational thoughts should be followed absolutely and logically."[20] It seemed at times as if he was the art world's satirist. When he gave interviews, he punched holes in the usual response script. Asked about the legacy of his native Hartford, Connecticut, a city that had once had a rich cultural identity, he responded, "Everyone is from somewhere."[21] He called out those who relied on art speak, "a secret language that art critics use when communicating with each other through the medium of art magazines."[22]

In 1993, the UK critic Rachel Barnes used the term "LeWitticisms" to describe his way of using language to break down barriers.[23] The natural enjoyment of art, LeWitt argued, is impeded by critical assessments that are heavy on jargon and short on clarity. He loathed such snobbish and dense interpretation and thought of art as universal: "Every person alive is an artist in some way. The way he thinks or walks or dresses or acts. We're all making art as we live. You furnish your house the way you want. You arrange your day, if you can, the way you want."[24] About critics, he said: "Artists teach critics what to think. Critics repeat what the artists teach them." He also commented, "When artists make art they shouldn't question whether it is permissible to do one thing or another."[25]

LeWitt's playfulness with language sometimes replaced one form of confusion with another, as his logical mind worked out mathematical formulas (even though he insisted he was not particularly interested in math). He typically used the same words as both the title of a work and instructions to the artists who were to complete it. For example, the full title for *Wall Drawing #211*, created for the Portland (Oregon) Center for Visual Arts in 1973, is: "A line drawn from a point halfway between the midpoint of the left side and a point halfway between the center of the square and midpoint of the left side to a point halfway toward the point where two lines would cross if they were drawn from the center of the square to the midpoint of the top side, and the second line from the point halfway between the midpoint of the left side and the upper left corner to the upper right corner."[26]

But the artists he hired to install these pieces understood and were grateful both for the work and for the interest LeWitt took in their own. His crews were largely female, a continuation of his early efforts to encourage many women who challenged the bullies of what was then an overwhelmingly male profession.

Even during his early days as an artistic loner when income was meager, LeWitt promoted the art of colleagues. As time went on and his income grew, he bought or traded pieces for such work, eventually collecting thousands of pieces. He also quietly paid the rent or hospital bills for friends and tuition for their children.

At the same time, he could have made a great deal more money to spend on his many causes had he not stood up to corporate power. Though he insisted his art was not political, it may be argued that the pieces he never undertook had political overtones. He refused major commissions from corporations that offended his liberal views on social justice or that endangered public health.[27] All this earned him respect and admiration from fellow artists. The minimalist sculptor Carl Andre spoke for many when he called LeWitt "our Spinoza."[28]

LeWitt asserted that objectivity and careful planning yield contemplative art. Hence, his work was often thought to be cold, impersonal, and even anti-art—a sequel, perhaps, to the emperor's new clothes. Later, however, the public embraced it as deeply personal. Many visitors to his exhibits are stunned by what they see, and children, attracted by the vibrant colors of the huge wall drawings, gasp and stretch their arms wide in delight. As Schjeldahl wrote in 2000, "If his art is without apparent emotion, that just leaves an inviting vacuum. Love rushes in."[29]

Contradiction is at the heart of the LeWitt phenomenon and the artist himself, and that became part of my impetus to connect his life and work. The difficulty in making that connection was expressed as early as 1993, when the British art critic Richard Dorment wrote in the *Daily Telegraph*, "There are few living artists that I admire more than the American Sol LeWitt, and few more difficult to write about."[30]

■ My pursuit of the LeWitt story has its roots in the last twenty years of his life. He and I lived in the same small town, Chester, Connecticut. We both belonged to the local synagogue, Congregation Beth Shalom Rodfe Zedek, whose new building he designed,[31] and attended Wednesday morning minyan services. On Passover, our families came together to celebrate the holiday and to invite commentary on the bondage and oppression that still persists in the world. Sometimes we read from a Haggadah that I wrote with Marilyn Buel and Jil Nelson—a play in which each person present was given a role. LeWitt was often cast as God. He took the part, though he grumbled about it.

Most often, though, I saw him mornings in his studio. He was always an early riser, so by 9:00 A.M. he had already put in three hours of work and walked with his dog, Lilla, to the middle of town to buy the *New York Times*, and he could accommodate a visitor—even an unannounced one. Sometimes I watched as he attended to his tasks. Sometimes we sat and talked. He did not use these occasions to complain about the art world or difficulties with his installations. I didn't use them to express my own professional frustrations at the time, trying to keep *Northeast*, the *Hartford Courant*'s Sunday magazine, alive as newspaper economics collapsed, or to discuss the challenges I later faced in the books I was writing. We talked instead about current events, music, and literature. We compared stories about our service in the US Army Quartermaster Corps (LeWitt during the Korean War and me during the Vietnam War). We shared our passions and regrets as two rare Connecticut fans of the Cleveland Indians.[32]

On a few occasions I couldn't help asking about his work. In 2005, I saw a pencil sketch pinned to the wall behind his desk. It looked to me like a variation on a series of wall drawings he had recently created, but somehow it seemed a little more complicated, something like interwoven figure eights. "That's for a ceiling," he said, "in Reggio Emilia." I waited for more explanation, but he said only, "Maybe you can see it when you go to Italy this fall." The work would be installed on the ceiling of the reading room of the city's eighteenth-century public library. What I didn't know at the time was that I would view the completed piece before he did. A crew of mostly young Italian artists, following LeWitt's meticulous instructions, finished *Whirls and Twirls* that summer.[33] I saw it a few weeks later, but LeWitt didn't learn how his plan worked out until late 2005, when he took his last trip to Italy.[34] Several years later, one prominent Italian collector, Giuliano Gori, who had commissioned LeWitt to do site-specific work on his property in Pistoia, referred to *Whirls and Twirls* as "LeWitt's Sistine Chapel."[35] However it was labeled, its power had a great effect on me.

As a writer, if I experienced what I called a religious experience—having nothing to do with theism but instead referring to the state of being deeply moved—I inevitably wanted to bring readers into that moment and share that epiphany with them. In the case of *Whirls and Twirls*, unapologetically bold and colorful and floating above the library patrons below, I thought, "I must write about this."

But there was more that drove me to write this biography. As I see it, LeWitt transcends categories. Yes, he was a member of an elite group. But with his personal characteristics and the inspiration that resulted from them, he serves as an example for anyone who wants to create—not only painters, sculptors, musicians, and writers, but also teachers, researchers, and entrepreneurs in search of new ideas and techniques and eager to break barriers.

LeWitt once said, "You shouldn't be a prisoner of your own ideas."[36] This is not a comment limited to art styles. It is instead a call to think freely and honestly every day. Indeed, it is LeWitt's sense of authenticity in a world of moral complexities and unrepentant egotism that makes his example compelling. A comment he made to the Hartford curator Andrea Miller-Keller seemed to sum up both his ambition and his sense of humility. In response to questions she sent him in Italy in the early 1980s, he said, "I'd like to create something that I wouldn't be ashamed to show Giotto."[37]

His life story, then, should interest anyone who wants to succeed but is afraid of breaking rules. After all, shy and humble Sol LeWitt broke a rule that had held since the Renaissance—that the artist's hand is the primary force in Western art.[38]

Many of LeWitt's peers had, in his view, more natural talent and had grown up without the hardships he had faced. But to him the struggles of childhood and later made his growth as an artist possible. Without struggle, he said, greatness can't be achieved: "Talent is a curse."[39]

Even LeWitt would have agreed, if reluctantly, that his personal decisions and generosity advanced the careers of many colleagues—most significantly, the women he mentored at a time when most female artists were ignored. In part, because of his own questioning, he understood the weight of their pursuits. His support of others also created a financial substitute for the cult of personality, creating momentum through a large circle of artists who promoted each other's work.

■ The deep friendship between Sol LeWitt and Eva Hesse, as well as the relationship of their respective oeuvres, has lately has been a subject of major art exhibits and film documentaries. Both rejected long-held tenets of art, and Hesse did so within a system that shunned her. When she wrote from Germany that she was at the breaking point, LeWitt replied. The first half of his long and passionate letter (reprinted in full in chapter 6), with its forty-five consecutive gerunds (many of which would have come as news to Noah Webster), is the part that is often quoted and has even been made into a punk rock video[40] and become a performance piece for the actor Benedict Cumberbatch.[41]

The letter foreshadows the intense adventures in variation (or, as it was generally referred to, seriality) that LeWitt would later pursue, as if he were Johann Sebastian Bach (his favorite composer), not a maker of images. But it is the second half of what he wrote to Hesse, which is almost always missing in commentaries, that underscores the connection between the person making art and art itself. In it, LeWitt refers to his own doubts; like Hesse, he had considered himself an outsider.

LeWitt's struggle is metaphorical, one that can be understood outside the world of art. For example, in his letter to Hesse he delivered advice in one brief sentence that should serve everyone who yearns for self-discovery and authenticity: "You belong in the most secret part of you." For him there would be no rut, no "if I could only do what I want to do." Yet, in this contradictory man, there was another side to him, one that could be cold or dismissive.

As his longtime business manager, Susanna Singer, told me, "Yes, he was an extraordinary man, but Sol was not a saint."[42] I came across lingering resentments in other interviews. As his conceptual colleague, Lawrence Weiner, said in the documentary film *Sol LeWitt*, made by the Danish director Chris Teerink and released in 2012, "Art is made by human beings, not machines," and therefore is subject to all human frailties.[43] Scholars certainly would point out that, in regard to notable achievers, image and reality are often at odds. One might even cite a line from Tom Stoppard's *Travesties* in which the characters clash over art's meaning, and one of them remarks cynically, "The idea of the artist as a special kind of human being is art's greatest achievement."[44] Yet in the case of LeWitt, the adoration of colleagues seems not only lavish but genuine.

Some of LeWitt's frailties, to be sure, came to the fore in his romantic relationships, most significantly in his very brief first marriage. And the artist offered an unsparing self-assessment to one of his lovers, referring to himself as "old, bald, deaf, fat, pig-headed, clumsy and at times self-absorbed."[45] Yet he attracted as romantic partners some of the most accomplished women in Europe and the United States. And though much has been written about the deep friendship between LeWitt and Hesse and his influence on her work, nothing has been published that makes any significant reference to his many love interests or how they affected him.

To be sure, dozens of exhibition catalogues in a variety of languages about his work contain scholarship and ruminations about key issues of modern art. LeWitt's own writings and interviews illuminate a great number of key points about the process of making art in the modern age. But the human element makes only cameo appearances.

I subscribe in this biography to the idea I have always practiced as an editor and writer — that is, to humanize subjects and articulate the personal stakes involved in their pursuits, an approach that can make even the most arcane subjects accessible and compelling to readers.

In the case of a man at the center of a complex art revolution, such an approach seems indispensable. The critic Robert Rosenblum began his 1978 Museum of Modern Art catalogue essay for LeWitt's first retrospective this way: "Conceptual Art? The very sound of those words has chilled away and confused spectators who wonder just what, in fact, this art could be about or whether it's even visible." Rosenblum also wrote, "LeWitt's art may be steeped in his cerebral, verbal and geometric systems, as was that of so many great, as well as inconsequential, artists before him, but his impact is not reducible to words."[46]

But what is reducible to words is a story of obstacle and triumph. The artist, after all, led a purposeful and generous life. He overcame setbacks and doubt — phenomena that are nearly universal — and he mastered the delicate balance of sticking to his principles while using flexibility to his advantage. Sometimes, however, the line between sticking to principles and flexibility seemed blurred.

You will read in chapter 14 about LeWitt's seventieth birthday celebration, an event he didn't want to attend. That night at the Wadsworth Atheneum Museum of Art in Hartford, stunned guests watched as the guest of honor did all he could to ruin the party. During the low point of the evening, when the artist sabotaged the planned tributes, most invitees didn't know whether to laugh, be outraged, admire the man's singular personality, or feign concentration on their strawberry *dacquoises*.

Afterward Carol said to me, "You've got to write about this." However, I hadn't attended the event in my professional capacity at the time (as editor and columnist). Nonetheless, what had just happened ranked with other significant events in the history of America's oldest public art museum.

So I wrote a draft piece on the party and called LeWitt to tell him I had done so. His response was gruffly authentic: "Why?" I replied, "Well, I had the instinct to do so," thinking that the word "instinct" might resonate with him. But then he asked, "Do you always follow your instincts?" I thought that was an odd question, coming from a man who had a reputation for doing just that. Perhaps sensing that the question was full of irony, he changed his approach: "Well, if you've written it, the least I could do is read it." I didn't mention that journalism ethics discourage giving subjects of pieces access to advance copies to protect the work's integrity. But as it seemed unlikely that the column would ever run, considering LeWitt's outrage over it, what was the harm in showing it? I went to his studio the next morning and delivered the piece. He said he would read it in due course.

Days later, having by then embarked on a trip to Israel, I discussed the matter with our rabbi, Doug Sagal. Though much younger than LeWitt and me, Sagal was widely respected for his wisdom. At the time of our conversation, we were in Jerusalem, in the midst of a congregational tour (the LeWitts were not among the group). Sagal and I had a private moment in the hotel lobby, and I explained the background of the seventieth birthday piece and that I was wrestling with competing forces. He was silent for a moment and looked out of the window in contemplation, in the way that rabbis do. Then he turned to me and said, "Well, maybe you will publish the piece. When the right time comes." I knew what he meant.

When I next saw LeWitt several weeks later, he asked, "Are you going to run that story you wrote?"

I said, "No, I don't think so."

He replied, "Why not? I thought it was pretty good."

Welcome, then, to the world of Sol LeWitt.

Sol LeWitt

ONE

THE LIFE OF STUFF

In 1980, a book was published that can't be read. Though it consists of 128 pages, *Autobiography*[1] contains not a single word of narrative, and there is no hint on its cover as to its author. Bookstore browsers, then, can only satisfy their curiosity by opening the volume to the title page, where the mystery is solved. Sol LeWitt is the author. However, a second enigma soon becomes apparent. What is the significance of the 1,125 black-and-white photographs that follow? None of them bears a caption. Most are of ordinary items that would be found in a house or artist's studio. Each photo is the same size, three inches by three inches. There are nine on each page, in a grid formation that mirrors the artist's reliance throughout his career on the cube—a form that he admitted was uninteresting in itself, which he decided made it ideal as a building block for art.

Autobiography is the life story in pictures of the artist Sol LeWitt (what he referred to as his only self-portrait) until the age of fifty-two. In this effort, he was influenced by a relatively new literary movement beginning in the 1950s, the Nouveau Roman, which abandoned all of the accepted tenets of storytelling.[2] His contribution to the effort was to tell a story wordlessly.

This is a record of much of LeWitt's personal inventory at the time— his way of telling his own story without the intrusion of the English language or sitting for interviews that never turned out to be accurate, in his view. In these photographs, he lets the reader make sense of where he came from and where he was going. He does this without the usual documentation and mention of his milestones to that time.

For example, there is no mention of his being born in Hartford in 1928 to immigrants prominent for their achievements—his mother having been a nurse in World War I, and his father becoming one of the most respected physicians in Connecticut. To be sure, there are visual elements that refer to Abraham and Sophie LeWitt. But there is no accounting of what befell his father when his only child was just five years old, or the greatly reduced circumstances that followed in an industrial city far from Hartford not in distance but in culture. A "reader" of *Autobiography* won't come across anecdotes about Sol LeWitt's childhood in New Britain, the industrial town that spurned modern art; his years at Syracuse University, starting in 1945, when he tried to learn what he didn't want to learn; or his first trip to Europe in 1950, when his eyes were opened to the Renaissance masters Giotto and Piero della Francesca, and he saw in each ideas for the future. LeWitt surely had good stories to tell about being shipped off to the Korean War and, along the way, finding inspiration in Japan; and his first years in New York City, when he felt, as usual, an outcast yet met and dated a string of beautiful and accomplished women. At the same time, he joined the staff of the Museum of Modern Art (MoMA), helped develop a circle of young and visionary artists, and wrote his iconic "Paragraphs on Conceptual Art" and then obliterated his first wall drawing—to the horror of the gallery owner. In *Autobiography* there is no mention of the harsh criticism of his bold idea that ideas are what matters in art, not the finished piece itself. He does not document how his work caught the eyes of international dealers or when he fell in love with Italy—and then, at the age of fifty, as if right on time, was given a MoMA retrospective that had visitors raving about what they saw. And he surely does not provide details about why, in frustration, he was about to leave the city.

The book instead provides visual memories and practical details about his studio on Hester Street, in New York's desolate Lower East Side—where, illegally, he also slept. The timing of the publication was no accident. The book appeared just as LeWitt and his future wife, Carol Androccio, were planning to take up residence in Spoleto, Italy, where the artist already owned a house, and where their two daughters would be born. His life in New York City had become increasingly complex and nearly intolerable because of many professional demands. As Carol LeWitt recalled, "Sol was driven out of New York by graduate students who told him, 'I'm writing my thesis on you.' By then, he was hellbent on Italy."[3] The artist was a little more expansive, but he focused more on what he saw as New York's professional limitations. But one thing he could manage at the time was to portray a sense of order. *Autobiography*, then, provides clues about the details of the first half of his long career and of his way of living up to that point.

A man whose private life had always stayed private displayed much of it on these pages in black and white, even though not a single easily recognizable image of the author is present. Readers, then, are free to draw conclusions about the life that these pictures represent. Here are nine such conclusions:

LeWitt didn't lack for organization. There are pictures of neat shelving; cans of goods placed on top of each other; and, it might seem, enough tools to stock a small store. There is a portrait of a Stanley box cutter made in "The Hardware City," where LeWitt grew up. Pencils sit inside a Three Fruits Marmalade jar. Art pens fill a Japanese tin — a relic, perhaps, of LeWitt's first trip in 1951 to a land that inspired him. The compass surely came in handy in LeWitt's mathematical schemes for wall drawings, and the gesso may have been left over from his attempts, with hideous results (by his own accounting), at abstract expressionism.

He wasn't exactly a starving artist. His kitchen yields but a hint of his developing taste for haute cuisine. Here are Japanese tea, brewer's yeast, and Olio Castelvetrano. There are mugs on hooks, sponges in buckets, an Italian coffeemaker, a colander, an array of pots, and a nutritional chart showing "Correct Food Combining." Also, a hint — a bottle of Brunello — of his interest in Italian red wine.

He had a well-worn wardrobe. There are a slicker, a rain hat, two pairs of ice skates used in Central Park, moccasins, sneakers; slippers, boots, woolen socks neatly rolled, a backpack, and the sport coat that his cousin bought him so the artist could have something appropriate to wear to his own 1978 MoMA retrospective.

He owned no early American furniture. But he had a simple wooden chair with paint drippings all over it, an original LeWitt, an original Mies van der Rohe, and an old armchair — the kind that his physician father sat in while fretting over bills related to his real estate holdings or dreaming up another tool for surgery.

Looking at the overstuffed bookshelves, one can understand why LeWitt spent every afternoon reading. He admired the dialogue of Dashiell Hammett and Raymond Chandler and the sturdy histories of Barbara Tuchman and William Manchester. He was inspired by Lewis Carroll's imagination in *Alice in Wonderland*. And he had two helpful tomes, *The New York Times Complete*

Guide to Home Repair and one that indicated his handicap in the anticipated move to Spoleto, *Parla Italiano*.

Ephemera endured. These included postage stamps (another boyhood passion); the Manhattan telephone number of Mimi Wheeler, a flame of his in the late 1960s and early 1970s; a chart of typefaces in alphabetical order; invitations to his exhibit openings; a front page of the *New York Daily News* featuring the tragedy at Chappaquiddick of Ted Kennedy and Mary Jo Kopechne; a list of books from the nonprofit company he had founded that promotes the works of artists; and an old copy of the leftist French publication *La Liberation*, edited by Jean-Paul Sartre, for which LeWitt raised money.

For a man who was hard of hearing, he heard music. The composers included Bach, whose work occupied much space, Schubert, Beethoven, Mozart, and other famous ones, but also those less often collected: Smetana; Bloch; Villa-Lobos; Boccherini; Gluck; Britten; and the edgy ones such as Philip Glass and Steve Reich, who benefited from LeWitt's largesse.

Inspiration was all around him, including the work of Eadweard Muybridge, whose serial photography influenced LeWitt's thinking; a clipping about Robert Rauschenberg's being given an award; a poster with the wording "If you cut your foot a dead cockroach will draw out the infection"; Italian calendars; a text painting by his friend Gene Beery ("Watch this canvas. Appearing SOON an amazing painting to revolutionize visual experience, start preparing yourself to dig NOW!"); and a mezuzah on the doorpost. There are no photos of automobiles, as he never bought one for himself.

He left very personal things that could intrigue a future biographer, such as the office sign from his father's practice, saying "Doctor A. LeWitt. Walk In.," and a photo of Carol LeWitt. By 1980, the artist had been with Carol for nearly two years. Not long afterward they would have two daughters: Sophia and Eva. There is no photograph indicating LeWitt's earlier (brief and exceptionally unhappy) marriage.

Though much can be read into *Autobiography* that may stray from what LeWitt had in mind, evidence shows that he thought the work explicit enough. In an interview, he said that a much better picture of him emerges from the photographs of his Hester Street life than could be gained in any other way. If that is so, then one can surmise what also might be obvious from so much of his art—that in a world of chaos, where everything cries out for attention, artists can restore order. In *Autobiography*, for example, Carol gets as much space as a Stanley hammer. As he wrote in "Paragraphs on Conceptual Art," "To work with a plan that is pre-set is one way of avoiding subjectivity."[4]

If *Autobiography II* had ever been published—say, in the year of his death—LeWitt might have included photos that would only have heightened public curiosity. Perhaps there would be some of his studio in Spoleto, where he hosted many of the most creative people in the art world. There might be photos of his banned "peep show" installation at the Smithsonian or of the logos of the Philip Morris Company, 3M, Nestlé, or other conglomerates that offended him with their policies to the point where he rejected their huge checks. He might have shown the instructions for a piece of art that represented the first time that Christie's auctioned art with no physical presence. Or there could have been a photo indicating his challenging Germany to examine, through the lens of art, its Holocaust legacy. He might have included the design that led to his being rejected by his hometown or photos of some of the young artists he employed or influenced—including one he never met, a Portuguese man who testified in an international art magazine that LeWitt had literally saved his life. There could have been photos of intimate corners of the house in the country where he and Carol lived during the last years of his life; of the studio he built there; and of his little shadow —Eva, his younger daughter. The photos could have shown his only architectural work, the synagogue that he designed and where he became, against all of his instincts, a member of the design committee. There might have been photos of the many artists, composers, and photographers whose work he championed, such as Chuck Close, Pat Steir, Mel Bochner, Robert Ryman, Lawrence Weiner, Eva Hesse, Vera Lutter, and Romare Bearden; or of the authors who affected him personally and professionally, including Michel Butor, Karen Armstrong, and Samuel Beckett. He could have shown the experimental pills or special brownies he relied on during the advanced stages of colon cancer, evidence of the enormous art collection he and Carol had built, or a dollar bill (representing the idea of making money by not caring about making money). There might have been photos of the old friends who rallied around him during his final days or evidence of how to create art after death.

TWO

SOLLY

In May 1935, a six-year-old boy in Connecticut used red and black pencils to draw a Mother's Day card that featured a heart on the cover.[1] When he finished his work, he gave the card to the woman who read Russian novels to him in the original language, cooked him borscht with potatoes and onions, and provided other homemade comforts in a period when, much too early in life, the child learned the meaning of bereavement. The Mother's Day drawing, then, is both Sol LeWitt's oldest surviving work and a symbol of the enduring bond between a mother and son.

That rendering of a heart, however, provides little evidence that its artist was a prodigy who one day would create a new definition of art. It is a little unusual, yes—instead of a wide and ebullient heart in the style of most childhood versions, it is narrow and deep, as if stretched from top to bottom.

On the back of the card is this handwritten message: "ROSES ARE RED / VIOLETS ARE BLUE / YOU ARE THE BEST MOTHER / I EVER KNEW."

Many decades later, after the adult LeWitt was identified as a pioneer in two of art's many "isms," the critic Peter Schjeldahl said: "The Minimalists scared me to death. Except for Sol LeWitt, who must have been dropped on his head as a kid. He's the sweetest, most decent, most intelligent man in the world, and he's a minimalist. How does that work?"[2]

Dropped on his head as a kid? In a way, yes.

■ Solomon LeWitt, called "Solly" by the immediate family, was the only child of two refugees who emigrated from Russia but didn't meet until they were living in the United States. Like all new arrivals from a different culture who spoke a different language, they had much to overcome. Each, though, set examples for their child about the need for independent thinking, taking personal and professional risks, and performing *tikkun olam* (Hebrew for "repair of the world").

One piece of memorabilia from those days is a formal black-and-white photograph of a man dressed in a tailored woolen suit and waistcoat. It shows that Dr. Abraham LeWitt had angular cheekbones, an imposing forehead, a well-groomed mustache, and lips that were slightly downturned but indicated a bemused countenance.

At the time the photo was taken, circa 1930, Dr. LeWitt; his wife, Sophie; and their son lived at 3333 Main Street in Hartford, the "Insurance City," which then was one of the richest communities in the country in terms of household income.

Connecticut's capital city had had a run of good fortune that extended back into the Gilded Age, fed not only by the insurance giants Aetna, Travelers, Hartford Fire (as it was known before it became the Hartford), and others but also by the nineteenth-century publishing empire that benefited writers who remain among the city's most luminous figures: Mark Twain and his neighbor, Harriet Beecher Stowe — the author of *Uncle Tom's Cabin*. Even in the Great Depression Hartford remained a city of distinction. It was sometimes called "the Athens of America," largely because of the work and vision of A. Everett "Chick" Austin, the director of the oldest public art museum in the United States, the Wadsworth Atheneum. Indeed, members of the LeWitt family were in the audience on the night in 1934 when the museum's theater hosted the world premiere of *Four Saints in Three Acts* by Virgil Thomson and Gertrude Stein, the first opera with an all-black cast.[3]

The home of Abraham, Sophie, and Solly was two miles north of the museum. Like many of the single-family houses in Hartford's prosperous north end, the LeWitt home was spacious — occupying 2,818 square feet and containing four bedrooms and two baths[4] — reflecting Abraham's standing as a surgeon and one of the founders of Mount Sinai Hospital, then a new institution, where he served as medical director. Even then, however, Dr. LeWitt found himself under great stress, a circumstance that he well knew could exacerbate his condition — he had been diagnosed with arteriosclerosis in addition to colorectal cancer.

How much of the details of Abraham's life story were passed along from Sophie to her son is unknown, but it appears that some important information was omitted. In the artist's later years, he said that he had few memories of his father, and he was uncertain about where Abraham had been born. He thought it was Turkey, as the birth certificate specified,[5] yet there had never been any stories passed down in the family about that country. However, among the documents the family kept was a copy of a certificate from an official registry in Istanbul that listed Abraham's father, Simcho, in the year 1891:

Eligibility to vote: None
Religious Affiliation: Jew
Date and Place of Birth: Ottoman Calendar 1247 (1832/33) Austria
Trade and Qualifications and Means of Livelihood: None
Age: 60
Father's Name and place of residence: Avram
Name and Reputation: Simchi [*sic*] LeWitt
Type of Residence: House
Street No.: 23
Street: Bath House
Neighborhood: Dark Mustafa Pasha the Archer
District: 6
City: Istanbul
Permanent distinguishing mark: None
Moustache and Beard: Red Beard
Eyes: Hazel
Height: Medium.[6]

Sometime after this certificate was issued, however, the family moved from Istanbul to Palestine, taking up residence in Hebron, where Abraham was born. Thus the confusion. At the time, Palestine was a part of the Ottoman Empire, and this fact, presumably, led the artist to believe that Turkey was his father's birthplace.

Abraham LeWitt left Palestine after becoming one of the few Jews accepted to study in Russia at the Samuel Poliakov School of Mining Engineers, in Gorlovka, from which he graduated with highest honors in 1890.[7] Later that year, he and his mother, Hinda, sailed from Hamburg to Liverpool on the passenger ship *Warrington*. In Liverpool they boarded the *Pennsylvania* and sailed for New York City, where they lived with Abraham's sister, Bella, in an apartment on East Thirty-Ninth Street.

Abraham worked with his brother, Michel, in the latter's Brooklyn jewelry store, which eventually moved to New Britain.Abraham was briefly employed after that as a mining engineer near Scranton, Pennsylvania, but then, wanting to be near members of his family, took a job at Russell & Erwin Manufacturing Co. of New Britain. There, his work on cylinder locks led to patents held by the firm. But he had plans to become a physician and enrolled in the first class at the new Cornell

University Medical College in Harlem. Two years later, in 1902, the State of New York issued medical license number 4230 to Dr. Abraham Le-Witt. Once again to be near relatives, he moved back to Connecticut. In a relatively brief time, he became one of Hartford's most prominent physicians, specializing in maladies of the eyes, nose, and throat, and also practicing surgery. He invented several medical devices, including clamps used in eye surgery and a girdle harness that helped intestines heal after abdominal surgery, which led him to become one of the city's wealthier residents. He invested in real estate, particularly apartment buildings, a financial plan that worked well for a time. He intended to stay single until his mother died.

■ Sophie (a nickname for Sofia) Appell was born in 1890 in Rostov-on-Don, in western Russia. She was one of the seven children of Solomon and Elizabeth Appell. After the assassination of Tsar Alexander II in 1881, for which many Russians incorrectly blamed the Jews, pogroms proliferated in cities and villages across Russia. In 1892, Solomon parted from his wife and children to see if he could find a place in the new world for them.

Baron Maurice de Hirsch, a Jewish German banker, had devoted some of his enormous fortune to helping Eastern European Jews emigrate. Initially most of the Jews moved to Argentina, Canada, and Palestine, but many were also immigrating to the United States by the 1880s. Other charitable and humanitarian efforts were begun, and Jews from Russia began to settle on American farmland that was largely available because it was too difficult for others to till.

This is how Solomon Appell ended up in Colchester, Connecticut, along with many other Jewish farmers. By the end of the nineteenth century, his farm had become a working concern, and shortly thereafter he sent for the rest of his family. The timing was fortuitous. Soon afterward, nearly 150 citizens of Rostov-on-Don were slaughtered in a pogrom.

Sophie was sixteen years old when she left Russia for America in 1906, traveling from Hamburg with her brothers Sam, Moses, and Aaron aboard the *Graf Waldersee* (their mother would come later). In Colchester she worked on the farm, but she also studied nursing.

A little more than a decade after that she was back in Europe—France, specifically—serving as a nurse during World War I. Her three brothers, Sam, Harry, and Louis served as soldiers toward the end of the war. A story in the *Hartford Daily Courant* indicates that the Appells made one of the largest American family contributions to the war effort. The account details the service of the brothers—a quartermaster sergeant, a machine gunner, and an army hospital worker—and then offers the following description of their sister:

> Sophie Appell has done valiant service. She was graduated from Mount Sinai Hospital at Philadelphia, Pennsylvania. After being called to service, she was temporarily on duty at Cape May, N.J., General Hospital #11 and was sent from there to France. Her letters tell of the wonderful morale of the American soldiers. She expressed pride in New Britain boys with whom she came in contact. A recent letter tells of having met David Rosenberg, Fred Ward, John Storey, Edward Hayes, Joseph Farr, and John Kerin, all well-known young men of the city.
>
> That Miss Appell was popular with her associates at Camp May is evidenced by the fact that in recognition of her service overseas, they named one of their rooms in the quarters at General Hospital #11 in her honor.[8]

Later in the piece, Louis Appell is quoted on the progress of the war, and the family spirit: "Never fear. We have [them] on the run, and we will be among the first to enter Berlin. Don't worry. An Appell can always take care of himself or herself."

When Sophie returned she had received a Red Cross commendation: "Sophie Appell—foreign service certificate . . . September 1918 to August 1919. The American National Red Cross tenders this expression of sincere appreciation for the faithful and efficient services rendered by you to this organization in its work overseas connected with the great European War when you served in the Nurses' Bureau. Certificate of identity, no. 22842, Nurse, Base unit 60 at Hoboken. . . . One scar over left cheek, one mole under left eye."[9]

The unofficial record consists of postcards from the war zone. One of them indicates that in France Sophie met a suitor. But the romance wasn't going to go anywhere as he was not Jewish but a Christian from Texas, and her family objected.[10]

A year after her return, when she working as a nurse in Hartford, she met the confirmed bachelor, Abraham LeWitt, who had treated Sophie's father in his medical practice.[11] Nineteen years her senior, the forty-five-year-old the doctor was an adventurer who had traveled to

Berlin and Vienna to investigate up-to-date surgical techniques and other new methods of treatment. He had been one of the first residents of Hartford to own a high-end automobile—a Knox,[12] made in Springfield, Massachusetts—and among the first to be a victim of auto theft (someone stole the steering mechanism) and to be thrown from a car at a railroad crossing after a collision with a freighter (he suffered only minor injuries).

After his mother died in 1920, LeWitt proposed to Sophie Appell. The two were married on January 16, 1922, at the home of Rabbi Abraham Nowack, and honeymooned in Florida.

In addition to his career as a doctor, Abraham took up writing, apparently as an avocation. In a 1933 essay he foresaw a time when the automobile and incompetent or inebriated drivers would be at the heart of a great number of deaths.[13] What is exceptional about the essay is the amount of research he had done to bolster his argument.

He also wrote a short story telling, in a foreshadowing of his son's eventual passion for social justice, of a doctor faced with an ethical dilemma common in that time: how to protect a deeply distressed woman about to give birth who was unmarried at the time she conceived. The story that ends with the mother being sent off to an institution, an outcome the doctor deeply regrets.

The tale may have been based on a real Hartford incident, and it might indicate that that one night, after a hard day, Abraham at last found a way to address an issue that had troubled him—and, it may reasonably be inferred, left him with a guilty conscience. In any case, there is no doubt that Abraham's final years were stressful.

He also was unfortunate with his real estate investments—which probably led to Sol LeWitt's later expressing a reluctance to own real estate. Abraham's investments were largely in properties in Hartford's north end. Though these provided the level of income that allowed him and Sophie to travel as well as enjoy other luxuries, they also appear to have contributed to his eventually fatal medical condition. He was highly stressed as a result of at least two lawsuits filed against him, as a result of his inability to collect rent from his tenants in the heart of the Great Depression. One lawsuit was filed by the Society for Savings, a Hartford institution that had loaned Abraham money. The other, more crushing, suit was filed by his brother, Michel. On August 11, 1934, Abraham LeWitt collapsed at his home and died of a heart attack.[14]

In the following months, Sophie tried to avoid financial ruin. The only way she could manage was to try to collect rent herself: She had to go door to door begging people to pay, and hated it.[15] Eventually, she realized that she would not be able to remain in her home.

■ When young Solly made his 1935 Mother's Day card, he and his mother were living temporarily in a small apartment owned by Sophie's sister, Luba Appell. She had taken them in after Abraham's death, but she did not have substantial means either. Luba, who had lived alone, owned a small grocery store on the first floor of an apartment building, but she performed acts of charity, extending credit to those who in the midst of the Great Depression couldn't pay their bills.

The view from Aunt Luba's kitchen table in the spring of 1935 resembled New York as portrayed by painters in the Ashcan school.[16] New Britain was a city of soot, but it had jobs. During the Great Depression the number of workers fell by a third, but the city's factories still employed 11,000 men making hand tools, ball bearings, refrigerators, pots, machine parts, razor strops, coffin trimmings, and other items that had turned the city into an international destination for blue-collar workers.[17]

Downtown the sidewalks were crowded with people on their way to buy pirogues, sausages, or dark European bread; to go to the clothing shops; or to visit the Polish-language movie theater on Broad Street or the jewelry and optician shop owned by the LeWitts—members of Abraham's extended family, which owned a variety of enterprises in the city and lived in much nicer housing than Luba's. The circumstances of Sophie and Solly improved, if only modestly, when Sophie found work as a school nurse in 1936 and they moved to a second-floor apartment of their own, at 51 Cedar Street, off of West Main. The artist would recall in 1974, "I . . . remember living in a part of town that really wasn't a very good part of town. It wasn't so bad really. But I remember that people were out of work."[18]

The Cedar Street location had at least one advantage: It was within easy walking distance of the library and the New Britain Museum of American Art. Few people could afford automobiles in the 1930s. Sophie would never learn to drive, and neither would her son (though certain people in rural Italy could testify that he foolishly took the wheel of a car at least once). The art museum was a community gathering spot, as in those days admission was free—primarily as a result of the generosity of the hosiery manufacturer John Butler Talcott and the philanthropist Grace Judd Landers. And as it turned out, it wasn't the city's manufacturing that made it a national sensation during those years, but an art exhibit.

Many decades earlier, in 1851, the *Hartford Times* had described New Britain as "a moral, well-regulated community."[19] That view held for a long time. Eventually, as both a teenager and a mature adult, Sol LeWitt would offer related descriptions that put the *Times*'s observation into an artistic context — the city could stifle ideas, especially those of young artists.

In 1929, the city became the focus of a national art story. What was then called the New Britain Institute, founded to offer educational opportunities, developed a small art collection. Its first curator, Fanny J. Brown, organized an ambitious temporary exhibit that featured the words of Picasso, Matisse, Chagall, Braque, and Modigliani — a real coup for a small, working-class city. But the head of the New Britain schools' art program, Dewey Van Cott, considered the exhibit a travesty.[20]

Van Cott wrote a scathing letter to the editor of the *New Britain Herald*, arguing that works of the artists represented in the exhibit ignored "such utterly unessential things as how to handle brushes, how to draw, what the principles of good design are and what constitutes good, harmonious color."[21] The controversy earned the Hardware City a national reputation for provincialism. *ARTNews* reported that the Van Cott's criticism "might have been quoted from the Boston papers of 1913 when the Armory show invaded the sacred city."[22]

New Britain was hardly alone in its provincialism. Just nine miles away, in the more sophisticated Hartford, Chick Austin, the Wadsworth Atheneum's director, was testing the patience of the institution's trustees when he paid $399.65 for a painting by Mondrian — just one example of his devotion to modern art. In fact, the trustees were no more welcoming to expensive traditional paintings. When Austin paid a whopping $17,000 for a Caravaggio, the brilliant *Saint Francis of Assisi in Ecstasy*, an investment that secured the museum's place as a repository of important art, the board objected to his profligate spending.[23]

In such an atmosphere, the odds seemed against any young person's being inspired to think outside the rules of art as they were accepted at the time. Indeed, on the roster of native sons and daughters of New Britain who became nationally prominent, there is no prominent artist. To be sure, the city produced Walter Camp, often referred to as the "father of American football," and two national political figures

—Abraham Ribicoff, who was governor of Connecticut, a US senator, and secretary of health, education and welfare in the administration of President John F. Kennedy; and Paul Manafort, who served as chairman of Donald Trump's presidential campaign and in 2018 was convicted of several felonies. Even if adopted sons and daughters are added to the list, only one child of New Britain became an artist of international status. He was the child of a mother who never stopped doting on him and a father who never had the chance to do so.

■ When a boy loses a father at a tender age, there is often speculation about the effect of the loss and the legacy of the father. The earliest evidence shows that the young Solly seemed withdrawn. This is apparent in the testimony of childhood friends and school records. Anna Foberg, principal of Lincoln Elementary School, wrote:

> Solomon did a very good job as a traffic officer. He was pleasant, not too bossy and kept his head at all times. He watched the children do things and talked about it in the meeting instead of picking small flaws. He needs to take his work less seriously and learn to smile. He also needs to step up and take charge of things as he finds that may be needed. He is apt to do just the ordinary job until an older person shows him where he may do things on his own. He was elected to the Safety Council by the votes of 200 children's teachers of the upper grades. He was chosen second best in a group of four.[24]

Miss Brown, a teacher at the school, wrote: "Solomon is a sober little fellow. He needs to smile and enjoy other boys and girls. He does very good work but acts too old for his age. Not a very tidy housekeeper. Had to be reminded to come back from traffic and clear away his work."[25]

As years passed, however, he occasionally showed signs of an emerging sense of humor. Walter Friedenberg, Solly's boyhood friend and classmate at Central Junior High, remembers: "He was not loquacious, and his diction was slurring. But he was alert, companionable, and witty. He had a giggle. That little giggle."[26]

Friedenberg remembers the games that their group played. There was football at Walnut Creek Park and baseball wherever the kids could play it. In those games, Solly LeWitt fit in nicely.

No doubt, however, he was different from other boys. Perhaps the clearest example is his choice of which professional baseball team to follow. New Britain is halfway between New York City and Boston, and the loyalties of the Hardware City's residents always have been split between the Yankees and the Red Sox. Solly, however, supported the Cleveland Indians, whose home games were played hundreds of miles away. This wasn't because of the physical and historical connection between Connecticut and Northeastern Ohio. Solly wasn't even aware at the time that that part of Ohio had once belonged to the Constitution State — it was its Western Reserve, where Cleveland sits. He told his friends simply that a person should think for himself. And when he thought for himself, he liked the Tribe, led by the farm boy wonder, Bob Feller. He never saw the Indians play in person, and this was long before televised games. So he followed them only in radio broadcasts and the box scores and brief game accounts in the *New Britain Herald*. This loyalty earned Solly a healthy dose of abuse, something he laughed about later — but he remained an Indians fan until his death.

Entering his teens, Solly became a member of the Boy Scouts and went several days a week to Hebrew School at Temple B'Nai Yisrael, the Conservative congregation of New Britain. The city had two synagogues at the time, the other Orthodox. And in early October 1940, Solly was called to the Torah for the first time as a bar mitzvah. Among other duties, he delivered a short speech that Saturday morning. It clearly indicates the views of a boy who understood what his mother had done for him. As his cousin Celeste LeWitt would say decades later, "Sophie's whole life centered on her one child," and she never walked past him without giving him a hug.[27] Friedenberg recalled, "The way she looked at him and spoke to him with great affection and love . . . I thought of her as a very warmhearted person."[28] This was obvious in the speech, which read in part: "Spare, I pray Thee, my dear mother for many a year. Bless her for the tender attention and selfless care she has given me to this day. May it be Thy will that she live many years to witness the results of her toil so that she may see that she has not labored in vain."[29]

It certainly appeared that Sophie had not labored in vain. Solly's early report cards were promising (with As and Bs). He received As for effort, obedience, courtesy, and cleanliness. Oddly, he earned Bs in penmanship, in which he later excelled and used in dramatic fashion in much of his work. And he did well in the Boy Scouts, earning merit badges in athletics, cooking, pioneering, safety, public health, bird study, personal health, swimming, lifesaving, handicrafts, first aid, stamp collecting, rowing, reading, civics, reptile study, path finding, scholarship, and camping.

Solly's interest in stamps and the passion he demonstrated for his collection may easily be viewed as a part of a behavioral pattern, since he would eventually collect art obsessively. His passion to own beautiful stamps is reflected in a letter he sent in 1941 to Reverend H. G. C. Hallock, a missionary in Shanghai, China, who immersed himself in Chinese culture and collected local ephemera:

> Dear Sir, I received your address through D. Mayer's friend in Lenox Hill Hospital. Although I know you are quite busy I was wondering if you could possibly send me some extra stamps you have lying around, because I am a stamp collector and have a quite large collection. My age is 13. To get back to my stamps, I have a few (14) covers from throughout the world and I thought it would be nice to have some from China. Will you please acknowledge this letter. I would appreciate it very much.
> Sincerely,
> Sol LeWitt
> 51 Cedar Str.
> New Britain, Conn., USA[30]

In school he took art classes, and many of his drawings survive. They show a very different Sol LeWitt—one who, in art anyway, was either obliged to or decided to think conventionally. He did portraits in pencil of famous men in public life: James Madison, Daniel Webster, Henry Clay, Andrew Jackson, John Marshall, Thomas Jefferson, Andrew Jackson, and Simon Bolivar.[31] It is not known whether he was free to choose his subjects, but if he was the choices indicate an early interest in history and politics that stayed with him. The portraits were straight-ahead drawings whose style would surprise no one, yet one could draw an obvious conclusion: the boy had talent, something that he dismissed in adult interviews as something everyone has. But the drawings he did at the age of fifteen stand out for their originality, attitude, and invention.

The portrait of James Monroe was reflective, to be sure, of images of the sixth president at the time in terms of the facial shape, hair, and so on. But the young LeWitt's portrait of Monroe added elements showing that at an early age the artist had begun to form ideas about the world. It shows Monroe as the mastermind of the Monroe Doctrine, standing tall on a map of America that features a sign: "Warning!! You are now entering the Western Hemisphere. . . . Leave Guns and Knives at Home." In this drawing, the United States is surrounded by a fence with its posts dug into the ocean. That ocean was also a theme for him in the sense that historic boats became subjects for his work. There are pencil sketches of a Spanish warship, the *Matthew* of Bristol (similar to the *Santa Maria*), an English warship of 1560, and a Roman warship dated 60 B.C.E. All of the vessels were sailing, perhaps, from landlocked New Britain. Unlike some of the other work, these maritime images have a great amount of detail. An observer studying LeWitt's ships and the intricate if much more abstract designs that emerged in his art decades later might conclude that the artist's mature vision of art began to develop in childhood.

In the summer between his junior and senior years of high school, Solly worked at manual labor he despised. He spent his free time expanding his views, commenting on present-day world affairs—which were dominated, of course, by World War II.

This sixteen-year-old, who had never traveled beyond the boundaries of Connecticut, had sophisticated ideas. A cartoon he drew on August 13, 1944, shows the metaphorical ship *Germania* sinking, with a few people on board representing Hungary, Bulgaria, and Finland. Private LeWitt's advice appeared below: "You'd better jump while you've got the chance." A few days later, Solly drew Hitler with his hands to his head and the Grim Reaper about to hand him a death cocktail. The title of the drawing was *The Day of Reckoning*.

But subtlety and a grasp of how people acquire and retain power were also evident. In another August 1944 drawing, Solly shows two German men in suits talking about the war. The death camps had recently been discovered, and news of disappearing Jews had certainly reached 51 Cedar Street. One of the men in the drawing whispers to the other: "I never would have imagined. Goodness." The other whispers back: "Und der Russians vant to Communize the United States und Britain—and the Jews vere the only vons to profit in the war. And that's not all . . ." Below is a quote attributed to Hitler: "When you tell them a lie, tell them a big one." Perhaps the most sophisticated drawing from that breakthrough summer shows an American businessman in a stupor, popping his vest buttons and railing, "Down with Russia, down with England, let the rest of the world go to hell." The title was "Hitler's Rear Guard—The Isolationist."

Mort Jaffe, one of Solly's high school friends, doesn't remember these drawings. Jaffe recalls only the European piece that hung near the kitchen table at 51 Cedar Street. He didn't know who had drawn it, but he didn't like it. It was sketchier, not intended to be representational, in the manner of schools of art that emerged after the impressionist period: "It was an ink drawing. A lot of white. It didn't make sense to me, as compared to Rembrandts."[32]

Jaffe was at the house because Sophie LeWitt, whom he recalls as being "a very liberal parent," was the only mother in the neighborhood who allowed the boys to play seven-card stud poker any time they wanted. They came in not through the living room door but through the back door, "in the European fashion," Jaffe recalls. "We played there maybe twice a week. Five of us — Wilbur K. Williams, Bill Rachlin, Samuel Abrahamson, Sol, and me. Only we never in those days called him Sol. We knew him as Saul. Just Saul. Like the king. I was surprised years later when his name was spelled S-O-L, because I never knew him that way."[33]

Friedenberg, who several decades later became publisher of the *Cincinnati Enquirer*, said: "Why did I like Sol? Because he was quiet, reserved, good-natured, witty and Jewish — and I was taught at home to be friendly and nonprejudiced toward Negroes and Jews." He offered the following reminiscence:

It was an early fall day, probably a Saturday, as I recall, when we were in 9th or 10th grade. Ten or a dozen schoolmates — boys only of course — would gather in Walnut Hill Park for a game of touch football. . . .

One day, for the first time, Sol showed up to play. I was surprised because he was conspicuously non-athletic, but I was glad to see him, as were the others. He was on the opposing team from mine and like me was a lineman, blocking and tagging the runner when we could. He seemed to be not quite in a flow of play, doubtless because he was the only one of us wearing eyeglasses, and they were of a definitely unfashionable rimless kind.

It started to rain lightly, but of course we kept playing, like real football teams do. Our hair, our clothing, our shoes, the grass, the ball all got wet, but we played on. Then on the next play, Sol and I were on the scrimmage line facing each other, and I noticed that the rain had coated his glasses with water, and I thought, "Heck, how can he SEE?" Yet he was still in there, playing with all his heart. My esteem for Sol went up.

Then, after the game was over, Sol invited me to his home, and I was pleased and accepted. It was an unpretentious apartment in a small building on a side street near the park. We were greeted by his mother, a kindly woman who continually gave me a blissful, serene smile and served me and Sol a cup of hot chocolate and a pastry with nuts and apples. She didn't say much but seemed very pleased that Sol had invited me to their home. I didn't say long because I had to get home.

It was only when we were in the army and became solid friends, Sol told me his mother was a nurse and that his father, a doctor, had died when was just starting school. I thought then that maybe [the reason] Mrs. LeWitt smiled so much was that she was pleased that Sol had a friend.[34]

However, Solly's schoolwork during this time was certainly not up to Sophie's expectations, as she held onto her hopes that he would eventually decide to go to medical school. His final grades for his junior year, 1943–44, were:

English: B
Physics: C
French 1: C
Chemistry: B
American history: A

His grades improved somewhat in his senior year, when he had the chance to take electives — including, for the first time, the field in which he would excel:

English (college prep): B
Physical education: A
Physics: C
Art: A
Latin American history: A[35]

The report cards reveal his two lasting passions: art and history. What they don't necessarily show was his emerging interest in international affairs. At some point in high school, he entered an essay contest. How he fared isn't clear, but essay is still in existence. In it is a deep sense of humility and questioning that would become one of LeWitt's trademarks:

Not the kind that preaches that everyone should love me, but that which teaches each to love all. . . . A tolerant person sees at once

all sides of a question and at the same time sees the right one.
That which benefits the greatest number of people. A tolerant
person does not consider himself any better than his associates
and his race and nation no better than his neighbors. Freedom
and peace follow naturally from tolerance. It sounds simple but it is
the most difficult of things to do. Men's minds are hard to change,
especially when they live in the past.[36]

The essay is astonishing for its maturity and the glimpse it provides
into the artist's career and personal values. In arguing for the spirit of
tolerance, he refers to what would become a lifelong quest. In addition,
a reader of the entire essay would see a fierce originality in it—unlike
the bar mitzvah speech a few years earlier, which seemed more scripted.
Solly understood complexity but at the same time argued that complexity should be no impediment to righteous action. This is early evidence
of his independent thought and an indication, in his assertion that he
doesn't need to be loved by everyone, that he understands going along
with the crowd can take an unthinking person in the wrong direction.

When Solly entered the essay contest, friends assumed that if he won
he wouldn't want to read his work aloud at an assembly. But he proved
to be no recluse.

Like most of the Jewish male students at New Britain Senior High,
Solly joined a Jewish club. His had about forty members. Jaffe, one of
the members, recalled:

Every Monday we had a meeting in the Main Street office of the
B'nai B'rith which sponsored us. You could play pool, cards. We
had a Ping-Pong table, and it was a place where we could meet and
talk . . . not much else to do in the middle of the war. Nobody had
[a] car, gasoline was rationed, so very little dating was done. Even if
you had a car, the kids didn't have driver's license[s]. The ration was
something like three gallons per week. We had parties—very few.
Later on we had basketball uniforms and played other sports. Sol
played in some of it. In baseball and football, he was a not a star.[37]

And, Jaffe says, Sol never wanted to play quarterback or be the leader.
That was the quality that led to a deep misunderstanding between the
two that threatened their friendship. The annual election for officers of
the club was coming up. To the surprise of everyone, particularly Jaffe,
Sol decided to run for president against his cousin, David Sokol, and

asked for Mort's vote. As Jaffe recalled: "I told him I couldn't do it. He asked me why not. I told him, 'I never thought you would run. And I already promised your cousin my support.' Well, Sol lost by two votes. If I had voted for him, it would have been a tie. After the election he came over to me and was very angry. He said, 'Well, *you'll* never be president.' Then a week later, I came to a poker game. He gave me a dirty look as if he was going to kick me out, but he didn't."[38]

Jaffe would go on to become a professor of marketing at Baruch College, part of the City University of New York. He kept in touch with his old friend through the years and sometimes expressed surprise that LeWitt would want to be so famous. That had not necessarily been his goal when he applied for college at sixteen (the age at which he graduated from New Britain Senior High). His mother; his much older cousins, Bella and Nellie; and other relatives urged him to follow his late father's path and go to medical school, but he had no interest in it and instead wanted to pursue art. He once told an interviewer, "I couldn't think of anything else."[39] But that response downplayed or ignored the passion and cleverness he had shown in art classes. A family compromise was finally reached: LeWitt would apply to Syracuse University, where he would get a solid education, but where there was a respected school of art.

On May 29, 1945, the New Britain seniors graduated. A special edition of the *Red and Gold Review*, the school newspaper, featured details about the commencement, photographs of and pieces by seniors, and local advertisements. On page 3 were twenty photos of seniors who received scholarships and awards. LeWitt's photo is in the third row, second from the left, and the paper reported that he had received the Parker Reading Prize, "given through a competitive examination under the supervision of the head of the English department."[40]

There is also a quote from LeWitt: "Let us search continually for Beauty. For it is only in Beauty that we shall find full happiness. If we are unable to find Beauty in the Arts, we should keep searching and perhaps it will appear in the commonplace. Let us always try to enrich our thoughts through new experiences: for thought is really Life's only reality."[41]

Here, then, is direct evidence of his ultimate pursuit — art as thought rather than as object. It may be reasonably presumed, of course, that this was only a notion at the time. But here an entry in a school newspaper is a serious statement from a young man who will make ideas his life's work.

His mother, however, still hoped that her only child would follow her late husband's path. As LeWitt put it in a 1974 oral history interview at the Smithsonian:

> In a way I was rebellious, because my family was middle-class, and my mother really wanted me to become a doctor, and one thing I didn't want to do was to chop open people and look inside of them. . . . I didn't think that that was any good. I didn't want to be in business; it was a boring kind of a life, it seemed. [Being an artist] was a way of asserting my independence. . . . It was something I could do. I wasn't precocious at all.[42]

There was nothing for him in New Britain except his mother's love, which he treasured, and the affection of a handful of relatives. The city itself held no opportunity in his view, because of its archconservative tastes in art and the laborious summer jobs he needed to take that had him sweeping streets and clearing manhole covers. Jaffe thought that there was some kind of family conspiracy: although the LeWitts and even the Appells had a variety of enterprises, Sol was never invited to work at any of them.

Aunt Luba might have been able to use him in the grocery store, but she continued to struggle, particularly after becoming the defendant in a lawsuit. A customer complained that she had bitten into a piece of bread made by the Schneider and Pomerantz Baking Company and was injured by a tack. She won her lawsuit against Luba, who was not able to recover the money from the supplier until much later.[43]

Aunt Luba adored Solly, as did Bella and Nellie, who helped fill in what was missing in his family. Even so, the teenager never warmed to New Britain, though he was respectful in his public comments, and apparently resentment to the city mounted.

In the first major interview that the adult LeWitt granted (in 1974 to Paul Cummings for the Smithsonian Institution), he specified his frustrations:

> I reached the point in high school where I had to go away to school, and by that time I had gotten to the point where it wasn't so much that I wanted to be an artist, it was just that I couldn't stand the life of the town, of this society. I just couldn't. It was more of an act of rebellion I think than a positive act of wanting to be an artist. . . . If I were living in these days, I would go into some sort of political

activity, or say, in the '60s, I certainly would be in some political activity. Although I was interested in politics or political activity, there just wasn't any real road that I could see. Being an artist is something that was in a way rebellious, in a way individualistic, and, in a way, it was an act of rebellion against . . . the bourgeois kind of society I was brought up in.[44]

Thirty-three years earlier, he had expressed this view in a very different way. Before he left for Syracuse, he wrote a poem, called "Ode to My Home Town," on the same typewriter that his father had used for his short stories:

New Britain, oh New Britain,
You moth-eaten town,
Your dirty old buildings,
Should all be torn down.
Your winters are cold
Your summers are hot,
The air is so foul
With mildew and rot.
The land of bad colds
Of sore throats and the flu,
Of sick aching headaches
And pneumonia, too.
You're a blot on the landscape
The nation's eyesore,
Your people dull-witted
And God what a bore!
The home of dumb cops
And bumpy thoroughfares,
With your stinky old busses
And ten cent fares.
You live among filth
And you don't mind the smoke
You thrive on the filth
And to you it's a joke.
Your beautiful starlings
Fly through the trees,
And the smell from the shops
Is what you call breeze.

You make us pay double
For all you can sell,
But after the war
You can all go to hell!
And when you reach Hades
And Satan greets you,
You'll feel right at home —
He's from here too.
The worst of it all,
You think you are swell,
You think you are perfect
And that gripes like hell.
You're dead and you're rotten;
You think you're alive.
You think you're a place.
Instead, you're a dive.
You're not worth this paper,
You're not worth this ink,
You can take it from me,
NEW BRITAIN YOU STINK![45]

Whether LeWitt ever showed this "ode" to his adopted town to anyone is not known. And although it certainly reflects his attitude at the
time, it wouldn't be his last word on the place—far from it. He would
one day be ranked among the Hardware City's greatest benefactors.

THREE
THE BOY FROM SYRACUSE

When sixteen-year-old Solly LeWitt arrived on the campus of Syracuse University for the first time in the summer of 1945, escorted by his loving older cousins Nellie and Bella LeWitt, he became one of the youngest students in the oldest fine arts educational institution in the country.

At that point, he knew little about the university except that one of his uncles had attended it, and that it was far enough from New Britain (about 275 miles) to suit him. He also knew that the Syracuse art department was strong, with a highly regarded faculty.

His first impressions, to be sure, were positive. In later years, LeWitt said that he thought the city was handsome and the countryside of hills and lakes even more so. He made no specific references in interviews to the campus architecture, but considering his eventual interest in the subject—including his evocation of architectural elements in his cement block pieces—it seemed that Syracuse had been a good choice.

The Romanesque Hall of Languages, the school's only building when it first opened in 1873, was large enough to accommodate classrooms for 2,000 students. Nearby Crouse Hall, where the college of Fine Arts and Architecture was housed, was built in 1889 of brownstone and had a medieval atmosphere with its dark, rounded arches; carved woodwork; and high ceilings.

Syracuse, like many other private universities, had suffered financially in previous years, because so many of the young men eligible for enrollment were fighting in World War II. As a result of returning soldiers and the promise of a GI Bill, campuses were soon overwhelmed by larger and much more diverse student bodies. At Syracuse, whose undergraduate population nearly doubled in size to about 16,000 over a period of months, a shortage of housing meant that some classes (including some in art) were held in Quonset huts.

Martin Greenberg, who also came from Connecticut, met Solly LeWitt in the summer of 1945. Greenberg recalled that the housing shortage for freshman was so acute that the two of them were assigned to rooms in Sigma Alpha Mu, a Jewish fraternity. "It was a house on a nice, tree-lined street of big Victorians," Greenberg remembered.[1] It was also headquarters for what became LeWitt's circle of friends.

If he was looking for fellow artists, he found them instantly. Leon Morgenstern, Edward Feldman, and Russell North became buddies. On the fringe of the group was a young man from Massachusetts named Hilton Kramer, who planned to become an art critic. A few students pursuing degrees in other subjects were part of the circle, too. Deborah Faerber was an English major and prospective teacher; Alan Nevas would pursue a career in the law and become a judge; and Arnold "Libby" Libner would go on to establish many businesses, including a prominent firm that manufactured bird feed. Sydney Geffen, a veteran who owned a car, provided the wheels for group outings to Warren Street (also known, Faerber remembers, as Fluid Street because of its multitude of bars).

Libner, a cousin of Greenberg, might have been the one who grew closest to the young student from New Britain. "Arnold was quite literary," Alan Nevas recalled: "He fancied himself a writer, and he wrote in a very flowery style, lots of flourishes in his fiction and nonfiction."[2] Libner also had a reputation, his cousin said, for being "biting and acerbic."

Nevas recalled that this circle of friends often went to clubs, shepherded there by North, who yearned to introduce his pals to the pleasures and complexities of bebop. "This helped us all," Nevas said. "None of us were big socializers. One of the reasons was that right after the war all the soldiers had come back, so the coeds our age that we would normally be dating were more interested in twenty-one- and twenty-two-year-old veterans. Guys like Sol and I were left behind socially. Besides, Sol was shy, not a pushy guy. We sort of connected on that level. So our substitute for socializing was listening to jazz."[3]

LeWitt's other passion was sports, both as a player and a fan. At Syracuse, he quickly adopted the Orangemen, as the football team was known at the time, and he went to games at the old Archbold Stadium, though in the postwar years the team was weak and rarely won.

The rub was academics. As LeWitt said in 1974, "Well, I was quite young when I went and . . . it just took me quite a while to get adjusted. And then I didn't have much art training. That was very tough on me because it was a very academic school. There was a lot of cast drawing and stuff like that, painting in a very academic way. And I was never very good at that. So that all made it more than usually difficult."[4]

Naomi Bragman Stern, who took some of the same classes at the time, recalled, "Hour after hour, we drew from the same plaster casts of Greek statues. It was all very traditional."[5] Cecile Gray Bazelon, who enrolled in the art school the same semester as LeWitt did, remembered that students were required to produce a work in the Renaissance style.[6] The faculty had relied for years on conservative stalwarts and taskmasters — "hard core old boys," as another student of that period, Morton Kaish, recalled.[7]

Unada Gliewe remembered that many of her fellow students in the pared-down freshman class in painting switched to liberal arts because of the strictures of the faculty. The schedule, she said, was rigorous: "Freshman year, we had cast drawings 9 to 12 Monday through Friday. Boy, you learned to draw. First two years were things like that, basic courses. I had illustration from 2 to 5 every afternoon. Every month you had to turn in sketchbooks. Friday they came around critiquing. Dr. [Frederick] Haucke we had for that. That man had the broadest thumb in creation. To make his point he would drag his thumb through the wet paint."[8] Haucke is remembered by others, such as Gray Bazelon, as an excellent teacher and one of the few in the first year or two of study who required students to use their imaginations.

Gray Bazelon and Kaish were two students who took the classic approach to art and appreciated the school's direction. They had the ability to copy styles of the masters. Those who earned the top grades were the ones who could render representational images without great difficulty. Kaish remembers that in such circumstances LeWitt had a difficult time:

> We all worked in light-filled high-ceilinged rooms dedicated to
> Old World discipline from a faculty largely composed of formalists.
> It was all about drawing from plaster casts, figure drawing. As the
> first such art school in America, [Syracuse] wanted to pass along the
> classic approach. I loved it because that's what I was interested in
> and could do. Unlike Sol. The thing I remember about him is that he
> was an intellectual — very thoughtful, quiet, not one of the student
> stars. I also remember his paintings at the time. He was struggling.
> We still worked from the model. Sol always painted their heads very
> large, pretty much in a modified monochrome, earth colors, grays.

It was astonishing in that he did it his own way even in the face of criticism of the faculty. What Sol wanted to do was more expressive.[9]

Indeed, LeWitt would later say in an interview that the longtime dean of the college of fine arts, Lemuel C. Dillenback — hired by Syracuse in 1934 to teach design — thought that the student from New Britain might become a great success — if only he would choose a field other than art.[10] This was the view not only of the authorities but also of some of his classmates. Gray Bazelon, reflecting on LeWitt's rise to fame, said, "What Sol LeWitt became afterward had no relationship with who he was at Syracuse. He was a nonentity for four years. We couldn't believe it [when he became famous]."[11] She had not wanted to spend time with him as she had with other students, such as one who "could draw like a Renaissance master."

It was a considerable service that the curriculum was focused on Old World art. How could a young person prepare to become an artist or art teacher without being knowledgeable about Rafael, Giotto, Caravaggio, Rembrandt, and the movements that stretched from the Renaissance to the eve of Modernism? But the eve of Modernism was the limit at Syracuse. By 1945, other universities' fine arts programs were teaching about what had happened since the Paris Salon dropped its requirement that to be exhibited, works of art had to be idealistic. In other words, the definition of art, as the years passed, changed dramatically from work that was representational to work that was affected by other elements, and ideas became as prominent as renderings.

What did it mean, Syracuse students may have wanted to know, when Paul Cezanne's green blobs represented trees; Georges Seurat extended the gap between artist and viewer with white space between dots and trusted the viewer to make up the difference; or when Marcel Duchamp decided that a urinal could be shown in an art gallery, turning both the object and assumptions about art upside down? What about the pranksters of Dadaism and the innovators of futurism, Fauvism, surrealism and other isms that led to the revolution of the abstract and its offshoots? Weren't they important as definitions (and collections) of art were changing dramatically?

In the years that followed, LeWitt became passionate about the foundations of expression. He wrote, as a kind of career statement, "I'd like to produce something that I would not be ashamed to show Giotto."[12] As he learned more about the world and traveled as much as any young artist of the era did, he understood that he was part of a continuum and found breathtaking the meticulous work of the masters, particularly those of the Italian Renaissance. His career, however, did not depend on his ability to learn their techniques. He grew to admire their achievements, but appreciating them, learning from them, and being inspired by them are quite different from copying them.

At Syracuse, the work that he was required to do meant that his freshman grades were mediocre at best.[13] He received a D in design and Cs in still life and other art courses. In his sophomore year his performance improved a bit, though he still got Cs in his portrait and watercolor classes. He got Bs in still life, illustration, and art history. And his best grade of all reflected the dean's opinion of his capacity outside the art world: LeWitt earned an A in English literature.

In the later 1940s, something of a revolution occurred on campus that changed LeWitt's outlook and prospects. Syracuse's chancellor, William Pearson Tolley, decided that the art school had to adopt a more contemporary view of art.[14] Kaish said, "My recollection is he put together a search committee, which came up with a recommendation that he chose not to follow."[15] Tolley brought Norman Rice to Syracuse, who in turn brought members of his Art Institute of Chicago circle, and Rice made the art program more innovative and diverse. Among the new faculty members were Merlin Pollack, Dean Butler, and George Vandersluice. Kaish recalled, "I liked the conservative guys, but suddenly they were out."

Kaish came back to campus for his junior year and saw dumpsters out in front of the school:

> At first, I was dismayed and overcome by sadness. I loved the old
> way, and I didn't really know how much I loved it until it was gone.
> I loved that there was no freedom and experimentation in the way
> you looked at things, or in the material we used. After the change,
> we began using new ways to think about design and color as
> opposed to the accuracy of shape. We were no longer documenting.
> We were interpreting and transforming. Eventually it all became
> very exciting, but some people never got over the change.[16]

LeWitt did. Of the new faculty members, he said: "They had decided that anyone who was in school before that was totally lost. They really didn't give a shit at all, and we didn't get very much instruction, which was the best thing in the world for me at the time."[17]

In his third year, LeWitt's grades improved, though not dramatically.

He still got Cs for anything that had to do with detailed portraiture, but in the class on form and expression he received an A. His senior year was by far his best, with all of his grades As, except for a B in esthetics. And he proved outstanding in his newest discovery, lithography. (Throughout college his grades in courses outside of art — history, English, and philosophy — were consistently high.) He didn't think he showed nearly as much talent as many of his classmates: "Some [of the other students] were really very good, but most of them didn't turn out to be artists after all. Some of the best ones never did. One guy became a window designer. There was one guy who did Lord & Taylor ads for a while. Then he started doing paintings, which were not so good."[18]

Theodore Salz, by consensus the star of the class, never became a full-time artist, though Gray Bazelon recalled, "We stood around awestruck looking at his drawings."[19] Other star students put their talents to use in various ways. Marvin Israel became art director for Vogue, Sydney Tillim was a long-time teacher at Bennington College, and Josh Fendell taught for nearly thirty years at the Maryland Art Institute. Kaish was one of the few who had major success in the art marketplace. Gray Bazelon's paintings became valuable commodities in New York City. And Kramer landed his dream job as art critic for the *New York Times*, though during his long tenure there he never let his friendship with LeWitt soften his views on the artist's work.

When asked why some of the best students didn't become artists but went off into the academic world, LeWitt's reply was one that ought to give hope to anyone who does not fit into the category of prodigy:

> Well, I think the reason they were very good students was that they had a great deal of talent; they had a great deal of facility. Having a great deal of facility, there wasn't the sense of struggle or sense of desire to improve that other people who didn't have this facility or natural talent to do things had to struggle a lot more. And merely doing things well in school is not the program of being an artist. It's a good program for being a student . . . because you do get very good grades and you do what's expected of you. To be an artist you probably need a little more rebelliousness. . . . Most of the artists I know, well, some of them never went to art school at all. Most of them weren't the best students.[20]

The interview in which he said this, by Paul Cummings, avoided most personal subjects, like all of the interviews of LeWitt. If Cummings,

   SOL LEWITT

going out of character for such interviews, had asked this question: "So, Sol, during your four years at Syracuse did you attract the attention of any lovely coed?" LeWitt might not have answered, or he might have responded with something less than a full accounting. Indeed, he did attract such attention. Gray Bazelon recalled—in contrast to how LeWitt would think of himself in later years—that the quiet young man had "handsome features." She herself had no interest in him—"the ballsy guys were the ones I was attracted to."[21] (She later married the classical composer Irwin Bazelon.) But another pretty student from New Rochelle became a LeWitt pursuer, up to a point.

North, LeWitt's friend and fellow art student, was the matchmaker. He talked to Naomi Bragman about a Syracuse junior art student who just might be interested in a date. When LeWitt met Bragman formally —they had previously seen each other at Crouse Hall—he told her his story in a few words. He spoke of his physician father, whom he'd never really had the chance to know. Bragman's father had been a physician, too (a psychiatrist), and, again like Abraham LeWitt, had met with an untimely death. Naomi had been only nine years old at the time.

She told LeWitt that her family had moved from Syracuse to Binghamton, New York, when she was a young girl, and that her father became the first person to have a psychiatric practice in that city. In the evenings, she, her sister, and their dad formed a chamber group, the Ill-Harmonic Trio, with herself on clarinet, her sister on piano, and their father on violin.

She said that after his devastating death, from pneumonia, the rest of the family moved to Manhattan and, like the LeWitt family after Abraham's death, found themselves in reduced circumstances. In Manhattan she attended PS 9, where the teacher used to let her go to the back of the room and copy pictures while everybody else was doing math.

Her interest in art continued through school, and she applied to only Brown University (which did not appeal to her) and Syracuse (her father's alma mater and her preference), because she intended to major in art and the tuition at Syracuse at the time was reasonable.

As she explained more than sixty years later, she took an instant liking to the much more introverted LeWitt, who, as she remembered, was seldom seen in art classes by then: "He spent hours in lithography. He was often the only person there. I don't now if he ever went to class. When I think about him at Syracuse, I think he was basically a self-taught artist. He didn't get anything out of Syracuse except a degree."[22]

They were opposites. "I was not introverted," Ms. Stern said:

That's what appealed to him. We often double-dated with Russ
North and his girlfriend at the time, Debbie [Faerber]. Russ had this
car, which only had a front seat. So I had to sit on Sol's lap all the
time. I even wrote a poem about it. I remember the legal drinking
age was nineteen. I was old enough, but the guys weren't, so they
would drink beer. I hated beer. I drank whiskey sours because you
can't taste the whiskey. We used to go out to the really cheap bars
near the campus.

Sol was really poor then, but so was I. We went to a lot of free stuff
—to hockey games and lacrosse games, and I never even heard of
lacrosse. The rest of the time we used to sit on the back stairs of my
sorority, Phi Sigma Sigma, and neck. I wasn't really the sorority type.
I joined just to see if I could get in.[23]

She described LeWitt at the time as "cute but not handsome. His hair was
going already. But he had a lovely smile. And he was in love with me."

Here, however, is the information that Naomi didn't give him at their
first meeting—she already had a beau, Ted Stern, back in New York
City. He had graduated from Cornell, was living at home and working, and was "waiting for me so that we could marry. I used to argue
with Ted, and every time we argued I was very happy to go out with
Sol. When I told Sol about Ted, though, it didn't bother him."[24] It was as
if this quiet young man from Connecticut had a confidence even then
that he could win her.

But it wasn't to be. When she graduated, Naomi announced, in a
tearful scene, that she did indeed intend to marry Ted: "Sol came to the
sorority house later and handed me this bundle, and then left. He was
on his way to Illinois, he said. He won a teaching assistant's spot there,
and would get his master's. The bundle he left with me had a dozen
lithographs and an oil painting. The painting was done with a palette
knife, and it was of an old woman in a black cloak, somber, depressing.
When I showed it to Ted, he hated it."[25]

Indeed, LeWitt's lithography work at this time was dark. Much of it
featured loosely drawn groups of people in gloomy atmospheres, such as
in *Street Scene* (1949). Scholars who examined that work later noted the
apparent influence of German expressionists such as Max Beckmann.

Despite the unpromising reaction from Bragman, LeWitt kept knocking on her door:

A month after Sol graduated, he was still thinking he could win me back. He came to New Rochelle and surprised me in the store where I was working, Sylman's, selling cheap clothes. I thought I would fall through the floor. He'd hitchhiked from New Britain. I had to find a place for him to stay—a friend of Ted's took him in. But I told him I wasn't going to marry him, that I was in love with Ted. I said, "I'm not going to see you anymore." Ted knew, of course, and had been very jealous. Ted was an engineer, who worked in a family business. He had money, and Sol was totally broke. He lost me, and he was still smarting because he was certain he was going to get the senior art prize at Syracuse. But Mort Kaish beat him out.[26]

The 1949 Syracuse yearbook makes no mention of the senior art prize, or of LeWitt. He didn't show up for his senior picture, making it the fourth straight year he'd shunned the camera, and the beginnings of a lifelong habit.

FOUR

THE ART OF WAR

NEW BRITAIN (Special). For outstanding art ability and promise, Sol Le-Witt, son of Mrs. Sophie LeWitt of 51 Cedar Street, has won three art prizes and scholarships for which he competed in recent weeks. This week he was notified that he had won a cash award of $300 by placing second in an oil painting and progress competition conducted by the John F. and Anna Lee Stacey Scholarship fund in Los Angeles, Calif.

Earlier, LeWitt won the $1000 scholarship of the Louis Comfort Tiffany Fund in New York for graphic arts study and a University of Illinois art scholarship for lithograph work. Native of Hartford and graduate of New Britain schools including the Senior High School in 1945, LeWitt was graduated from Syracuse University last June. He is now doing graduate work in art at University of Illinois.

Hartford Courant, October 6, 1949

A reader of the *Courant* at the time would get the impression that young LeWitt, rewarded for his diligence and academic record, had embarked on a steady path toward success—at least, as success is generally measured. The scholarship for work in lithography also came with a teaching assistantship, which ensured that two years in Illinois would be comfortable enough. But it wasn't to be—at least not for more than a few months.

LeWitt's comments over the years about going to Illinois show that his attitude about the experience ranged from ambivalent to extremely negative. In 1974, he said of the Illinois opportunity:

I thought it was good luck at the time. But it was the opposite. . . . By that time I was just plain fed up with school, and I didn't really do very much. I wasn't very popular with the faculty. And then I had gotten the thousand dollars, and, by the time Christmas came, I was so fed up, I just left school completely. Then I thought, "Well, I really wanted to do some more lithographs," so I went to the Hartford Art School, and I just asked them if I could use their press, and I made some sort of deal with them. I don't know whether I paid them or what. But I did that for a few months. Then I took off and went to Europe.[1]

But even his recollections of Europe, where he saw great works that he had previously seen only in textbooks, were not very positive. He described the trip briefly to Paul Cummings in their interview:

MR. CUMMINGS: Was that just to travel and look around?

MR. LEWITT: I had that thousand dollars so I figured, "Well, I didn't expect to get it so I might as well do something I didn't expect to do."

MR. CUMMINGS: Well, in the 1950s you could do a lot with a thousand dollars in Europe.

MR. LEWITT: Right. It lasted pretty much the whole time.

MR. CUMMINGS: Where did you go and what kind of activities did you do?

MR. LEWITT: Oh, I went to England and France, Italy, the Scandinavian countries. Oh, I don't know, I wasn't really interested in seeing museums and things like that. I saw some, and I just wanted —

MR. CUMMINGS: To see what the rest of the world was like.

MR. LEWITT: And at that time the Korean War had started so when I returned I knew I was going to be drafted.[2]

There is no reference here to the two college buddies who went with LeWitt, Alan Nevas and Russell North. Nevas, the surviving member of the three, recalled, "I was in law school [at New York University], and our pal from Syracuse, Russ [North], was also living in New York. He called one day and said, 'Sol and I are going to Europe. Do you want to go with us?' I was working my tail off in law school. It was very hard. And though my parents wouldn't give me any money at the time, I had saved some, and I thought, why not [take the summer off]?"[3]

Nevas recalled that the trio arranged an economical voyage, securing triple-decker bunks in the hold of the *Washington*, originally built as a battleship for World War II and was newly recommissioned as a transport. Nevas said:

The ship was loaded with young people going to Europe for the summer. The voyage took about a week. We stopped first in Ireland, let people off, and then [went on to] Southampton. From there, we took the train up to London and stayed at the YMCA for about a dollar [a] night. We went to galleries during the day, and it was my introduction to art. One night at a pub we met an English guy who latched on to us, and he took us to other pubs and clubs. He had been in the [Royal Air Force] and took a liking to Americans. He told us there was a softball game at Hyde Park every Sunday morning. So we played there. Russ pitched. Sol and I played outfield.[4]

LeWitt provided some details about London and what followed in a sketchbook.[5] One sketch, drawn on June 10, 1950, shows a double-decker bus at Trafalgar Square, and another from the following day shows a view from Waterloo Bridge.

Nevas recalled:

From London we took the train to the Channel, and then an overnight ferry to the hook of Holland. We bought the cheapest tickets so we had no bed, just chairs to sit on. So that night, Sol [and] I were determined to find a place to sleep. We went to the upper deck, where the staterooms were—which of course you had to pay extra for. We tried all the doors until we found one that was unlocked, and [the room] was unoccupied. We went in, locked the door, and went to sleep. The next morning we found Russ. He'd been sleeping downstairs, on a chair.

In Amsterdam, we went to the Rijksmuseum. For me, I was along for the ride. Sol stayed in the museum for hours.[6]

Nevas didn't recall how long his companion spent with the museum's many masterpieces, such as Van Gogh's *Self Portrait* (1887), Rembrandt's *The Night Watch* (c. 1642), Vermeer's *Woman Reading a Letter* (1663), and Fra Angelico's *Madonna of Humility* (1434–35). But it was hard to get LeWitt out of the rooms that contained these paintings. His sketchbook shows no record of the museum visit but does contain many views of the city, including church steps, crowded streets, a canal, and a Newfoundland dog.

In Paris, the trio stayed in one room at the Hotel Noailles but often split up—LeWitt going to the Louvre or other museums or galleries; and Nevas and North assessing beauty in a different way, at the city's cafes and bistros. At night LeWitt and North went to jazz clubs, while Nevas stayed at the hotel: "Sol and Marty saw [the clarinetist] Sidney

Bechet perform at least five or six times."[7] LeWitt's drawings show no Louvre masterpieces but include whimsical images of the visitors to the museum. There are many more sketches of Paris and its environs: Place Pigalle, a flea market, Versailles gardens and a sculpture in one of them, a Montparnasse scene, and a flamenco bar. He made no sketch, though, of a headline in the Paris edition of the *Herald Tribune* that would affect him significantly.

There was startling news from the Korean peninsula. About 75,000 North Korean troops, aided by China and the Soviet Union, crossed the thirty-eighth parallel, the line that divided North and South Korea. Pressure mounted on the United States to react to what the United Nations termed an invasion. The action was seen in the United States as hard evidence of the Soviet plan to spread communism worldwide and, hence, required an armed response. President Harry S. Truman, articulating what eventually became known as the domino theory, said, "If we let Korea down, the Soviets will keep right on going and swallow up one [place] after another."[8] The military draft, the infrastructure of which was still in force from World War II, began to target hundreds of thousands of young men. The three potential draftees from Syracuse tried not to dwell on the inevitable as they made their way via train toward the south of France.

In Nice they rented bikes and rode along the Riviera to Cannes. Nevas recalled: "We were riding along. Coming in the other direction were guys on bikes. They stopped when they saw us. One of them was Bob Sugarman, who was a friend of Sol and Russ. Imagine that. We all stayed together on the beach. It's the first time we saw bikinis and topless women. As I recall, Sol wasn't interested."[9] (This point, though, is undermined by the evidence of a sketch: LeWitt drew a woman in a revealing bathing suit, though most of his subjects were less titillating—such as a man on a motorbike, a market, and the view from the hotel window.)

"We'd talk to women, try to connect, but Sol would hang back," Nevas added.[10] This portrait of the young LeWitt as shy around women is in direct contrast to what would happen in later years.

The trio then took the train, stopping off in Florence to spend time at the Uffizi Gallery,[11] and then going on to Rome and Venice. "Every city, we stayed at a cheap place," Nevas recalled. "In Venice somebody sent us to this place, a dollar a night. We went to sleep and, during the night, we heard footsteps back and forth in the hallway. We realized it was a whorehouse, and the people going back and forth were customers."[12]

Though Nevas offered no specific references to LeWitt's art discoveries in Italy, there is evidence that this trip proved greatly influential. LeWitt's sketchbook shows more drawings from this part of trip than any other, including a visual accounting of a day in Assisi. At the Basilica di San Francesco, LeWitt saw the frescoes that many historians attribute to Giotto, who is considered the first of the great artists of the Italian Renaissance and who set, in the view of the awed young LeWitt, an unreachable standard.

Other works that stuck in LeWitt's mind from his initial visit to Italy included many by Piero della Francesca and Sandro Botticelli. In an interview in 1993 he said, "Piero appealed to me for his sense of order, superimposed on which was a sense of passion and ritual."[13]

From Venice (LeWitt, of course, sketched gondoliers), the three young travelers took the overnight train to Munich. In the morning they saw a bombed-out city, still in ruins five years after the end of World War II. The city gave Nevas chills, particularly when he heard a frequently used word, "*Achtung!*" That proved to be the last destination on his foreign tour before returning to Paris for the trip home. LeWitt and North went on to Scandinavia, as he headed back alone to the United States to get ready for his fall semester. Nevas recalled, "Somewhere along the way, I can't remember where, we'd met some English girls, and they were planning to see them. When they got back to the States, they told me they did."[14]

It was an ironic last party before heading off to a different war, because draft papers were indeed awaiting LeWitt.

By the end of 1950, the profound difficulties of the Korean War had become clearer—even to some hawks who, still brimming with pride about American accomplishments in World War II, had argued that the job could be finished in relatively short order. This view proved wildly optimistic. In November, US Marines and infantry troops were surrounded by Chinese Communist forces at the Chosin Reservoir. Three days later, at a press conference, President Truman admitted that the United States was considering use of the atomic bomb. Three weeks later he declared a state of national emergency, and by the end of the month the evacuation of Seoul, the capital of South Korea, was being planned.

This was a situation that LeWitt and other draft-age men couldn't escape. As with his comments on his education and his trip to Europe, LeWitt made matter-of-fact references to his life as a soldier. His New

Britain classmate, Walter Friedenberg, who was drafted at the same time as LeWitt, prepared a more vivid account of the time for the purposes of this biography:

January 10, 1951, a cold morning. A special bus was parked in front of the Burritt Hotel just off the triangular main square in New Britain. Twenty or so men in their early 20s, shivering on the sidewalk. A couple of Army non-coms with a list of names. Induction Day.

And there was Sol LeWitt! We spotted each other right away. We had not seen each other since 1945, the year of our high school graduation. We greeted each other warmly and even before we boarded the bus began to get caught up. [I learned that] Sol had studied art at Syracuse. I had gone to Wake Forest College and was working as a reporter in Winston-Salem.

We discovered we had the same attitude toward being drafted. We had no dread of being killed, wounded or becoming a POW —that seemed distant and unlikely—but simply detested the idea of being in the army, with its regimentation and loss of freedom to continue the civilian work we each enjoyed. We gave no thought to —or I should say we did not discuss—the probability that the army intended to teach us how [to] use weapons and kill North Koreans and Chinese. We weren't in the least bit patriotic about becoming soldiers, but neither could we claim to be conscientious objectors. So [we] were inducted. We shared a mood: reluctant and resigned.

We were bussed to Fort Devens, about thirty-five miles northwest of Boston, and got off into six inches of snow and the same biting cold. The rows of barracks, the headquarters buildings, the olive-drab trucks and jeeps, the olive-drab soldiers everywhere—we were in the army now. . . .

After just a few weeks of drill-marching in the snow, chowing down . . . we got the word that we were to be sent to California as "fillers" for the 40th Infantry Division, which we were told was the Southern California National Guard. . . .

The troop train was composed of several shopworn passenger cars. As it headed west, it became obvious there were a lot of New Yorkers aboard. There was a lot of poker playing and arguing. . . .

By luck of the car assignment and some selection on our part, Sol and I became acquainted with two kindred spirits: Harry Ekblom, a New York lawyer, and Bob Fithian of, I recall vaguely, the rural

Midwest. We were set apart by having completed college and started on careers, and [we] had similar attitudes about being in the army, and about life in general. We spent the daylight hours talking or reading [all the way to the destination, Camp Cooke, in Southern California].

That sprawling Army base (now Vandenberg Air Force Base) was located on the Pacific coast nine miles northwest of Lompoc. Doubtless because we were college graduates, we were assigned to a high level headquarters rather than an infantry line outfit, and in a group of 30 or 40 recruits were given basic training: marching in drills, firing rifles[,] etc.

Sol made an inept soldier. He couldn't remember to start marching by putting his left foot forward, instead of his right foot. Our drill sergeant, a three-striper, once became so annoyed by Sol's indifference that he halted our unit, picked up a grapefruit-sized rock and put [it] in Sol's left hand with the advice/warning, "Here, that's your left. Start with your left." It seemed to work.

All four of us quickly concluded that the 40th Division, or what we saw of it, was a slipshod organization, not well disciplined or demanding. Taking advantage of the "wait" part of "hurry up and wait," Sol carried a sketchpad and pencil in the thigh pocket of his fatigues and often sketched away (without showing his drawings). During downtime in the barracks Sol would frequently sketch on larger paper.

(Sol made a pencil sketch of me. Through the years I treasured it, but through many packings and storings the bottom edge became frayed, so I finally trimmed it off, including Sol's signature. Years later, after Sol became famous, I wrote him jovially to ask if he would re-sign it. He wrote back, in the same tone, "I'd have to see it first. I might not want to." The drawing is framed and on my study wall, as is, and I occasionally tell a new visitor, "This my LeWitt.")

After a few weeks we recruits were let out for a weekend and the four of us headed to Hollywood. We got as far as Santa Barbara. We were all so entranced by the Spanish Colonial–style architecture that we got no farther—that weekend or the next two weekends. We all loved drinking in quiet bars, eating in pretty-good restaurants, and lolling on the beach.

[One day] Sol invited me to accompany him on a visit to the Santa Barbara Museum of Art. With Sol leading the way, we cursorily toured the exhibits, then headed to what few Impressionists and Post-Impressionists there were. As we left, Sol said of the museum, "Not much." Out of the blue he said he greatly admired the paintings of Albert Ryder, for the finesse and feeling of his moody skies.

After perhaps three months, word got around that the 40th was to be shipped to Korea. That came as a scary bit of news for many of our fellow-recruits but not for the four of us, for we believed that we would stay far from combat, assigned to some higher-up headquarters, probably as clerks.

(I was less optimistic and concluded that if I would have to fight in a war I would have to learn how to do it, which our lackadaisical basic training did not teach us, so I volunteered to go to infantry Officers Candidate School at Ft. Benning, Ga.).[15]

By the time the two recruits from New Britain reached California, the involvement in Korea, though never declared a war by Congress, had intensified. Things had not gone well for the allied South Korean and US troops. Positions were seized, held, and then lost. North Korean troops were well trained and equipped, and they inflicted a great number of casualties. The war that supposedly pitted good against evil was not going as planned. Moreover, Mao Zedong had ordered Chinese troops to the peninsula as a result of what he considered to be armed aggression against Chinese territory.

For the 40th Infantry Division headquartered in California, going to Korea seemed inevitable—even though, as Friedenberg reported, it was not an elite outfit at the time. To be sure, the division had served with valor in World Wars I and II, but its leaders and composition had changed. It would be necessary to train the division's members not only in California, but also in Japan, before sending it to the Korean Peninsula.

LeWitt's account of the period, as recorded in letters to his Syracuse pal and fellow draftee Arnold Libner, begins with impressions of the domestic training and advice for his friend:

> January 26, 1951
> Hi Lib,
> Here I am, sprawled out in my barracks, aching all over, and we haven't even started our basic [training] yet. I got out here last Sunday after a five-day train trip. Before that I was at [Fort] Devens for a week. It's hot as a crap-shooter making his twelfth straight pass

with loaded dice in the middle of July out here. . . . We've been doing
KP, digging ditches, shoveling gravel and drilling all the time. We do
anything to keep us busy. . . .

I have been assigned to Division Headquarters, which might
turn out to be a good deal. Try and do as best you can on your
classification tests that they give at the induction center — it might
keep you out of the infantry.

I have saluted two officers so far and try to avoid them by
pretending not to see them, walking across the street or about 50
yards out of my way.

There are a million rumors as to where this division is going
when it goes. I won't believe anything till I get on a boat. . . .

Let me know when you expect to be inducted. Don't go!
General Ike[16]

The next update was sent from Camp Cooke a month later, when Libner was training at Fort Devens, Massachusetts:

Dear General,
The shit has really been flying thick and fast since last Saturday
when they announced that we are shipping out for Japan (and
points west). I am not going with the division in March but will
continue my training until the end of May and then join the division
in Japan or wherever they are. I am still in HQ but all my training has
been Infantry. . . . We have been getting different kinds of combat
courses such as the infiltration course where you crawl 70 yards
through barbed wire, over logs in sand while they fire machine guns
over your head and TNT charges explode all over the place. When
you're through your rifle is still supposed to be clean. . . . We had
another dandy, charging down a field and up a steep sandy hill
firing from the hip — then double timing about a half mile. After that
getting shot by some North Korean would be a pleasure. . . .

As you was, Sol

On June 11, 1951, LeWitt and other late-arriving members of the 40th
boarded the *General J. C. Breckenridge* in San Francisco, bound for Yo-
kahama, Japan. When they came aboard, they were given a copy of the
ship's newsletter, with its welcome message: "May you look back on our
16-day voyage together as an opportunity to have met new friends, seen
the vast Pacific, and travel by water to the Orient. We thank you for your

cooperation throughout the trip and all of us about the GB wish you: the best of luck, happiness, and success in your new ventures."[17]

In anticipation of the "new ventures," the crew of the *Breckinridge* tried to provide the troops with a sense of home and comfort. The crew organized an orchestra, featuring Private Edwin J. Costa, of New York City, who had played vibes and piano with the Sam Donahue ensemble; Private Elmer "Skip" Allbrook, of Portsmouth, Virginia, who played violin and had toured with Dick LaSalle's band; and others with significant credentials.

The newsletter staff quickly expanded and included a new cartoonist, introduced to the passengers as: "Pvt. Sol Lewitt, age 22, of New Britain, Conn., assigned to HQ Co., 40th Div., Japan. Sol was an artist before entering the Army and attended Syracuse University, N.Y." His prolific output during the voyage expanded his penchant for wry commentary.

Among his cartoons is one of soldiers trying to sleep during a rainstorm. One of them says: "I had a very restful sleep last night on one of the hatches. The gentle pitter-patter of the rain on my sleeping bag made me sleep all the better." LeWitt also showed the cramped conditions on board with a sailor holding a whip and saying, "After I woke up and took a leisurely shower I got into the chow line which really moves fast because it is a single line and no one crowds it." Another chow line drawing was accompanied by the following text: "And the KPs and cooks are nice to us. Even though there are no cups or bowls and silverware they let us go thru the line anyway. The dining room is a huge, spacious place, air conditioned and filed to overflowing with smiles, and we talk about politics and world news." In yet another cartoon about the chow line, he shows a lieutenant colonel saying to a much younger officer, "I'm sorry, Lieutenant, the cook says you can't have any caviar."

The newsletter included updates from the war, indicating the participation of Chinese troops. It is particularly candid for an official Navy document: "War News: U.S. 8th Army Headquarters, KOREA, June 26, 1951—Chinese forces formed a still resistant line against patrolling and attacking United Nations units on the central and western fronts yesterday and early today. Communist units offered light to heavy resistance in the area north of Wachon and northwest of Hangue while enemy activity was confined to platoon-sized engagements against Allied patrols from the east coast."

When the voyage ended at Yokohama, Private Solomon LeWitt rejoined the 40th as it trained for duty in Korea. Japan would have an inspiring effect on him, some which is reflected in his letters to Libner. The only one that survives from Japan was written about the time the division shipped out for Korea. LeWitt's arrival in Korea was about week after that of the new commander, General Matthew Ridgway, who replaced General Douglas MacArthur after he had been fired by President Truman.

> December 28, 1951
> Dear Lib,
> . . . Right now the section is embroiled in a mighty production called "Once Upon a Holiday." It is a real stinker by any standards except for a couple of numbers. I am property man — which means I get a free TDY [military shorthand for "temporary duty assignment"] to Tokyo when the show plays there on New Year's Eve. We don't come back until Jan. 5, which means one big last fling before we ship out. . . .
> I really was beginning to enjoy Japan, too. But I won't be in any great danger [in Korea], since I think I'll be in the PX section [post exchange]. . . .
> GENERAL KIMBELL (I think.)

The 40th Division was sent directly to the front in Korea, relieving the 24th Infantry Division. Over the next several months, the 40th participated in the battles of Sandbag Castle and Heartbreak Ridge, and while it inflicted heavy casualties, it suffered about 400 fatalities, with many more wounded. LeWitt, assigned to headquarters company, worked behind the lines, designing posters for events and working at the post exchange, where he was in charge of the warehouse in which general supplies and whiskey and beer were stored. Behind the lines, though, was not necessarily a safe address, as the next letter indicates.

LeWitt received his first promotion, to private first class, but he was still slightly outranked by Libner, who had yet to go to war. The letter begins with a mockery of Army regulations and refers to the point system — when soldiers received enough points, largely measured by in-country service, they were eligible to go home. And it is signed with the nickname of Dwight Eisenhower, former general and president:

> To Pfc. Arnold Libner, 53rd Quartermaster Co.,
> Fort Drum, NY,
> Dear US51090148,
> . . . Our division "rear" unit (mine) is moving about 7 miles to

Chunchon which is closer to the 40th front than we are now. The place we have in Chunchon is supposed to be real jolly. . . . One side is the largest oil dump in Korea. On the other side is a large oil seaport. [Enemy units] apparently swoop down on the place. They also like to pick off guards. . . .

We just finished our inventory here and happily were only a couple of hundred dollars behind. We aren't supposed to make money here and are allowed one and one half percent loss—about $2,000. . . .

With any luck I'll leave this favored land in the middle of summer. That is if 36 points are still the criteria. I now have 24 points.

The only contact I still have with the army is guard duty but even that is a joke now. We show up late to our posts, don't bother sleeping in the guardhouse, always have dirty weapons and sometimes don't even bother to blouse our boots [arrange fatigue trousers so they puff out a bit at the boot line]. When on our posts we sit around and talk to other guards. Due to our semi-blackout we can hear the officer of the guard coming before he can see us. . . .

Love and kisses,

IKE

April 4, 1952
PFC Sol LeWitt to CPL Arnold Libner
Fort Drum, NY
53rd Quartermaster Sub. Support Co.
Dear Stonewall [referring to Stonewall Jackson],
. . . At the end of this month the Lt. [lieutenant] promised me 10 days off in Japan. I don't think I'll have much difficulty in finding something to do.

Nothing new in the PX business except I'm glad to be here even at 2 points a month. However, when I get out and people ask me about my peonage in this wonderland, I'll say, "I'd rather not talk about it," with an expression on my face that could be interpreted as "God, why must they crucify me by making me think about it." It ought to be good for at least two or three pieces of ass until they begin to catch on. . . .

Well, all's well that ends, or so they say,
Yours truly,
Phalanx T. Phalanx

Before he wrote the next letter, LeWitt had received another promotion, to corporal, and had further explored Japan's lures—cultural and quite otherwise:

May 4, 1952
CPL Arnold Libner,
53 Quartermaster Sub Sup Co., Fort Drum, NY
From CPL S. Lewitt
Hello Hector,

Just returned from Japan a couple of days ago after five days of uninterrupted bliss. It was like climbing out of a cesspool into a pink, scented cloud. A young lady friend and I did the town up and down with a couple of sideways thrown in. Never walked more than six feet, took cabs. Saw Kabuki theater, very nice but very long—started at 4:30, ended at 9:30. Slept between sheets for the first time in four months. Had a steam bath at the notorious Ginza Center, was massaged by two winsome flowers of Nippon. Took a motorboat ride thru the canals of Tokyo, almost as much algae floating around as there was in the water at Nice. . . . Drank many whiskey sours at Tokyo's plush EM Club at 25 cents a throw. Missed May Day riots by a day, had to fly to Pusan to catch a batch of whiskey. Sent it off by boxcar, saw my Pusan girlsan, flew off to Seoul, then caught another plane to Chuchon, where I live (temporarily).

Tomorrow I go to Inchon to order and draw the division PX supplies. Will see my Ong Dung Po concubine if she hasn't run off with the captain I am sharing her with. . . . Things could be worse.
*Cuttah Sipcio,
Edgar
*Go way, please (Korean)

Nov. 3, 1952
CPL Arnold Libner, Camp Drum, NY
Dear Libber,

As things stand now I'll be out of here in nineteen days which isn't bad when you consider that I started counting days at 140. Since I'm shortly to rotate I haven't done "dick" in the last month.

. . . I'll be home by Christmas and I hope that we'll be able to get together for New York and have a ball, so to speak.
Yours for smaller armies,
Sol

The letters to Libner obviously serve a different purpose than analyzing the influence of the war on a supply corporal. Eventually, LeWitt reflected on that experience, notably in 1974 when he was asked in an interview about the effect his service had had on his work and way of thinking. He offered two responses, one of them general: "I think everything we do has some effect if you want to look into it." The other specifically related the impact of Asian culture on him. He said of Japan: "It was really just a beautiful way of life that the people had. They still have quite a bit of the old tradition, class, dress, manners. There was a very aesthetic sense of life and . . . everything had a certain rightness to it and there was a simplicity, and everything was done with the most high sense of beauty. Which is kind of a relief from our civilization, which is quite the opposite."[18] Or, as he would write in more succinct fashion to a girlfriend twenty years later, "Japan makes Europe seem like New Jersey."[19]

It was while he was in Japan that he began to collect art. He bought woodblock prints there wherever he could find them and shipped them back to New Britain. At that point he didn't know much about them, but he thought they were exquisite — which was enough for him.

In all, LeWitt's experiences in war and on its fringes of war provided him with training if not for military victory, at least for survival in his next tour of duty — trying to make a living as an artist in New York City.

FIVE

LOST IN THE CITY

LeWitt didn't often speak of his early years in New York City. But the impression he left with friends and in interviews is that it was a deeply frustrating period artistically and, from a personal point of view, a lonely one. Not that he was isolated. He developed friendships, pursued romances, and even succumbed — if briefly and exasperatingly — to the institution of marriage. But in recalling those days in conversation, Le-Witt was uncharacteristically downbeat.

In 1953, he rented his first apartment — at 115 East Thirty-Fourth Street, near Lexington Avenue, in an affordable building. There was enough space to work, though at first he had no idea what work he would do. By then, abstract expressionism had been the primary movement in modern art for nearly a decade, but he soon discovered that he had no interest or skill in producing works in that style.[1] Indeed, many other young artists descending on New York at the time felt the same way. Jasper Johns and Robert Rauschenberg, then in their late twenties, found it very difficult to sell their work and had to make livings designing store window displays, among other tasks. The work they were developing — Johns featuring common symbols such as the American flag and bull's-eyes, and Rauschenberg focusing on "combines," for which he used materials and images not usually associated with art — were sometimes referred to as "anti-art" by critics. More charitable observers called their output Neo-Dadaist,[2] considering it to reflect elements of the prominent international avant-garde period early in the twentieth century that was known for its irrationality, humor, and elements of protest.

LeWitt, who had not yet found any ism that he could embrace, recalled later: "I spent all the money I saved and went through unemployment. . . . I also went to a school, and that was kind of a fiasco."[3] The school was what was then called the Cartoonist and Illustrators School.[4] Though eventually LeWitt would later teach there, as would others of his circle, his experience as a student on the East Twenty-Third

Street campus proved unsatisfactory: "I really wasn't interested in being an illustrator, but it was the closest school to where I was living, and I just wanted to survive, I guess. I wanted to get the GI Bill money, which wasn't very much, but at least I could live on it. It was the same sort of academic bullshit I had [at Syracuse and Illinois], so I got tired of that very quickly."[5] In a 1977 interview, he summed up his art training, saying that he "probably would have been better off studying something else."[6]

However, one advantage of the route he took was that he could make enduring friendships. He kept in touch with old friends from Syracuse, for example. Martin Greenberg, Russell North, Alan Nevas, and Deborah Faerber often got together in the city to see movies or go to a bar, to enjoy Greenberg's cooking, or indulge in whatever cheap entertainment was available. At the time Greenberg and Faerber were dating. As Greenberg recalled, "Everyone fell in love with Debbie. She was darling —short, cute as the dickens, an All-American girl, smart, funny, easy going."[7] And she was soon intimate with LeWitt, making Greenberg jealous—though he said, many decades later, "It didn't come between me and Sol."

In the spring of 2007, Deborah Faerber Evans read an obituary of Sol LeWitt in the *Miami Herald*. She hadn't known that he had been ill, so the news of his death came as a shock. A few minutes later, she went through her LeWitt inventory, rediscovering memories. She kept letters from LeWitt on the top shelf of a closet with a piece of art, albeit informal, that had never been shown in a gallery.[8]

Evans thought back to "the coterie of Syracuse pals" who had stayed close in the years after graduation, and to her own days in New York before moving to southern Florida. She thought, "How young I was. How immature."[9] And she thought, too, about the choices she had made.

She and LeWitt had gone to plays, museums, and bars together. One memory in particular had stuck with her. One night they were having drinks in Greenwich Village,

> when some guy tried to hit on me. Sol objected, and the guy left. I said, "I wonder what that guy does for a living." Sol said, "He's a horse's ass. That's what he does for a living."
>
> I knew that Sol was creative, and that he thought in ways that other people didn't. I was drawn to him, but I was too much of an idiot to recognize that. We were talking marriage but I was not mature enough to even say I wasn't interested in marriage.[10]

Instead, she decided to let her travel itinerary send a clear message. She bought a ticket on an ocean liner bound for Europe, where she planned to spend four months. LeWitt gave the impression that he supported the journey and, using his 1950 experience as inspiration, gave her a creative going-away gift.

It was an eight-page letter with drawings and commentary in the vein of some of the work he had done aboard the *Breckenridge* a few years earlier, but more pointed and clearly showing affection for the recipient.

The first page shows an ocean liner with an American flag and the words: "So . . . now you too are going to Europe. Well . . . Here are some helpful hints to make your visit happy." The inside features a line drawing of Europe, intentionally out of scale. Accompanying his detailed sketches of the Eiffel Tower and the Arc de Triomphe, LeWitt wrote: "There are many strange and wonderful things to see but you will become sick to death of them." He shows a variety of different foods of the continent (fish, bacon, croissants, and so on) and says, "The food and wine is [*sic*] famous throughout the world, and will make you very ill." One page shows a man playing an accordion and another man dancing. The text said, "See the real people in their native costumes — they will like you because you have American money." Another page features a rendering of a passenger train on an overpass. LeWitt's comment was, "Trains are lots of fun but you won't mind if they are just a little slow and sooty . . . the wooden seats are nice to sit on." The final page shows a woman climbing up one big Alp. LeWitt concluded: "Above all, have fun."[11]

From Evans's account of the journey, it was clear that she did have fun. When the ship returned on December 8, 1954, she was jostled during the disembarking process and was the last person to leave the deck. When she walked down the ramp, LeWitt was waiting for her. "Anybody else would have left by then," she said.[12]

However, LeWitt's attempts to woo her failed. And not long afterward, Evans, who went to work in a newspaper office in New York, met a "tall, dark, handsome and stupid reporter" whom she married, a union that lasted only two years.[13]

There may have been more depth to her relationship with LeWitt than she acknowledged at the time. But that depth certainly comes across in a 1954 letter she wrote to LeWitt on *Miami Herald* stationery, while she was waiting for her divorce to become final. The letter also suggests, in a wry tone, an idea for art, absurd as it is:

It is with some reluctance that I take pen in hand, for thus occupied I cannot tear great shreds of skin off my back, my pastime of these last few nights. Fascinating, destroying myself on even a small scale. . . . I feel hurt, my sense of purpose lags and a grim anger for the elements. . . . Two girls, lately of the *Herald*, just stopped in and drank the rest of my beer. I forget what we talked about. Nothing is new with my divorce. I just sit it out for 80 days. The lawyer called me a few days ago to say my ex-boss had called him to ask how I was and how in Hell did I get a job on the *Herald*. Everybody is so nice. The lawyer said he'd buy me a drink later in the week and then didn't call. If he weren't charging me nothing, I'd take my business elsewhere. . . . Thank you for the temperance lecture. My god, I wish I had a bottle. When the hurricane comes, you shut all windows except one in the bathroom, fill the tub and sink with water or whatever you prefer, and sit and wait in darkness. I may just do that tonight. Who could have thought that a mind, blank non-directional me, was an eight ball? . . .

Why don't you put the end tables in the middle of your living room, place a bottle of gin on one, Vermouth on the other, and tiptoe out of the room for seven or eight minutes. If, when you creep back in, and the room is empty and the skylight is broken, go up on the roof with a water pistol and squirt the hell out of any pigeon that can't fly a straight course. Then make some more end tables and repeat the experiment but sell tickets.

It is hot and I am running out of cigarettes. . . . I have a date with a fellow sot tomorrow and Tuesday. . . . Three weeks in this town and I haven't located a subway entrance yet. Entirely too above-board. Something fishy. Good night.[14]

How LeWitt could support a wife or a family had yet to be determined. He had come to New York because of its vitality, and specifically because it had become the new center of the art world, but unknown artists were at the bottom of a fixed hierarchy.

The movement toward New York began before World War II, when many prominent European artists and teachers emigrated to escape fascism. Among the most influential were Josef Albers, Max Ernst, Marcel Duchamp, Piet Mondrian, and Salvador Dali. This was followed by the emergence in the city of artists such as Franz Kline, Robert Motherwell, Lee Krasner, and Jackson Pollock—all of them championed by the critic Clement Greenberg, whose influence was as outsized as his personality, and who argued that the art world was now in the hands and imaginations of about fifty abstract expressionists in studios south of Thirty-Fourth Street.

Some of the personality of the city that emerged during the period was captured by writers such as Mary McCarthy, who in a 1947 *Partisan Review* piece, suggested how she could explain the character and vitality of New York — particularly its cosmopolitan nature — to a French intellectual: "Sukiyaki joints, chop suey joints, Italian table d'hotel places, French provincial restaurants with the menu written on a slate, Irish chophouses, and Jewish delicatessens."[15]

In addressing the flurry of creativity in New York, the poet John Ashbery wrote in an essay:

> My arrival in New York coincided with the cresting of the "heroic"
> period of Abstract Expressionism as it was later to be known,
> and somehow we all seemed to benefit from this strong moment
> even if we paid little attention to it and seemed to be going our
> separate ways. We were in awe of de Kooning, Pollock, Rothko and
> Motherwell and not too sure of exactly what they were doing. But
> there were other things to attend to: concerts of John Cage's music,
> Merce Cunningham's dances, the Living Theatre, but also talking
> and going to movies and getting ripped and hanging, and then
> discussing it all over the phone.[16]

LeWitt was drawn in particular to the work of Kline and Willem de Kooning and the earlier work of Pollock. "But," he said, "there weren't too many second generation Abstract Expressionists who I thought were very good."[17] He never felt that he was equipped to be part of the movement—he described his attempts as complete failures. In addition, he professed disdain for many of its painters: "Most of them were so arrogant and loud. Because the Abstract Expressionist has a way of living and a way of talking and a way of arguing and a way of doing everything that was just so completely different from me that I just never could get with it."

To make his rent payments, he had to find steady work. In 1954 he found a job at *Seventeen,* the first magazine founded specifically for a teenage audience. LeWitt's primary task was to run the photostat machine. Rather than finding this work tedious, he discovered a way to occupy himself and to experiment with technology: "I used to do superimposing of photographs. They ended up looking like Rauschenberg's. The kind of stuff he was doing later on. I would take whatever photographs were around and superimpose them on one another. . . . Then I would sometimes draw on it while it was still in the liquid. So that was the only kind of art I was really doing because I really wasn't too interested in painting. I felt that I should or else there wouldn't be any reason for my existence."[18]

Eventually, other members of the magazine's staff recognized that their photostat man had more to offer than making copies, and he was promoted to the art department. There he helped with production and was asked on occasion to draw small illustrations for feature articles.

In an interview he gave to the curator Gary Garrels in 2000, LeWitt revealed that some of the things he learned at *Seventeen* influenced his later work.

> GARY GARRELS: Photography is something that you have come back to from time to time in your work. . . .
>
> SOL LEWITT: I learned something when I worked at *Seventeen* magazine. They had a man who would take pictures of objects and they used these as a kind of editorial idea of objects that were available to buy. The idea of photograph as a recorder of objects was something I thought was a basic premise of the medium, and I wanted to try to use it in different ways. Later I started to incorporate it into books because I started to be involved with the seriality. . . . I still make photo pieces, though I don't think of myself as a photographer. In fact, I don't think of myself as a painter or a sculptor. I think of myself as an artist who can use any of these media, materials and techniques as I wish, without pinning myself down to the name.[19]

A year before LeWitt came to *Seventeen*, the artist Eva Hesse (then seventeen) served as an intern there. Hesse and LeWitt, who would become the closest of friends, never met at *Seventeen* in person, though as the curator and author Veronica Roberts pointed out in 2014, they met "on the page."[20] After Hesse left the magazine, it did a feature article on her, calling her a young artist to watch. As a filler on the last page, LeWitt drew an elaborate birthday cake in pen and ink. It was his first signed professional piece. A few months later, he drew a writing desk using the same sort of elaborate design, making full use of classical patterns and, perhaps, a foreshadowing of ideas he would expanded upon one day.

In 1955, LeWitt was offered the position of art director of *Fashion and Travel* magazine—but for only one issue, as at the time the magazine rotated talent. He recalled: "They had very good people, like [Richard] Avedon, people like that doing photographs. Perfectly respectable, except the hiring and firing policy. But it was a good experience."[21]

Afterward, he collected unemployment insurance until "I met someone who said the architectural firm of I. M. Pei was expanding its graphic design department, and 'Why don't you go?'"[22] By then, LeWitt had developed a keen interest in layout and typefaces, so it seemed like a sensible idea. He secured a position in the firm in 1955, where he was one of five artists in the department, but he found it tedious and frustrating:

> The first job that they asked me to do was to design a letterhead. So I just designed a very simple letterhead right across the page in small type, and the guy who was the head of the graphics department [Don Page[23]] told me I had to do something else. There were three or four people working on this, some of the most God-awful things, embossing and, you know, logotype things. After six months they went back to the very first design. That was the one that was accepted. I was so pissed off at that, and it was such a waste of time. The whole thing was like that. Everything was just done, and redone, and overdone. Usually the first solution was best.[24]

In general, the working atmosphere was tense. LeWitt recalled, "Architects and artists are mortal enemies (at least many architects think so)."[25]

LeWitt also produced brochures and did specialty work on projects such as the Roosevelt Field Shopping Mall, in East Garden City, Long Island:[26] "The only thing that I did was to make a directory to be placed throughout the shopping center. You would push a button and the store . . . would light like a big pinball machine."[27] He also worked on symbols to be put in storefronts, illustrating what that store sold (a shoe, for example), but they were never installed: "The head of the department had this kind of idea, and then he just sent everybody to work on it. That kind of treadmill just turned me off: doing stupid things endlessly." There were other stupid things, however, aside from the work, one of which involved an impersonation.

Martin Greenberg recalled that during their conversations on East Thirty-Fourth Street, LeWitt revealed that Pei, who became one of the world's most acclaimed architects, was also "a notorious scofflaw"—in that he accumulated dozens of parking tickets, and never paid the fines. "The police were after him and he had to go to court." LeWitt often told the story to friends, and always had a laugh over it. He said Pei refused to go and sent instead an intern of Italian descent to pay the fines, instructing him, "When they call my name tell them, you're me." When he got in front of the judge the intern was very nervous. The judge asked, "Is your name I. M. Pei?" The intern said he was. The judge said, "Are you Italian?" The intern said, "No, I'm Chinese."[28]

Over the years, interviewers asked LeWitt whether his I. M. Pei experience (it lasted just one year) had a strong impression on the work he would eventually do. The question seems pertinent enough. LeWitt has often been compared to an architect in that, in particular for his wall drawings, he conceived the plan, did the preliminary sketching and wrote the instructions, and then let other people carry out the work. But LeWitt played down this notion. However, many decades later, while reflecting on that time in an interview for his 2000 retrospective, he surmised that the Pei experience must have affected his thinking.

During his time there, LeWitt became close friends with Tony Candido, a staff architect who was also a painter in his spare time. Candido had studied architecture under Mies van der Rohe, but he wanted to get back to his first love, seeing what he could create at an easel. The two became what Candido described as "painting buddies—there was a time we saw each other every night."[29]

As LeWitt later described it, Candido provided the impetus for his own ultimately unfulfilling return to painting: "So I got really turned on to doing art again. I started painting. And I got really interested in Abstract Expressionism. I did it long enough to discover I couldn't do it. But at least it got me going."[30]

LeWitt persuaded his old college acquaintance, Hilton Kramer, now a critic for the *New York Times*, to come to Candido's studio to see his work—the sort of generous gesture he would later become famous for among artists. LeWitt and Candido went to exhibits on Fifty-Seventh Street, and down to the Cedar Tavern on University Place, a hangout for the likes of Kline, Rothko, Pollock, and other art luminaries. LeWitt talked to none of these artists at the time, but the bar was nevertheless a source of inspiration. As the sculptor Tom Doyle recalled, "This was the artist's living room."[31] The artist Mercedes Matter later called it "the cathedral of American culture of the '50s."[32] It didn't look much like a cathedral. Nor did it have the amenities of most bars—there wasn't even a jukebox. It did have a clock on the wall that sometimes ran backward. In his description of the place (always referred to by patrons as the Cedar Bar, rather than Tavern), the art historian Jed Perl listed it among the hangouts that "offered opportunities for friendships and love affairs to begin or flourish or end, for careers to get going or jump forward or derail."[33] The writer Robert Katz described it, in part, by saying that artists could "breathe the same boozy oxygen once breathed by Pollock and still breathed by Rothko, de Kooning, and Kline, where in art salons Clement Greenberg and Harold Rosenberg handed down the immutable laws of flatness, inscribing in extravagant prose meant to be eternal how utterly marvelous it was."[34]

It was at the Cedar Bar, that LeWitt met his mentor, Earl Kerkam. Candido remembered Kerkam as "an original Damon Runyon character with a slouched hat, swaggering torque, a New Yorker through and through, unpretentious. Earl knew his stuff. He had a bad arm but he drew like an angel. He was a strange guy. I got the impression he was lonely."[35] By then, Kerkam had shown his work at important galleries (including the galleries of Betty Parsons and Charles Egan, and the Poindexter on East Fifty-Seventh Street), but he was known to other artists primarily as a fixture on a bar stool and a man of wisdom and good counsel.

Thomas B. Hess, the editor of *ARTnews*, wrote as a tribute to Kerkam that he was "an old man who can nurse a beer for hours at the Cedar Bar, listening to the conversation of his newly famous artist friends."[36]

Even well-established artists turned to him for approval. Pollock had already become a New York icon when he received a postcard from Paris written by Kerkam that praised the younger artist for his canvases displayed in the City of Light. The painter Louis Finkelstein, writing about Pollock in *ARTnews*, quoted his reaction: "Overjoyed, he waved it under the noses of the boys at the Cedar Bar, shouting, 'Earl says it's not bad.'"[37]

LeWitt described Kerkam as "an old man. He was really very independent. He hated the Abstract Expressionists for one thing. He would paint—he had a flower in a Coke bottle, and he would be painting that all the time. Very funny. He wasn't much of an artist, but he certainly was a personality. He really helped me a great deal, not in any specific way, but he was very encouraging. He said he liked what I was doing."[38]

This was so, even though the work that LeWitt was doing at that point was derivative and unsatisfying to its creator. For a time, inspired by

Giacometti and others, he experimented with still life, but with an abstract bent. In a way, Kerkam was an ideal mentor, in that his own work seemed to reject the standards of the times. In painting nudes and wildlife he rejected the idea of nostalgia and any sense of the common consensus about what makes something beautiful. Although LeWitt never remarked on this, other than to say that he didn't much care for the work, it's not a leap to suggest that Kerkam's willingness to cast aside conventional thinking influenced the younger artist. One can imagine Kerkam waving a glass in the air and saying, "Screw them all. Do what moves you." Even so, that work went nowhere either, and none of it remains. Still, LeWitt felt supported by fellow artists.

During his stay at I. M. Pei, LeWitt was encouraged by Robert Slutsky. The latter had studied at Yale University under the German-born artist and teacher Josef Albers, one of the many talented immigrants from Europe, and in time gained wide recognition for his innovations with color and shape. A few years later, Slutsky would help put LeWitt and Candido on the exhibition map.

LeWitt's tenure at I. M. Pei also made it possible for him to discuss great books with avid readers. At the time, LeWitt read Albert Camus and all the works of Samuel Beckett. With Candido and another avid reader and artist, Dan Graham, LeWitt also became fascinated by the work of Michel Butor, a French novelist whose writing had just been translated into English. One book in particular spoke to him. He passed it along to LeWitt.

The book in question — Butor's *Passing Time*, published in English in 1961, is the story of Jacques Revel, a Frenchman who takes a low-level position in a fictitious English city. Revel is not confident about his ability to speak the new language, and he also feels overwhelmed by his circumstances. The novel challenges the reader to solve a puzzle — that is, it makes the reader something of a partner in the storytelling. It's not hard to imagine why LeWitt, who considered himself an outsider in New Britain, at Syracuse, in the army, and during his early years in New York, might see a little of himself in Revel and admire the precision and depth of Revel's creator. As Graham pointed out, the protagonist in the novel "got lost in the city. It was like a labyrinth."[39]

Moreover, Butor was an experimentalist who believed that novels could be collaborations — as LeWitt would later believe about art. Butor worked with painters, musicians, and photographers on projects that defied boundaries and categories. This kind of thinking and breaking the mold intrigued LeWitt. (Many years later, he may have been thinking of Butor's work when, for example, he collaborated with the choreographer Lucinda Childs and the composer Philip Glass.) Influences such as Butor, Beckett, and others inspired LeWitt.

He made a decision that is necessary for almost anyone who would create art. Yes, Wallace Stevens could be a bond surety executive for the Hartford Fire Insurance Company in the daytime and create poetry on his way to and from work, and Charles Ives could hold an unrelated full-time job and write music at the same time. But for ordinary mortals, working and succeeding in any art field requires immersion during the most creative hours of the day. LeWitt understood this and came to the realization that working in graphic design offered him a highway to nowhere. He thought: "I don't really want to do this. I don't like it. So I just quit, and went back on unemployment and started painting."[40]

Even so, he struggled — or, as he put it, "I was floundering."[41] Abstract expression still held no interest for him and did not suit his talents. As he later said, after achieving some measure of success, "Abstract Expressionism was the most simpleminded kind of art imaginable."[42] Besides, the movement had had its day, and that day was ending. Recalling his fascination with the Italian masters, LeWitt decided to create work based on some of their canvases but with his own distinctive touches. Indeed, a drawing after Piero della Francesca that he finished in 1958 attracted a good deal of attention and comment more than four decades, later when LeWitt's work was celebrated in his San Francisco, Chicago, and New York retrospective.

The reason the drawing was included was that the work of Piero turned out to be a crucial influence on LeWitt's development as an artist who could discern a disciplined sense of order in narrative scenes. For example, when LeWitt worked on his own version of *Story of the True Cross*, one of Piero's frescoes in Arezzo, Italy, he saw the creator of the original as partly a mathematician devoted to geometric laws. The art historian Horst Janson put it this way: "This mathematical outlook — we read of Piero — permeates all his work. When he drew a head, an arm, or a piece of drapery, he saw them as variations or compounds of spheres, cylinders, cones, cubes and pyramids, endowing the visible work with some of the impersonal clarity and permanence of stereo metric bodies. We may call him the earliest ancestor of the abstract artists of our own time."[43]

 SOL LEWITT

■   LeWitt's downbeat recollections of his time at I. M. Pei may have been partially the result of the domestic crisis he faced at the time.

In the summer of 1955, he had gone with other artists to Fire Island, off the southern shore of Long Island—which had become a destination not only for gay city residents escaping the heat of the summer but also for many artists.

It was during that summer that LeWitt met Alma Reilly, who what was what they called in those days a "looker." Candido referred to her as "an Ava Gardner type."[44] A native of New Rochelle, New York, she was then twenty-seven, the same age as LeWitt. However, she had been married before for a short time and had gotten a divorce on the ground of mental anguish (unlike incompatibility, an accepted reason for divorce at the time).

Then as in his later years, LeWitt did not speak about the details of this part of his life, except to refer to a brief marriage (he never mentioned the name of his first wife in interviews), and his friends could only speculate about how and why the union occurred. The best witness might have been LeWitt's old friend Russell North, who served as an official witness at the marriage ceremony at New York's City Hall on August 22, 1956, but who died many years before LeWitt.

On one of the very few comments LeWitt ever made about his first marriage was to the photographer Vera Lutter many decades later. She recalled: "I asked him if he had ever been married. He said, 'It was summer, and we shared a house, and then we were doing our thing, and we thought ok, now you've got to get married.'"[45] Others remember him saying something like, "I didn't know what else to do at the time."[46] That is, he saw no alternative to succumbing to the convention of marriage. A biographer playing psychologist might suggest that LeWitt was rebounding from the end of his relationship with Evans and wanted to be sure his solitary days were over—or that, as certainly was the case later in his life, he found some deep sense of purpose in the rescue of a needy lover. What is known for certain about the first marriage, which lasted officially for two years but in effect was over after a few months, was that the couple lived on Avenue C, in the Manhattan neighborhood of Alphabet City, during this time; that the husband and wife were ill-suited for each other; that LeWitt's friends were surprised that he had taken this step; and that his mother, who seldom disapproved of his actions, did so in this case. Sophie LeWitt expected the best for her son, and in her view the best bride—a Jewish woman—was still out there somewhere. LeWitt later lamented that he had found himself lonelier as a husband than he had been as a single man.

After his stint at I. M. Pei's office, LeWitt worked briefly as promotion art director at Barker Levin and Company, a marketer of Lassie coats for women, but he later offered no recollections of this time. During these months, he tried to get professional representation for the work he was doing, and he eventually found Charles W. North Studios, a producer of promotional materials for businesses. His arrival as a client was announced in hyperbolic fashion, in an advertisement that listed new artists and applied lavish adjectives to each. Robert J. Berenson was a "photographer of unusual talent." Haskell Goldberg was a "distinctive illustrator." Sol LeWitt was "a prize-winning painter and graphic designer."[47] This connection lasted only a few months.

LeWitt's personal living circumstance improved if only in that he was able to find a place that suited only him. After the failure of his marriage, he moved to a loft on West Broadway in the neighborhood that would later become famous as SoHo.[48] At the time it was a rundown section that had none of the busy character of uptown. Many buildings were shuttered, and particularly at night, there were few pedestrians on the sidewalks, except for the members of the growing community of artists.

It was during a walk to the hardware store that LeWitt met the artist Marjorie Strider. After a brief conversation about tools, he got right to the point: "Would you go out with me?" However, she was engaged to the artist Michael Kirby, who, like Strider, would become an important cultural figure in Manhattan. (In later years Strider's work was often exhibited with that of pop artists Tom Wesselmann and Roy Lichtenstein.) She told LeWitt, "You might consider my sister, Nancy." Like her sister, Nancy Strider had come to Manhattan from Oklahoma. She had worked first for American Airlines as a stewardess (as the job was called then). "She was quite attractive," Marjorie said of her sister, and added, "Not that I wasn't."[49]

As LeWitt learned, Nancy had gone through a difficult time emotionally. She had been engaged to be married and the reception had been planned. Then she discovered that her husband-to-be had been married before and had four children.

Nancy Strider recalled that in any case she wasn't the kind of person who wanted to spend the rest of her life in Guthrie, Oklahoma: "So I followed my sister to New York. I came only because she was here, and [I] stopped working for the airlines."[50] She did this though her job had opened up, if not the world, a considerable part of the United States to her, a "girl who'd never been out of Oklahoma, except to visit my sister in Kansas City," and she had found herself partying regularly in Santa Monica. You could get a job, she recalled, "if you were good looking. But there were restrictions. You weren't allowed to gain weight and you had to wear a girdle, which I didn't do." When she'd had enough, Manhattan looked like a good alternative: "When you grow up in Oklahoma, New York is a very glamorous place." She moved in with her sister on Green Street and got a job right away as a secretary at a construction company.

Living with her sister made Nancy almost a character out of a Broadway play. She was *My Sister Eileen*, transported from the backwater, seeing the city as a naïf, and trying to make it. She recalled:

> All of my sister's friends were artists. They had a much different lifestyle than I did. I always had a self-esteem issue. I had been brought up, in the fashion of those days, to be seen and not heard, to not have opinions.
>
> To me these artists were intellectuals. That's not quite totally true, but they had different interests than I did.

When she met LeWitt, he put her at ease:

> He made fun of snobbery. He was so unassuming. Almost anti-intellectual, but he read widely, and was knowledgeable about many things. And he made me feel wonderful. He was dismissive of me feeling as if I was an inferior intellect. He introduced me to his friends, and to the films of [Ingmar] Bergman — I hated *The Virgin Spring* and I'll never forget it. There was also Bob and Ray on the radio — I thought they were hilarious. And there were the records of Elizabeth Schwarzkopf — I had already become a fan of the opera.

Strider never met Sophie LeWitt, but she remembers that Sophie often sent her son homemade baked goods and other treats from New Britain. The food was something of an education for Strider, who had been brought up Presbyterian: "There was only one Jewish family in Guthrie." And she had never tasted anything from a traditional Eastern European Jewish kitchen. Borscht and brisket were revelations.

The fact that she had been brought up in a town segregated by race and ethnicity left a mark: "It flabbergasts me that I never questioned it." But the time with LeWitt opened her eyes to a world well beyond anything she had known: "New York is total diversity, which is wonderful."

Strider remembers LeWitt experimenting with his work during this period: "He was painting with a flat palette knife, small paintings, with color put on thickly." How his work developed after that remained a mystery to her. After two years, their relationship ended. She was ready to be married, and LeWitt, still smarting from his venture into matrimony, couldn't bring himself to play the groom again.

Strider never saw him after that, though she followed his work—even, on one occasion, all the way to Bilbao, Spain, on a trip she made with her daughter (LeWitt had provided a work, *Wall Drawing 831, Geometric Forms*—for the Frank Gehry-designed Guggenheim Bilbao). However, she retained an important souvenir from the time she'd spent with the man who showed her life's possibilities.

LeWitt had just gotten a new job—one that would lead directly to the break he needed—but he hadn't forgotten her. For her birthday, he sent her a drawing of plants in his loft with the word "Joy" on top of it. It would become a gift that she could eventually pass along to grandchildren—who, Strider hoped, wouldn't have to wait as long as she had to take advantage of opportunities to grow.

SIX

STIRRINGS

While LeWitt and Strider were together, they saw the exhibition *Sixteen Americans* at MoMA. The featured artists[1] challenged long-held assumptions about the very nature of art. The exhibition attracted large crowds and much negative criticism. In a letter to Dorothy Miller, the show's curator, the *New York Times* critic John Canaday wrote, "For my money, these are the sixteen artists most slated for oblivion. There is not a single painting, and very little sculpture, that I could imagine living with."[2] But LeWitt reflected in 1974, "It was probably the most influential show of the decade, or of many decades, because it was the opening of many new ideas."[3]

At the time, LeWitt was still trying to discover his own direction and vision but confined by the past, still copying Renaissance masters and thinking within strict artistic boundaries. Abstract expressionism was ebbing, but what would replace it? The answer took years to develop, and LeWitt would be in the middle of it. But in 1959, when *Sixteen Americans* opened, he was just a bystander, struck by what he was seeing.

Among the most notable works in the exhibition in terms of the attention they received and the impact they made were those by the young Frank Stella, who at that point had exhibited only two paintings in two New York City shows and who apparently considered black the new primary color. Jed Perl described it this way: "The very look of this downtown bohemian world—its streets, its homes, its style of dress— was anti-picturesque."[4] Ad Reinhardt, another artist who influenced LeWitt, had experimented with shades of black. But Stella's work was more intense and stark, and it was eventually considered by critics to be the beginning of minimalism—though at the time it was considered by some to lack minimal qualities of art.

As the critic and historian Robert Rosenblum wrote twelve years later, "To most eyes [the paintings] appeared monotonously simple and inert, a bewildering impoverishment of art."[5] He quoted the critic

Dore Ashton, who had asked, "Is it really important for the public to see the work of a 23-year-old boy who has been painting for three or four years?"[6]

Artists in attendance admired the work, as it seemed to signal a new freedom. Blackness was a theme that LeWitt would use in different ways over many decades.

The exhibition also featured Jasper Johns, whom LeWitt also held in high esteem. As he later said, in the 1950s he often went to Tenth Street, where galleries showed the new and unconventional, to see Johns's work, and he remembered in particular seeing the early versions of American flags: "Of course I didn't understand it at all. I didn't know what it was all about. [Even so] I was really a big fan of his."[7]

A LeWitt work from the middle of his career, *Wall Drawing 599*, at the Jewish Community Center on New York's Upper West Side (his twentieth New York public installation), more than hints at the influence of Johns's bull's-eyes. Just as important, perhaps, was Johns's artist's statement in the catalogue for *Sixteen Americans*, especially when taking into account LeWitt's later pronouncements about the making of art. Johns related how he created his paintings: "Sometimes I see it and then paint it. Other times I paint it and then see it. Both are impure situations, and I prefer neither."[8] The comment signaled his freedom from traditional thinking and exposes the folly of explanation—a view that LeWitt often expressed.

None of the negative comments about the exhibit in the press mattered to LeWitt or to other young artists who saw it. The question of inspiration is of course an important one. There is the kind of inspiration that comes from seeing the work of Johns, Stella, and fourteen others at MoMA, in the studios of friends, or on Tenth Street. This sort of inspiration can include the charge, earned or not, of stealing ideas. Indeed, such a charge would be leveled at LeWitt many years later when, as may be inevitable in art, the lines blurred between inspiration and piracy.

There is also the kind of inspiration that is intensely private, a product of the artist's mind and heart when they are free to roam into dark or light corners whenever the mood strikes. And there is the unpredictable phenomenon of happenstance and good luck. What would have happened to LeWitt as an artist, for example, if he hadn't had certain pieces of luck? For example, would he ever have gotten himself out of the doldrums if a person he had never met hadn't left behind a rare book in the crevices of a couch while moving out of his furnished downtown apartment?

It was LeWitt's old Syracuse pal Russell North who found the book after he moved into the apartment. He showed it LeWitt, who in later recounting the episode, said, "I borrowed it. I should return it. I hate to return it."[9]

The book was a first edition of photographs by Eadweard Muybridge, the pioneer with the camera who had been born in England but lived most of his life in America. The volume showed photographs as LeWitt had never seen them before: in series, creating a narrative structure. For example, there was a horse running in several sequential frames. LeWitt had been born in an era when the motion picture was well established, but he knew that it was composed of still frames, and that Muybridge's work seemed to have been a precursor. Indeed, he was sometimes referred to as "The Father of the Motion Picture."[10]

In the 1880s, at the University of Pennsylvania, Muybridge worked on a series of photographs that would make up a sort of encyclopedia of motion. This included photographs of 20,000 positions assumed by men, women, and children, sometimes clothed and sometimes naked, and by birds and other animals. All this and much more was done before Thomas Edison began his experiments with motion pictures in 1888.

"At that time [North gave him the book] I had never heard of Muybridge," LeWitt said in an interview in 1999, but after that he was "always trying to think of ways to incorporate [some of Muybridge's ideas] into the making of art."[11]

"I think that Muybridge was really the biggest influence on my art of any older artist," he told Paul Cummings in 1974. "The logic of the serial image was the important thing to me. At first it was the image, but then it became the fact of seeing things from three different angles, as they emerged and changed. It had a beginning and an ending. A kind of philosophical realism. . . . He called his work a figure in action, in motion, or animals in motion. Of course they were still photographs. . . . It was right on the edge of photography and motion pictures."[12]

In the early 1980s, LeWitt expanded his view of Muybridge's influence, when he told Andrea Miller-Keller, curator of the Wadsworth Atheneum's new Matrix Gallery, that the photographer offered a way of creating art "that did not rely on the whim of the moment but on a consistently thought-out process that gave results that were interesting and exciting. . . . [It was] a precise way of making art which was logical rather than rational." He said that up until then there had been two systems of making art: making decisions at every moment — "a circle here, a square there"—or spreading painting everywhere (as in the work of Jackson Pollock, for example). But "Muybridge offered a third system."[13] In short, the most important part of the artist's anatomy is not the hand but the brain. And to the brainy LeWitt, this was a revelation that, after a period of failure that made him question his abilities, gave him a new path to pursue.

What struck him, as well as other members of the circle that developed around him, was that somehow art was at a dead end. They felt that the role of artist was to invent, not copy. But invent what? As LeWitt explained to Gary Garrels in 2000, what happened next—the development of what was called minimalism—was not some new advance on what had come before but, in a sense, a going backward, stripping art down to its bare essentials.[14] In effect, it was a process of looking at art, and the idea of art, as if it had never been invented.

In the early 1960s, LeWitt experimented with the idea of applying Muybridge's ideas to his own developing interests. It was the first time he had had a sense that, though inspired by the work of another artist, he could create something all his own.

In 1961, he made several pieces, including *Muybridge 1* and *Muybridge 2*, using photographs. For the first one he made a box about ten feet long, one foot high, and ten inches deep. He divided this into ten compartments, and in each he inserted a photograph of a model walking toward the viewer in sequence. "It was a process of enlargement," he explained.[15] (The process and the result would become notorious three decades later in a prominent public debate.)

He started expanding his work that featured one figure in action. A running figure, for example, was repeated, and often in three-dimensional paintings that included words of explanation and symbols such as arrows. In the documentary film by Michael Blackwood, *Sol LeWitt: 4 Decades*, the artist describes the conception of the work. He started with the running figure by Muybridge but added elements of depth and dimensionality: "Receding color, something introduced by Joseph Albers, was important here. In this piece, color and form played with one another in terms of recession and advance, the idea of objectivity rather than subjectivity, in three-dimensional forms."[16] As a result, what the viewer saw in this piece and others that followed was not a flat canvas but one that receded or came forward toward the viewer at various points in the work. Even so, this was just a step on the way to a more inventive use of this process.

Early structures, attached to walls, were simple. LeWitt used basic forms. The idea of seriality developed as time went on and was represented in *Autobiography* and so much of his work later on, with "the idea that each individual part was equally important, and that all parts were equal, with nothing hierarchal. A man running in Muybridge was the inspiration for making all the transformations of a cube within a cube, a square within a square, a cube within a square, etc."[17]

The cube became the primary building block of LeWitt's structures, which in itself created something of a visual riddle. As he would write in 1966, "The most interesting characteristic of the cube is it is relatively uninteresting. Compared to any other three-dimensional form it lacks any aggressive force, implies no motion, and is least emotive. Therefore it is the best form to use as a basic unit for any more elaborate function, the grammatical device from which the work may proceed. Because it is standard and universally recognized, no intention is required of the viewer."[18]

In terms of evolving images, the process by which LeWitt turned ideas of Albers and Johns into his own involved addition and subtraction, though his explanation seems like a riddle:

> The thing about Albers that I couldn't grasp was that if he has colors that were receding they should, I thought, physically recede . . . rather than [serve as] an illusion. This, I think, was partially from [my] understanding of what Johns was doing. . . . Then I thought, well [Johns] should be applied to Albers. In the meantime I had all these Muybridge ideas in my head, so it actually came off much more simply than it seems. They had just too many things going on, too many ideas in them. Then I discarded the figure, and the word, and the symbol, and just started doing three-dimensional things. . . . I just had to make decisions and the main decision was that one had to simplify things rather than make things more complicated. One had to figure out what one wanted to do and then simplify it in that direction.[19]

Simplicity, he thought—what a remarkable concept, particularly after the anything goes, look at me and what I'm doing abstract expressionist period.

■ At the time of *Sixteen Americans* LeWitt was once again collecting unemployment benefits, or the Rockefeller grant, as they were sometimes referred to by the cultural crowd. The reference was to New York's governor, Nelson Rockefeller, who by then had also earned the unofficial title of governor of the arts.

The city entered a new cultural era in terms of infrastructure and momentum. The Solomon R. Guggenheim Museum, twenty years in the planning, finally opened on Fifth Avenue. Lincoln Center was in its nascent stage and eventually would become the home of the Metropolitan Opera, the New York City Ballet, New York City Opera, and the New York Philharmonic. And the Rockefeller family collectively gave about half of the $25 million needed to expand MoMA, the cultural temple that the family had helped found and fund in 1929.

MoMA had earned a reputation of connecting modern life to art. It elevated the idea of design—industrial, graphic, and so on—allowing it to be recognized as a legitimate art form. The museum had architecture, photography, and film departments, which was unusual for the time. As Thomas B. Hess wrote in 1957 in *ARTnews*, "The Museum is the sum of its Christmas-cards and upholstery-fabric competitions, Mondrians, automobiles and Pollocks, Latin-American watercolors and Picassos."[20] Alfred H. Barr Jr., the museum's founding director, was still there, and its employment policies helped promising young artists willing to take entry-level jobs.

In that time, making a living as an artist in New York was an arduous task, even for some of those at the top. For example, though Pollock's canvases eventually sold for millions of dollars, during his lifetime they seldom were sold for more than $1,500. For younger artists, the economic outlook was far worse.

LeWitt was first mentioned in the *New York Times* in an article by Nan Robertson that was published in July 1961. Robertson wrote:

> The public view of painters and sculptors often focuses on two extremes, both sentimental. One is the glamorous beatnik sipping espresso into the late hours on Macdougal Street. The other is the artist struggling, starving and suffering alone in abject, but poetic, poverty.
>
> The truth is that even the most dedicated artists in New York waiting for discovery must and do work part-time as teachers, illustrators, museum guards, house painters, carpenters, salesmen, antique restorers, truck drivers, waiters, bakers, barbers, masseurs, plumbers and fashion models.[21]

Robertson's piece cited a study made by Bernard S. Myers, a professor at the City College of New York. Myers had discovered that over a five-year period only 8 of the 112 artists he tracked had earned more than $3,000 annually.

LeWitt was among the many artists that Robertson interviewed. The *Times* noted under the photo of the artist in his studio: "Sol LeWitt earned $1,000 last year, the first money he has ever taken from sales of his paintings."[22]

When he applied to work at MoMA in 1960, LeWitt was thirty-one, near the end of the "young" range. He contacted his cousin, Pell LeWitt, who worked in the museum's publicity department, and who helped arrange an interview.[23] And the idea of entry-level work didn't faze the artist. He recalled in 1993: "I asked for the job and got it. That was great. I wouldn't have to come to work until 5:30 p.m., and I'd work until about 10 or 10:30 p.m. . . . This job was the best one I got because it was sitting at the desk in the office building part in the evenings and after the offices were closed. There was nothing to do but read and be there. So I saw every exhibition that they had at the time and saw a great deal of film."[24]

In all, from 1960 to 1964, he served in a variety of capacities: bookseller, night receptionist and watchman, and all-around clerk. In the last year he worked at the museum, he was recruited to teach a class in drawing "to mainly suburban housewives" in a school run by Victor D'Amico, a tenant in the building: "I had all to do [my own work] and I made enough money, living very frugally, to live fairly well."[25]

LeWitt recalled a time of great worry at the museum during the Cuban missile crisis in 1962, when it seemed as if the United States was on the brink of war with the Soviet Union. At the time, LeWitt was stationed at one of the desks. One night "they were taking paintings out, the Picassos, Matisses, Schwitters—all the great masterpieces—and substituting a sort of the second string. Alfred Barr was coming through and I said, 'Excuse me, Mr. Barr, where these paintings are going, that's where I want to go, too.'"[26]

The coterie of low-level MoMA employees banded together artistically. Others with entry-level positions (including serving as guards) included the young artists Robert Ryman, Dan Flavin, Robert Mangold, and Gene Beery. The circle also included Lucy R. Lippard, who worked in the library and eventually became a writer and art critic who documented the minimalist and conceptual periods. Lippard wrote that

MoMA became "the hub" and "the beginning of our art world lives."[27] In 1993 LeWitt said, "It was an important little cell of art at that time. The ideas that were talked about amongst ourselves turned out to be of some significance, because at that time art was changing a great deal, and some of the more important people of that generation happened to be here at that time."[28] In the same year he recalled: "The discussions at that time were involved with new ways of making art, trying to reinvent the process, to regain basics, to become as objective as possible."[29] This idea was in direct contrast to the highly subjective and self-aggrandizing abstract expressionist movement.

A different form of influence developed in this circle, which expanded beyond MoMA employees: artists wrote about each other's work in art journals. Mel Bochner and Robert Smithson, for example, wrote about LeWitt, who in turn wrote about Ruth Vollmer. Many of the artists curated shows in new downtown galleries that included the work of their colleagues.

Because these artists got to know each other and began to gather in their respective lofts, it is tempting to think of scenes from *La Bohème*, with young impoverished dreamers struggling for their art and love. Indeed, there was even a tragic Mimi figure, Eva Hesse. But reality offered its own drama. And the jobs the artists secured gave them living wages, even if low ones, and time during the daylight hours to tend to their own work and invite their museum colleagues into their studios.

One of LeWitt's first close relationships from that period was with Flavin. Together they explored a simple idea: simplicity itself. This would be clearly manifested in Flavin's work, in which he featured arrangements of fluorescent lights that baffled many viewers.

LeWitt recalled that Flavin often quoted philosophers when he wasn't expressing his own opinions. LeWitt listened, apparently endlessly, to his new colleague: "One didn't talk very much with Flavin; one listened."[30]

LeWitt often went to Flavin's house for dinner, as the latter's wife at the time, Sonja Severdija, was an excellent cook. Flavin was "always interested in art and would talk about it. These weren't always one-sided conversations, but his egotism was not fully developed at the time. He was working on it."[31]

Loquaciousness aside, Flavin became a big influence on LeWitt, who in a 1993 interview said: "Flavin's piece [*Nominal Three*] using a progression of one, one-two, one-two-three [fluorescent lights], was an important example for me. It was one of the first system pieces I'd seen. [Donald] Judd's progression pieces of that time were also very important. I began to think of systems that were finite and simple. This was the basic difference between the idea of simplifying form to become less expressive, and the idea that the form was the carrier of ideas."[32]

The LeWitt-Flavin relationship developed at the same time that pop artists, as they would be referred to, were producing work that—in contrast with the general response to what came before it—was crowd-pleasing stuff. In a self-contradictory recollection, LeWitt said: "I always liked [Roy] Lichtenstein, and I still do. And I like [Claes] Oldenburg and [Andy] Warhol, too. . . . On the other hand—the theoretical sense—I didn't care for the whole idea of what they were doing, but I could see they were very serious people who were doing something really interesting."[33]

The momentum of pop art and then op art,[34] a spinoff that featured optical illusions and abstractions in contrast to the former's recognizable images, helped create the belief (at least in some circles) that the art world was on the brink of nothing less than revolution. The critics Harold Rosenberg and Clement Greenberg, champions of the old ways, were passé. Pop art was among the phenomena that helped build a bridge from what had come before. As the BBC art critic and author Will Gompertz wrote in *What Are You Looking At?* a capsulized history of modern art, "Lichtenstein's paintings were a very long way from Abstract Expressionism. Where the art of Pollock and Rothko had been all about existential feelings, Lichtenstein and Warhol focused purely on the material subject; removing all trace of themselves in the process."[35]

Still, how would these young artists—LeWitt being the oldest, and something of a father figure to the others—contribute to this new momentum, as they weren't interested in turning Brillo boxes into subjects? And how would they do it without falling prey to what they despised, the self-congratulatory, celebrity-driven marketplace that ranked the artists' lives as more important than their work? How would the work of the LeWitt circle become noticed? A significant part of the answer would be in the slow and steady process of relationship building.

■ There is some uncertainty about how LeWitt met Eva Hesse. In *Converging Lines: Eva Hesse and Sol LeWitt,* Veronica Roberts credits Robert Slutsky with introducing the two to each other. Lucy Lippard writes in *Eva Hesse* that Harvey and Ellen Becker did the honors. But there is no doubt that from the moment LeWitt met her, Hesse affected him deeply.

In some ways their work seemed very different from each other's. His was primarily finished when the plan was finished. Hers depended heavily on decisions made during the process of putting pieces together. But they shared common goals otherwise and were intellectually in sync.

The art historian Kirsten Swenson argues that this relationship is a microcosm of change: "Throughout the 1960s Hesse and LeWitt were engaged in an ongoing dialogue and artistic exchange, navigating the era's social and political upheavals as well as the changing values of the New York art world."[36] She also notes that "the work of Hesse and LeWitt insisted on open-endedness and ambiguity; irrational or absurd art rejected interpretation."[37] The two sympathized with each other about the difficulties of their formative years, and Hesse's deeply affected her mentor.

As a child, she had emigrated from Germany with her sister in the *Kindertransport* and was later reunited with her parents, who came to America to escape Nazi persecution of the Jews. Her grandparents, however, did not survive the Holocaust. And when Eva was twelve years old, her mother committed suicide. After that Hesse's life went in two directions, that of an art prodigy and that of a person burdened by family history and her own self-doubt.

She began to study art at the Pratt Institute when she was sixteen. She later said: "The only painting I knew, and that was very little, was abstract expressionism, and at Pratt they didn't stress painting at all. When you started painting class, you had to do a lemon still life and you graduated to a lemon and bread still life and you graduated to a lemon, egg, bread still life and this was not my idea of painting. I was also much younger, at least emotionally, and chronologically, too, than everybody else."[38] She got the job at *Seventeen* when she wasn't yet seventeen: "For some strange reason they hired me. I think it was just because of the gall of coming up there." She later studied design at Cooper Union Art School, which she loved, and then she went to Yale University, where she earned a bachelor of fine arts degree and became a faculty favorite. She recalled: "I loved Albers's color course but I had had it at Cooper. I was Albers's little color studyist—everybody always called me that— and every time he walked into the classroom he would ask, 'What did Eva do?' But Albers couldn't stand my painting and, of course, I was

　　　　　SOL LEWITT

much more serious about the painting." At the time she met LeWitt, she was also trying to make it as a painter. And like him, she had taken jobs in Manhattan to pay the rent — in her case first at a jewelry store and then as a textile designer.

In one of his last interviews, in 2001, LeWitt described meeting Hesse: "She was really cute, very pretty, very alive, very hip at that time. She knew a lot of people because of being at Yale . . . even though what she was doing was kind of still-school stuff, I thought it was really pretty good."[39]

From his own testimony and from that of the sculptor Tom Doyle, who later married Hesse, LeWitt fell hard for the young artist. Many men did. In 1972, the *New York Post* reported, "There is no one who doesn't mention Eva Hesse's beauty — a dark, brooding, 5-foot-3 beauty, with dangling earrings and clunky shoes and Bohemian — but always stylish — clothes."[40] LeWitt said in 1972, "Yeah, well, I was sort of wowed by her, but unfortunately she wasn't wowed by me."[41] Doyle's explanation of why Hesse had no romantic feelings for LeWitt was that "she said Sol reminded her too much of her father."[42] Nevertheless, LeWitt and Hesse had a deep relationship, which eventually helped both struggling artists discover new approaches to their work. Like all female artists of the time, Hesse had an extra burden as she tried to succeed in a male-dominated field.

The fact that LeWitt would come to help her and then other female artists before the dawn of feminism earned him many admirers. In 1978 he wrote, "It was my friendship with Eva that made me aware of the problems that women artists face in a world dominated by the male hierarchy. . . . There seems to be an implicit rule (even among female critics, etc.) that a woman can never be considered the dominant practitioner of a style or idea."[43]

■ LeWitt met Doyle in 1961 and immediately started talking football. Both were avid fans, and both had played the game — though LeWitt's artistry on the gridiron was hidden in the middle of the line, and Doyle's wasn't. As a wide receiver (then simply called an "end") for Miami University, in Oxford, Ohio, his exploits had been clearly seen, and he retained an insider's knowledge of the game. But he had been the only wide receiver in the Mid-American Conference to become more interested in making sculpture than in scoring touchdowns. He was also — no minor point, from LeWitt's point of view — in love with Hesse. Lucy

Lippard described Doyle's appeal when Hesse met him at the opening of his first show, at the Allan Stone Gallery. He was "a lively and charming Pennsylvania and Ohio Irishman, several years older than [Hesse], a dedicated sculptor, good talker, Civil War buff, and Joyce addict."[44]

Doyle and Hesse soon married, and worked and lived at first in a loft on Eighteenth Street near Fifth Avenue, moving to the Bowery in 1963. "The trouble was it was against the law to live in a loft," Doyle recalled.[45] Artists were supposed to limit their time in such venues to working and live elsewhere. Far from having the cachet that it now does, in those days lofts were mostly dingy firetraps in down-and-out neighborhoods. "Artists specialized in hiding things from inspectors," Doyle said. But he was not very talented at this: "One time a fireman came to my loft and asked me, 'You got a stove? You got hot water? What about that bed, there?' I shrugged. He said, 'You artists—you don't have nothing but a good time.'" Robert Barry's solution—when he had an apartment on the corner of Grand and the Bowery with no heat and only cold water, for $70 a month—was to take a $20 bill out of his shirt pocket and hand it to the inspector. As a result, he never had any trouble, except for the time when he was instructed to put a screen around the potbellied stove.[46]

LeWitt had faced similar problems, but he used his wits instead of his bank account to solve them. Once when an inspector came to his own dilapidated studio and living quarters, he had to figure out how to avoid a summons to court and, at the same time, not present false testimony as he had in the I. M. Pei case. According to Doyle, when the inspector asked, "Do you live here, too?" LeWitt replied, "Would you live in such a place?"[47] This answer, apparently, solved the issue.

In those days, as no artist in the circle could afford extravagance, they helped each other as best they could. For example, LeWitt became part of the construction crew when Doyle and Hesse moved from Eighteenth Street to the Bowery, an area where the rents were cheap, the working spaces were ample (their place, though ramshackle, had wide floorboards and two fireplaces), and the conveniences of life scarce. So was privacy and a sense of safety, though Doyle said, "the bums were so drunk they wouldn't bother you."[48]

Doyle had just finished building a studio for the jazz saxophonist Ornette Coleman, and he needed immediate help to make a studio space for himself and Hesse. LeWitt arrived at the right time. He helped install plumbing in the bathroom, repair the plaster walls, and put in a toilet and bathtub. Doyle very much appreciated the help, though he noted that "Sol wasn't a great mechanic."[49]

When everything was done, Doyle and Hesse set up shop, with space enough to invite others in who had worked alongside of them before the move. So Grace Bakst Wapner and Ethelyn Honig also did their artwork in the Bowery district.

Still in her mid-twenties, Wapner became part of the LeWitt-Doyle-Hesse-MoMA circle in 1960 without any real intention of doing so. Though she had graduated with a bachelor of arts degree from Bennington College a few years earlier and had taken courses in sculpture and ceramics, she had followed a conventional path for young women at the time—marrying young, having children, and thinking of art as something of a hobby. She was convinced that her own talent, whatever it was, should be confined to producing things that would never be seen in public. Her attitude, in short, was a common one among female artists in a male-dominated profession.

Even so, on weekdays she took the kids to school and then rode buses from the Upper West Side to the Lower East Side to work on her art and pursue her blossoming friendship with Doyle, LeWitt, and Hesse.

LeWitt was known throughout this period and later for providing encouragement to artists without regard to gender, a rare gift in those days. Both Hesse and Wapner were recipients of his guidance. Wapner recalled:

> I was a totally immature artist then, just beginning to find my way. I didn't know Warhol, Lichtenstein, or [James] Rosenquist. Sol deliberately took me around to meet various artists: Judd, Flavin, [Carl] Andre. I remember that we had lunch with Carl, and he doodled on a napkin, and then Sol picked it up and put it in his pocket.
>
> Sol helped me a great deal. There was something about his mind and the way it worked. We spent a lot of time together, he often came with me to pick up the kids from school, and we talked about everything.[50]

LeWitt gave Wapner other rare gifts. On Mozart's birthday, he brought her keys from an old piano. And he gave her lists of books to read by Leo Tolstoy, Joseph Conrad, and Gustave Flaubert, as well as Jane Austin's *Emma*. He was a Henry Higgins to her Eliza Doolittle, but much kinder than Higgins. He was also something of a Harry Houdini, or perhaps merely an ordinary thief.

One day Wapner discovered that "I was missing a piece from my [sculpture] work. There were a lot of scraps I had been putting together. I was sure I had this piece there somewhere, but couldn't find it. Two weeks later, Sol showed up with box of primary colors on the outside, and little holes to peek through."[51] On the bottom it said, "The most important thing is on the inside." It was her missing piece. Three years later that missing piece was still in the box that LeWitt had borrowed from her so that he could include it, titled *Cube with Random Holes Containing an Object*, as one of two pieces in his first gallery show—a piece that, obviously, asked the viewer to go beyond what could be seen.

Honig's path to the Bowery differed from Wapner's, but it also illustrated the particular obstacles that women faced when trying to be taken seriously as artists. Honig had studied not art but sociology and psychology at Sarah Lawrence College, and for a time she had thought she might go into acting. Like Wapner, she married early, at the age of twenty-one. Her husband was a physician, both an internist and gastroenterologist. It had been "an arranged marriage. My mother met his mother at the hairdresser. I only knew him six weeks before the wedding day."[52]

Honig and her husband had two children, but like Wapner, Honing was itching to expand her vision beyond the home. She had always liked to draw and had taken art classes at Sarah Lawrence and then Bennington, "though I didn't understand a thing [the professors] were talking about."[53] Instead she did her thesis on the fascist personality.

But once back in New York City, she found work as a gallery assistant, and in that capacity she met Eva Hesse, "who was absolutely gorgeous."[54] Her relationship with Hesse led to their sharing an interior space in the Bowery studio of Doyle and Hesse. "The width of the place was twenty-five to thirty feet or more, with a huge window in Eva's area. Grace and I had no windows. There was curtain erected around Tom and Eva's bedroom, and Tom's big work space was filled with wood."

Honig remembered that friends who dropped by "always went into Tom's studio, never Eva's."[55] LeWitt was an exception: "Sol came around pretty much every day and talked to us. Grace was asking for guidance, but I wasn't. Even so when I did talk to him he always offered support." She also recalled that at the time LeWitt was still working on his Muybridge-inspired pieces, and that he used tools borrowed from Doyle and Wapner. With them, he "made some boxes pierced with holes and placed [objects] inside the boxes. The only way one could see the [photo or object] in the box was to look through the holes. Much later when Eva made her 'Accession' pieces, I was to think of Sol's boxes again." Hesse's pieces were square boxes made of galvanized steel and vinyl.

Hesse, Honig recalled, was needy: "She was very angsty. She said to me, 'You can make a home. I can only make a studio.'"[56]

Hesse's diary is full of anxiety and doubts. In 1963, she wrote: "There is a tenseness and anxiousness that never leave me. . . . I am constantly dissatisfied with myself and testing myself. I have so much anger and resentment within me. Why still now. . . . It is difficult to be an artist's wife and an artist also."[57]

Indeed Lippard, who chronicled Hesse's life, confesses that when she first met Hesse, she thought of her as "Tom's wife," rather than an artist of equal, or better, caliber.[58]

Wapner's relationship with Hesse also yielded insights into the troubled artist. They had met in Woodstock, in upstate New York, where Wapner and her family always summered.

Wapner and Hesse quickly bonded, though they were of different temperaments and different worlds. "There were times," Wapner recalled, "when she was almost incapacitated, and times when she was full of life and warmth and could be very encouraging."[59] But then Wapner, like many others, could only imagine the emotional cost of Hesse's seriously interrupted childhood. Wapner saw Hesse as innately talented, unlike herself: "It had never occurred to me that I could be an artist. I could just make art. Whereas for Eva, art was her self-definition. She didn't think she could be a mother. I think it was because she felt she wouldn't have the patience, the energy, the concentration. She was too occupied with work and didn't have those reserves of selflessness. I just did work whenever I could, and when I came home my children were primary to me."[60]

Wapner and others sensed a certain tension between Hesse and Doyle. Theirs had been a whirlwind romance — they were married six months after they met, and though they were passionate about each other, they turned out to be fiercely competitive in their art — particularly when Hesse began to receive more attention than Doyle.

LeWitt, of course, was the son of a woman who long ago had managed both to master the challenges of motherhood (and to do so particularly well, given that she had to undertake the task without a partner) and to carry on her career as a nurse, in the New Britain schools. Such a balancing act was not common in those days and may have contributed to her son's sensitivity to the struggle of women who faced both discrimination in the workplace and internal questions about how to pursue passions outside of family life.

His most dramatic effort to provide such help came in the case of Hesse. In early 1964, she and Doyle had gone to Germany, where the industrialist Friedrich Schiedt had offered free studio space in a factory near Düsseldorf in exchange for works of art.

From time to time LeWitt kept in touch both of them, updating his friends on US news; his work or nonwork; his political takes, always from the left. One letter followed the Harlem riots in the summer of 1964 and referred to the convention that nominated Barry Goldwater to be the Republican candidate for president:

> July 20, 1964
> Dear Eva and Tom,
> Very good to hear from you—nice letter. Summer is a pisser
> —very, very hot—sit around in my jockey shorts, watch TV, drink
> beer, work a little in AM, drink beer. I get good breeze in the back of
> my place. Watched Republican convention some on TV. Surrealist
> nightmare—endless bullshit. Eisenhower incredible master of
> non-speech and non-interview, can talk for hours and say nothing.
> G'water could win! If all bigots vote for him, he'll win in landslide.
> All whites who are afraid of negroes or afraid of anything whoop it
> up for him. Oh well. Can't live forever. Understand Europeans are
> shitting in pants (except Germans—they find something appealing
> in G'water and he in them). Riots in Harlem this past weekend—
> all middle class solid citizens diving for foxholes, hoping G'water
> will restore law and order. . . . Maybe stay in Europe for the next
> 8 years.[61]

LeWitt also included in the letter specific news about his circle, which he titled: "Society Notes From the Bowery." An excerpt: "The Robert Rymans are vacationing in Maine and have been up there for the past three weeks. They are laughing at weather reports from NY. . . . The Ray Donarskis have dragged into town but I haven't seen them—so fuck them. Little Irwin Flemminger has found a loft of good size (25 feet by 90) on the Bowery near Houston."[62]

LeWitt's letters to Hesse to this point had little practical effect. She continued to struggle as both an artist and a wife during this period. Her diary and letters refer to her difficulties. In diary entries in 1964 she lamented that she was doing little work, was depressed, and was reading a good deal. In the space of a month or so, she finished two Katherine Anne Porter novels, *Pale Horse, Pale Rider* and *Ship of Fools*; Kingsley Amis's *Lucky Jim*; John Braine's *Vodi*; and Colin Wilson's *Adrift in Soho*.[63] She also listed the dates when Tom disappeared or was drunk, as well as the intrusions of visitors and obligations. Once, when she sold a piece, she could feel the tension because on the same day a work of Tom's was rejected. To distract herself from her own intensifying confusion and sadness, she read Mark Twain—first *Pudd'nhead Wilson* and then the iconic writer's autobiography.

Her work suffered. Doyle recalled, "I told her why don't you try [using] some of the shit lying around here [in her sculpture]. They're tearing up the old weaving things in the factory. . . . We could use anything we wanted. The workers all brought us stuff they thought we'd like—they were breaking up machines. There were miles of that string there. The string is what got her going."[64]

Even so, she wrote to Honig in March 1965, "A woman is sidetracked by all her feminine roles from menstrual periods to cleaning house to remaining pretty and 'young' and having babies."[65]

In another letter to Honig written in the same period, Hesse said she dwelled on "the female struggle" all the time and referred to the difference between her outlook and her husband's: "My determination and will is strong but I am lacking so in self-esteem that I never seem to overcome. Also competing all the time with a man with self-confidence in his work and who is successful also."[66]

And in April 1965 she wrote to LeWitt and quoted from her diary with only a few small changes to correct grammar. The letter makes clear her despair and self-doubt:

> Day after April Fool's Day
> Dear Sol,
> It is to you I want to talk about what is on my mind. It is because I respect and trust you, and also in this case you are one who understands somewhat me personally and my art, existent or nonexistent.
> Also, we strike some diametrically opposed balance, reacting emotionally so differently yet somewhere understanding. I know I

kind of went down in your estimation but I feel deservedly so. Like I disappointed you and myself as a person in many ways! Still, I feel in some ways you are with me. Be that as it may I want to explain (try to) what I am going through in my work or non-work.

I trust myself not enough to come through with any one idea; or maybe a singular good idea does not exist. And if there would be one among the many I don't think I could recognize it. So I fluctuate between working at the confusion or nonworking at the confusion. When not actually at work I nevertheless struggle with the ideas —like I'm hip—maybe too much so—grasping everything and nothing in the hope of finding self. At this time I can no longer see what I have done nor distill the meaning. I want to too much and try too much—the joke is on me, constant frustration and failure.

I wonder at my trying so hard. It is likely for the wrong reasons I feel. But when one doubts oneself as much as I do one can wonder what is a rationalization justifying what—like maybe that is just the way struggle is supposed to be, nothing more nor less. But I cannot sustain the desire to work long enough to solve anything, and maybe I don't love it enough to try.

But then, what else shall I do? I read and worry and it goes in circles and the thought crops us, work it out and you shall find out. But then I am alone with myself and it is unbearable for me.

I don't want sympathy but I don't want you to laugh at me. I would only like to be able to show you what I have done here and ask you what you think. That is impossible so I am talking with you.[67]

Hesse went on to describe some of the work she had been producing, thinking it worthwhile at times and worthless at other times. There are scores of drawings using loose ("free and crazy") forms, and for two solid days she'd been working on "a dumb thing which has three dimension, supposed to provide continuity with the last drawing. It actually looks like a breast and penis—but that's OK, and I should go on with it. Maybe it or they would make it in another way but I don't know where I belong, so I give it up again. All the time it is like that!"[68] Later she added: "Anything is better than the inactive or no ending suffering of not knowing and trying to know. To decide on a purpose and way of life, a consistent approach to even some impossible end or even imagined end."

It was a week later when LeWitt received the letter on Hester Street, and a few weeks after that when his response was on its way to Germany. The first part of the response is the one that artists around the world often quote to each other whenever they are stuck. It also reflects the permutation idea that began with the Muybridge inspiration and that would be so dramatically explored in LeWitt's grids, boxes, and wall drawings. The second half of the response, however, may be just as valuable, as it is much less of a rant and reveals LeWitt's own struggles and doubts, and shows how, in time, he pushed through them.

In a 2001 interview LeWitt reflected on what he had written Hesse: "I had, really even before she went away to Germany . . . recognized that she had something extraordinary about her work and I just couldn't see her frittering it away with self-doubts, which were a big thing in her life. She was going to these therapy sessions her whole life. The thing is she never really got rid of all these kinds of [fears]."[69]

Compounding the problem was Hesse's struggle with being a wife and an artist, at a time just before the feminist movement gathered momentum — which presumably would have allowed her to feel permitted to follow her instincts.

Wapner's experience was more typical of the way talented women sublimated their desires to address important family issues. But Hesse eventually forged ahead. LeWitt said: "She was a symbol, an example of a career, or a way of being in the art would that would not have been possible before. Before she was working, I think the male-dominated art scene would not allow a woman to be a great, important artist. They [women] could be subsidiary; they could do good art, but not something that was really tremendously important. [Hesse] did, and in a very brief time."[70]

It will never be known with any certainty whether LeWitt's now famous letter became the primary spur or whether, as LeWitt later surmised, that some people (like Mozart and Gershwin) may instinctively know that their time on earth is short, and they must produce: "You do have all these examples of people rushing back to their studios and other people leisurely going through their lives, producing things as they go along, without any hint of somebody tapping on their shoulder and saying hurry up."[71]

LeWitt's letter also is an inspiration for people today who have never worked in a studio but who are in any field in which subjectivity rules, and where self-confidence is a fragile commodity. Here is the full text:

Dear Eva,

It will be almost a month since you wrote to me and you have possibly forgotten your state of mind (I doubt it though). You seem the same as always, and being you, hate every minute of it. Don't! Learn to say "Fuck You" to the world once in a while. You have every right to. Just stop thinking, worrying, looking over your shoulder, wondering, doubting, fearing, hurting, hoping for some easy way out, struggling, grasping, confusing, itching, scratching, mumbling, bumbling, grumbling, humbling, stumbling, numbling, rumbling, gambling, tumbling, scumbling, scrambling, hitching, hatching, bitching, moaning, groaning, honing, boning, horse-shitting, hair-splitting, nit-picking, piss-trickling, nose sticking, ass-gouging, eyeball-poking, finger-pointing, alleyway-sneaking, long waiting, small stepping, evil-eyeing, back-scratching, searching, perching, besmirching, grinding, grinding, grinding away at yourself. Stop it and just DO!

From your description, and from what I know of your previous work and your ability, the work you are doing sounds very good. "Drawing-clean-clear but crazy like machines, larger and bolder . . . real nonsense." That sounds fine, wonderful — real nonsense. Do more. More nonsensical, more crazy, more machines, more breasts, penises, cunts, whatever — make them abound with nonsense. Try and tickle something inside you, your "weird humor." You belong in the most secret part of you. Don't worry about cool, make your own uncool. Make your own world. If you fear, make it work for you — draw and paint your fear and anxiety. And stop worrying about big, deep things such as "to decide on a purpose and way of life, a consistent approach to even some impossible end or even an imagined end." You must practice being stupid, dumb, unthinking, empty. Then you will be able to DO!

I have much confidence in you and even though you are tormenting yourself, the work you do is very good. Try to do some BAD work — the worst you can think of and see what happens but mainly relax and let everything go to hell — you are not responsible for the world — you are only responsible for your work — so DO IT. And don't think that your work has to conform to any preconceived form, idea or flavor. It can be anything you want it to be. But if life would be easier for you if you stopped working — then stop. Don't punish yourself. However, I think that it is so deeply engrained in you that it would be easier to DO!

It seems I do understand your attitude somewhat, anyway, because I go through a similar process every so often. I have an "Agonizing Reappraisal" of my work and change everything as much as possible and hate everything I've done, and try to do something entirely different and better. Maybe that kind of process is necessary to me, pushing me on and on. The feeling that I can do better than that shit I just did. Maybe you need your agony to accomplish what you do. And maybe it goads you on to do better. But it is very painful I know. It would be better if you had the confidence just to do the stuff and not even think about it. Can't you leave the "world" and "ART" alone and also quit fondling your ego? I know that you (or anyone) can only work so much and the rest of the time you are left with your thoughts. But when you work or before you work you have to empty your mind and concentrate on what you are doing. After you do something it is done and that's that. After a while you can see some are better than others but also you can see what direction you are going. I'm sure you know all that. You also must know that you don't have to justify your work—not even to yourself. Well, you know I admire your work greatly and can't understand why you are so bothered by it. But you can see the next ones and I can't. You also must believe in your ability. I think you do. So try the most outrageous things you can—shock yourself. You have at your power the ability to do anything.

I would like to see your work and will have to be content to wait until Aug. or Sept. I have seen photos of some of Tom's new things at Lucy's [Lippard]. They are impressive—especially the ones with the more rigorous form: the simpler ones. I guess he'll send some more later on. Let me know how the shows are going and that kind of stuff.

My work has changed since you left and it is much better. I will be having a show May 4–9 at the Daniels Gallery 17 E. 64th St. . . . I wish you could be there. Much love to you both.

Sol[72]

"I will be having a show . . . at the Daniels Gallery"—this information is passed along in a matter-of-fact way, without much attention called to it or any hallelujahs. At the relatively advanced age of thirty-six, he was about to have what was only his second group show, but the occasion called for no boasting or celebrating in light of Hesse's depression, and in any case doing so wasn't his habit.

Hesse responded to LeWitt's urgings. In a letter she wrote to her friend Rose Goldman, she said she was "working like crazy."[73] She used a variety of materials in her new work, including pressed wood fibers, cord, acetone varnish, enamel, ink, electrical wire and papier-mâché.

From then on, LeWitt and Hesse's correspondence and contact was constant. In the late 1960s LeWitt's first foreign show, in Düsseldorf, quickly gave him an entrée to the world. His postcards to Hesse during this time were postmarked from Kyoto, Tunis, Rome, Marrakesh, Amsterdam, Tangier, Granada, Barcelona, Leningrad, Helsinki, and Lima. Some of these trips were related to work (he had pieces in shows or sales), but most were the result of LeWitt's continuing urge to travel.

When Hesse returned to New York and her marriage ended, she relied heavily on LeWitt's support, and they were in nearly daily contact. For Hesse, the following years proved that LeWitt's confidence in her was not wasted. After she returned to the United States, she became a central figure in what became the post-minimalist movement. Her drawings and structures (made of materials such as rubber, papier-mâché, wax, wire mesh, enamel, and cheesecloth) were exhibited (though never, during her lifetime, in a solo show), and she gave LeWitt credit for his influence and support in her exhibition texts. However, on occasions when her work was not included in major shows, she became distraught. After feeling snubbed by the influential gallery owner Virginia Dwan, who did not invite her to participate in the 1966 exhibition titled *10*,[74] she wrote notes of frustration in her journal. She said that she felt like a "non-artist" and that "they all forget me. . . . This includes Sol, yes loyal Sol. He neglects me socially with Virginia. I too am forgotten. Yes, even Sol."[75]

Dwan later said, "My artists [at the time] were LeWitt and [Carl] Andre. . . . My eyes weren't ready for Hesse at that point."[76]

During this time Hesse experimented with materials in her sculpture and often used latex though she worried it was too impermanent. In an audio interview given in the late 1960s that has been preserved by the San Francisco Museum of Modern Art (which mounted a Hesse retrospective in in 2002), she said after talking of her use of latex, "Life doesn't last, art doesn't last."[77] The latex, then, had become a metaphor.

The fact that she began to experiment with fiberglass led to speculation that toxic materials she worked with could have caused or contributed to her illness. It was then, after all, that she complained to LeWitt and others of severe headaches. In later years, fiberglass would be classified as a health hazard, tied to serious lung conditions and cancer. (The sculptor Duane Hanson, who also worked extensively with fiberglass, was diagnosed with cancer, and the connection between such maladies and certain kinds of plastics were made in a variety of authoritative studies.)

As the years passed, and particularly in the first part of the twenty-first century, Hesse's stature and legacy as an artist grew as the art world recognized her innovations. As LeWitt said, "she fired peoples' imaginations."[78] In 2009, the art historian Briony Fer wrote about the variety of work and materials displayed in a 2002 exhibit of Hesse's work at the Tate Modern in London: "A collection in miniature of Hesse's art. . . . I don't think it's too much of an exaggeration to see their combined effect as a small bomb exploding the category of things called sculpture."[79]

On several occasions Hesse's work has been exhibited with LeWitt's, most significantly in the 2014 show mounted by the Blanton Museum in Austin, Texas, that traveled to the Addison Gallery in Andover, Massachusetts, and then to the Cleveland Museum of Art. A documentary film, *Tracing the Rope: Eva Hesse Life + Work*, was released in 2015 and received enthusiastic reviews.[80]

Members of the LeWitt circle considered many questions over the years, including how high Hesse's star would have risen if she hadn't died from the effects of a brain tumor in 1970. For many of the artists, LeWitt included, her spirit and innovation endured. LeWitt often referred to her as his best friend and a great artist, and he saw her as a central figure in his own development. In particular, Lippard describes *Metronomic Irregularity II* as "square grey panels connected by dynamic lines of white wire, like brain waves working overtime."[81] According to Veronica Roberts, its ideas may well have influenced LeWitt in the creation of his first wall drawings.[82]

Honig remembered Hesse as an inspiration not only for her but also for many other artists, female and male. Honig went on to exhibit her work in scores of shows including those at MoMA and the Musée d'Art Moderne de la Ville de Paris, and she returned LeWitt's many favors by publishing his first public print portfolio in 1970.

Wapner—the woman who didn't think she could be an artist—went on to place her work in more than a hundred solo or group shows and has published many essays on art and the women and men who make it. She retains a vivid memory of the meaning of the multicolored box, *Cube with Random Holes Containing an Object,* with the "most important" item inside. She remembers that she took it home on the bus one day to show her family, and that a fellow rider was certain that the mysterious object "must be a pussy cat."[83]

SEVEN

"WHAT WOULD SOL DO?"

In the early 1960s, Gene Beery, a guard at MoMA, patrolled the galleries with curiosity about their contents but not much else. "I didn't know anything at the time," he recalled. "I was a rube—a Catholic conservative Republican nitwit from Wisconsin."[1]

He was also an aspiring artist, and he liked what he saw on the walls and in the museum's garden. But Beery would not have been able, had a visitor asked, to explain the significance of, say, the vast art collection of James Thrall Soby, of Hartford, that became part of the MoMA collection and went on display in a 1961 exhibition. Soby, who had worked at the Wadsworth Atheneum in Hartford before becoming a curator at MoMA, had purchased works for himself by Picasso, Balthus, Miró, Calder, and Dalí.

Beery yearned to know more about the 300 photographs by Edward Steichen that went on display in March and the futurism show that spring—the Italian artists Giacomo Balla, Umberto Boccioni, Luigi Russolo, and Ardengo Soffici used modern technology and movement as inspiration. Gallery talks were scheduled daily on Picasso's *Guernica*, Matisse's *Red Studio*, and other masterpieces. An aspiring artist needed to know about these, and about how the past affects the present and the future.

Beery could also learn from music. The Thelonious Monk Quartet was coming to play at the museum,[2] and there would be a concert of compositions by John Cage—whose most talked-about piece at the time was titled *4'33"*, during which not a note is played for almost five minutes. What kind of music, an artist might well have wondered, is that? And what freedom is a visual artist granted? If a composition has no music, could a painting have no paint? There was so much to know, see, and hear, but Beery's job prevented him from being in the audience. The "rube" needed a mentor, and there was an older man (in his early thirties) at the desk who, Beery recalled, "watched people come in and out of museum . . . and he seemed to have plenty of time on his hands, and was easy to talk to."[3]

So Beery, an aspiring artist from Racine, Wisconsin, and Sol LeWitt, an aspiring artist from Hartford, Connecticut, began the first of their many conversations during their hours on duty at MoMA, and LeWitt did for Beery, in a larger sense, what Earl Kerkam had done for him.

LeWitt filled Beery in on much of what he needed in the way of art history. He also introduced Beery to the writings of Samuel Beckett; Eugene O'Neill; Michel Butor; and another French author, Louis-Ferdinand Céline — the pen name for Louis Ferdinand Auguste Destouches, a brilliant novelist and virulent anti-Semite.[4] The two men talked of other LeWitt passions — Johann Sebastian Bach; an array of classical, romantic, and modern composers; and jazz, discussing themes and variations on themes, ideas that both would pursue in their work.

In short, Beery received what he had come to New York to get, including encouragement for his own painting. LeWitt liked the way his new friend was thinking, incorporating words into his images — an idea that LeWitt had tested in a different form. Both men would explore language's relationship to art, Beery in a more obvious way than LeWitt.

In 1961, a few Beery pieces were chosen for a figure painting exhibit at MoMA. When the show went up, he was in the unusual position of standing guard over his own work. He was shocked when one visitor — no less a person than Max Ernst himself — offered $100 on the spot for one of them, a deal it was impossible to refuse, and the transaction conferred on him the exalted titled of artist.

Beery had come a long way in a short time, and he provided something important for his mentor — the news that an apartment was available in his building at 117 Hester Street. At the time, LeWitt had been renting nearby, on Montgomery Street, and paying $23.50 a month (rats included); he was seeking a better space.[5]

Hester Street was in the heart of the Lower East Side neighborhood that had been a refuge for many European immigrants — notably, Jews leaving the oppression in Eastern Europe. Many Italians and members of other ethnic groups had moved in since, but there were still a kosher meat market, Orthodox synagogues, and a shop that sold egg creams as well as turkey and duck eggs. And there was a firehouse down on Canal Street from which, Beery recalled, "The damn engines would go out at two in the morning, with the firemen blasting their horns just to wake everybody up."[6] His building's first floor was occupied by Meyerhoff Butter and Eggs. But many people remember the neighborhood at the time as dangerous—needles were found in the street, and people were afraid of going out at night.

Still, LeWitt was intrigued, and he rented a third-floor apartment there for $45 a month (he could have moved to an apartment on the seventh floor instead, which—because there was no elevator—would have been $28 cheaper). Beery remembered buying scraps of lumber from the bums on the Bowery to produce heat from the wood stoves. This history may come as something of a surprise to the buyers who in 2015 secured a condo across the street of roughly the same size for $1,800,000.

Beery was delighted that his museum colleague would be so close, but he didn't anticipate that he would soon have to call on his friend to bail him out of deep financial trouble.

As time passed, Beery had won a bit of success as an artist but not much income. When he fell two months behind in his rent, "the land-lord gave me an ultimatum. I had a lot of art there, my 'masterpieces,' and the landlord said, 'OK, sorry—I'm sending everything to the Staten Island dump,' including my paintings. But Sol intervened and saved quite a few. He put them in his place, and then he paid me for them— six grand for ten paintings. That was a lot of money. He eventually gave these paintings to the Wadsworth Atheneum."[7] LeWitt had become able to buy art and support friends by selling a few of his own works and living frugally—not spending money on chic living quarters, trendy consumer goods, or automobiles.

Beery remembers that LeWitt's apartment became a gathering place for many people from MoMA, including the aspiring writer Lucy Lippard, who lived nearby. Two other regular visitors were Robert and Sylvia Plimack Mangold.

Robert Mangold, like LeWitt, found the working arrangements at MoMA ideal for his schedule and needs of the moment. As a guard he was a union member, and for the first time he had health insurance— an important consideration, as he and Sylvia would soon have a child. The hours were convenient as well, as the museum was open only from 11 A.M. to 5 P.M. This gave Mangold, as it did LeWitt, time early in the day to tend to his own art. Like all guards, Mangold was assigned to varying work stations. Sometimes he would be in a gallery, sometimes in the movie theater, and occasionally an elevator. In the course of his day, Mangold would often see LeWitt sitting at a desk, reading a book. During breaks and at other times, the two artists talked. When they compared notes on art, they seemed to be in sync, and they became close friends. Mangold's education and struggles in some ways mirrored LeWitt's and led him to the same point in his artistic career.[8]

Mangold had grown up in Buffalo: "I came from a family in which everybody worked in a factory. I didn't want to be a factory worker."[9] So he went to the Cleveland Institute of Art and "started hanging out with painters and sculptors. . . . I saw that the teachers in Cleveland taught two or three days a week, and I thought I could have that life, too. I'd be a teacher-painter." But what these teacher-painters were doing, Mangold discovered, was limited in scope: "It was very academic. Figure drawing was king. All traditional things. So I also wound up doing still life paintings—pots and pans and draperies."

In 1955, Mangold visited nearby Pittsburgh for what was then an annual event, the Carnegie International Expo—first held in 1896 and the oldest recurring exhibit of contemporary art in America. That show opened Mangold's eyes and imagination:

> They had Kline, de Kooning, Pollock, and artists who painted in Europe including Picasso. It was an amazing juxtaposition from the world of Andrew Wyeth. I wanted to know about abstract expressionism, the New York School. But the faculty in Cleveland wasn't interested. I wanted to understand the new way of painting. But the way to understand is to do it. And so I did. One teacher was sympathetic to me. In referring to other faculty members, he said, "They all think you're terrific, but they don't like what you're doing. They don't like New York artists." So there was this rub.[10]

Mangold knew he had to move on, and he got that chance when he received a scholarship to study for a master's degree at Yale University. It was during his time in New Haven, Connecticut, that he met Sylvia Plimack, who had been a classmate of Eva Hesse at Cooper Union and who had also had come to New Haven to study.

After finishing at Yale, Mangold and Plimack moved into an apartment on Eldridge Street, in the same Lower East Side neighborhood where LeWitt, Beery, and Lippard lived. And they saw the work of other artists in the expanding MoMA circle.

Mangold recalled: "There wasn't envy or jealousy back then. Everybody was supportive of each other, back before people started having covers on *Artforum*."[11] He remembered long and sometimes contentious discussions about the future of art. When abstract expressionism petered out, there was controversy among critics, museum directors, gallery owners, and artists about the potential endurance and worth of the pop art and op art phenomena and what "ism" would be next. Mangold was experimenting with monochromatic pieces and trapezoids, and his work was certainly not part of what was catching on at the time. However, he found comfort and support in the emerging circle of MoMA artists, the oldest of whom was LeWitt.

"Sol was a real leader in that community," Mangold said. "I can remember that whenever a decision had to be made, we'd ask ourselves, 'What would Sol do?' How would he handle this? He seemed to have such a clear head emotionally. For example, artists could get angry at this group or that group, but he was open to their ideas in a way that we weren't."[12] In terms of LeWitt's support of women, the curator Marcia Tucker wrote, "He had a kind of sensitivity and awareness that was unusual at the time."[13]

LeWitt emerged as not only the father figure but also one of the few artists of the time who could be counted on to have a cool head. Lawrence Weiner, another member of the growing group of upstarts, recalled that "socially, Sol had a lot of warts," referring to his lack of interest in, even disdain for, social conventions. He continued: "But I adored Sol for one reason, the way he acted at times of difficulty. He controlled his jealously, controlled his anger. He literally controlled himself. Sol was not a saint. But his caring—that's what made him such a decent human being."[14] Wherever possible, he pointed to possibilities as opposed to limitations.

Sylvia Plimack Mangold remembered the challenge that LeWitt gave her when he visited her studio and told her that she had more talent than she thought she had. According to her, "if you were his friend, you were his friend for life."[15]

These friends were all involved in the same adventure—they were artists who didn't easily fit into the categories that to then had been so well defined. And none of them, LeWitt included, had earned anything close to a glamorous living by pursuing their individual passions.

■ LeWitt and others who punched MoMA's time clock produced their artwork during their off-hours, but who would notice it, and who would buy it? These artists had two common goals: making sure that their work was seen and, in a celebrity-driven market, avoiding calling attention to anything but their art. That approach worked for J. D. Salinger after publishing *The Catcher in the Rye*, but LeWitt hadn't produced anything iconic, nor was he a recluse—just someone more comfortable making art than making small talk or mastering the art of glad-handing.

Who would know about and verify the worth of his efforts by actually writing checks? Would Dan Flavin's fluorescent lights, arranged as art rather than office illumination, catch a collector's imagination? Would Robert Ryman's fiercely monochromatic paintings; Mangold's trapezoidal panels; or LeWitt's representations of somersaults or other images, his drawings of irregular lines and progressions inspired by Muybridge, or some of his new work—a combination of painting and, as he would call it, structure—that had no category? As Weiner, another of the artists who emerged during this period, recalled, "The only audience we really had was other artists."[16]

What these artists and a few others connected to them wanted to do was, in effect, to start over, rethink the idea of art, and redefine the process of making it—to go back to the beginning. In 1993 LeWitt said: "My thinking was involved with the problem of painting at the time: the idea of the flat surface and the integrity of the surface. By the end of the Fifties abstract expressionism had passed, it was played out. Pop Art was more involved with objects. I wasn't really that interested in objects. I was interested in ideas."[17]

The idea that ideas are more important than anything else was not unprecedented. In fact, it had been expressed first by Leonardo da Vinci. In his 2017 biography of Leonardo, Walter Isaacson worked directly from the artist's diaries and posited that he was more interested in concepts than execution.[18] But at the time LeWitt talked of concepts, ideas were buried. What was clearly on the surface was execution, the discoveries made by modern artists as they painted (or dripped) on their canvases, not beforehand.

Even so, a viewer of his art at the time might well have been confused about his process and the results of it. It was, in LeWitt's own view, neither sculpture nor painting, though it looked like both. For example, *Running Man*, a three-dimensional work completed in 1960, uses words and figures. LeWitt would explain years later: "As the colors advanced and receded visually the forms did so physically, projecting from the frontal plane or receding behind it. The pieces are referred to as structures because they are neither paintings nor sculptures, but both."[19] But that's not what art publications were writing about. Instead, as had been the custom since art criticism first instructed and baffled readers, critics and commentators defined what was worthy and what was not.

Most serious art collectors then, as in every period, were more comfortable investing in the known and easily labeled (whether they were drawn to it or not), rather than works in any avant-garde, unpublicized genre created in studios in unsavory parts of town. Nonetheless, a huge opportunity was coming for artists of all stripes in the sense that collecting art, for the first time in America, was becoming a widespread practice even among members of the middle class. A combination of factors was responsible, including a change in tax laws and the emergence of the idea of art as investment—something akin to a savings account but with potentially greater payoffs, and having the added bonus of being an investment you could look at every day instead of one socked away in a bank.

However, there was trendy art and art that was too far out for the general taste. What would eventually be labeled as minimalist or literal art—and what some called a violation of the principles of art—would never be confused with works from the earlier celebrity-driven and crowd-pleasing periods. As the artist Jo Baer would say in 1995, "the minimalists were placing themselves as Puritans against the hedonists."[20]

Tastemakers—critics such as Clement Greenberg (sometime referred to derisively as "Pope Clement"), Harold Rosenberg, and later Rosalind Krauss and Hilton Kramer were prominent among them—would determine what should be seen and admired. Moreover, they couldn't see everything, and what they couldn't, or wouldn't, see included an array of the work by those labeled minimalists. They had been kingmakers (indeed, the male reference applies here), and everywhere in midtown kings held court.

A commentary by John Bernard Myers in *Art and Literature* that reflects on the cultural season of 1963–64 reveals the results in a kind of religious journey, naming the artists and the galleries (in parentheses), mostly mainstream, that showed their work:

> The seekers of culture promenade Madison Avenue stopping here
> for a moment or there for ten minutes. Starting from 57th Street
> they look at the plaster effigies of George Segal (Green Gallery), the
> laminated wood figures (faucets for penises) of Mike Nelson (Amel),
> the object-painting of Appel (Jackson), D'arcangelo (Fischbach),
> the flowers of Hartl (Peridot). . . . Up the Avenue go these pilgrims,

seeing special grace, trying to "know themselves." Their eyes are greedy . . . their fervor rarely slacks. Up, up, up the Avenue, sometimes making a foray to the left or right: Moskowitz's window shades (Castelli), [Robert] Indiana's exhortation to Eat/Die (Stable), Rosalyn Drexler's painting-over cut-out lovers (Eldon). . . . They buy with the mixed feelings of a New Jersey dry cleaning tycoon who gives liberally to Our Lady of Perpetual Help—just in case.[21]

There were some confrontations between downtown and uptown, Greenbergian and otherwise, establishment and avant-garde. Lippard went to a midtown opening with LeWitt in the mid-1960s, where they ran into the color field artists Kenneth Noland and Jules Olitski, part of the Greenberg crowd. Noland pulled no punches when he saw Lippard, telling her, "Everything you write is beneath contempt, and you have mean little eyes." As she recalled this pronouncement, she said, "I'm so glad Sol was there to put his arm around me or I would have burst into tears or kicked Noland in the balls." She remembered that when she was introduced to Olitski, "we looked at each other, and then Olitski said, 'I've got to go take a piss.'" Encounters with Greenberg himself went no better. Lippard attended a lecture by abstract expressionism's biggest champion in which he talked about quality art, and during the question-and-answer period she asked, "So how would you define quality?" He replied, "If you don't know what quality is, you don't know the difference between red and green."[22]

Lippard also recalled that Kramer said that "it looked like I was going to be a leading art critic until I fell victim to the radical whirlwind."[23]

Yet she did become a leading force by writing voluminously in magazines and eventually publishing more than two dozen books. She interpreted the work and showed how the artists of the LeWitt circle struggled to discover and refine his or her unique talent.

One of the artists who always had a streak of independence was Robert Barry, whose story helps illustrate how artists who had the same interest in thinking for themselves found each other and, in doing so, the mutual support they needed.

Barry's Irish-American father and Italian mother (she had emigrated to the United States) had no objections to his pursuing art, and after a stint in the army after the Korean war, he pursued a master's degree and looked for a way to stray from the crowd. He had come under the tutelage of Tony Smith, the sculptor and architectural designer, and the abstract master Robert Motherwell, and Barry's ideas about making art early in his career caught the attention of people of influence. But if his art was different and independent, his attitude about art in the marketplace was even more so. After taking a teaching position at his alma mater, Hunter College, he had little interest in selling art, only in doing it and having people see it. His work from the start was shown around town, most significantly uptown in the Westerly Gallery. At the same time, a new gallery had been opened by Seth Siegelaub nearby.

In a 2015 interview, Barry said he knew of Siegelaub's reputation as an art promoter and writer and, lately, someone who had been in the trenches of the retail business:

> I remember going into his gallery to introduce myself. It was a loft-like type of space, oriental rugs on the floor. Good quality work in the gallery, but nothing outstanding. But one painting was odd and different. I remember that Seth was sitting at a desk with a glass of coffee, smoking a cigarette. He was a little guy, and fast talking. When I pointed to the piece I liked, he said, "That's a Lawrence Weiner."
>
> So I found out if you hung around with Seth, you soon came to know everybody. His gallery only lasted a couple of years, but he used to have Sunday afternoon soirees at his apartment on Madison Avenue, and he'd show the work of artists there.[24]

This, then was, part of the momentum that contributed to what would eventually become — in hangouts as varied as Max's Kansas City, the Upper East Side, and former tenements and factories downtown — a group that in the opinion of many observers helped bring about an era of art that in terms of new ideas and boldness rivaled Paris in the late nineteenth century.

■ On a frigid January day in 2008, Dorothy Vogel opened the door of the rent-controlled one-bedroom apartment on East Eighty-Sixth Street that she and her husband, Herb, had lived in since the early 1960s. The afternoon had been set aside to talk with a biographer about LeWitt, but it began with taking in the phenomenon of the Vogels themselves.[25]

The apartment looked to any first-time visitor as if it was a warehouse that hadn't been put into order, with boxes and cartons of art everywhere. The walls were full of paintings, with no space left bare. The kitchen was not a kitchen but a storage room, with canvases piled on the stove and in places where cereal boxes or spices are usually found. Chuck Close said in a documentary film about the Vogels, "Even their bed would get higher and higher as they shoved more art underneath it."[26] Although the increasing height proved an exaggeration, it was true that the Vogels slept over an array of pieces they had collected, including a LeWitt structure painted black that the artist, hoping to remove any trace of such structures in that color, later replaced with a white version.

And all of this was in the apartment though a few years earlier five full-size moving trucks stuffed with art from the apartment had headed for the National Gallery of Art, in Washington. The phenomenon of the Vogels was by then well known to everyone who made art in Manhattan.

"Herbie's not feeling well," Dorothy told me. "He's resting in the bedroom."[27] So sitting at the only spot available, a table near the entrance to the apartment, she began to recount the story of how the two of them, unlikely prospects, had amassed one of the largest collections of contemporary art in the world. That, of course, was what the world wanted to know—how a postal clerk (Herb) and a librarian (Dorothy) could come to donate more than 4,000 pieces to the National Gallery and still have enough in their apartment so that there was no room for dinner parties.

LeWitt had remarked on the Vogel phenomenon a year or so before he died, when he wrote to the director of the documentary. He said it was likely Earl Kerkam who had introduced him to Herb Vogel. As he later recalled, "At the time, I knew almost no one [at the Cedar Tavern] so talking to Herb was something better than listening to other painters' bullshit." LeWitt made his first sales to them.[28] Herb Vogel, after all, had not come to the Cedar Tavern with a long art résumé. He had taken a course at the New York Institute of Art but not one in art history. "I'm not interested in that," he told LeWitt. "I'm interested in what's happening now."[29]

Herb's obsession with emerging art preceded Dorothy's arrival on the scene. But when they married in 1961, they made a decision that would eventually turn them into cult figures. They would live on one of their salaries and use the other exclusively for the purchase of art. At the time, Dorothy was more drawn to bookstores and the theater than to galleries. But her husband was consumed by the idea of filling their house with what he considered beautiful things, though other people didn't put much of what they collected in that category. As Close said, they often bought "the most unlikeable, least decorative stuff."[30] They were so passionate about art that even when their meager bank account was empty, they found ways to buy it—often borrowing against their life insurance policies, as Christo and his wife, Jeanne-Claude, recalled.[31]

Dorothy Vogel's recollections on that cold day in 2008 were interrupted by the arrival at the table of her husband. Herb was dressed in tan shorts and a T-shirt, as if he was going to walk to the beach. As he sat down in the only other available chair, he made no reference to how he was feeling. Instead he said, "I only have one thing to say—Sol LeWitt was the most generous man I ever met."[32] And then he talked for forty-five minutes without interruption, often tossing out his hands for emphasis.

He recounted how he and Dorothy had begun collecting by going to the galleries on Fifty-Seventh Street, the center of the established art mart. But then they left the horde and spent much of their time exploring Greenwich Village and going to the area that would become known as SoHo. In the early 1960s, they were the first collectors to come to 458 Broadway, where LeWitt then lived and worked.

Herb Vogel was drawn to LeWitt from the start. As LeWitt said many decades later: "He wasn't much for small talk. Maybe that's why we got along."[33] Vogel recalled, "I didn't meet anyone else like him. He was a giant of an artist and a giant of a person. He gave support to a lot of people."[34]

When Vogel asked to come to LeWitt's studio, the artist explained that he would have to lower a key on the end of a rope so that the Vogels could get through the front door. In time, the Vogels made weekly visits downtown, and their regular connection with LeWitt endured for decades. (In later years, there was a weekly phone call, usually on Saturdays.) Vogel said, "Sol was the first artist I really came to know. I didn't feel it was difficult to speak to him. He was always himself, a listener, an absorber."[35]

Herb Vogel was drawn not to abstract expressionism but to something "more radical." At the time, LeWitt's work seemed different enough. In 1962, for example, he completed *Wall Structure Blue*, a colorful square within a square, that presaged his later three-dimensional work with cubes. Though Herb and Dorothy made the purchases together, he said: "I'm the one who picked out the drawings."[36]

LeWitt made his first sales to them. LeWitt recalled in a letter in 2005:

My talks with the Vogels concerned theoretical and technical
matters but also [were] about the usual kind of social events such
as shows, openings, birthdays, etc. The Vogels were not much into
ideologies or intellectual shoptalk but were very involved with the
art that came out of it. They had a sharp appreciation of new art
and genuinely felt a great affinity to it. I think Dorothy's reaction
was more intellectual. She would question ideas more than Herb,
who had a more visceral reaction to the work. They had little
money to spend, but the artists in whom they were interested did
not care about that. They (we) liked people who noticed our art.
I would make a drawing on the backs of the ten-dollar checks they
left with me as part payment for the work they got [sometimes for
as little as $50].[37]

Herb Vogel's testimony about LeWitt's generosity no doubt had its
roots in the way the artist — though getting great attention from the Vogels and grateful for their regular, if relatively meager, financial support
— used the opportunity to promote other artists. Vogel said, "Sol was
the first to introduce me to other artists."[38] And so they began collecting works by Robert Mangold, Richard Tuttle, Dan Flavin, Mel Bochner,
Carl Andre, Robert Smithson, and others. And they became friends of
many of these artists.

Some of the Vogels' shopping tours, however, were resisted and re-
sented. Mary Peacock, a magazine editor who dated LeWitt in the
mid-1960s, said in a 2013 interview: "What popped into my mind is the
relentless rounds of the Vogels, trying to get cheap art. On the one hand,
they were admired and tolerated. On the other hand, there was a kind
of scavenger quality trying to get things cheaper. . . . You'd see them at
openings, and everyone understood they had no money. But they were
relentless."[39]

In an interview in the same year, the artist Marjorie Strider said: "I
felt [the Vogels] were taking advantage of artists. Artists thought, well,
there's that postman who loves art. Sol sent them to my studio. But I
wouldn't sell anything for their price. Sol called me and said they don't
have any money. I said, 'Well, if you don't have any money you don't
buy art.'"[40] Even so, most of the artists in the circle relied on the modest fees the Vogels paid and were grateful to LeWitt for the connection.

None of the artists that the Vogels bought from were media darlings or had been anointed important artists, but that didn't matter to

Herb: "We went to places with our eyes and our hearts, not because of critics."[41] And though he didn't study the history of art, he was quite aware that the new is always problematical: "If it's serious and profound [work], it takes time to recognize." He was also wary of artists who were excellent promoters of themselves: "The mediocre get people to talk about their work. That's the way our society is, promotion. But very few at the top [as a result of such promotion] will last. The others will disappear."

In 1995, the Vogels caught the notice of the staff of *60 Minutes*, and Mike Wallace came to the apartment to do a segment on the phenomenon of the postal clerk and the librarian taking their place alongside Charles Saatchi, Paul Allen of Microsoft, a gaggle of investment bankers and hedge fund directors, and other high-profile collectors.

Wallace was the program's hardest-hitting interviewer. As the Vogels had expected, he viewed much of the work in the apartment with skepticism. When he stopped to look at a Richard Tuttle piece that features a piece of rope, he asked, "What does this signify?" Dorothy told Wallace that it didn't signify anything: "It's art, Mike."[42]

People at the National Gallery weren't so skeptical. After the Vogels, who have no children, decided to give their art to the nation, it was the National Gallery whose moving trucks picked up so much of their collection. The museum was short on contemporary work, and the 4,000 pieces donated by the Vogels could easily fill that hole. In addition, the Vogels wanted to make it possible for museums in all fifty states to have pieces from their collection. The National Gallery agreed, and as a result work from the Vogel collection can be seen in museums nationwide.

There was talk early on about paying for the collection, but the Vogels refused, settling only for a yearly stipend to help with their finances (they were relying entirely on their pensions). They had never been art investors, as they had never sold a piece: "We wouldn't do that," Herb said.[43] However, the Vogels didn't use the income from the National Gallery to pay the rent or medical bills or to buy food. They now had their own hole to fill: an apartment that had been largely emptied of art. So every dollar they got from the National Gallery went to buy new art.

One of their treasured pieces was never removed, as it couldn't be transported in a moving truck. The Vogels bought *Wall Drawing 65)* by LeWitt in 1971—or at least the instructions. At the time, LeWitt believed that, armed with the instructions, anyone could finish the piece. Dorothy tried her hand at installing it on a bathroom wall. "When Sol saw what I had done," she recalled, "that's when I think he changed his policy—no more trusting amateurs."[44]

Though the Vogels stood out as collectors for their unusual ways, they were far from alone in joining a collecting revolution that came along just as the artists in the LeWitt circle were emerging. In 1963, *Life* announced that "more buyers than ever [had] paid into a broadening [art] market."[45] Two years later, *Newsweek* reported that it was suddenly fashionable to collect art, and for the most part it was economical to do so because most artists set their prices very low with the goal of establishing their reputations and getting the word out about their work. In *Notes on Patronage: The 1960s*, Francis O'Connor wrote: "This new audience was made up of young, mobile, affluent, highly trained technocrats, eager to enjoy the comforts of their class—one of which was art. Art magically combined characteristics irresistible to these nouveau riche: it was prestigious to own and conspicuous to display, and vied with the stock market in investment potential."[46]

There was also a revolution in how they bought art. Previously, critics like Rosenberg and Greenberg had greatly influenced artists' success or failure, but the market was becoming much more independent. In *Conceptual Art and the Politics of Publicity*, Alexander Alberro wrote: "The critic, who had had a continuing importance throughout the era of the New York School, was no longer the primary arbiter of artistic success. . . . What emerged was an increased collusion among dealers, collectors, curators, and artists, where value was fixed by 'trendiness' and, ultimately, by 'marketability.'"[47] In *Culture Making: Money, Success in the New York Art World*, Steven Naifeh wrote: "An article in *Time, Life* or the *New York Times* was more useful to a dealer than an article in one of the art journals. Ironically, articles which criticized an artist's work began to have the same effect as articles which praised it: both brought the artist to the public's often casual attention."[48] To add to the momentum, large companies were beginning to commission works for their offices and lobbies, a phenomenon that ultimately would benefit LeWitt.

However, it wasn't the artist who at first became primary beneficiary of this new marketplace hierarchy. Siegelaub—who as a writer, collector, and exhibiter was crucial in the promotion of conceptual art—said in a 1969 interview that collectors told artists, "Sell it to me very cheaply because you'll be in my collection."[49]

However, the Vogels had not been among those collectors. They had no interest in the value of works, except for the value at the time of buying. No doubt the value was higher than the price they offered, and they took advantage of the multiple needs of the artists they focused on—for recognition, self-esteem, and enough money to eat for a week.

At the time of the Vogels' first visits to his studio, LeWitt was technically represented by Charles W. North Studios. In terms of shows, solo or group, the relationship yielded zero results. LeWitt's first public showing came about only because of personal relationships—specifically, those he had forged with Tony Candido, Robert Slutsky, and Harvey Becker at I. M. Pei, and later with Dan Flavin and Dan Graham.

Slutsky arranged for a small show in 1963 at St. Mark's Church-in-the-Bowery in Manhattan. He did so in a hurry, as part of the intent was to include the work of Becker, who was dying of cancer. There is no available documentation about that show, except for Candido's memory of it and that it drew some, but not wide, interest. LeWitt's references to it are few, except to mention Becker's illness and to say that he liked Becker's work.

At the time, LeWitt's work not only made references to Muybridge but was also beginning to be inspired by the things he read. In addition to the work of Beckett and texts about Russian painters in the pre-Soviet era, he responded to events that moved him. Candido referred to work that LeWitt may have destroyed—an homage to the executed Spanish poet and playwright Federico García Lorca, "an earthy painting with text. Sol wrote something in the paint." The reason it was likely destroyed was that LeWitt was moving everything to his Hester Street apartment and taking only the things he thought successful. Even so, the St. Mark's show was, Candido recalled, a modest one.[50]

Following that, LeWitt invited Flavin and Donald Judd to Hester Street in the hope that they would support his new efforts (wooden structures), leading to an exhibit in a well-established gallery. At the time, Flavin and Judd were doing work that LeWitt felt picked up on Muybridge's idea of seriality. This reinforced his ideas that led to his seriality work on structures.

The meeting with Flavin and Judd tested LeWitt's credo that was emerging at the time: that the idea was more important than the execution in a work of art. Based on the evidence, Judd and Flavin agreed with him. LeWitt's ideas for his pieces, they said, were a lot better than the execution, which they dismissed as crude. LeWitt never presented himself as the ideal craftsman with wood or any other material, but, as James Meyer notes in *Minimalism: Polemics and Art in the Sixties*, "the meeting did not go well."[51] Nevertheless, the friendships endured, and when Flavin helped organize a group show at the Kaymar Gallery in 1964, he invited LeWitt to show his new work, along with that of other friends: Robert Ryman, Judd, Larry Poons, Frank Stella, Darby Bannard, and Jo Baer.

One of the pieces shown was *Nine Boxes*, perhaps LeWitt's seminal work of the time since it connected what he had taken from Muybridge and then Flavin — a sense of seriality — with a color palette that about three decades later would become his signature. There was also a foreshadowing of the sense of playfulness that would show up in his work regularly. Here were nine boxes arranged in a square and mounted on the wall. Each box had slats (which created patterns that would show up again and again in LeWitt's work) and contained an item that the viewer could only see partially, without being able to identify it. As Veronica Roberts pointed out in her essay, "Opening LeWitt's Early Boxes,"[52] the creation of this work coincided with the phenomenon of mass-produced toys and games — trains, yo-yos, Play-Doh, Hula-hoops, Barbie dolls, and so on — and *Nine Boxes* seemed to fit right in. Only the artist knew the contents of the boxes: a drawing by Grace Wapner's daughter, Erika, and items belonging to, among others, Robert Ryman; Tom Doyle; Luba Appell, LeWitt's aunt; Marjorie Strider; and Harvey Becker.

As Roberts explained, "If *Nine Boxes* operates like a web with threads radiating from LeWitt out to other artists, it also connects to later works of LeWitt's own making. The nine-square grid format, for starters, quickly became ubiquitous in LeWitt's visual lexicon."[53]

The reviewer Brian O'Doherty wrote in the *New York Times*:

One of the most provocative shows in town almost slipped by unnoticed, a tiny little space called the Kaymar Gallery, 548 West Broadway, one block south of Washington Square, which the show turns into an original Coolsville. . . . The outstanding picture is a recent Frank Stella that could, without much exaggeration, be called a masterpiece. . . . There are also excellent pieces by Danny [Darby] Bannard (creamy reserved subtleties out of Albers), Sol LeWitt (who kills the observer with his own curiosity), Irwin Fleminger (juggling yellow beads behind Plexiglas) and Leo Valledor (a perilous act of daring in hieratic purple).[54]

Graham wrote to Hesse after the show that "Sol, during 'an introspective period' about two weeks ago, conceived his next year's work.

It's based somewhat on his Kaymar Gallery piece—it's good—I can't entirely visualize it but shadows are important. I asked Sol how long it took him to get the idea and he said, 'about a millionth of a second.'"[55] It was Graham who arranged for it to be shown.

The direct result of that Kaymar group show for LeWitt was an invitation from Graham, who was helping run the Daniels Gallery, on Sixty-Fourth Street, to have his first solo show. The news meant a great deal to LeWitt, who admired Graham as an artist and thinker. "We shared the same interest in Michel Butor," Graham recalled.[56]

In an interview in *Bomb*, Graham said of LeWitt: "When I first met him, he was doing extremely interesting work on typewriter paper. He has a great mind. He did this kind of work long before anyone else. This work was the earliest form of the non-Duchampian type of Conceptual art that I had seen. It was very important to me."[57] But the good news that Graham wanted to exhibit LeWitt's work brought with it a healthy sense of panic.

LeWitt once said: "I've always worked out of terror. If I had a show coming up, I had to do something. I just accelerated what I was doing because I would know what the stake was, and I would know that I had to do several pieces."[58]

It was at the Daniels Gallery show that the few critics who showed up to see it noticed and interpreted something that didn't neatly fit into any convenient category. LeWitt's *Hanging Structure (With Stripes)* was his first ceiling work, a three-dimensional suspended construction of striped boxes, rectangles, and elongated shapes. Also in the show were simpler wooden structures attached to the wall, basic shapes along with a piece that resembled a hockey stick. Anne Hoene wrote that new phrases might need to be invented to address this phenomenon. She suggested "sculptecture" or "post-painterly relief."[59]

LeWitt sent his own account of the Daniels exhibit to Eva Hesse and Tom Doyle: "Even I have a couple of things in a new gallery . . . a big group show. Flavin had a fluorescent on the floor (yes) and it was stepped on twice and massacred. Someone sat on the Judd and cracked it. My piece is 8' high but by its nature and position most people don't see it. That is good to have something 8' high and still inconspicuous."[60]

Though that show didn't get a great deal of press coverage, it drew a great number of young artists—who, while not entirely knowing what to make of it, were nevertheless intrigued. Robert Smithson recalled that the exhibit "operated as a kind of catalyst. There was just a lot of energy generated around that time and a lot of people's works were re-ally starting to manifest themselves." He wrote in *Artforum* that some viewers were "left cold" by the exhibit or found it "too dreary," but that the work "stood as visible clues of the future."[61]

Among the visitors who weren't left cold was the artist Mel Bochner, a graduate of Carnegie Mellon University who was then twenty-five years old and eager to make his own way. Like LeWitt, he had gone through his schooling questioning the curriculum, which he later reported being dismissive of any contemporary movement after Mondrian. And like LeWitt, he had an interest in philosophy, history, and language.

Bochner would recall that he had tried to see LeWitt's work in the group show at the Daniels Gallery, but because of its irregular hours he never found it open: "The first work I did see was in a group exhibition at the Graham Gallery in the winter of '65. It was an ungainly thing—a low, black, open, gridded plane centered on top of a stack of two open black cubes. Like nothing I had ever seen before, it resembled a three-dimensional skeleton of the Platonic ideal of a table. I was intrigued be-cause I couldn't imagine what line of thought could lead someone to make an object that looked like that."[62]

Bochner also recalled his first meeting with LeWitt: "I don't know what I was expecting him to look like or to be, but it wasn't the utterly unpretentious and totally straightforward person I met. Sol put on no airs and assumed no attitudes. From the moment we were introduced it seemed that we had always known each other. That was so common with Sol, because other people told me they had the same experience."[63]

When the Daniels show ended, LeWitt offered a hint of what was to come in the way of the ephemeral nature of his work, though he wasn't entirely serious when he told Graham that the wooden structures should be recycled as firewood.

Also among the admirers was Virginia Dwan, who in a short time had become a prominent gallery owner. As heiress to the Minnesota con-glomerate 3M, she had inherited a fortune, and she devoted her time and money to creating a gallery in Los Angeles that reflected her own increasingly adventurous tastes and her passion for supporting artists who had something new to say. Beginning in 1959 in Westwood Village, near where the University of California, Los Angeles was going to build a medical school, she had exhibited work by Robert Rauschenberg, Yves Klein, Ad Reinhardt, Larry Rivers, Philip Guston, and Claes Olden-burg, among many others.

Though Dwan would be a gallery owner in Los Angeles and later New York for only twelve years, she became well known in the art world for her critical thinking, risk taking, and support of promising artists whose work had been spurned or dismissed by the establishment—even those, such as LeWitt, whose career had barely begun. She was a key figure in the transformation of how the public was introduced to artists' works.

In the early 1960s, public attention had turned from abstract expressionism to pop art, as it was much easier to grasp. Though there was debate in critical circles about the artistic worth of replicating images from the mass culture such as household products and celebrity portraits, or creating cartoonish narratives, pop art represented a distinct turn from the response to abstract expressionism to something easily recognizable, if still a little baffling. (Why is a painted Brillo box art?")

In a way, the minimalists who followed seemed influenced by at least the ordinariness of objects (such as Brillo boxes), materials not thought of as art that nonetheless could become art.

But the ordinariness of the materials the minimalists used wasn't intended to contrast with the vibrancy or perhaps instant aesthetic appeal of pop art. Though of course there had been exceptions, it was still the norm to ask, when considering the worth of a piece of art, "Is it beautiful?" The idea of idealism had faded a decade earlier, but beauty was still a hallmark, even part of the definition, of art. Abstract art could certainly be beautiful, as in the case of Pollock's drippings. Pop art featured brilliant reds (Tom Wesselmann's lips) and yellows (Roy Lichtenstein's cartoons; and James Rosenquist's vibrant, hot-colored images, similar to the hues that LeWitt would eventually choose for hundreds of wall drawings). However, what would become known as minimalism was nothing like pop art and, on its face, was much less appealing.

In a symposium at the Getty Center in Los Angeles in 2004, Dwan provided a summary of scores of critical reviews:

The following are some of the descriptions I have found for art of this period in books and magazines: bleak, numb, severe, hollow, morbid, useless, coffins, oppressive formalism, deadly, programmatic, closed system, didactic, deductive, anti-compositional, not-enough-art, not-enough-work, theatrical, ordinary, bland, neutral, redundant, austere, literalist, authoritarian, non-emotional, anti-emotional, static, frozen, deadly, industrial, hermetic, inscrutable, depersonalized, unmodified, middle-brow, novelty, capitalistic, reductive, endgame, comatose. So what could have possessed me to devote myself to such works?[64]

Yet she also wrote: "I did not approach this art as a movement. Rather I was engrossed by each person's unique vision. It was their individual genius that involved me. For me it was a grand adventure to take part in the realization and presentation of their works."[65]

This certainly turned out to be the case in terms of her involvement with LeWitt and his work. While visiting New York, where she would open another gallery, Dwan had seen LeWitt's solo exhibit at the Daniels Gallery: "I had just happened into that gallery knowing nothing about it and had seen that work. It was [LeWitt's] white work [his structures] that interested me, and I just had a feeling about it. It was a feeling something very important and that I wanted to be able to represent this." She wasted no time acting on this feeling: "It was one of the few times that I went to a studio and immediately said, 'Let's have a contract,' all within a few hours. And I think Sol was quite taken aback because he hadn't had that kind of response up until then."[66]

LeWitt recalled that Dwan "asked me in February [1966] for a show in May, and I didn't have any work. Well, I did have work, but I said to myself that I wanted to do new work, not show any old work [from] the other shows. . . . I just decided that I had about three months, and I worked really very hard, and I did all the work. So it just accelerated the pace of things."[67]

Dwan produced a show in October of that year (simply titled *10*) that featured the work of ten artists, including LeWitt. She said in a speech in 2004:

These works seemed to share a look or attitude that I would, again, call "quiet" as well as appealingly cool, self-contained, and highly resolved.

Outside the atmosphere was charged and chaotic. It was the time of the Vietnam War, race riots, demonstrations for women's rights marches, for gay rights, student uprisings . . . marches in Selma and on Washington and the assassinations of three American leaders. There was a sense of values in upheaval and of disillusionment. The standards and actions of the very government were in question. But in this bewildering whirl there were some still, silent points appearing in art. And it was into this maelstrom that

Sol LeWitt appeared with his methodology, his reassuring logic, his aura of tranquility and humility.[68]

In all, LeWitt would have five exhibits at Dwan's gallery in New York, each drawing more attention from critics and the public at large. The shows featured his skeletal structures at first and eventually his wall drawings.

Bochner saw the paradox of combining the simple with the complex: "The accumulation of facts collapses perception. The indicated sum of these simple series is irreducible complexity. And impenetrable chaos. They astound."[69] Smithson put his finger on what was changing—the relationship between artist and viewer, and how both contribute to the effect of the piece: "the structured space, made formal and visible, caused the gallery-goer to become acutely aware of the phenomenon of perception, his place in space and time."[70]

In 1968, Peter Schjeldahl, at that time a reviewer for the *New York Times*, wrote about a Dwan exhibit that featured an array of LeWitt cube variations and, significantly, a table-top model showing how the finished product was conceived:

No one is likely to dream about Sol LeWitt. Confronting his work
—so canny, intelligent, and cold—is an occupation reserved for the
decidedly wide-awake mind. . . .

What [LeWitt] is offering with this show is a sort of specimen of the creative process, turning art, as it were, inside out for our scrutiny. As an experience, LeWitt's art is astringent, to say the most. As an essay on esthetic brinkmanship, it is both instructive and engaging.[71]

Such reviews, emphasizing LeWitt's thought process, began to separate him in the public mind from the traditional image of the artist.

About Dwan, who served as his dealer during that period, LeWitt recalled: "She was very fair, she was very open. She showed stuff mainly of very good people, but not always. I tried to get her interested in Bob Ryman, but she couldn't see it quite right. I introduced her to Bob Smithson, for instance, and they became very good friends."[72] Dwan and sometimes LeWitt accompanied Smithson to sites where he worked on his earth sculptures, and provided assistance, such as Captiva Island and the Great Salt Lake where he produced his *Spiral Jetty*.[73]

LeWitt said: "I kept talking to [Dwan] about Flavin because Flavin at that time was with Kornblee [Gallery]. Well, he had his eye on

[Leo] Castelli. He ended up with both galleries. [Dwan] was very open-minded and quite intelligent about art. Only some people bamboozled her; she took on some not so great artists. But in the main she had a very good gallery."[74]

Even though Dwan championed this work, she wasn't able to sell much of it. LeWitt said, "She wasn't much of a salesperson."[75] Also, gallery crowds at the time seemed more interested in drinking the wine at openings than in buying the art. Larry Bell, who was using cubes of glass in his work at the time, recalled in 2014 that "the openings were raucous affairs, with a lot of people. They came to party, not to buy art."[76] Bell heard this question about his cubes more than once: "When do you put the fish in these glass boxes?" LeWitt never got a fish question, but he did witness a lot of blank stares.

Some observers who were watching closely noticed that LeWitt's work had taken a dramatic turn, exploring seriality in a way he hadn't yet done. Writing about that period, Charles Haxthausen, an art professor at Williams College, argued: "The decisive breakthrough in LeWitt's development came with the aptly titled *Serial Project 1*, a complex three-dimensional work of cubes in baked enamel on aluminum, in 1966. It is with this piece that he definitively established the principles of his serial art."[77] It resembles an architect's model of a small downtown, using cubes as the basic design but in a variety of heights and rhythms. To a viewer at the time, its design might have seemed pleasant enough, but its intent wasn't clear — a circumstance that the artist anticipated. LeWitt pointed out:

> The aim of the artist would not be to instruct the viewer but to give
> him information. Whether the viewer understands this information
> is incidental to the artist; he cannot foresee the understanding of
> all his viewers. He would follow his predetermined premise to its
> conclusion avoiding subjectivity. Chance, taste, or unconsciously
> remembered forms would play no part in the outcome. The serial
> artist does not attempt to produce a beautiful or mysterious
> object but functions merely as a clerk cataloging the results of his
> premise.[78]

Mel Bochner's review of LeWitt's work in the Dwan show in *Arts* showed Bochner's own developing ideas and his use of words as art and served to demonstrate the support that some artists were providing each other by enthusiastically getting the word out. Yet it also demonstrates the difficulty in putting LeWitt's ideas into a language ill-equipped to adequately account for the experience of the viewer. (As Bochner writes, "Their presence prevails over description."). Bochner was experimenting with a new form of writing that he felt was reflective of the new art trends (though readers of Samuel Beckett may see a relationship between the two authors in terms of style.):

> Sol LeWitt: Grid. Cube. White. Wood.
> Intersection. Joint. Obstruction.
> White wood grid cubes and other
> structures which are not cubes. On the
> floor. In corners. Against walls.
> Floor to wall. Wall to wall. Ceiling
> to floor. Their presence prevails
> over description. Sol LeWitt's white
> wood grid multiple structures are
> computations of interstices, joints,
> lines, corners, angles. They
> constantly permute. Binocular vision
> destroys regularity. Vision unlocks
> within impassable areas. There is
> no invitation. Formality is a guise.
> Space tenses: past, present-
> future, plural-present. Perceptual
> phenomena: indeterminate sequence,
> infinite invention, coordinate
> disorder. Everything is still.
> Everything is repeated. Everything is
> obvious. The accumulation of
> facts collapses perception. The
> indicated sum of these simple series
> is irreducible complexity. And
> impenetrable chaos. They astound.[79]

Although LeWitt despised the culture of personality, he was as good as, or better than, most artists in getting the word out about his work. As he explained to Lippard at the time, "These variations would be read by the viewer in a linear manner. . . . It can be read as a story, just as music can be heard as a form in time. The narrative of a serial art works more like music than literature."[80]

Here again is how LeWitt explained, in a 1966 article in *Art in America*, his decision to make the cube the basic element whose permutations he would explore. The explanation sums up in a single paragraph the relationship between simplicity and complexity, and that between logic and absurdity—at least in terms of how he thought about it:

The most interesting characteristic of the cube is that it is relatively uninteresting. Compared to any other three-dimensional form, the cube lacks any aggressive force, implies no motion, and is least emotive. Therefore it is the best form to use as the basic form for any more elaborate function, the grammatical device from which the work may proceed. Because it is standard and universally recognized, no intention is required of the viewer. It is immediately understood that the cube represents the cube, a geometric figure that is uncontestably itself. The use of the cube obviates the necessity of inventing another form and reserves its use for invention.[81]

One of LeWitt's cube structures was included in what became a seminal show of contemporary art, *Primary Structures: Younger British and American Sculptors*, at the Jewish Museum in 1966.[82] The show included work by Donald Judd, Carl Andre, Larry Bell, Tom Doyle, and several others who defied traditional tenets of art, and it caused a media stir. Pieces in *Time* and *Newsweek* about the show, titled respectively "Engineer's Esthetic" and "The New Druids," called attention to this new movement.

But even among the artists in the show there was some tension. One of the artists, Mark di Suvero, said that "*Primary Structures* is the key show of the 1960s" but also offered a qualifier: "My friend Donald Judd cannot qualify as an artist because he doesn't do the work."[83] This of course was a reference to the same idea LeWitt had, which was to conceive of the piece and let someone more skilled at finishing it carry on from there. Judd retorted: "The point is not whether one makes the work or not . . . I don't see . . . why one technique is any more essentially art than another."[84]

Kramer, writing in the *New York Times* about LeWitt's second solo show, featuring his expanding use of cubes and their variations, said that "the basic concept is a boring one, though the artist deserves a bit more expressive mileage from it than you might think possible."[85]

LeWitt faced questions similar to those Judd received. One story comes from Mary Peacock, his girlfriend for a time in the late 1960s. She remembered that "he was part of a panel discussion at Cooper Union when a student got up and said, 'I just don't understand how this can really be art if there's no touch of the artist's hand in anything —if you didn't build it yourself.' Sol responded in his typical fashion: 'Well, I use my head instead of my hands.' Then he sat back down, his explanation over."[86]

In the late 1960s, LeWitt's work was the subject of scrutiny in mainstream publications, among them *Artforum*. His MoMA friend Lippard wrote in that magazine: "His white structural skeletons are the most unsecretive of objects, their interior and exterior components laid bare to the eye; yet he does know how to handle such total revelation and retreats rapidly to its single viewpoint."[87] In that sentence, she summed up LeWitt's intriguing qualities that would transcend media and time.

It seemed as though the momentum of the small group of artists who had been outcasts was carrying them, and those associated with them, to a new place.

But then came sour news: Virginia Dwan decided to close her New York gallery in 1971. LeWitt wrote her as soon as he heard: "I feel like a New England mill town which has just been told by the Textron Corporation that the plant is being shut down & moved south."[88] Yet by then, members of the circle had broken out in ways that required no single champion to speak for them.

■ In a way, Carl Andre made his work with his own hands. That is, he arranged materials that had been originally manufactured for other purposes, including fireplace bricks, railroad ties, scraps of metal or wood, and even debris that he picked up on walks through Hell's Hundred Acres—the area in lower Manhattan of abandoned factories and other buildings that had gone to seed that eventually became known as trendy SoHo.

The name Hell's Hundred Acres came from fire wardens' idea had that artists' quarters were full of bales of rags soaked in combustible fluids. But the area was also called that because it was a perilous neighborhood in those days. Yes, it was cheap to live or work in. But you got what you paid paltry sums for.

In contrast to LeWitt, Andre had come to Hell's Hundred Acres through the railroad yards, where he had worked as a brakeman until he was found culpable of pulling the wrong switch and causing an accident. The former Phillips Academy and Kenyon College student would use that experience in his work.

The relationship between Andre and LeWitt, alternately close and cold, could be tracked in a way through the bar scene: Andre was the consummate bar customer, and LeWitt, though occasionally with him, chided him for that.

In a 2012 interview, Andre remembered going once or twice to the Cedar Tavern with LeWitt and encountering a particular bartender with whom he had some trouble: "He had a pathological hatred of artists. He thought we were parasites, that we didn't do any real work. And he didn't want to serve us."[89] Perhaps the bartender could sense Andre's real intent in coming to the hangout.

"I went to the Cedar bar to pick up girls," Andre said, referring to the time before his marriage to the artist Rosemarie Castoro. "Girls from Barnard would hang around the artists. Sol never approved of this. He thought I had too many girlfriends."[90] This was a reference to Andre's habit of stringing women along while he carried on affairs with others. To be sure, LeWitt would have many girlfriends, but he subscribed to the idea that this mating business should be done sequentially—rather like his art—not all at once. "Sol thought I was sexually immoral," Andre said. This, he thought, was the source of LeWitt's "underlying antagonism."

As it turned out, however, Andre would eventually provide LeWitt, and tens of thousands of others who were interested in his work and that of others labeled minimalists or conceptualists, plenty of reason for antagonism.

Meanwhile, LeWitt managed in his own quiet way to attract some of the most interesting women in Manhattan, though generally one at a time.

EIGHT

PARAGRAPHS OF ART

The editor has written me that he is in favor of avoiding the notion that the artist is a kind of ape that has to be explained by the civilized critic. This should be good news to both artists and apes. With this assurance I hope to justify his confidence. To use a baseball metaphor (one artist wanted to hit the ball out of the park, another to stay loose at the plate and hit the ball where it was pitched), I am grateful for the opportunity to strike out for myself.

Sol LeWitt, "Paragraphs on Conceptual Art"

As the number of his exhibits increased, LeWitt quit his position at MoMA to devote his working hours to making art, though he also taught an evening class for adults ("I didn't like it too much") at the museum. In recalling this period and the requests for shows that came in, he said, "I almost always accepted them, not knowing what I'd be doing but knowing I'd be doing something."[1] The decision to take on everything that came his way led to his projects for the printed page in addition to those for the gallery.

Calling on skills he had developed long before, LeWitt also took on freelance illustration work for magazines. The most prominent of these efforts appeared in *Harper's Bazaar*, whose literary editor, Dale McConathy, sought to publish the work of high-profile and emerging writers and cutting-edge artists.

"The magazine was very sophisticated," recalled Mary Peacock, who worked there as an assistant in the literary department. "If the agent couldn't sell [the piece] to the *New Yorker*, they sold it there [*Harper's*]."[2] She described herself at that time "as a good little English major from Vassar" and her job as one that required her to sort through submitted short stories and excerpts from novels and present what she thought were the best to McConathy. In this work she had help from other staff members, including Julie Judd, the wife of Donald Judd, and Nancy

Holt, the wife of Robert Smithson. "The department was a hotbed of art girls," Peacock recalled.

These connections, she surmised, must have led LeWitt to the *Harper's Bazaar* offices to illustrate several pieces and provide a few independent drawings. This work also coincided with his growing interest in publication as a way to bring art in an economic fashion to those who had no capacity for buying it.

When LeWitt came to *Harper's Bazaar* for the first time to discuss this work, Peacock was taken with this quiet man whose work she had seen first at the Daniels Gallery: "He was very bright, very nice, and talented. You could just tell he was a decent and honorable person, not a smarty-pants."[3] And soon the two began to date.

When asked why LeWitt, who never saw himself as much of a ladies' man, had many smart and talented women as lovers, Peacock—who went on to help Gloria Steinem found *Ms.* in 1972—said: "A big part of his appeal to women wasn't all about 'How soon can I get you in bed?' and to do so, 'I must strut around and brag.' Sol was just Sol. He wasn't wishy-washy, and he didn't put on airs."[4] In short, he was not typical of artists of the time in this way: "He was not aggressive like Carl [Andre]. Carl was predatory." She also commented: "A lot of people make the mistake of assuming that because you are a terrific artist you must be a terrific person. No one seemed to consider at the time that you could be a fantastically gifted artist and a total shit, as in 'I am the Great Houdini.' Sol could admire Carl's work but also kick him in the shins when he thought he was being a shit."

However, none of this prevented LeWitt and Peacock from being part of the groups that had pasta dinners, along with Andre and Rosemarie Castoro. Other participants on such evenings included Ruth Vollmer, Dorothea Rockburne, Lucy Lippard, the Smithsons, the Judds, Hanne Darboven, Dennis Oppenheim, Jan Dibbets, Robert and Sylvia Mangold, Virginia Dwan, John Weber (who followed Dwan as a significant exhibitor of LeWitt's work), and others central to what was becoming a prominent—if not entirely adored—group of artists, writers, gallery owners, and collectors.

Also in the crowd was the architect Susana Torre, newly arrived from her native Argentina, and her husband at the time, Alejandro. LeWitt had met Torre in 1968 when he traveled to Argentina because he had a piece included in a Buenos Aires exhibit.[5] As she recalled in 2015:

We knew about and admired Sol's work. Our favorite art magazine was *Art International*; the articles that interested us the most were by Lucy Lippard, which I translated for our artist friends. There were not many people at the Di Tella exhibition center that day that could speak English as fluently as I, so I approached Sol while he was working on his installation to see if he needed help. I found out that the organizers had pretty much left him to his own devices, with the exception of an invitation to the opening cocktail party and dinner. I decided to give him a tour of Buenos Aires, including the shantytowns in the outskirts, so he could see what surrounded the glamorous center. . . . I told Sol that we'd be in New York before the end of the year, and he, being as generous as he was, encouraged me to let him know in advance so he could help us. . . .

I remember the first time Alejandro and I visited Sol in his Hester Street loft. We had just arrived in NY and our previous visit to the city had been limited to museums and tourist sights. That evening the Lower East Side seemed positively dangerous to us, and we couldn't believe that an artist with an international reputation, and whose work appeared in magazines, could live in such a grimy building. Once inside, Sol's world, populated by hundreds of classical music records, works by artist friends, books, a few potted plants (including a small marihuana one) and Native American rugs, made us feel instantly at ease. I remember a large worktable, a kind of makeshift kitchen, a sleeping area, windows covered with folding grilles, a patched up tin ceiling and Puss, his cat. And Sol welcoming us to New York with the gift of a Muybridge print he had framed with a white wood molding. . . .

He enjoyed women's friendship, a fact his girlfriends accepted. I remember especially Mary Peacock, a fashion writer for *Harper's Bazaar* who was always distributing among friends the expensive items that would have been discarded after a fashion shoot. I have big feet, so I got my pick of beautiful shoes I would have never been able to afford on my own. Mary was critical of the fashion industry, and ended up founding *Rags*, a newsprint magazine that documented street fashion. It created some shock waves in the industry.[6]

Peacock had by then intimate knowledge of trends and of what some of the hip people were wearing. During the years she was with LeWitt, they went to many art openings that drew a cross-section of Manhattan residents and had dinner at Puglia in Little Italy or at Max's Kansas City, the successor to the Cedar Tavern as the hangout of artists and celebrities.

Peacock recalled that once at Max's Kansas City there was a discussion between LeWitt and Robert Smithson on entropy and thermodynamics and their applications to real life and art: "It was all quite nerdy. Smithson carried on, and Sol was fascinated by what he was hearing, and [while] exploring the intellectual constructs behind their work."[7] These two were drawn by the world of ideas, not, Peacock said, "like Jeff Koons and others whose interest was in calling attention to themselves."

She continued: "I felt rapport with that kind of world, even though many people thought that the art that came out of it was a joke. People at the time thought minimalism was a crazy fraud. . . . A couple of florescent bulbs [Dan Flavin], white paintings [Robert Ryman]. It made no sense to many. I really don't know what I would have thought of it if I didn't know the people involved. But I had the privilege to understand it from the inside. It wasn't the excruciating glamor of it—it wasn't glamorous at all."[8] It was just hard-nosed straight-ahead work: "So many artists focus on being famous and making money. They get into a thin idea and are willing to do the same thing over and over again as long as somebody can peddle it. There are enough artists like that. These artists weren't that way at all."

The relationship between Peacock and LeWitt ended in 1968, on more than decent terms. LeWitt and a variety of friends helped her move to a new place on Grand Street. When he learned that she had no sofa or coffee table, he built one of each for her.

And as it turned out, though his relationship with one literary staff member at *Harper's Bazaar* was over, he wasn't yet finished with the "hotbed of art girls."

In the meantime, he had a very full social life. His daily calendar for one month alone, January 1969, shows a plan for every night, except for January 17—he recorded "nothing" in the space for that day.[9] Among his evening appointments and get-togethers in that month were two dinners with the Mangolds, a meeting with Flavin, going to Max's Kansas City with Grace Wapner, dinner with Russell North, going to a party for Robert Smithson, going to a Twyla Tharp performance and another by Yvonne Rainer, meetings with Jo Baer and Sam Hunter, dinner with Andre and Castoro, a meeting at the Solomon R. Guggenheim Museum,

Michael Kirby's birthday party at Max's Kansas City, a meeting with Weber, and even a fashion show. There were a variety of dinners with people identified only by last names. The shy LeWitt was obviously not reclusive. He had no problem making friends or working on the marketing of his own work and that of others, even though he would still not submit to the rites of the celebrity culture.

The fact that many of his artist friends were female made him unusual for his time. Many of them credit him for encouraging them, though in some cases that encouragement went for naught. Such was the case, he felt, in regard to Lee Lozano. She had turned to art after studying philosophy and natural sciences, and by 1966 she was turning out raw stuff, much of it sexually suggestive. She turned rebellious, as indicated by the instructions she wrote to herself in 1969: "GRADUALLY BUT DE-TERMINEDLY AVOID BEING PRESENT AT OFFICIAL OR PUBLIC 'UP-TOWN' FUNCTIONS OR GATHERINGS RELATED TO THE 'ART WORLD' IN ORDER TO PURSUE INVESTIGATIONS OF TOTAL PERSONAL AND PUBLIC REVOLUTION. EXHIBIT IN PUBLIC ONLY PIECES WITH FUR-THER SHARING OF IDEAS & INFORMATION RELATED TO TOTAL PER-SONAL AND PUBLIC REVOLUTION."[10] LeWitt recalled his relationship with Lozano in 2001 in *Artforum*:

Back in the '60s, I used to visit Lee Lozano's studio pretty regularly. On some of these visits, she would present you with three objects —abstract objects, like small cubes—and tell you to arrange them on a tabletop. I remember her doing the "Wave" paintings, which I was very impressed with—and their premise. When they were first shown, everyone agreed it was a major statement. Lee's relative disappearance from the historical records is sort of mysterious; the work was hardly negligible, so it's hard to say why she didn't have more of a career. It was definitely hard to make it as a woman artist, and she herself really withdrew from the world. The thing about not speaking with women went way beyond an art project. I remember sitting in a restaurant with her once and a waitress came to the table; not only would Lee not talk to her, she would hide her eyes. She had an extreme dislike for the company of women, thought they were evil. When she came to my studio, if my girlfriend opened the door, Lee would turn on her heels, run down the stairs, and be gone. Her wounds were self-inflicted; the withdrawal from the art world and the antifeminism. Eventually she stopped making artworks altogether. She became a spirit who would appear and then vanish, but her work was saved by friends and those who had faith in her vision.[11]

■ In 1966, Smithson had urged *Artforum*, the most influential American magazine about contemporary art, to invite artists to explain their ideas and novel approaches to new work. This effort was a direct result of the emergence of the concept that the idea, rather than the execution, was the heart of art. When the magazine agreed to do this, LeWitt was among those who wrote their thoughts.

Just a year earlier, he had been quoted in an exhibit catalogue as having a rather hazy idea of what he was doing: "I find it difficult to write a statement that will be a correct summation of my philosophy of art. The work itself seems to subvert such statements, while the total of one's work creates its own philosophy."[12] Within a year, however, he had changed his mind.

The result of LeWitt's effort, "Paragraphs on Conceptual Art," was published in *Artforum*'s April 1967 issue and became a foundational document. To be sure, the words "conceptualism" and "conceptual" had been used to refer to art for some time, dating back to Marcel Duchamp's work with his "readymades."[13] The term "concept art" had been used by Henry Flynt, a philosopher and avant-garde musician, in a 1961 essay titled "Concept Art (Provisional Version)." It was reprinted in La Monte Young's *An Anthology of Chance Operations*, a book that documented Duchamp's work and the movement called Fluxus—a development of experimental and interdisciplinary ideas developed by artists and composers such as John Cage, George Brecht, Yoko Ono, and Joseph Byrd.[14] But LeWitt's definition of the term expanded Flynt's idea, focusing primarily on the way artists do their work, and it was intended, as LeWitt wrote in one of a series of letters to Andrea Miller-Keller, who curated his work at the Wadsworth Atheneum, "to redirect the emphasis to idea rather than effect."[15] In a 1993 interview LeWitt expanded on this: "Duchamp was making a different kind of art derived from Dada and Surrealism. These forms are absolutely conceptual but I was not interested in them."[16] He also articulated his rejection of pop art as a form. His view was that it "had too much to do with the reaction of the viewer, to make an impression on the viewer in order to turn things inside out. I was interested in the work of art itself, not in the creation of the viewer. You know in Dada or in the beginning of Pop Art or

Conceptual art the thing was to freak out the viewer, you know that was the main thing for [Andy] Warhol."

Nor were LeWitt or his friends interested in subscribing to what Clement Greenberg and Harold Rosenberg saw as the essential definition of art, the idea of formalism, or the view that a painting is a painting and nothing else. Seen in that light, a painting is a commodity clearly identified as art — something apart or aloof.

For artists, critics are of course a necessity. But LeWitt and many others saw limits to critics' wisdom. In "Paragraphs on Conceptual Art," he tackles them head-on:

Recently there has been much written about minimal art, but I have not discovered anyone who admits to doing this kind of thing. There are other art forms around called primary structures, reductive, ejective, cool, and mini-art. No artist I know will own up to any of these either. Therefore I conclude that it is part of a secret language that art critics use when communicating with each other through the medium of art magazines. Mini-art is best because it reminds one of miniskirts and long-legged girls. It must refer to very small works of art. This is a very good idea. Perhaps "mini-art" shows could be sent around the country in matchboxes. Or maybe the mini-artist is a very small person, say less than five feet tall. If so, much good work will be found in the primary schools (primary school primary structures).[17]

At the time, LeWitt and others in the circle were developing a view of art that made it not so much a commodity as a community-owned entity. For example, LeWitt argued that everyone owns the *Mona Lisa* who has a mental picture of it. And Lawrence Weiner said, "Once you know about a work of mine you own it. There's no way I can climb inside somebody's head and remove it."[18]

There were other unthinkable ideas at the time as well. As LeWitt later wrote Andrea Miller-Keller, "It wasn't too important what a work of a art looks like."[19] That was clever, certainly, and something like Edgar Wilson "Bill" Nye's view that "Wagner's music is better than it sounds" (the quote is often misattributed to Mark Twain).[20] But what does LeWitt's comment really mean? Surely art is for the eye as well as the mind. Perhaps LeWitt was merely reinforcing his argument that meaning and contemplation had been underemphasized, and this was his way of restoring the balance.

Barrier breaking was a key to the LeWitt circle, whose members—
while respecting the art of the past and learning from it—considered
it to be largely irrelevant to the work they were doing. As LeWitt would
explain to an audience at MoMA in 1978:

> Especially at the time, in the '60s, the thinking about art had kind of
> constipated itself into a real formalism where painting was painting,
> sculpture was sculpture, and a painter has to do certain things, and
> a sculptor had to do certain things. Painting had to be painterly
> and sculpture had to be sculptural, and everything was, you know,
> handed down from above. At that time many people including
> myself wanted to get rid of this kind of thinking because it was so
> detrimental to thinking as such. That kind of thinking is still around
> and the products of that thinking are around and I think they are
> pretty boring. I think that unless the mind is made free, free of
> definitions, and free of all of what the definitions imply, then there's
> not too much chance. In other words, let's say, well, I'm a sculptor,
> that means that in a way you have to carry the whole history of
> sculpture on your back, or as a painter you have to say, well there is
> Mondrian and there is Monet and then there is, well, I have to think
> about all of these things. If you don't think of these things in terms
> of words and definitions, you say, well, I'm making art. What's art?[21]

In addition, LeWitt was pushing himself to declare in art what Samuel Beckett had declared on pages and in the theater. "Beckett was interested in absurdity as a way out of intellectuality," LeWitt said. "Even
a simple idea taken to its logical end can become chaos."[22] The artist
didn't talk about specific passages in Beckett, but one can imagine him
ruminating about this one from *Worstward Ho,* a late novella: "Ever
tried. Ever failed. No matter. Try again. Fail again. Fail better."[23] This, in
Beckett's boiled-down language, is the essence of what LeWitt had advised Eva Hesse.

LeWitt read Beckett's *Molloy* trilogy and, it may be presumed from his
ideas that followed, identified with both the idea of the inner monologue
of the protagonist and the penchant of Molloy not to follow common
wisdom unquestioningly. In her 1977 essay titled "LeWitt in Progress,"
the critic Rosalind Krauss cited passages from *Molloy* in her discussion
of LeWitt's open cubes and their variations. In all, Krauss reproduces
four lengthy paragraphs in which the author recounts his experience
with sucking stones found on the shore: "Yes, on this occasion I laid in

a considerable store. I distributed them equally among my four pockets."[24] He goes on to say he has sixteen stones in all, four in each pocket.
If he took one stone from one of the pockets, he replaced it with another
stone from a different pocket, and so on, until he had run through his
collection. Yet he writes, "This solution did not satisfy me fully." He was
in search of ultimate arrangements, which seemed to elude him. In effect, this was also the result of LeWitt's incomplete open cubes.

The intersection of simplicity and chaos became the core of LeWitt's
discoveries over the next few years. In 1974 he said:

> All artists I think are mystics to the extent they do something that's
> never been done before, and I think of it as a leap. That Kierkegaard
> kind of thing. An artist goes off into some kind of unknown space.
> But I think a conceptual artist does it with concepts. He has to reach
> into some kind of unknown or something irrational. The trouble
> with most art, conceptual or any other kind of art, is that it's so
> predictable. Most second-rate art could be done by anybody. Really
> good art has a kind of extra leap into the unknown. That's what I was
> trying to define.[25]

When "Paragraphs on Conceptual Art" was published in *Artforum*,
it served as a manifesto for everyone who was open to the idea that art
transcends the physical product of the artist and enters mystical territory. Here are three key paragraphs out of the seventeen:

> I will refer to the kind of art in which I am involved as conceptual
> art. In conceptual art the idea or concept is the most important
> aspect of the work. . . . The planning and decisions are made
> beforehand and the execution is a perfunctory affair. The idea
> becomes a machine that makes the art. This kind of art is not
> theoretical or illustrative of theories; it is intuitive, it is involved with
> all types of mental processes and it is purposeless. It is usually free
> from the dependence on the skill of the artist as a craftsman. It is the
> objective of the artist who is concerned with conceptual art to make
> his work mentally interesting to the spectator, and therefore usually
> he would want it to become emotionally dry. There is no reason
> to suppose, however, that the conceptual artist is out to bore the
> viewer. It is only the expectation of an emotional kick, to which one
> conditioned to expressionist art is accustomed, that would deter the
> viewer from perceiving this art.

Conceptual art is not necessarily logical. The logic of a piece or series of pieces is a device that is used at times, only to be ruined. Logic may be used to camouflage the real intent of the artist, to lull the viewer into the belief that he understands the work, or to infer a paradoxical situation (such as logic vs. illogic). Some ideas are logical in conception and illogical perceptually. The ideas need not be complex. Most ideas that are successful are ludicrously simple. Successful ideas generally have the appearance of simplicity because they seem inevitable. In terms of ideas the artist is free even to surprise himself. Ideas are discovered by intuition. What the work of art looks like isn't too important. It has to look like something if it has physical form. No matter what form it may finally have it must begin with an idea. It is the process of conception and realization with which the artist is concerned. Once given physical reality by the artist the work is open to the perception of all, including the artist. (I use the word perception to mean the apprehension of the sense data, the objective understanding of the idea, and simultaneously a subjective interpretation of both.) The work of art can be perceived only after it is completed.

These paragraphs are not intended as categorical imperatives, but the ideas stated are as close as possible to my thinking at this time. These ideas are the result of my work as an artist and are subject to change as my experience changes. I have tried to state them with as much clarity as possible. If the statements I make are unclear it may mean the thinking is unclear. Even while writing these ideas there seemed to be obvious inconsistencies (which I have tried to correct, but others will probably slip by). I do not advocate a conceptual form of art for all artists. I have found that it has worked well for me while other ways have not. It is one way of making art; other ways suit other artists. Nor do I think all conceptual art merits the viewer's attention. Conceptual art is good only when the idea is good.[26]

In these paragraphs, LeWitt tries to define an area that had seldom been explored in the art world. That is, in terms of a finished product, the focus on the artist at the easel, say, blurs the distinction between the inspiration (or idea) and what appears on the canvas. But to LeWitt, with all key decisions made beforehand, it becomes much clearer what the artist is thinking.

For example, in his seminal *1966 Serial Project No. 1*, a structure (suggesting a city block) that was shown first in 1967 at the Dwan Gallery in Los Angeles, he clearly points out in a voluminous way the mental picture he has of the finished work. He wrote:

> The individual pieces are comprised of a form set equally within another and centered. Using this premise as a guide no further design is necessary. . . . The cube, square and variants on them are used as grammatical devices. . . . These pieces could be made without regard for their appearance but to complete the variations that are pre-set. . . . Each individual piece of the mine is autonomous and complete. All major permutations are accounted for within the set of 9. Four sets of 9 complete the idea. . . . The grid system is a convenience. It stabilizes the measurements and neutralizes space by treating it equally . . . etc.[27]

Yet as detailed as these descriptions are, LeWitt also provides plenty of contradiction in his definition of conceptual art. In his view, this category is partially defined by the idea that art does not need to be seen to be considered art. That is, an idea does not need to be executed; it can simply created in some way, just by thinking it up. In a dramatic demonstration in 1968, LeWitt showed that even when executed, an idea can be literally buried from public view. This was his goodbye to minimalism. It was essentially a performance: he buried a cube in a garden.

As LeWitt recalled his Netherlands work titled *Buried Cube Containing an Object of Importance but Little Value* in an interview:

> Well, it evolved this way. Bob Smithson, I think, around '67 decided, oh well, somebody asked him to design this airport that was eventually built between Fort Worth and Dallas. As part of his scheme, he wanted to have an Earth Show. Well, the whole thing fell through. But then he wanted to have the Earth Show at the Dwan Gallery. He wanted to have [works by himself], Carl, myself, and Bob Morris. I said, "Well, what I'll do is just bury a cube." So finally next year, around '68, there was supposed to be a show. I was in Holland at the time and [Martin and Mia Visser] were friends of mine and collectors, and they were remodeling their house, and they had it all dug up, so I had them build a stainless steel box, and I had them put something in it, and it was welded shut and buried.[28]

All of this certainly caught the attention of the art world in a way that was new. Unwilling to call attention to himself on magazine covers yet urgently wanting his work to be seen, he discovered ways to lure magazines and their readers into his world. Though an art lover wouldn't recognize him in a crowd, he or she could pick his paragraphs out of a text. Indeed, Robert Rosenblum would write that LeWitt's images, as explained, would rank with those of the philosophers Immanuel Kant and René Descartes, as well as the mathematician Euclid.[29] Many years later, Alexander van Grevenstein, longtime director of the Bonnefantenmuseum in the Netherlands, would write that LeWitt's "Paragraphs on Conceptual Art" and "Sentences on Conceptual Art"[30] "constitute the foundations of the new artistry, laid out for the first time and displayed in full context. There is hardly a 'manifesto' that has had so much influence."[31]

Even so, not all reaction to LeWitt's ideas was reverent.

In the March 1968 issue of *Art International*, LeWitt's colleague and friend Robert Smithson wrote: "Everything LeWitt thinks, writes, or has made is inconsistent and contradictory. The 'original idea' of his art is lost in a mess of drawings, figurings, and other ideas. His concepts are prisons devoid of reason."[32] For LeWitt, such reactions were not only tolerable but welcome, as a means of stirring the pot.

Indeed, two years after he wrote "Paragraphs on Conceptual Art," he wrote "Sentences on Conceptual Art," the first of which argued that conceptual artists are "mystics" rather than rationalists. This, no doubt, was a reaction to the view that this new art was cold. Another sentence was: "Illogical judgments lead to new experience."[33] He was clearly urging people to steer away from what is known and what is safe (and what is commercial).

These sentences also became influential, but, according to LeWitt's colleague John Baldessari, not well known enough, buried as they were in art publications, and Baldessari felt that they deserved a wider audience. Thus, he made a video in 1972 in which he put "Sentences on Conceptual Art" to music, taking popular tunes and giving them LeWittian lyrics. Baldessari sang all of the thirty-three sentences, including those that made some of the most innovative points, though none fit into to what any composer would consider a rhythmic order:

15. Since no form is intrinsically superior to another, the artist may use any form, from an expression of words (written or spoken) to physical reality, equally.

32. Banal ideas cannot be rescued by beautiful execution.

33. It is difficult to bungle a good idea.[34]

The manifesto aspect of LeWitt's writings contributes to the prevailing view that his work was removed from the intensely passionate approach of artists who came before him. But over the years, many people in the art world felt otherwise. One of them was Martin Friedman, long-time director of the Walker Art Center in Minneapolis, who said: "The main thing about Sol was on the one hand, abstract and depersonalized, but that's a complete fallacy. [His work] has recognizability and personality, the most elegant mixture of theory and practice. He is credited with the founding of conceptual art, which is presumably coolheaded [and] rational but at the same time was inadvertently sensuous and beguiling, and he moved from style to style with a kind of inquisitiveness. So he never became a prisoner of a style. He mastered it and then went on to the next thing."[35]

Nor did LeWitt always interpret or explain art in formal terms. In fact, in conversation he abhorred formality. Jane Rainwater, a student of his in the 1970s when he taught briefly at the University of Hartford, recalled in 2013 that someone asked him "What is art?" It is a question, of course, whose answer could fill volumes of the size Will and Ariel Durant wrote. But LeWitt answered that day: "Art is a big fluffy thing."[36]

As time went on, LeWitt also decried what he created. As Robert Barry recalled in 2015, "we all hated the term 'conceptual art.'"[37] That is, nobody wanted to be painted into a corner or labeled. No artist wanted to be called a minimalist or a conceptualist. But labeled and marketed (handsomely) they all were. And LeWitt's "Paragraphs" and "Sentences" were used over and over again as ways to make points that even their author couldn't decipher. Once, he confided to Barry, "I wish I had never written that shit."[38]

■ The same year that LeWitt wrote "Paragraphs on Conceptual Art," he exhibited *46 Variations on Three Different Kinds of Cubes* at Virginia Dwan's gallery in New York, an important piece because of the way it took Beckett's ideas and made them visual — using an ordinary shape, the cube, to explore mathematical absurdity. Baldessari recalled seeing the piece during its creation in LeWitt's studio. It showed the many possible permutations of the cube shape and, just as important, asked the viewer to in effect finish the work by imagining what was missing from each cube. Baldessari said: "What I saw is still imprinted upon my mind. My reaction was 'You can't do that!' I could either reject what I saw or change my mind about art making. I changed my mind, and his art would subsequently have a large effect upon my work."[39]

The show at the Dwan gallery attracted another disciple. At the time, Adrian Piper was a student at the School of Visual Arts, where LeWitt had briefly taught. She was twenty years younger than LeWitt, but the generational difference was no impediment in her connecting with his work. In recalling that work in a blog post after his death, she wrote:

> [The show] opened my mind, and revolutionized my practice as an artist. By presenting an ordered series of objects as exemplars of a personal but highly logical system of permutations, Sol demonstrated the potentially infinite number of ways in which reality could manifest [itself]. I remember as vividly as if it were yesterday the power of those austere white, four-foot high square columns of steel cubes, stacked in threes and set in rows of six, advancing toward me in direct frontal formation, each shaded slightly differently from the next, all displaying simultaneously the rigor of system and the playfulness of idiosyncrasy, filling the space with their authority. They radiated presence, significance, and also mystery, because the conceptual scheme they embodied was not perceptually obvious. In order to understand why these physical structures expressed meaning and order so intensely yet so privately, you had to be willing to study them, compare them, count them, organize them in thought; to think, to research, to consider carefully the unlimited variety of ways in which even the simplest object could have been slightly different than it was. Sol expressed this wonder at the infinite variability of the geometrical foundations of perception throughout all of his work, up to the very end. He conferred meaning and conceptual significance on the individual objects he fashioned through their relationship, not to the critical analysis of a third-personal viewer, but rather to the conceptual system that he as an artist also fashioned. Sol proved that we could be artists and theorists at the same time.[40]

Piper would go on to do work inspired by LeWitt: "I felt freed not only from technical and formal constraints of figurative art but also from my perceptions of what art had to be."[41] One of the first pieces she did in this time was *Sixteen Permutations of a Planar Analysis of a Square*, a

1968 work in which she enlarged a negative of diagrams and text that displayed variations on a square in three dimensions.

■   As Peacock mentioned, artists of the time, including LeWitt, had to steel themselves against harsh reviews. One of the fascinating aspects of LeWitt and this group is that the self-doubt they may have felt and the occasionally vicious criticism of others never appeared to sway them from following their paths.

This was the case when the critic Michael Fried wrote a blistering assessment of minimalism, which he called literalism, in an *Artforum* essay titled "Art and Objecthood." He argued that art and "objecthood" (the word he used to indicate a reliance on materials not associated with art) are incompatible, and that practitioners of literalist art (such as LeWitt, Judd, Flavin, and Morris) were compromising the quality of art because their work was too "theatrical" and their practice was impure.[42]

In her 2007 blog post, Piper wrote:

Rosalind Krauss wrote an unenthusiastic review of this ground-breaking show in *Artforum* in April 1968. [She wrote in part: "But there is really only one question that is finally relevant and that is: what does this cumbrous, mechanical joining or filling of content with form have to do with the enterprise of art?"[43]] . . . I didn't have the nerve to just call him up and console him; I knew who he was, but we'd never met. But I did write him a letter of consolation about how much I'd liked the show and how important I thought it was. I suggested that he ignore the review. He wrote back, thanking me and remarking that he didn't mind if the review was negative, as long as it was lengthy. He also enclosed two working drawings from the series, and suggested that we meet at the Bykert Gallery and go for a beer. We both arrived around the same time. Apparently he'd been expecting a man, because when I walked up to him, he did a double take and asked, "You're Adrian Piper?" I assured him that I was, and we went for our beer. Both Virgos, both lovers of [Johann Sebastian] Bach and Beckett, we bonded right away, while bickering about whether or not Bach's choral works (Sol's preference) were superior to his instrumental works (my preference at the time). Actually I didn't know Bach's choral works that well—I owe my love of them to Sol; but felt pleased that he pulled no punches in defending them and promised to reconsider *The Art of Fugue,* if

I would reread the works of Beckett I'd failed to fully appreciate, which were most of them. Sol was not as verbose as I'm making him sound. He was shy, and sparing with words, which he used plainly and to great effect. He asked for nothing but my friendship, and I asked for nothing but his.[44]

Piper's recollection about LeWitt's reaction to a negative review confirms what critics and historians later said — that getting the word out about the work was much more important than whether the reviewer held it in high esteem. Certainly reviews never diminished Piper's enthusiasm about LeWitt's work. When she moved into an upper-floor studio at 117 Hester Street, she "became a complete pest."[45] She borrowed his copies of Beckett's books and Bach recordings:

I watched so many old movies on his TV that in desperation he bought me one for my 20th birthday, and brought a chair upstairs for me to sit in so I could watch it. I also fed his cat, Puss, while he was away, and executed some of his drawings. In return for my being a pest and feeding his cat, and without my knowledge, he chatted up my work to all of his friends in the art world. I have no idea how many doors he opened for me. But I received invitations to show my work in all of the conceptual art exhibitions that were then taking place in Europe, and unsolicited visits from gallery owners, critics and curators from all over the world who knew him. Sometimes he would have such a person to lunch or dinner downstairs, and urge them to drop upstairs to see my work while they were there. In large measure I owe my easy admission into the art world, and my early success, to him.[46]

She recalled her "sympathy with the position on art taken by Sol LeWitt" in a lecture at Harvard University. Her work at the time focused on "the construction of finite systems . . . that serve to contain an idea within certain formal limits and to exhaust the possibilities of the idea set by those limits."[47]

In 1968, LeWitt exhibited an untitled structure of painted wood slats in a MoMA show called *The Art of the Real USA, 1948–1968*. The exhibit contained fifty-seven pieces by thirty-seven artists[48] and demonstrated a great change in thinking about the perception of art, and what it requires from viewers. E. C. Goosen, the curator and chairman of the Hunter College art department, wrote in the catalogue: "The new attitude [by the artists represented in the exhibit] has been turning art inside out: instead of perceptual experience being accepted as the means to an end, it has become the end in itself. . . . The spectator is not given symbols, but facts, to make of them what he can. They do not direct his mind or call up trusted cores of experience, but lead him to the point where he must evaluate his own peculiar responses."[49]

LeWitt's piece was featured, along with a work by John McCracken, in the exhibit's last gallery as a kind of final statement. The *New York Times* critic John Canaday, skeptical of the new wave of contemporary art, made much of that last room in his review, in a kind of summing up of his own: "Full enjoyment of the exhibition must depend upon one's readiness to renounce all expectations of humanistic expression in contemporary art."[50]

At the time of this exhibit, LeWitt was heavily involved in both trying to apply his conceptual ideas and, as in the case of Piper, encouraging others to do the same.

Dorothea Rockburne, who met LeWitt in 1965 and who eventually became godmother to his youngest daughter, Eva, recalled that LeWitt often visited her studio to ask about her work, "commenting on this, making suggestions on that."[51]

The aspects of LeWitt's personality that Rockburne most admired were "his independence of thought and stubborn unwillingness to accept the recognition due an artist of his stature. Sol didn't belong to any organizations that I know of. When he was put up for membership at the American Academy of Arts and Letters he refused to join. Yet he was very much part of the art machine—you know, the gallery system."[52] One group, however, that she remembered his being part of was an informal association of artists in the 1970s. "They were mostly Minimalists, who would get together to protest various things," she said. The group's strongly opinionated attendees included Judd, Flavin, Smithson, Morris, Andre, and Richard Serra. Rockburne noted:

I was the only woman there. The group had an official name, but I have no idea what it was. I nicknamed us the Art Scouts because I thought that was kind of funny. There was a series of meetings, but I don't think much was accomplished. There was a lot of b.s. going down, but Sol was always very careful to stop us from getting into self-aggrandizement and self-promotion, which could easily have happened in about two seconds. He kept the discussions very much on the straight and narrow. That's pretty much been his way.[53]

During the installation of Rockburne's first solo exhibit, at the Bykert Gallery, she recalled:

Sol stopped by to see how I was doing. The exhibition was an installation utilizing various materials and structurally based on mathematical concept of Set Theory. Having glued a panel of chipboard to the wall I had second thoughts about its placement. I decided to change its position in the room so I had to remove the panel and any glue from the wall and restore the wall to pristine condition — enter Sol. By this time he was traveling extensively for his work. Sol was aware of the time constraints for the installation. He promptly took off his jacket, got down on his hands and knees and helped me to carefully remove rubber cement from the wall. He stayed all day, volunteering to come back the next day, which fortunately wasn't necessary.[54]

LeWitt's Hester Street hospitality toward fellow artists had its limits, however. In his final interview, in 2006, he said:

I remember Mario Merz came to New York [to visit from his native Italy], and he stayed in my place endlessly and I had to tell him he had to go one day. It was so funny because his schedule and my schedule were so different. He would be coming home and I would be getting up, and I get up around six in the morning, and he was coming home from being out all night and he'd sleep all day and I worked. We were really opposite but after about four weeks or so I kicked him out and he was very nice about it, he knew it was coming.[55]

■ LeWitt's usual table at Max's Kansas City — he was always in the early dinner crowd, arriving about 6:00 P.M. because of his penchant for early rising, a habit that had begun when he was in the army — was near a fluorescent installation by Flavin. Chuck Close remembered that the Flavin piece "cast a pall over everyone, and that's where many artists sat because it made them look more sickly."[56]

Robert Rauschenberg and his entourage and Warhol with his groupies sat in other parts of the restaurant, holding forth much later in the evening and in the early morning hours. Close remembered, "There was a huge John Chamberlain sculpture that people used as a coat rack — it was like a Monet haystack."[57] The area around the cash register served as a photography gallery, with changing exhibits. Patrons passed two piranha-filled fish tanks on the way to the booths.

Owned by the flamboyant Mickey Ruskin, Max's Kansas City became, according to Warhol, the place in the city where art and artists "homogenized."[58] Ruskin filled his walls and spaces with art and traded food and drink for art—a policy that set him widely apart from fellow restaurateurs. LeWitt, Close, Weiner, and others usually sat near the Judd sculpture. Andre often brought in his French horn case filled with champagne. On the occasions when Lippard brought her young son, Ethan, the boy crawled under the table to untie everyone's shoelaces.[59]

Max's served regular meals. At the time, "Max's Own Kansas City Cube Steak," a specialty of the house, went for $7.95, but barbecued chicken could be had for just $4.95. Even so, artists with only small bank accounts occasionally made do with the chick peas that were gratis—"inedible," as Close recalled, "but if you were hungry enough they became your sustenance"—and nursed gin and tonics for two or three hours. Or they might have sipped a "Blondie" for $2.50, "a silky smooth bombshell with Galliano, Cacao, and a good head."[60]

Music played all the time, and the jukebox was a repository of classic songs. One night, Janis Joplin, with a bottle of Southern Comfort in her hand, sang along with Billie Holiday, tears running down her cheeks.

Sometimes the artists were overshadowed by living legends who came for dinner. They included Cary Grant, Dennis Hopper, Patti Smith, Bob Dylan, Joan Baez, David Bowie, and Lou Reed. Mel Brooks also came in, while working on a movie script called *The Producers*, and Alice Weiner, a waitress at the time (before she became a full-time artist) remembered him as a very big tipper.

Close described Max's atmosphere as often contentious: "We often talked art better than we made it, but there were fights. Everyone was asked to defend what they'd recently seen. If someone saw a show everybody wanted to know what it was like." Close recalled that Helen Marden, the wife of the artist Brice Marden, praised a Rauschenberg show, but Serra, the sculptor, challenged her on it to the point of rudeness—whereupon she threw her drink in his face. And "another time, Carl Andre was punched during an argument over art."[61]

Joseph Kosuth remembered the minimalist group made "quite a team." He said: "You would sit at their table, and would be just absolutely, you know, wiped out, like the fastest-gun-in-the-West art conversations . . . real pricks, real killers. Carl Andre, Smithson, Serra. I used to give them a fight but on the other hand I thought a lot of it was macho posturing, and not really that productive. But of course if there were, you know, attractive young ladies around, our masculinity was on the line, so we would have art battles."[62] Close said, "Sol, on the other hand, was a benign presence," never entering the fray.

Kosuth essentially claimed the title of father of conceptual art for himself and had used the term conceptual art to describe his own ideas.[63] He remains a central figure whose writings and work have been influential. There were many similarities between his view of art and LeWitt's, but there were also deep divides. One of them is illustrated by Kosuth's view that "the public isn't interested in art anyway . . . no more interested in art then they are in physics." He believed that "they either get it or they don't get."[64] According to LeWitt, the viewer of the art is part of the art—that is, he or she completes the art: "Once it is out of his hand, the artist has no control over the way a viewer will perceive the work. Different people will understand the same thing in a different way."[65] Debates about such points were common at Max's Kansas City.

LeWitt was also part of a small group of artists who had agreed with a marketing point raised by Rauschenberg. By the early 1970s, what was being called contemporary art—as opposed to previous labels such as abstract expressionism, pop art, and op art—was being sold at auction houses and causing a stir.

Sotheby's put up for auction fifty contemporary works owned by Robert Scull, known for his collection of pop art and minimalism. The auction drew an overflow crowd, including luminaries such as Lee Radziwill, the designer Halston, the architect Philip Johnson, and the influential gallery owners Ivan Karp and Leo Castelli. By the end of the evening, the take was more than $2 million, an astonishing figure for 1973. Among the pieces sold was one by Rauschenberg that Scull had bought from him for $900 in 1958; it went for $85,000. It was Rauschenberg's view that artists were entitled to some percentage—he argued 15 percent—of subsequent sales as a royalty. Scull did not agree, and accounts of the evening include descriptions of more than a little hostility between the artist and the collector. According to Anthony Haden-Guest, author of *True Colors: The Real Life of the Art World*,[66] an account of the era, Rauschenberg's view was later supported by LeWitt as well as James Rosenquist, Andre, and Hans Haacke.

This position could reasonably be assumed to be part of LeWitt's

     SOL LEWITT

emerging thinking on how to market his own work and keep some measure of control over it, something that eluded most artists.

LeWitt expressed his ideas in a statement at a public hearing held by the Art Workers Coalition in the School of Visual Arts, April 10, 1969, an event intended to address artists' rights and related issues:[67]

> A work of art by a living artist would still be the property of the artist. A collector would, in a sense, be the custodian of that art.
> The artist would be consulted when his work was displayed, reproduced, or used in any way.
> The museum, collector, or publication would compensate the artist for the use of his art. This would be a rental, beyond the original purchase price The rental would be nominal; the principle of a royalty would be used.
> An artist would have the right to retrieve his work from a collection if he compensated the purchaser with the original price or a mutually agreeable substitute.
> When a work is resold from one collector to another, the artist would be compensated with the percentage of the price.
> An artist should have the right to change or destroy any work of his as long as he lives.[68]

Though this marketing vision as a package was not adopted, it helped shape LeWitt's thinking about how to keep control of his work over the years, and it eventually led to an innovative plan for marketing his wall drawings.

■ Alice Weiner, then Alice Zimmerman, worked at Max's whenever she needed the money, wearing the mandatory red-and-black apron. In recalling those days and the first time she met the artist Lawrence Weiner, one of the leading figures in conceptual art, she said: "Lawrence and John Chamberlain were already drunk on margaritas by the time I started to serve them. So I was nasty to them. John said, 'I'd like to count your freckles in the moonlight.' Lawrence said, 'I love you.' I said, 'You don't love me. You love the drinks I'm bringing you.'"[69] Nevertheless, in the months that followed she changed her opinion, and the two were married.

This, then, was the kind of place that Max's became—a lifeline for many, including the artist Jackie Ferrara, who met LeWitt there and who found not only encouragement for her work but reaffirming payment as well: "He was the first person to buy my work."[70] At her show at Sachs Gallery in 1974, he bought three sculptures and a painting. LeWitt had seen the announcement for the show, which mentioned her plywood pieces, and "I guess he was intrigued, so he came to see the show." This gesture led directly to her next opportunity. LeWitt introduced her to the dealer Max Protetch, and he was Ferrara's dealer for many years.

There are hundreds of examples of similar purchases by LeWitt over the next few years, and many artists who remained grateful because he often used his wallet, not merely his lips, to verify their work. His growing private collection was amassed through purchases, trades with other artists, and taking works from gallery owners instead of payment for the works of his that they had sold.

LeWitt's entries in his informal account book reveal just how much of his income was spent on the art of others. For example, in a much later period, March 1985, he made a list of what he had collected or was still owed for a half-dozen pieces that had been sold by galleries. This amounted to about $70,000. He also recorded what he had paid for each of seven works by fellow artists, which totaled about $61,000. This meant that he had spent nearly 90 percent of his income in this way. The body of work as he built his collection reflected a wide array of styles, many of them revealing not only his taste in art but certain influences on him and his work. His purchases included one of Andre's ventures into free verse; a 1963 Jo Baer piece on graph paper that, in the use of line and grid, brings to mind later work by LeWitt; Barry's spare canvases that explore invisibility and elusiveness; several Bochner pieces that play with numbers and letters; Hanne Darboven's more extreme treatment of numbers; Jan Dibbets's explorations of perspective; Ferrara's Masonite pyramids; dozens of pieces by Eva Hesse (many of them untitled); Douglas Heubler's typewritten pieces (one titled "The above point normally exists halfway between the surface of this paper and Sol LeWitt and is only located on the surface itself when it is being looked at."); Richard Long's landscape sculptures, including *A Thirteen Hour Random Walk by Night Along Unfamiliar Roads and Lanes*; Sylvia Mangold's *Painted Graph Paper*, which uses her signature masking tape on borders — a touch that LeWitt encouraged her to adopt for much of her work; etchings by Brice Marden; Piper's 1968 *A Number of Variations on the Area of an 8" Square*, fashioned in the shape of a fir tree, which she created shortly after meeting LeWitt; more than a dozen of Edward Ruscha's portraits of Southern California; Smithson's *Mirror Vortex*, made

　　　　SOL LEWITT

of aluminum and stainless steel; Pat Steir's *Burial Mound*, an etching
that makes ample use of images, words, and numbers; Richard Tuttle's
enigmatic *Kinesthetic Drawings*; and Lawrence Weiner's *Two Minutes of
Spray Paint*, another demonstration of his belief—entirely subscribed
to by LeWitt—that art is not object but idea, which is a rejection of art
as commodity. According to Janet Passehl, curator of the LeWitt Collection, Baer had a box where she put things she wasn't happy with, and
LeWitt would go through the box and pick things out.[71] LeWitt often delivered art to colleagues not in trade but in appreciation, and it was one
such occasion in May 1968 that led to the idea that would become his
signature. The root of it was a year earlier.

NINE

UP THE WALLS

When LeWitt saw a 1967 show curated by Joseph Kosuth in Hanover, Germany, he was struck by the work of one artist in particular, Hanne Darboven. LeWitt recalled:

> She had a small group of drawings with her which she showed me. I was struck by the originality and depth. . . . I went to her studio some days later and saw many more drawings. I told everyone I knew about her work. One was Kaspar Konig. He called Konrad Fischer in Düsseldorf. Konrad gave her a show the next month. I am glad to have been able to start her art-showing life. Since then I've followed all of her work. She has been a close and dear friend.[1]

The episode typified LeWitt's efforts to arrange opportunities for other artists. Thirty-seven years later, he was still championing Darboven, as indicated by his tribute in the catalogue of her 2004 exhibit in Hanover:

> The architecture of time.
> Endless, remorseless, infinite.
> As vast as the oceans, as short as a wave.
> It includes all of our lifetimes, and more.
> Days, months, centuries. The remote past, the remote future and
>   now.
> As simple as a line on paper. As complete as a thousand pages.[2]

LeWitt's own international fame began in 1968. In June, Arnold Bode produced his final version of the the influential exhibit in Kassel, Germany, called Documenta. Bode, a painter and art professor, had begun in the mid-1950s a major effort to bring Germany back into the cultural discussion in the decade following World War II. In the Hitler era, the German public had had no opportunity to see work that the Nazis considered degenerate. So Bode's first Documenta, in 1955, drew 130,000 visitors who wanted to see what was meant by Fauvism, cubism, expressionism, or futurism. Encouraged by the positive reactions, Bode eventually produced the event every four years.

The 1968 show, his last one before passing it on to others to run, featured young artists, and much of the media attention was focused on Tom Wesselmann, Roy Lichtenstein, Andy Warhol, and Robert Indiana, though much of the focus of the exhibit was on works by Dan Flavin, Carl Andre, LeWitt, and others who were producing a new kind of art that appeared to increase the differences between European and American artistic values.

These elements were noted by Jef Cornelis and Karel Geirlandt, who interviewed artists including LeWitt, Christo, and Robert Rauschenberg and produced a documentary film. They played naïfs who put themselves in the shoes of the bewildered spectator, questioning the nature of minimalism. Feelings ran high from the beginning of Documenta IV. Opening speeches could not be delivered because they would have been drowned out by an angry crowd, in part fueled by the kind of anti-American attitudes that had disrupted the twenty-fifth Venice Biennale. Some of the same social and political upheavals that were obvious in the United States at the time were evident in Europe as well.

In the midst of the chaos, LeWitt's contribution to the show—the cube structure titled *Three Part Variation*—seemed quiet. However, it was noticed by a visitor to Documenta IV, the Rome gallery owner Fabio Sargentini, who would soon have ideas of his own about displaying works in this controversial new wave.

What happened next was the art world's version of "what goes around comes around." LeWitt's promotion of Hanne Darboven had helped forge a connection between LeWitt and Konrad Fischer—who with his wife, Dorothee, had just opened their gallery in the center of Düsseldorf.

Fischer's gallery was in a humble space—an alley enclosed at both ends by glass doors. But, as Daniel Birnbaum wrote in *Artforum*, it became the European center of cutting-edge American art.[3] Kaspar Konig, who advised Fischer, said at the time, "The amazing thing was that almost no American artists after [Kenneth] Noland and [Frank] Stella were known in Germany, so there were enormous opportunities."[4] Birnbaum added, "It's no exaggeration to say that Fischer's activities in the late '60s and '70s changed the course of art in Europe as well as, indirectly, in the United States."

Fischer invited LeWitt to come to Germany to be part of a group show of American artists. The Fischers would become champions of LeWitt, Lawrence Weiner, Robert Ryman, Andre, Bruce Nauman, and others.

LeWitt met Jan Dibbets when both had works at Fischer's gallery, and they became immediate friends. LeWitt stayed with Dibbets at his home in Amsterdam for a time. This was where LeWitt developed his taste for fresh herring, and where for Dibbets his new friend became a professional lifeline. The Dutch artist felt very much alone in Amsterdam. He had "nobody to talk to" about the kind of art he was pursuing. Dutch art, of course, has a rich history, but in terms of appreciation of and support for contemporary movements, Dibbets found, Holland was a lonely place. "I was trained as a painter," Dibbets commented, "but painting had no future."[5]

He said that "everybody was looking for something else aside from what was done before." What Dibbets found was a new way to think about photography, thanks to LeWitt. In 1969, when LeWitt came to Amsterdam again, he gave Dibbets a work by Eadweard Muybridge. Muybridge's photography had inspired LeWitt years earlier, and it also inspired the Dutch artist. "This gave me a good push," Dibbets said. "The seriality opened my eyes." Reflecting on the gift, an example of the thousands of gifts LeWitt bestowed on friends over the years, he said, "Where do you find a friend who gives you material that helps you in your work?" Moreover, LeWitt counseled Dibbets on how to keep going in the face of criticism: "There were two American artists joking and insulting me. I told Sol about it. He looked at me, and said, 'Why do you worry? These two, you know they are both full of shit.'"[6] If LeWitt did a lot for Dibbets, the younger artist returned the favor by literally giving him the space he needed.

On the day that LeWitt was scheduled to fly back to New York, Dibbets had to leave early in the morning to teach. He told his guest to "have some coffee, read a book, just close the door when you leave for the airport."[7] But instead of reading, LeWitt had another idea — to leave a gift for his friend.

When Dibbets came home that day, LeWitt was gone, but he had left behind a pencil drawing on a living room wall, "a checkerboard filled with diagonals."[8] It was, Dibbets decided later, a LeWitt experiment — one that later that year, across the Atlantic, would cause a sensation. But before that, LeWitt made a side trip that helped define his work and separate it from the crowd.

     SOL LEWITT

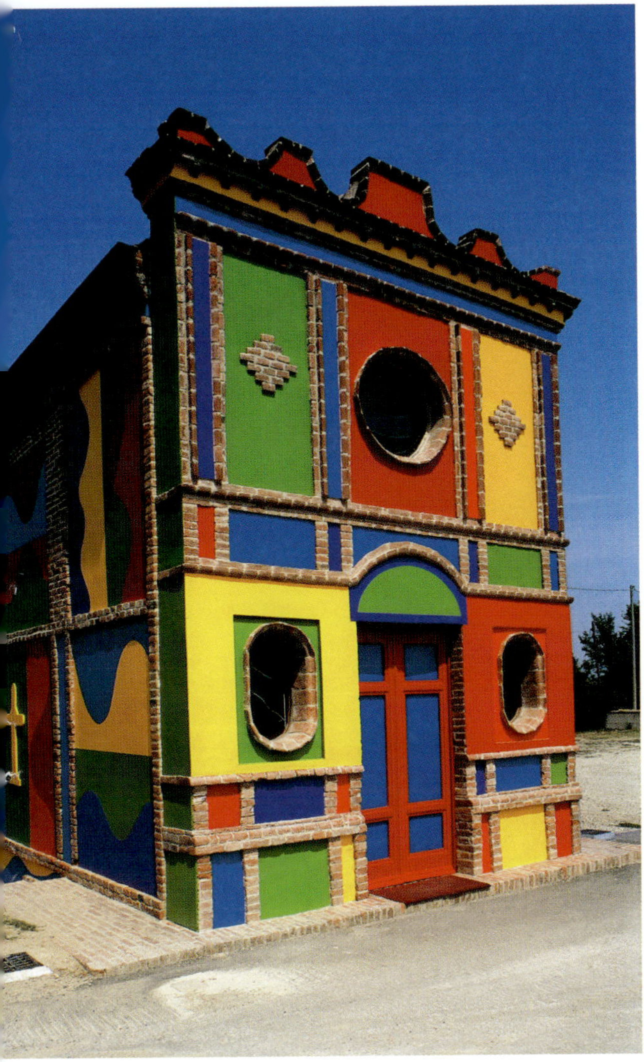

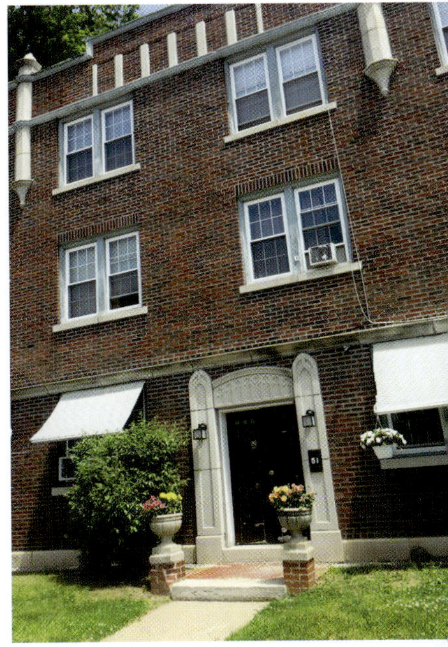

The Cedar Street apartment in
New Britain, Connecticut, where
LeWitt spent most of his youth. During
that time, the city earned national art
headlines for unflattering reasons.
(Lary Bloom)

LeWitt collaborated with David Tremlett to revitalize
a chapel in the village of Barolo, Italy.
(Universal Images Group North America,
LLC/DeAgostini/Alamy Stock Photo)

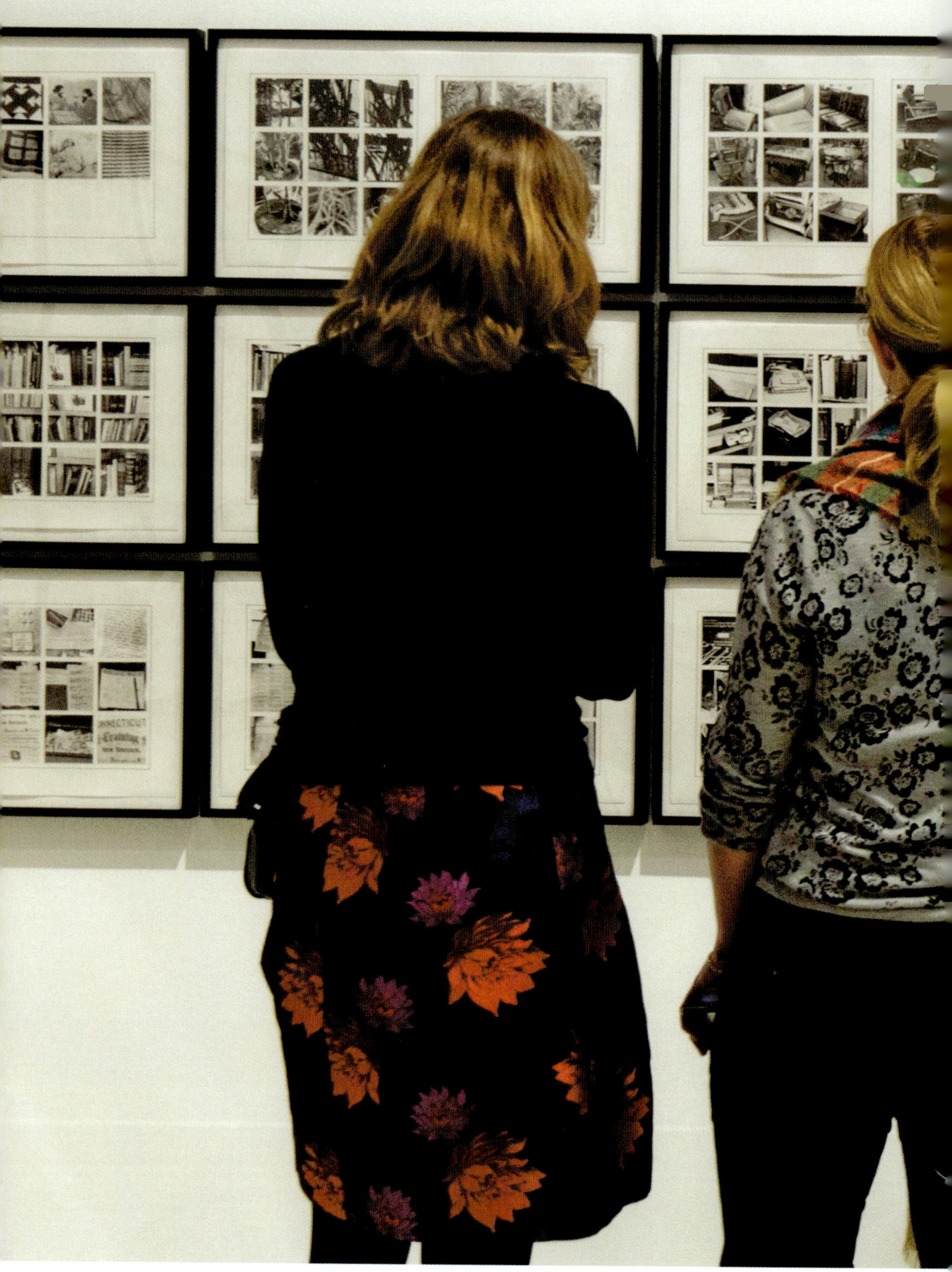

Pages from LeWitt's 1980 Autobiography, in which not a single word of text appears, went on display in London in 2015 in the exhibit Magnificent Obsessions. (ukartpics/Alamy Stock Photo)

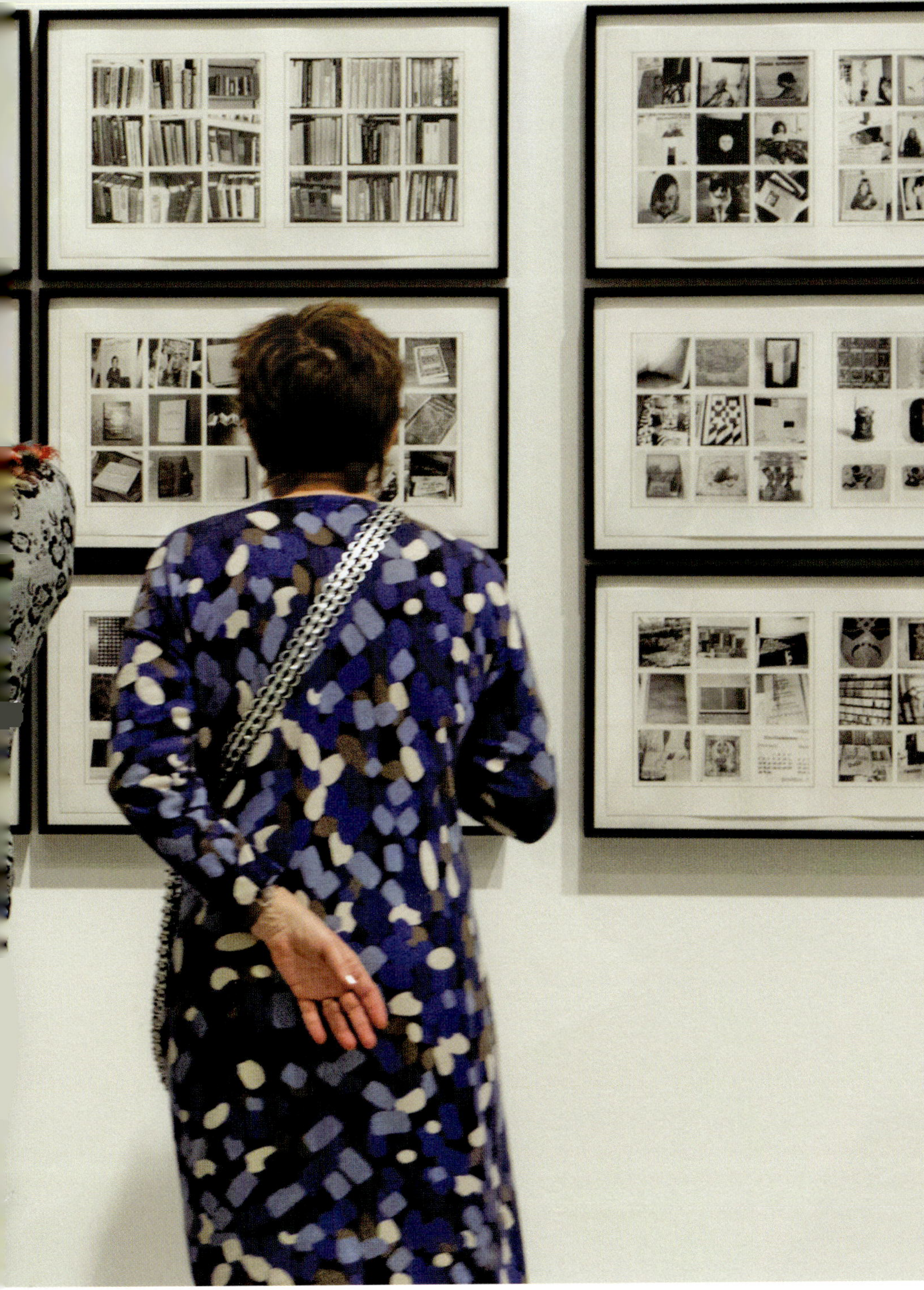

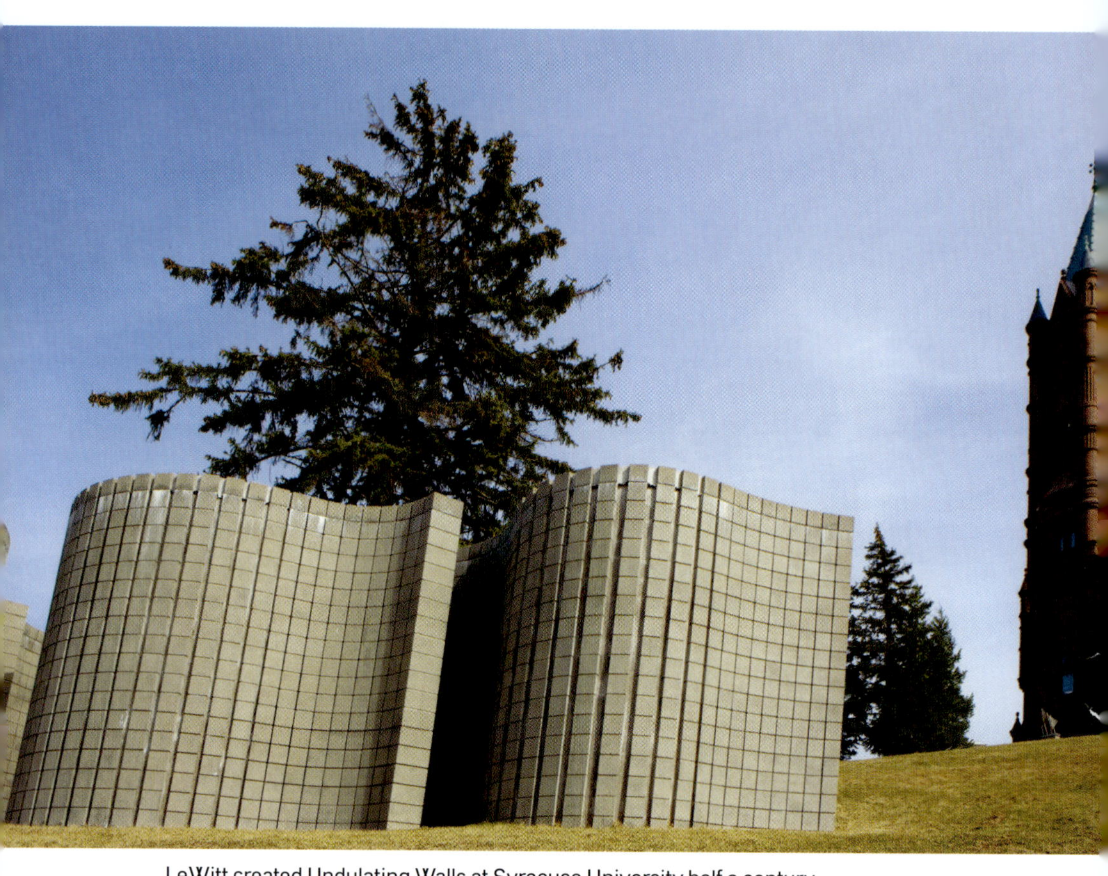

LeWitt created Undulating Walls at Syracuse University half a century after studying art there. (Philip Scalia/Alamy Stock Photos)

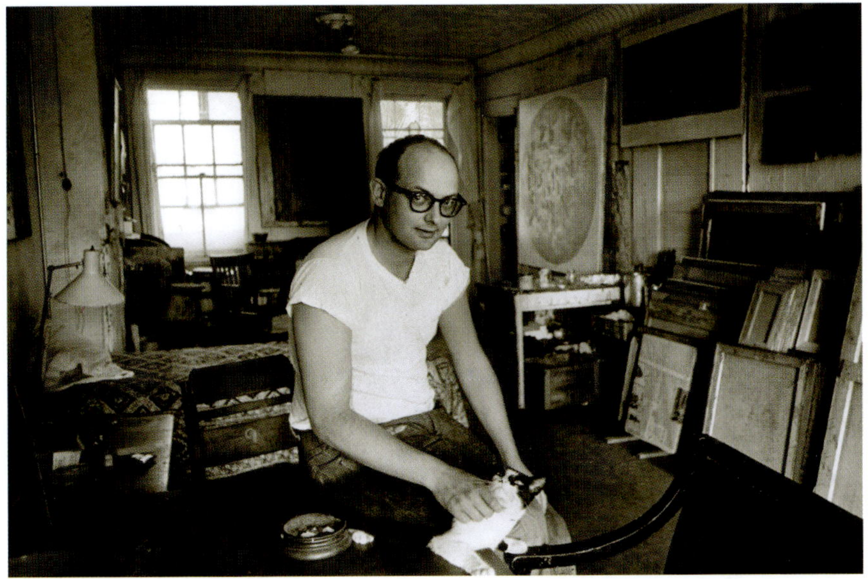

The first mention of LeWitt in the New York Times came in 1961, when he was earning less than $1,000 a year on his art. (Neal Boenzi/The New York Times/Redux)

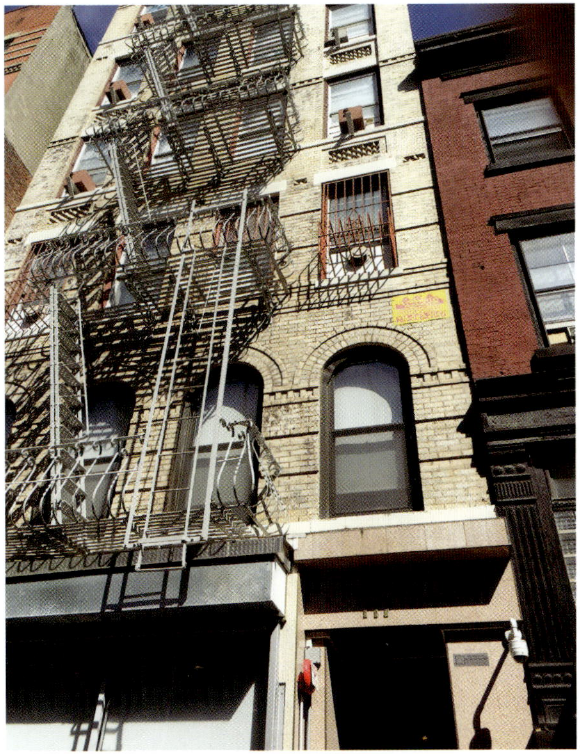

117 Hester Street, New York City, where LeWitt lived for twenty years, became the center of a nascent movement that stripped art down to its basics. (Lary Bloom)

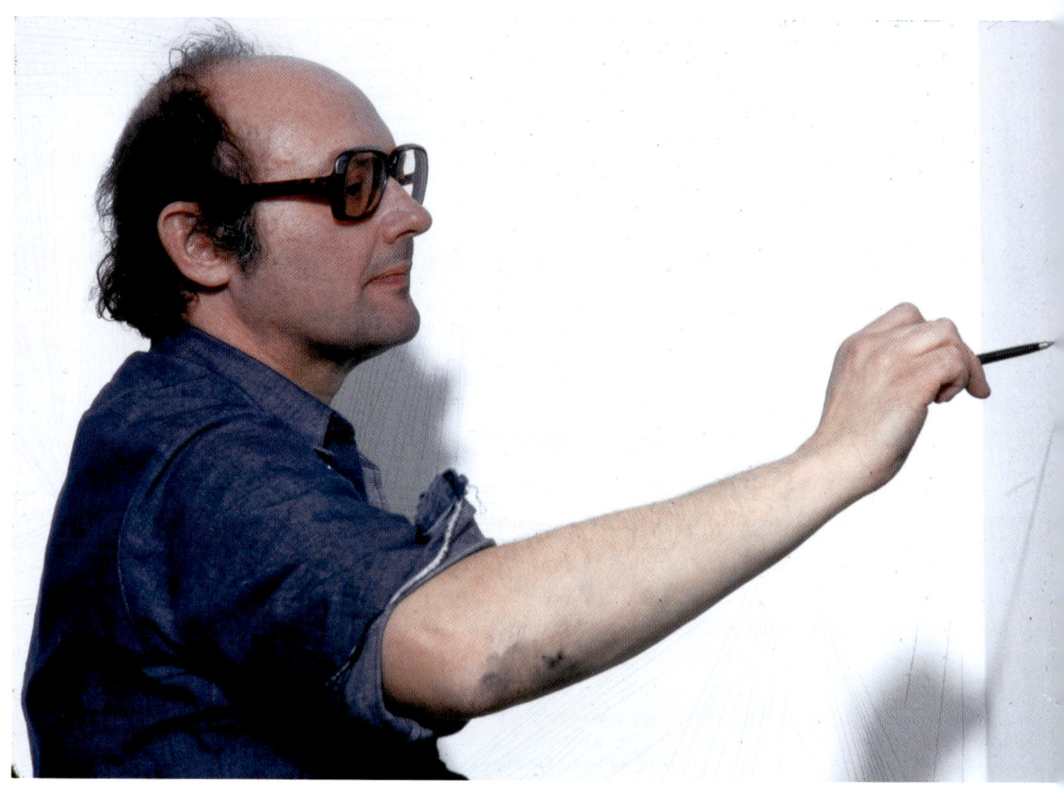

By the time of his 1978 retrospective at the Museum of Modern Art, LeWitt had long since farmed out wall drawing installation to assistants. But he joined the crew in this instance. (Jack Mitchell/Getty Images)

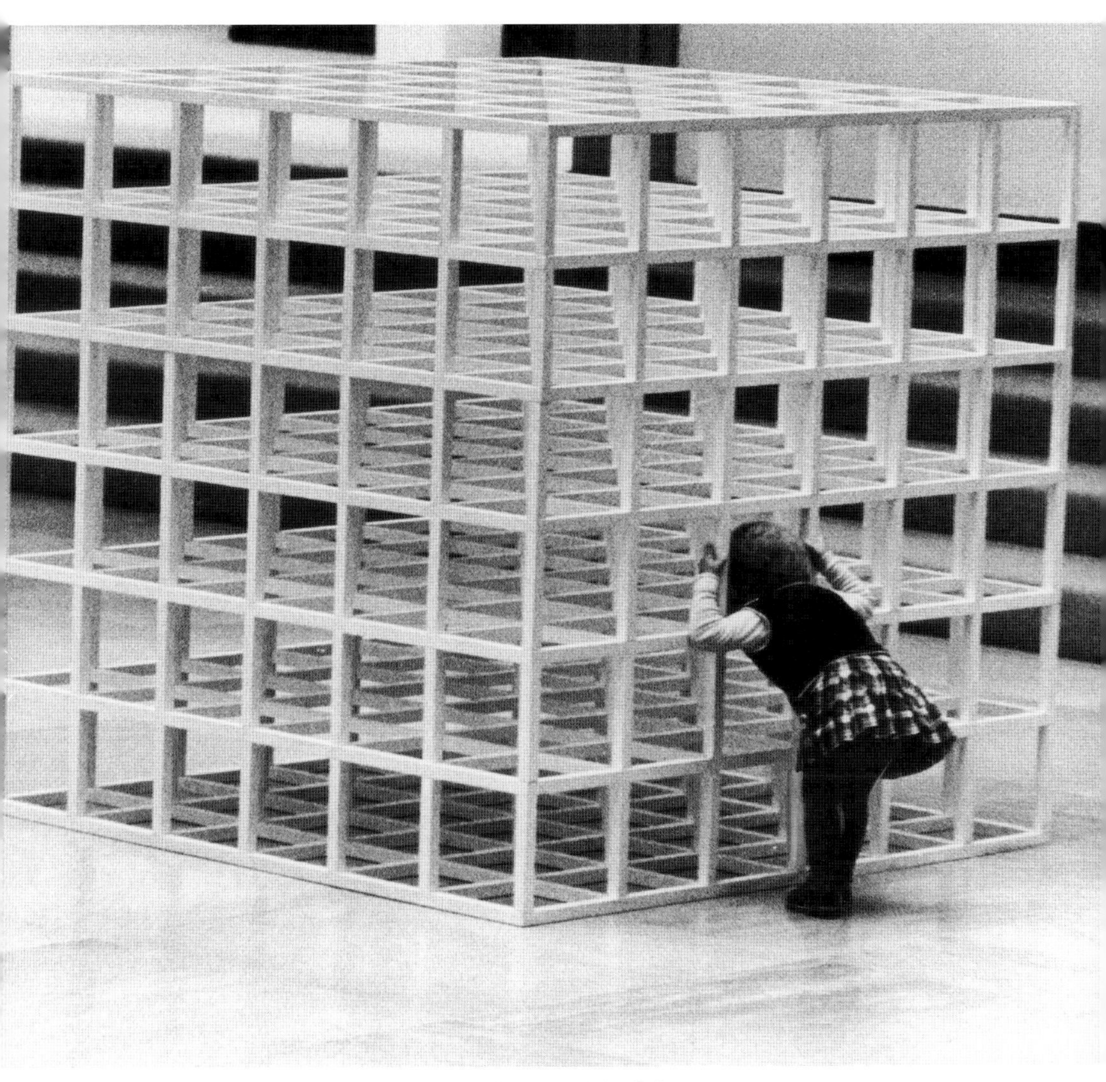

A child in Toronto sought the inside story on Open Modular Cubes.
LeWitt's variations on cubes became a primary early theme in his work.
(Reg Innell/Toronto Star via Getty Images)

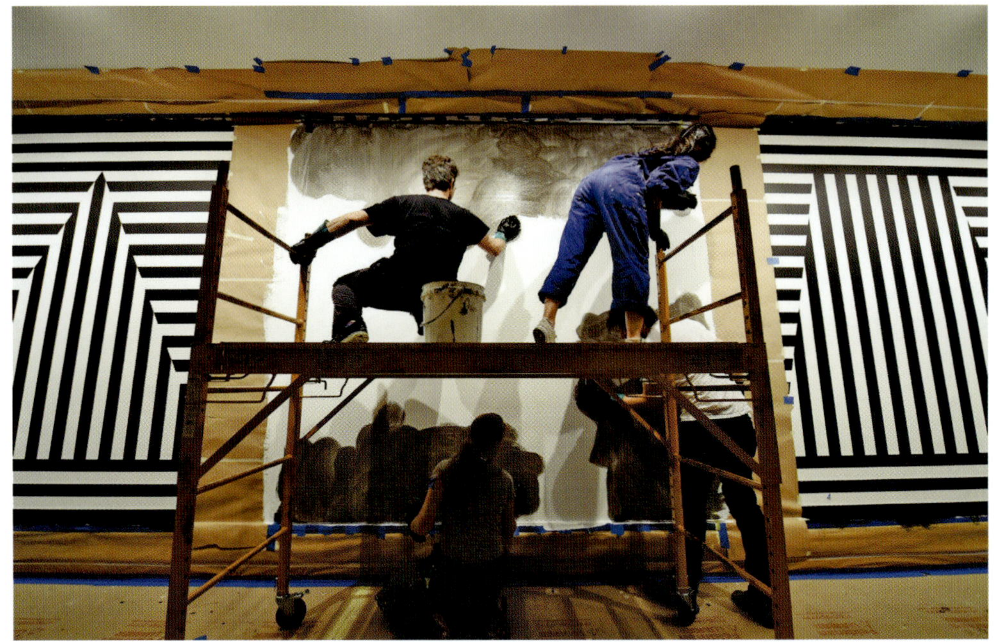

Wall Drawing 370, conceived in 1982, was installed at the Metropolitan Museum of Art in New York City in 2014 but obliterated, as planned, a year later. (Stan Honda/Getty Images)

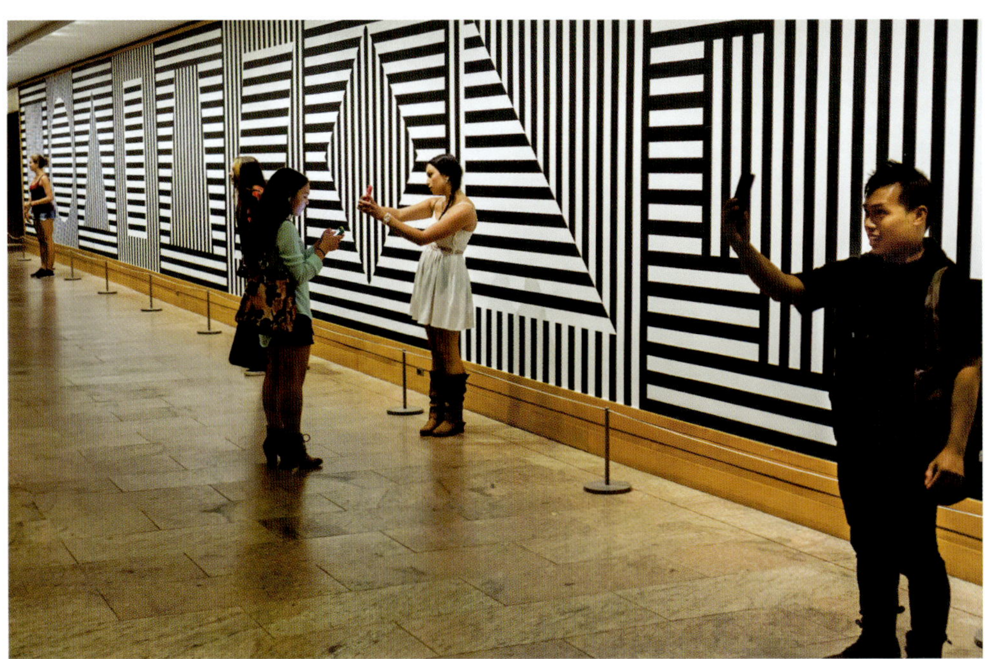

After Wall Drawing 370 went up at the Met, it prompted millennial selfies. (Richard Levine/Alamy Stock Photo)

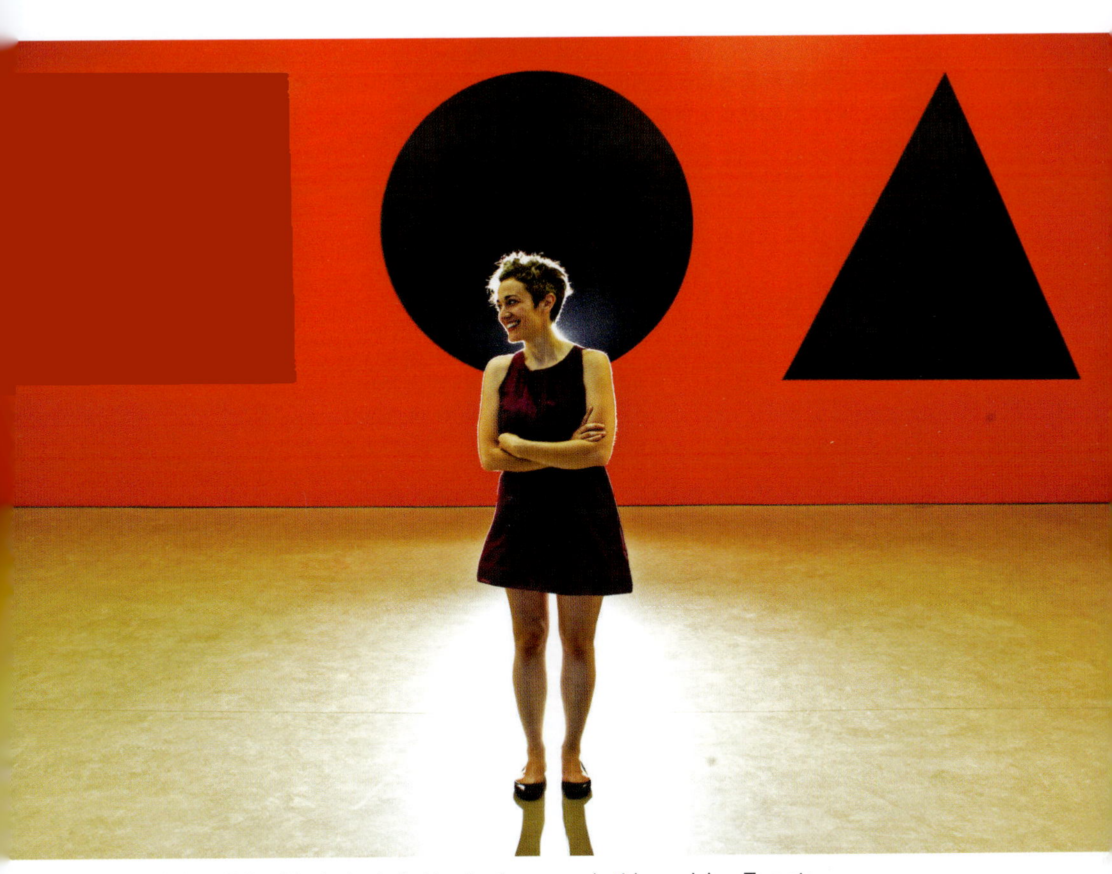

The artist's building blocks included basic shapes, as in this work in a Toronto exhibit arranged by Sarah Robayo Sheridan of the Mercer Union Art Gallery. (Tara Walton/ Toronto Star via Getty Images)

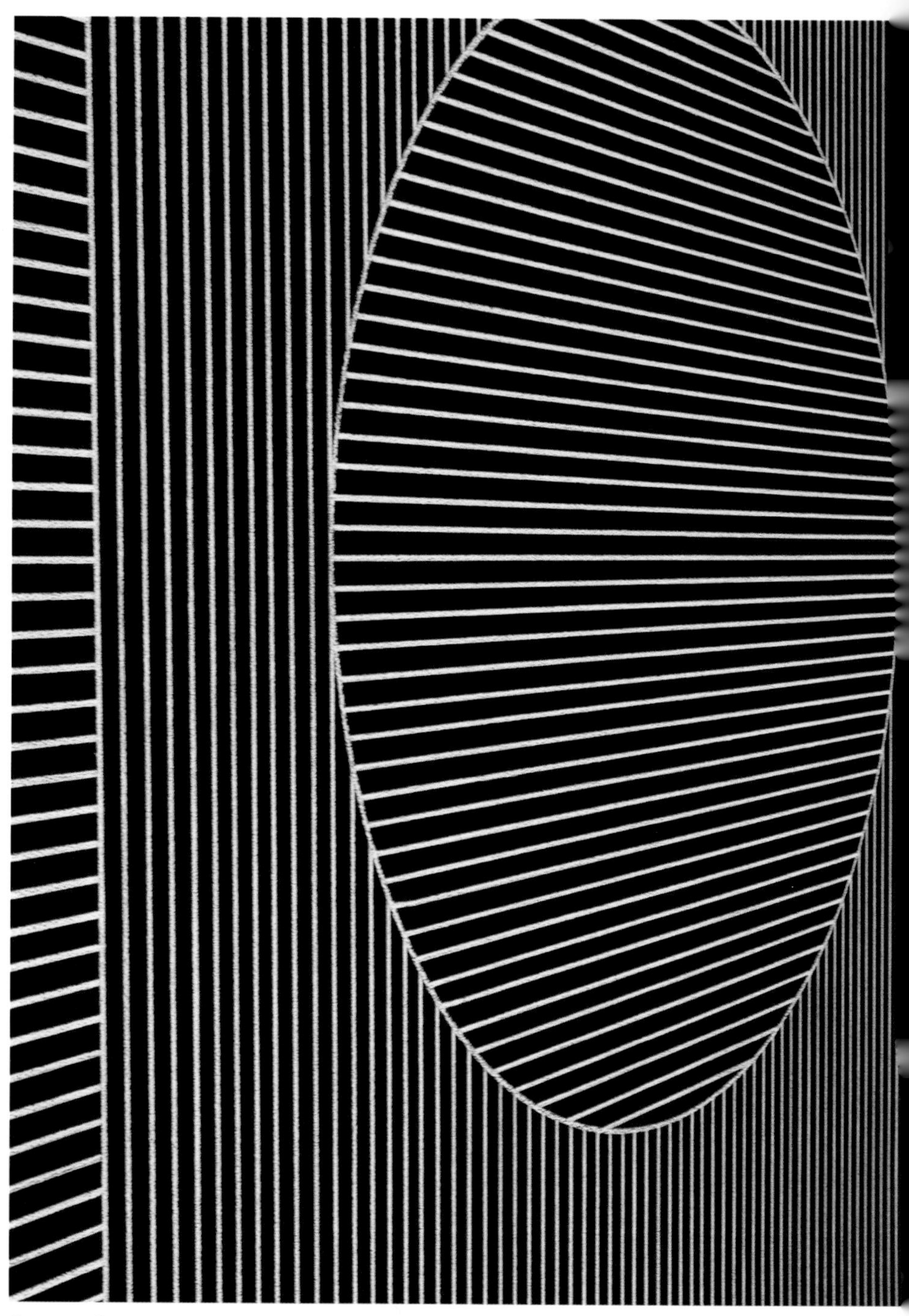

A twenty-five-year-long retrospective opened at Massachusetts Museum of Contemporary Art in 2008, featuring more than 100 LeWitt wall drawings that collectively cover about 27,000 square feet. (Randy Duchaine/Alamy Stock Photo)

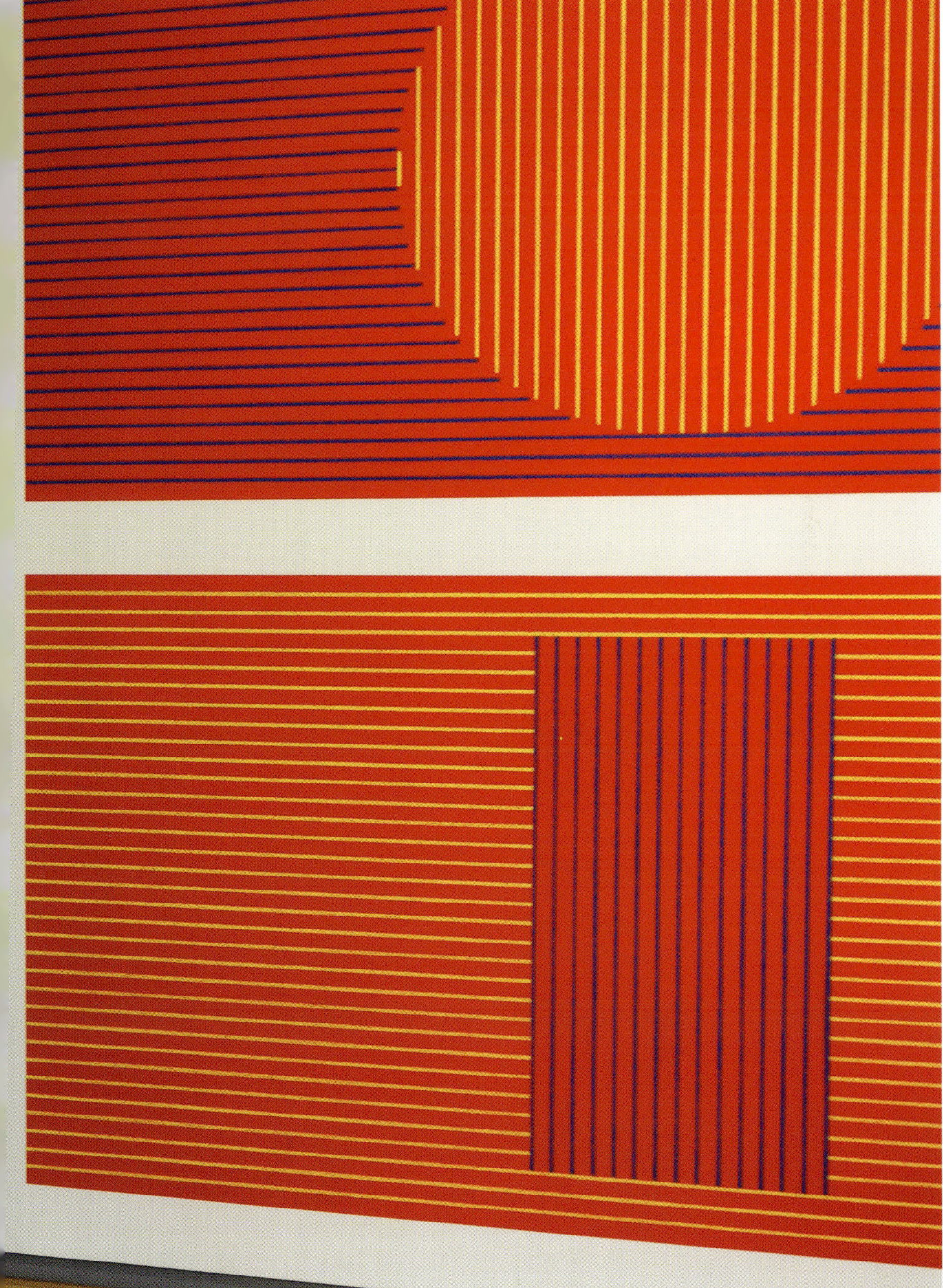

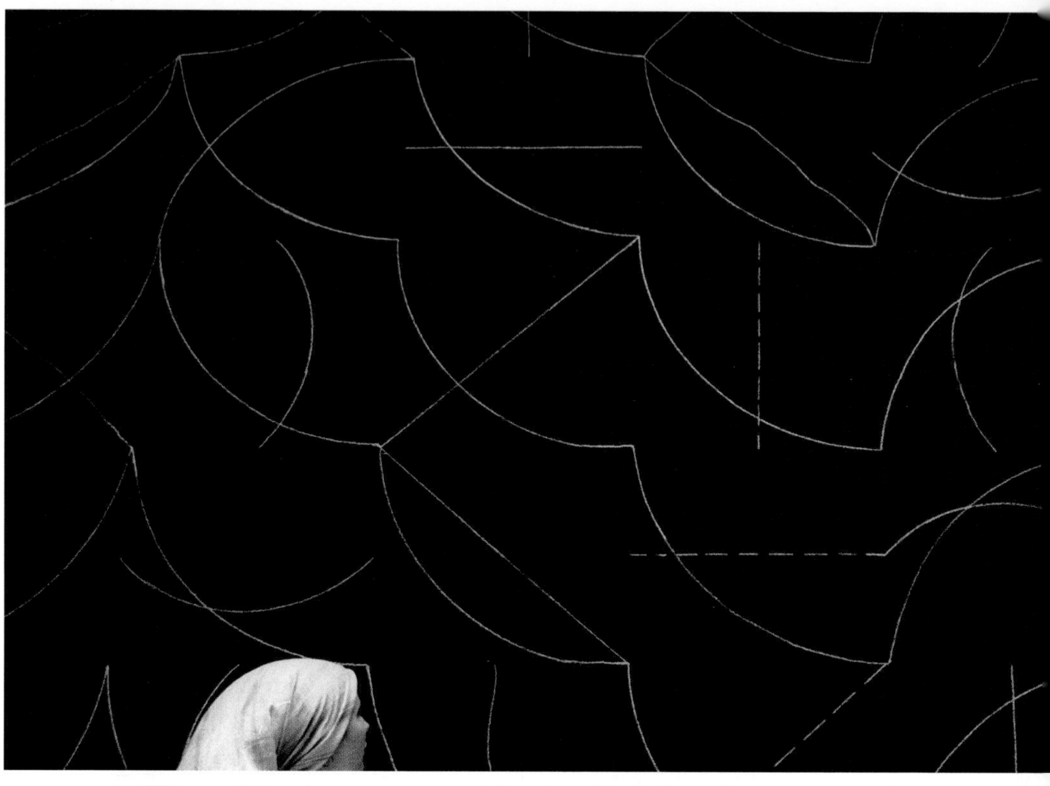

LeWitt was attracted at a young age to Italy, where his work proliferated. In 1976, he had this wall drawing in the Venice Biennale. (David Lees/Corbis/ VCG via Getty Images)

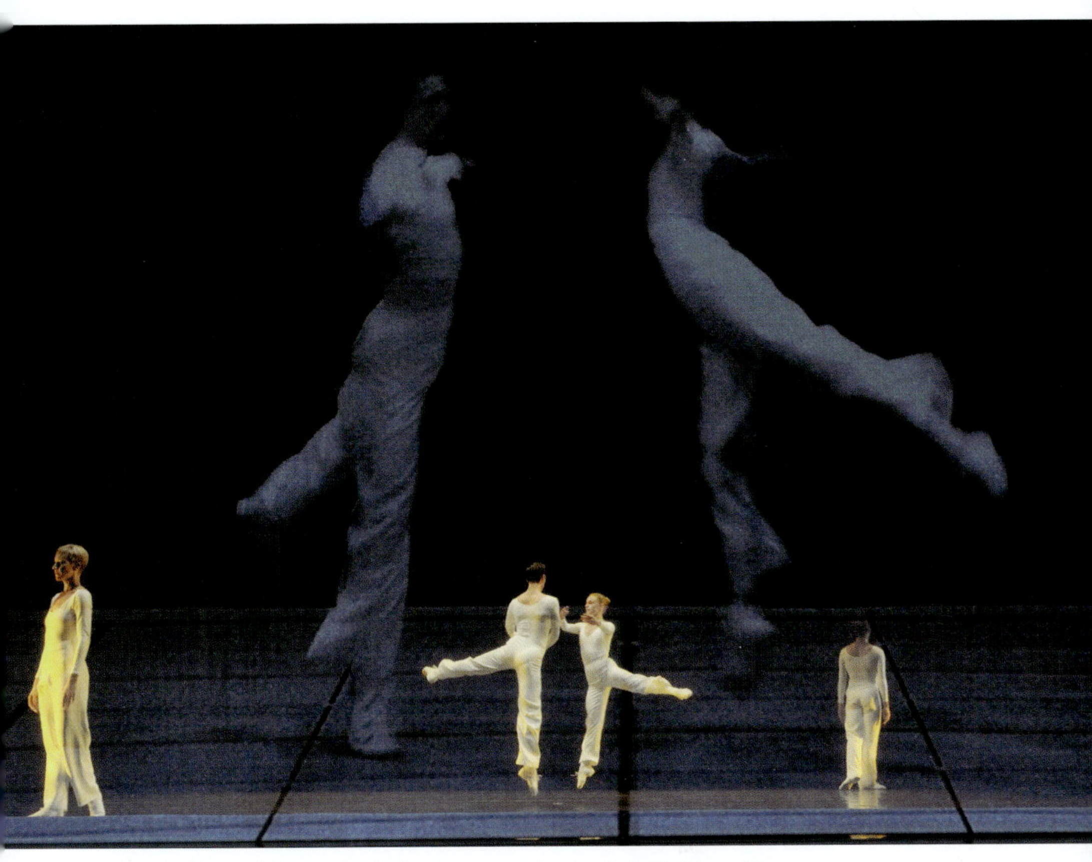

In 1979, LeWitt collaborated with the choreographer Lucinda Childs and the composer Philip Glass to make the film Dance, juxtaposing rehearsal film of performers with live images. (Sueddeutsche Zeitung Photo / Alamy Stock Photo)

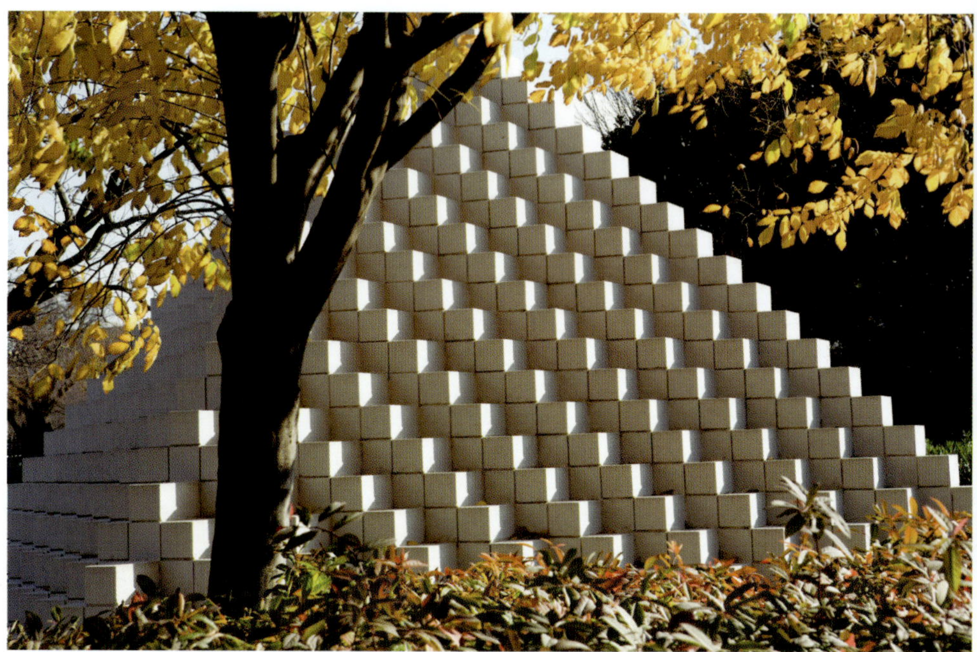

LeWitt's Four-Sided Pyramid in the National Gallery of Art Sculpture Garden in Washington, D.C. (Philip Scalia/Alamy Stock Photos)

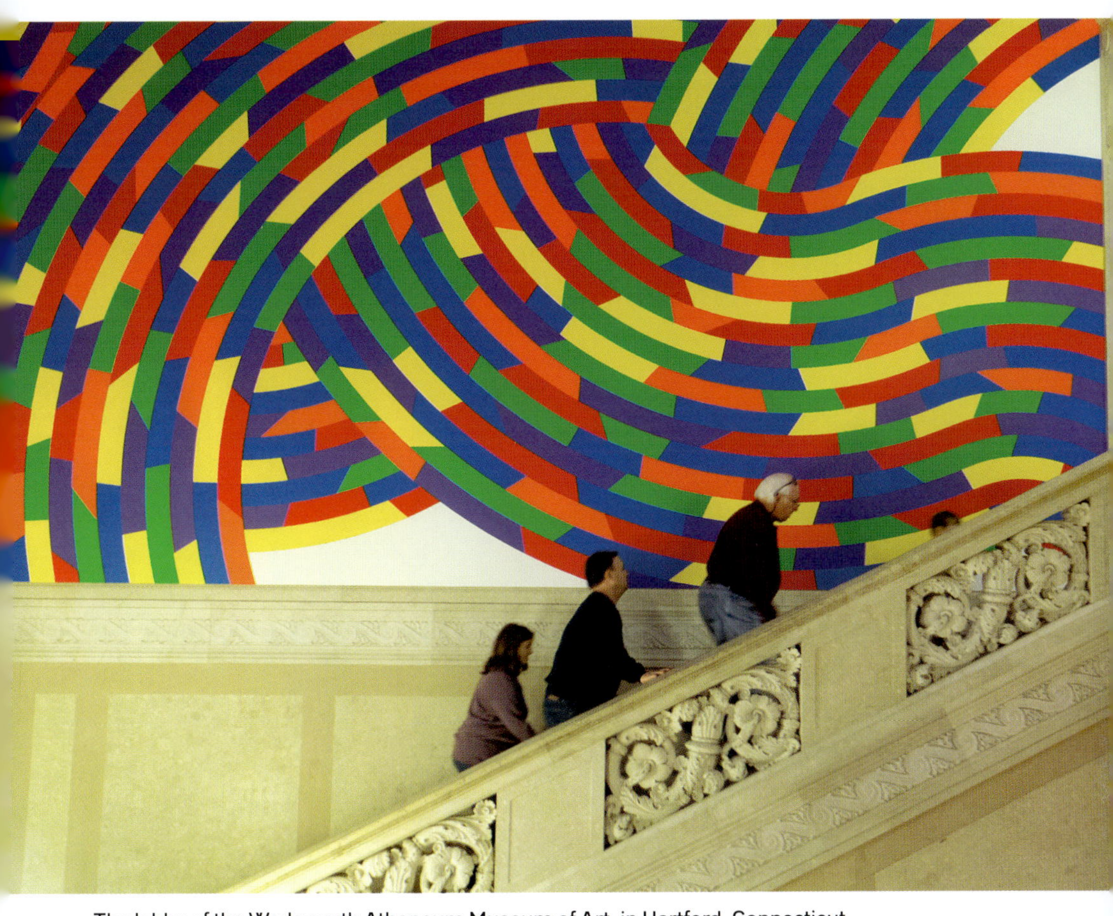

The lobby of the Wadsworth Atheneum Museum of Art, in Hartford, Connecticut, where as a boy LeWitt went to classes, features a wraparound wall drawing. (Randy Duchaine/Alamy Stock Photo.)

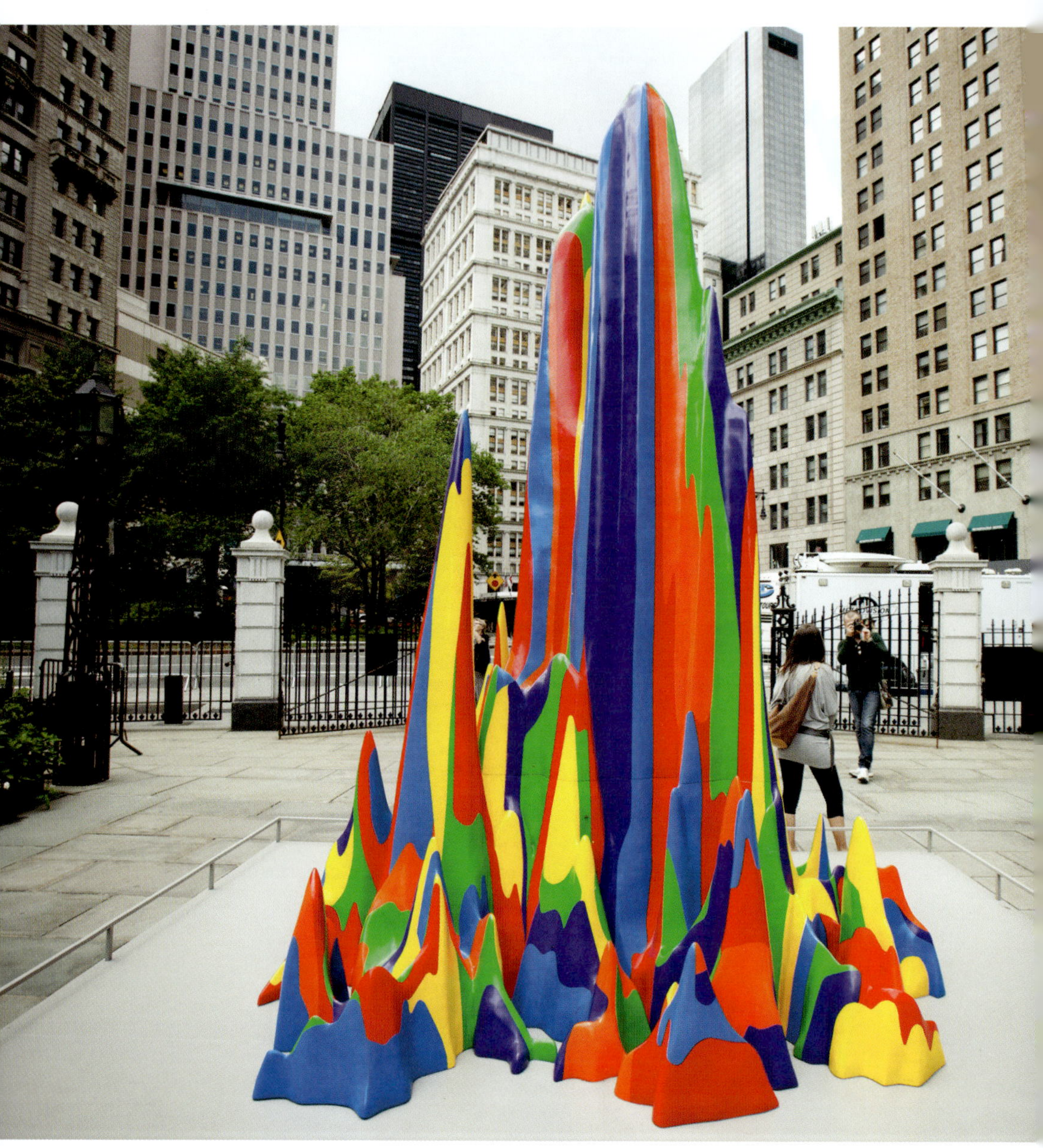

Completed in 2005 in City Hall Park in Manhattan, Splotch 15 is among the artist's body of structures inspired by urban architecture. (Richard Levine/Alamy Stock Photo)

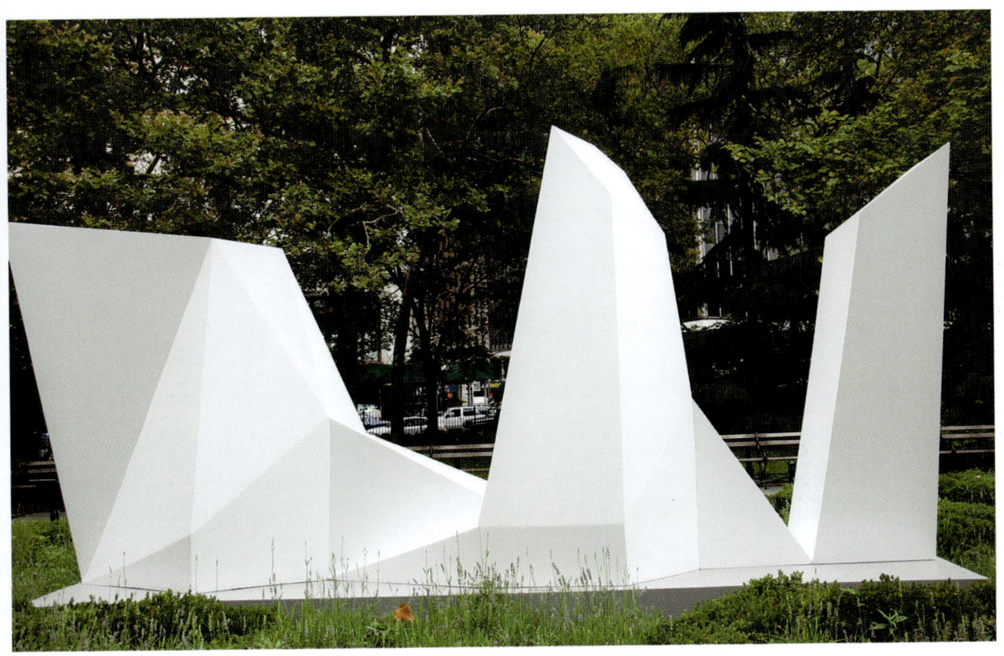

Complex Forms, a structure in City Hall Park, Manhattan, is one of hundreds of site-specific works. (Tracy Whitefoot/Alamy Stock Photo.)

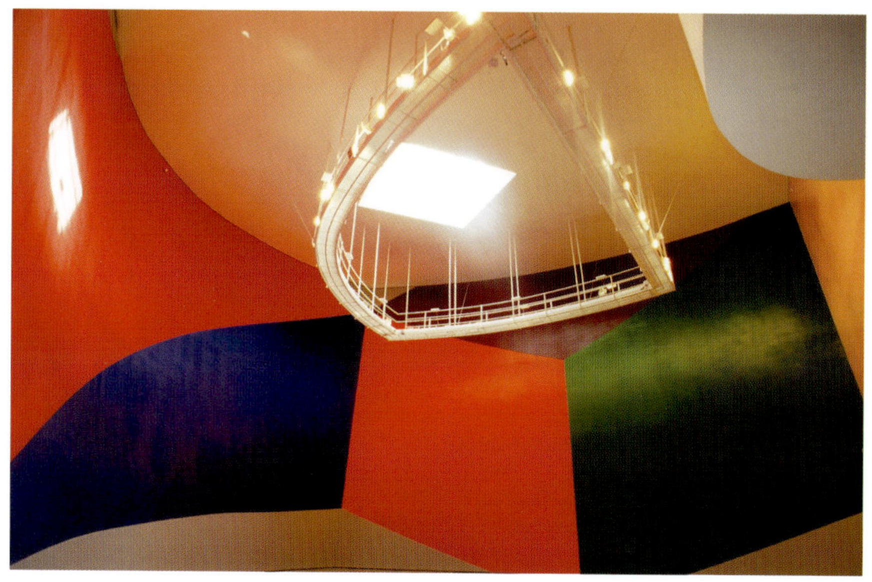

Architect Frank Gehry's Museo Guggenheim Bilbao includes Wall Drawing 837, Geometric Forms. (Eric Vandeville/Gamma-Rapho via Getty Images)

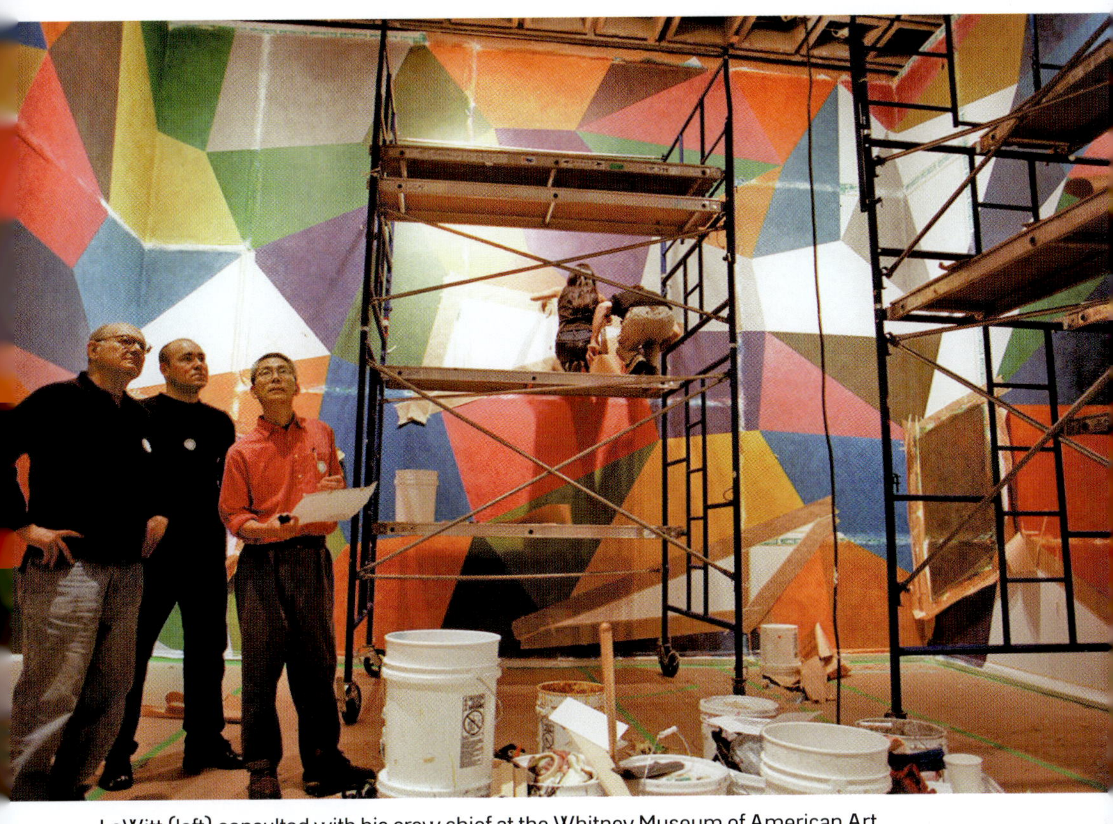

LeWitt (left) consulted with his crew chief at the Whitney Museum of American Art in advance of the final stop on his cross-county 2000 retrospective. (Librado Romero/ The New York Times/Redux)

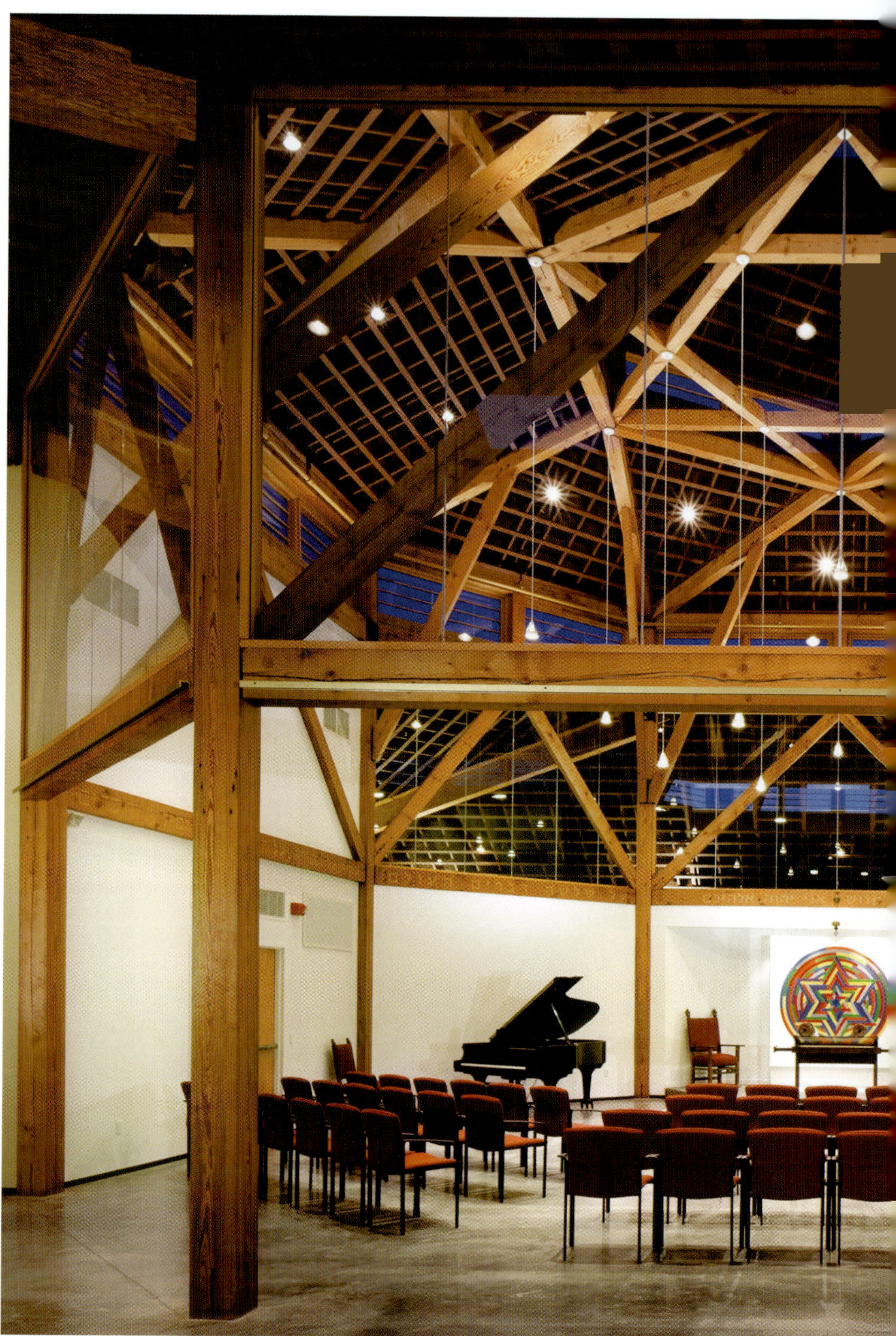

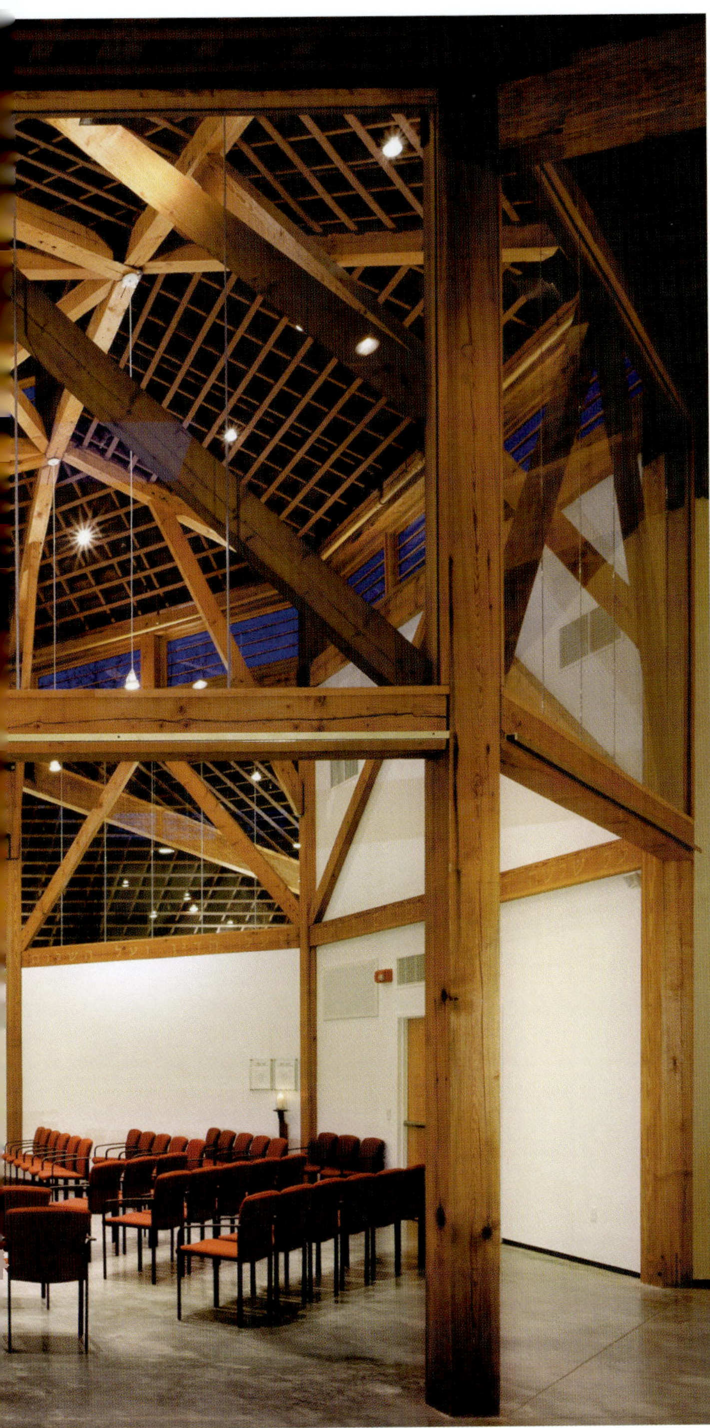

During his final years, LeWitt lived in Chester, Connecticut, and as a member of Congregation Beth Shalom Rodfe Zedek, he created the concept for its sanctuary and overall design. (Robert Benson Photography, LLC)

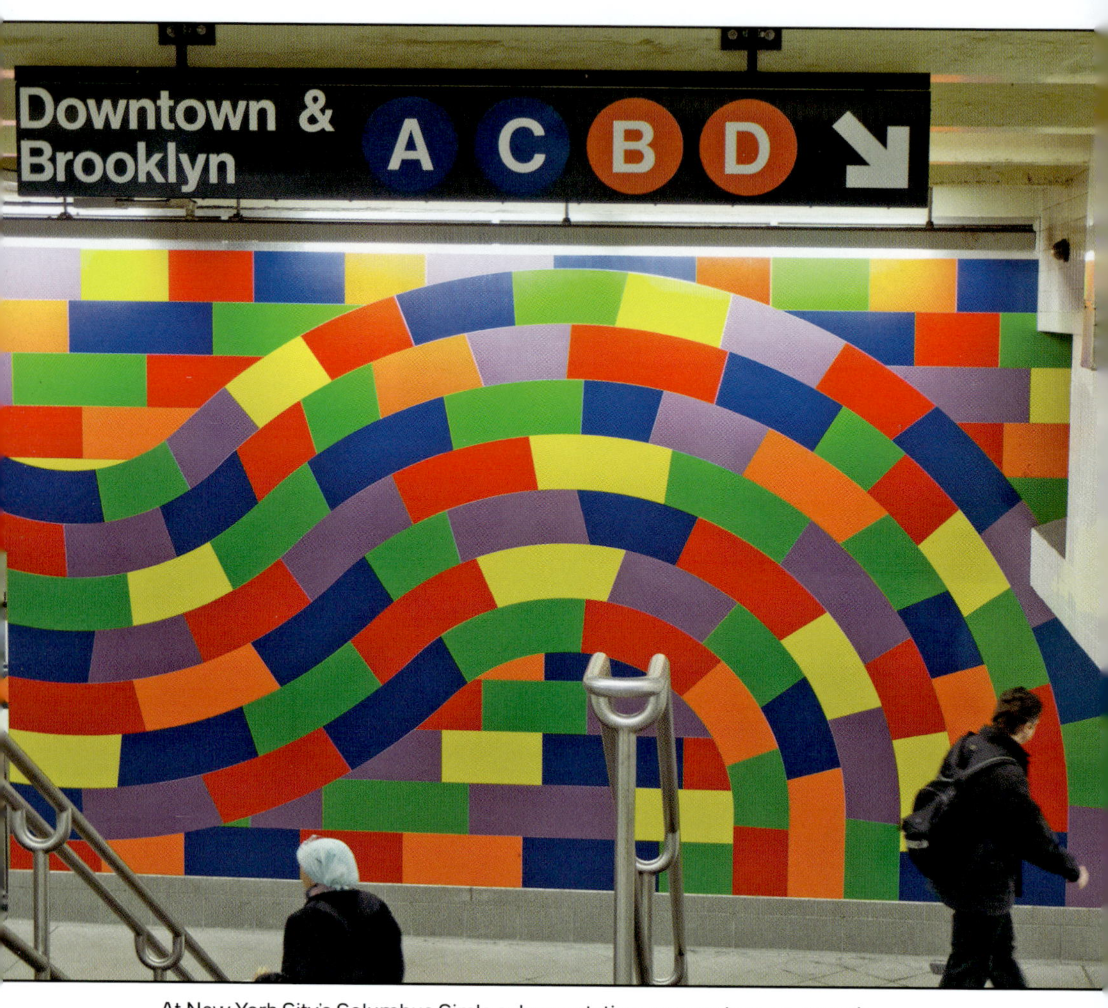

At New York City's Columbus Circle subway station, commuters see a work finished after the artist's death. (Randy Duchaine/Alamy Stock Photo)

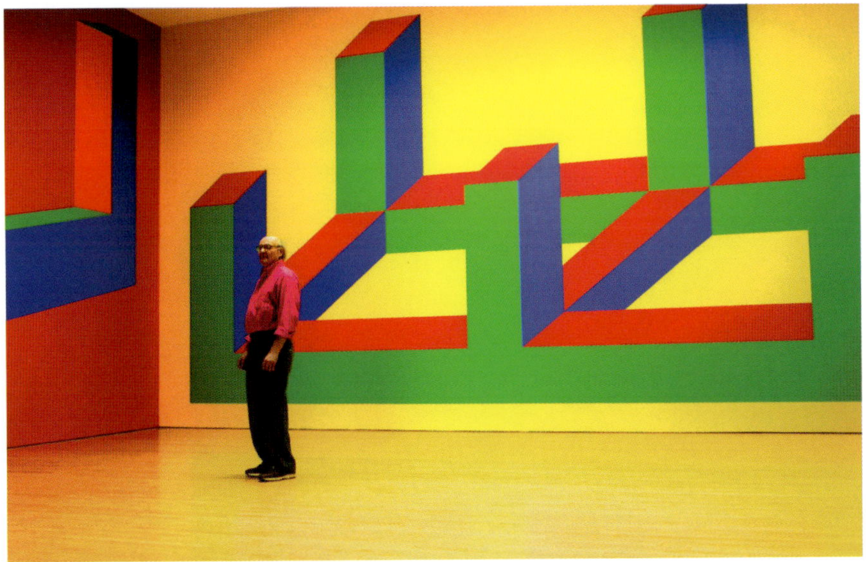

At the Margo Leavin Gallery in Los Angeles in 2001, LeWitt saw Wall Drawing 993 in finished form only after visitors had seen it. He said: "I try to imagine the outcome, but I'm always surprised when I see them." (Gina Ferazzi/Los Angeles Times via Getty Images)

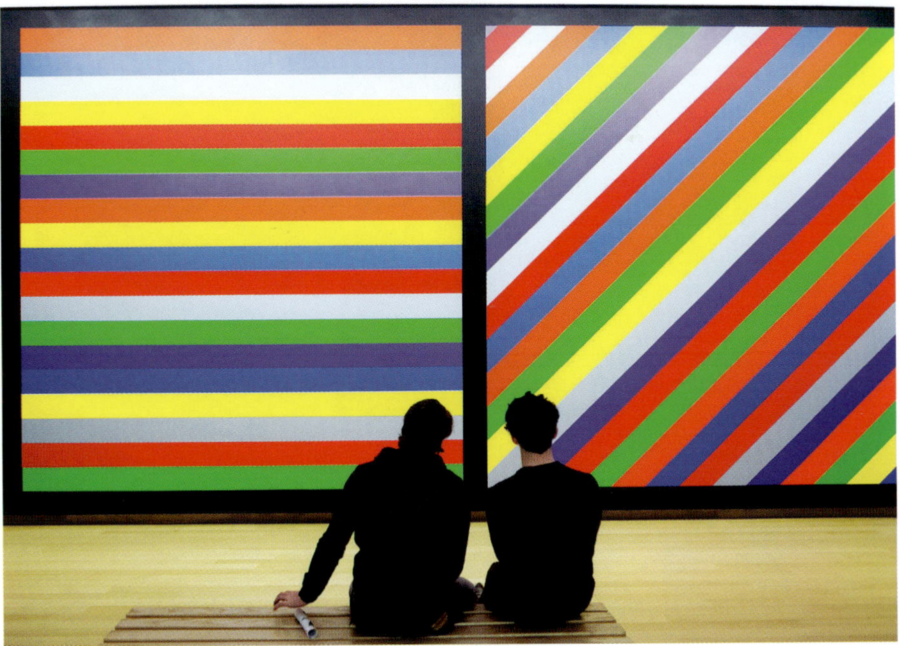

Of work by LeWitt and his circle, Rudi Fuchs, the retired director of the Stedelijk Museum in Amsterdam, said, "For [Europeans], it was liberation . . . this was something new, exciting." (Urbanmyth/Alamy Stock Photo.)

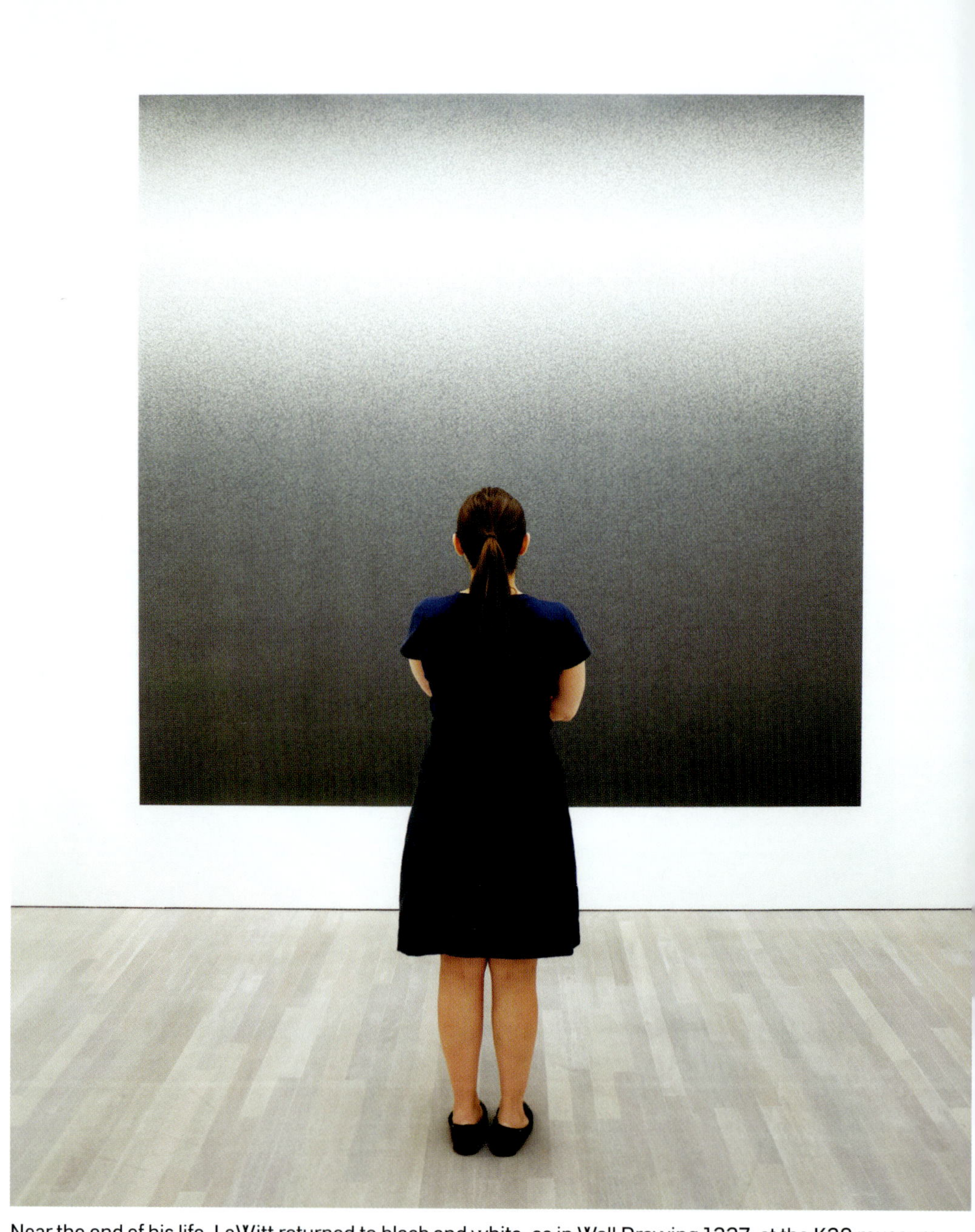

Near the end of his life, LeWitt returned to black and white, as in Wall Drawing 1227, at the K20 museum in Düsseldorf, the city in which his international career blossomed. (Urbanmyth/Alamy Stock Photo)

During LeWitt's time in Germany, Fischer took him to Nebato, an industrial factory in the Netherlands. The factory's chief foreman, Dick van der Net, had done work for Andre. LeWitt asked van der Net to fabricate *Serial Project No. 1*, and he did so quickly and precisely, according to LeWitt. Though the artist had used other people in the United States to do such work previously, he found that he got the best outcomes in the Netherlands and over the next year had most of his work done there.

This significant collaboration that became the underpinning of LeWitt's European presence was made possible by the owners of the factory, Martin and Mia Visser. Mia Visser served as the intermediary between the artist and the fabricator. LeWitt wrote careful instructions for each piece and sometimes worried that they were unclear. "Are you confused? Is it confusing?" he asked. But in an unpublished statement, probably composed in the mid-1970s, LeWitt explained a phenomenon that separated the artist from the finished product. Due to his collaborator's "empathy" and "understanding of the artist's intentions . . . the artist feels secure that his work will be well made even if he is not there to oversee all stages of its manufacture." But he also clarified the burden of the artist in such a case. The artist had to submit an accurate working drawing, and instructions for that drawing, "or take the blame for imperfect work."[9]

By the fall of 1968, though LeWitt's name was becoming more familiar in Europe, making a living in New York was still not easy for him. In 2015, Rudi Fuchs, the retired director of the Stedelijk Museum in Amsterdam, reflected that though Manhattan had a great collection of artists and they were on the verge of creating, in his view, "the best art since the Renaissance," Europeans seemed to embrace them much more quickly than Americans did: "For us, it was liberation. Dutch and European art was the art of memories, but this was something new, exciting."[10] Yet for most Americans the art was too scary, too hard to define, and certainly not chic in the way that works by Warhol and his crowd had been. Dibbets said:

> The war and fascism stopped cultural thinking for probably ten
> years in Europe. . . . Many great artists moved to New York. . . . You
> could see things happening [there]. . . . Americans profited from
> the war, we were vacuumed. After the war, it took a long time for
> Europeans to restore [their countries] . . . but they realized America
> was where it was [happening], but Americans weren't aware what

was happening under their own noses. Every time I went to MoMA there was never [a] painting by Ryman, never a sculpture by Andre, no Flavin, no Sol, no Weiner, no Kosuth. But Europe was full of it [contemporary art]. . . . As Carl Andre said, "The big city is more provincial than the province because the province looks up to the big city and the big city only looks to itself."[11]

LeWitt needed to make ends meet, and he did so in part by taking teaching jobs. He began a four-year stint as an adjunct professor, teaching each fall semester at the School of Visual Arts, and often team teaching.

He later said: "I talked to Carl Andre because we were both traveling a lot of the time, and we figured if one of us wouldn't be there, the other would be there, or both would be there, or none of us would be here. We didn't take attendance: we didn't give grades. We gave everyone the grades they wanted."[12] One of the students LeWitt taught was Laurie Anderson, who became a well-known performance artist and who remembered her time in class as inspirational. She and LeWitt later became close friends.

LeWitt sometimes offered his students a version of his famous line, "It's not too important what art looks like" — for example, telling them, "Don't worry what it looks like. You'll get used to it."[13]

■   Though most of LeWitt's circle at the time was composed of visual artists, there were exceptions.

LeWitt's music collection required a great deal of storage space. During the morning hours, as he worked, he often played music by Bach, Bedřich Smetana, or Béla Bartók at a volume that, because of his declining hearing, had to be turned down when a visitor entered. Some of his collection, however, was of more recent vintage, including the work of composers who had relied on him for encouragement and financial support.

In his early years as a composer, Steve Reich studied LeWitt's structures, and his music reflected certain ideas of LeWitt's — such as repetition, regularity, and variations. "Music," Reich would say, "is an art in time."[14]

Reich first saw LeWitt's work at the *Primary Structures* show at the Jewish Museum in 1966, while he was working on a piece called "It's Gonna Rain," and "I thought, well, we're kindred spirits." And as the years passed, he watched LeWitt's work proliferate as his assistants "followed directions in the same way that musicians follow notations."[15]

In 1970, LeWitt came to Reich's studio and living space, at Broadway and Canal—where because of the noise of trucks hitting potholes, he slept with earplugs. Reich was living hand to mouth. Composers can write all the music they want, but if no one plays or records it, it doesn't exist, at least in terms of valuable commodity. At the time, LeWitt didn't know what Reich was writing, but he wanted to purchase some of Reich's scores. "He bought the manuscript for "Four Organs," done in ink on onion skin paper," Reich recalled, "and they became part of his collection of artwork. He did beautiful things when people were in financial need."[16] Reich's career flourished afterward (for example, he won a Grammy), and he became known as one of the two or three most prominent minimalist composers.

Philip Glass harbors similar memories. He first met LeWitt in 1968, when he was living frugally with his wife and two children in the East Village and augmenting his income from composing (which was, as he recalled it, "not a dime") by doing construction work, driving a taxi, doing plumbing, and building furniture. He remembers: "Sol called me up and said, 'Can I buy a score?' I couldn't believe it. He bought basically all the scores I wrote for three years. He did that kind of thing with many people. Whatever he had [in the way of money or art] he shared with other people."[17] In Glass's 2015 autobiography, *Words without Music*, he writes that Sol "was an extremely generous man," and that his buying scores from struggling composers was "a way, actually, of giving us money."[18] To be sure, Glass also received support along the way from Serra, for whom he also worked. Yet such mutual support in the cutthroat world of "look at me and my work" remained an oddity.

Glass became a preeminent figure in American music, considered by many to be the greatest American composer of the modern era, and his work would be performed and celebrated internationally.

As for LeWitt, he received plenty in return for his investment in Glass, in terms of inspiration. He told Laurie Anderson, "I do my best work at Phil's concerts."[19]

■   By the time his structures were becoming his signature work, LeWitt was also thinking and talking about transferring his ideas of permutation to a different form. He wanted to try his hand at drawing again, but he wasn't interested in the traditional three-dimensional approach. In

1965, Donald Judd argued in "Specific Objects," "The main thing wrong with painting is that it is a rectangular plain placed flat against the wall."[20] LeWitt wanted to break free of that convention. He told Andrea Miller-Keller in 1983 that "it just made more sense to work directly on the wall than on an object to be put on the wall."[21] Well before that, in an interview a year after he did his first wall drawing with Patricia Norvell, then studying for her master's degree, LeWitt had argued that "the paraphernalia of the painter is an anachronism" and the last significant era of painting had ended with the cubists.[22]

Art historians would credit LeWitt with a breakthrough and the invention of a new genre. He would respond by disagreeing that wall drawings were breakthroughs, saying, "I think the cave men came first."[23]

There were several differences, however, between the cave painters and LeWitt besides venue and working attire. For one thing, cave paintings depicted scenes from the lives of people and animals, whereas the wall drawings LeWitt was conceiving at the time were made up only of lines. He would point out that depictions of people are just that—depictions, not meant to be real. But lines are real—they aren't being referred to by an artist, or interpreted by an artist, and they exist as a reality of their own.

Another key difference was that cavemen, by undertaking these drawings, hoped to leave a permanent record that could be interpreted and appreciated for generations to come. Indeed, much of the work has endured for millennia. This idea also drove the fresco painters and muralists whose site-specific work would remain in place as long as that place existed. LeWitt had the opposite notion: nothing is permanent, least of all a wall drawing in the art world. This is a lesson that the pioneer downtown gallery owner Paula Cooper learned when she gave LeWitt his first public wall drawing space.

In the area that would become SoHo, Cooper saw not only a desolate neighborhood but also an opportunity. She opened a gallery at 96 Prince Street, thinking that because the area was filled with artists, there were opportunities for gallery owners there as well—a view that turned out to be prescient but one that required a great deal of entrepreneurial courage to act on.

The art writer and critic Peter Schjeldahl would write a year later, "The Cooper is, if you will, an 'activist' gallery, aiming to reflect and influence the actual production of new art as much as its acceptance by critics and collectors."[24] It was, indeed, activist in many ways.

Cooper's first show, in October 1968, also signaled her intent: to make her gallery relevant and newsworthy. The title of the show was *Benefit for the Student Mobilization Committee to End the War in Vietnam*. With help from the activist David McReynolds, she and Lippard, the show's organizer, invited LeWitt, Judd, Baer, Flavin, Ryman, Andre, and others to participate.

The year had been a violent one in so many ways, beginning with the April assassination of Martin Luther King Jr., followed by that of Robert Kennedy two months later after a campaign speech, the brutality that marked the Democratic national convention in Chicago, and urban riots — with the Vietnam War, the most divisive foreign war in US history and a factor behind so much of the discord and destruction, still raging.

New York City — particularly in neighborhoods with large proportions of young people — became a cauldron. McReynolds had been protesting the war since its early days. In 1965, he was one of five protesters who burned their draft cards in a public display at Union Square. (He was the only one who didn't go to prison because he had just turned thirty-five and was thus beyond draft age.) Through connections with the photographer Karl Bissinger, another antiwar activist, many artists had been recruited at the time to become part of the peace movement.

Cooper's intent was threefold: to support an organization that opposed the war by raising funds for it; to draw crowds to view the work of artists she admired; and by drawing such crowds and some critics, to put her new and decidedly un-posh gallery on the cultural map. She succeeded in all three aims.

For LeWitt, the lure here was not political, except in the sense that he and the thirteen others whose work was displayed were all against the war, and therefore eager to participate in the show. He may have kept politics out of his art, but otherwise it was an obsession. As Bochner would say in his eulogy of LeWitt, "If you argued with him, especially about politics, you'd better know what you're talking about or he'd tear you apart. He was a no bullshit guy."[25]

The invitation to the opening reception read in part: "These 14 nonobjective artists are against the war in Vietnam. They are supporting this commitment in the strongest manner open to them, by contributing major examples of their current work. The artists and individual pieces were selected to represent a particular esthetic attitude, in the conviction that a cohesive group of important works makes the most forceful statement for peace."[26]

To be sure, LeWitt thought American society at the time verged on the dystopian. Earlier in 1968, in an interview in *Venice*, he said:

The American way of life is a myth. Even middle class people do not follow it and only give lip service to it. American life is rapidly breaking down. We have riots, wars, etc. The middle class morality is breaking down—it has not existed for a long time. There is no reason that the artist should feel he is part of something that is so decadent and so completely without any purpose. He cannot think of himself as defending the establishment because the establishment hardly exists any more in any real sense.[27]

That same year, prior to the Vietnam exhibit, LeWitt expanded on this in an interview in *Metro*:

The artist who is concerned with painting and sculpture just does his art and believes what he believes as a person. There are certain art forms like the cinema that are often politically and socially grounded. But when it comes to the sculptor or the painter they are asocial and apolitical. I don't know of any or painting or sculpture that has any kind of real significance in terms of political content, and when it does try to have that, the result is pretty embarrassing. In the future maybe artists will have it, but as it is now, I do not think there is anything that particularly would qualify as great social art or great political art.[28]

Yet LeWitt was connected to many causes. Looking back in a 2003 interview, he said: "The '60s were awash in politics and revolution. Not only in art of course, but feminism, racial equality and opposition to war. I, like almost all of the artists I knew, was involved in all of these movements and was politically left-oriented."[29] On a couple of occasions, he later broke his own rule about not being political in his art. But in 1968, he limited his views to his words, not his art: "Artists live in a society that is not a part of society. . . . The artist wonders what he can do when he sees the world going to pieces around him. But as an artist he can do nothing except be an artist."[30]

Yet the participation of LeWitt and the thirteen other artists in the Cooper Gallery benefit show certainly made its own statement about the need for artists to come to together and to call attention to a foreign policy that robbed the country of its treasury, young men, and reputation.

Lippard later wrote:

The slowly evolving public opposition to the Vietnam War . . . came
to a head, sweeping large numbers of artists into the resistance.
The assassination of Martin Luther King Jr. and events in Southeast
Asia made a newly conscious white constituency aware of the ties
between oppression of Third World people abroad and at home. . . .
Political consciousness and racial or sexual identity met to provide
a ground on which artists could relate. Similarly, many of us began
to understand how the power structures of the art world reflected
those of the world around us.[31]

But if the purpose of the Cooper Gallery show was to raise political
consciousness about the Vietnam War, this wasn't obvious from its content. Lippard, who organized the show for Cooper, said as much in an
interview in the *New York Times*: "It's a kind of protest against the pot-
pourri peace shows with all those burned dolls. It really looks like an
exhibition first, and a benefit second."[32] In short, artists were not making a very big sacrifice for the cause. Still, for Cooper, the show brought
much-needed attention to her new effort.

The daughter of a navy social worker, Cooper had always wanted
to help artists since she was living in Paris at the age of eighteen. She
looked at a lot of art in galleries and museums in Paris. But she also had
to make a living. "I was scared to death," she recalled in a 2012 interview. "I didn't know how to do anything. I couldn't type. I didn't want
to be someone's secretary."[33] She took a job at Chanel, first operating a
switchboard and then serving as receptionist.

However, she wanted to work in a gallery, and after a year at Chanel
(which she thought was "really boring") she found a job at a place that
specialized in primitive and pre-Colombian art. One day a Peruvian
gold mask came to the gallery—a mask that had been featured on the
cover of *Life*—and the excitement about this arrival made Cooper's gallery work, which until then had seemed perfunctory, exciting.

After she moved back to the United States, she took a menial job at
the Japanese Trade Center in New York ("I didn't know how to type but I
faked it") and then learned of a position at World House Gallery: "It was
from the first incredible. I learned so much. They showed Giacometti,
Max Ernst, Brancusi. We would lend works to museums. I worked with
the loans, the clients, and installed shows. I had one black suit. That was
my Saturday outfit."

During these years she was often treated with "a pat on the head" (a reference to the cold fact that art and the selling of art was a man's business), "but I didn't care." After she married—a scale manufacturer many years her senior—she told him of her idea to open her own gallery, but "he said I couldn't work." That marriage didn't last, and Cooper went to work for Park Place, an artists' cooperative gallery, until that folded.

She remarried and had a child "but wanted to do something." That something was to open her own gallery, but "I didn't have any money. I went to the bank and asked for $5,000. They gave me $3,000, and I started looking downtown. I looked from below Fourteenth Street to Canal Street, in the areas where the artists lived." The uptown galleries were little shops. Her idea was different: "I wanted a flexible program where I could sell the artists' work and where they could live. It wasn't very smart" or practical. It had to be a gallery only: "It was a funky space on Prince Street, on the third floor, a place where boxers used to hang out. It was near sweatshops and pocketbook factories. Nobody knew where it was. People told me, 'You're crazy. Nobody's going to come. But I said of course they will. I had 3,000 square feet for $150 a month, raw space, and I didn't have the money to fix it. The floors were splintery and I didn't have an office. But I didn't think about that. I didn't think about failure."

The Vietnam show was her first, and it became a legendary exhibit not only because it caused a political stir but for many other reasons—including the fact that it contained the first of LeWitt's over 1,200 wall drawings, a piece that built on ideas first expressed on Dibbets's living room wall, a gift to a friend that turned out to benefit the donor more than the recipient.

As LeWitt recalled in 1974, he was trying to break away from art's three dimensions: "In order to do something two-dimensional it had to be done directly on the wall. Because painting was always done as a three-dimensional object. There was always a stretcher, canvas, any kind of thing that made it into another dimension. I had thought of it quite sometime before, and I remember talking to Judd about it once and saying, 'Well, you know, what the hell.'"[34]

Cooper remembered: "Sol came, and he picked a freestanding awful wall, you could see my storage was behind it—the worst space, and he came and made a drawing on it. It took him two days."[35] During that time he carried out the tedious task of drawing with black pencil the straightest parallel lines he could, in an arrangement that would pre-figure the ideas in many of his works to come—horizontal, vertical, and diagonal. He never presented himself as the ideal draftsman, but some-one had to do the work if it was going to be done. He expounded on how he went about creating work and how his thought process evolved in the catalogue for a show two years later at the Pasadena Art Museum (now known as the Norton Simon Museum): "The draftsman and the wall enter a dialogue. The draftsman becomes bored but later through this meaningless activity finds peace or misery. The lines on the wall are the residue of this process. Each line is as important as each other line. All of the lines become one thing. The viewer of the lines can see only lines on a wall. They are meaningless. That is art."[36]

Barry, who was also asked to provide work for the Cooper Gallery exhibit, recalled in a 2015 interview seeing LeWitt working on the wall during the installation period: "I was kind of snooping around, trying to figure out what I would put in the show, and I saw him sitting on a stool, with only a pencil and a ruler." What he saw astonished him: "It just kind of hovered there on the wall. It was another kind of light. There was a feeling there which I think Sol would have hated. He would have said to me, 'These are just lines on a wall.' But this was something rare in terms of conveying a feeling, a way of seeing."[37]

The piece consisted of two squares divided into quadrants. Each quadrant was then divided into four squares each, in a way similar to previous black-and-white works by LeWitt. Though the lines were made with colored pencils, the finish was soft, hardly visible from several yards away. Up close, though, the viewer couldn't help seeing its intrica-cies and complexities. But if the viewer wanted to purchase what LeWitt cryptically titled *Drawing Series 11–14 (A+B)*, how could that happen?

The art, if present at all, was the idea, not the graphite on the wall, according to the artist. Cooper said: "Sol showed me a paper—the idea for the drawing—and we must have talked about what would happen if someone bought the piece."[38] After all, this sort of sale was something that gallery owners had no history with. How could anyone possibly buy a drawing that's right on the gallery wall? In a 1969 article for *Studio International*, LeWitt wrote, "Two-dimensional works are not seen as objects. The work is a manifestation of an idea. It is an idea and not an object."[39] How does an artist, then, sell an idea?

The way to do it, apparently, was demonstrated on the artist price list that visitors would see. For example, the sculpture by Andre had an asking price of \$1,500 (the gallery would take half of each price). Flavin's fluorescent light work could be had for \$2,000, Mangold's trapezoid for \$2,500, Ryman's monochrome piece for \$900, and so on. The "price" listed next to LeWitt's name was only "per hour"—as if he had been a house painter or a therapist. In short, the drawing wasn't an object but an image that could be transported anywhere.

When the show opened, it drew a large crowd, but nothing in the way of war protesters. Among the attendees were Herb and Dorothy Vogel, although at first it was only Herb who climbed to the second-floor gallery. A large dog belonging to one of the guests was perched on the stairway, and Dorothy, who was afraid of dogs, refused to come up until the dog was taken out by its owner.

Later that night, Herb Vogel approached Barry about buying some of his work, but Barry brushed him off: "I always avoided him because he was always coming on strong. Because I wasn't big into selling."[40] Financially secure from his teaching position at Hunter College, "I was militant. Nothing's for sale." Barry said he was bitter about the gallery scene.

At the exhibit's opening reception, LeWitt took Barry aside: "Sol told me I should talk to the Vogels, that they're putting together a very important collection, and that Herbie wasn't going to sell anything I sold him. That he's not a big-mouth jerk going around trying to hustle art." Barry also commented: "I listened to Sol, and [I am] so glad I did. He was our advisor. He was an extremely intelligent man, and there was a logic to his thinking, a straightforwardness I really liked. He could also be loose and fun, and critical of the art world."[41] The straightforward, logical pitch about the Vogels yielded good results all around.

The Vogels were able to buy many pieces by Barry—"always on the installment plan," the artist recalled,[42] with \$50 every payday—and many years later when the Smithsonian produced its show of the Vogels' collection, Barry was asked to design the poster for it. The poster became so popular that it sold out before the artist could secure a supply of them.

Ten years later, in the catalogue for MoMA's LeWitt retrospective, Bernice Rose, the museum's curator of drawing, wrote of that first wall drawing:

> LeWitt's transposition of his drawings from the restricted if
> traditional format of a sheet of paper to the architectural space
> of a wall with which it became absolutely identified was a radical

move. It suggests transformation in the role—and the very nature
—of the drawing medium, both within his own work and the history
of the medium. LeWitt's move was a cataclysm as important for
drawing as Pollock's use of the drip technique had been for painting
in the 1950's. Both opposed, through radical transpositions in the
way in which the thing is made, expectations of the way art ought
to look—what it ought to be.[43]

But when the show ended, Cooper was left with an unprecedented
situation. Some of the pieces had been sold, and about $30,000 had
been raised for charity, but the LeWitt work stayed where it was, un-
purchased. Even if it had been bought, what about the image that remained? She called LeWitt and asked him what to do. He told her just
to paint over it. "I can't do that," she said,[44] responding not only out
of respect for tradition but also out of the deep affection she had for
artists and their work and believing that gallery owners and curators
are charged with the care of art, not the destruction of it. In the end,
she asked someone else to do as LeWitt had told her. So *Wall Drawing 1* disappeared a few weeks after it was created. At least so it seemed
to everyone except the artist himself, although Dwan would eventually
write: "For me LeWitt's wall drawings recall Tibetan sand mandalas in-
sofar as they involve circumscribed, procedural, repeatable defined elements that, when erased, return to the invisible real of the conceptual.
The Tibetans, after long days of finally detailed, minute development,
brush up all their many colors into a brown-red-blue-yellow sparkling
heap of sand and throw it into the nearest body of water, but that exact
concept remains to be repeated later."[45] However, Tibetan sand mandalas had no resale value, unlike LeWitt's wall drawings as they began
to proliferate.

LeWitt did a second drawing a few months later at the Ace Gallery in
Los Angeles, and over the next year or two he refined his technique of
drawing on walls, beginning to rely on others to do the "perfunctory"
part—that is, the part of the project that comes after the idea is hatched
and then sketched out with instructions.

Rose wrote: "The size of the drawings was determined by the size
of the wall and its physical location. The $\frac{1}{16}$ inch interval between the
lines was determined by binding the group of leads together so that the
lines would be clearly distinguished from one another while an interval was maintained in which neither space nor line dominated. It was

important that, while the drawing did not disrupt the 'integrity' of the wall surface, it be clearly seen as linear."[46]

Though LeWitt left straightforward instructions for his assistants, he didn't often record the experience that ensued. He did, however, provide an account of an early drawing—the first for which he used assistants—created in May 1969 at the Cooper Gallery, which reveals the process and his thinking. It is also the first example of what became a LeWitt signature—lines in four directions. The title and the instructions, as would become customary, were the same: *Four part serial drawing. A wall divided horizontally and vertically into four equal parts, with three of the four different kinds of line direction superimposed in each part.*

The instructions indicate both the specific form of the drawing and the need for problem solving on the part of the individual draftsman as the work proceeds, as well as the way such work necessarily swerves from perfection, with its permanence as an idea and temporality as an object:

This wall drawing was executed by Adrian Piper, Jerry Oster and Sol LeWitt on the south wall of the smaller room of the Paula Cooper Gallery, 96 Prince St. It is part of an exhibition for the benefit of the Art Workers Coalition and was compiled by Lucy Lippard. This drawing is 16'8" × 6', composed of four sections, each 8'4" × 3'; and was drawn with 9H graphite sticks. The drawing is the width of the wall. The height of each section (3') indicated by the maximum length . . . a line can be easily drawn using a 45 degree angle as a guide. Each of the four sections has three crossing lines superimposed on one another (vertical, horizontal, diagonal right to left 45 degrees representing the basic corrections that lines can be drawn. These lines are drawn as lightly and as close together as possible ($\frac{1}{16}$"), The tonality of the drawing should be equal since there are an equal number of lines in each segment. However, the properties of the wall, in some cases, dictate the darkness of the line (i.e., if there is a trace of grease or foreign substance or if the wall budges out), [and] the pressure exerted by the draftsman is not always equal. Nor is the distance between lines always the same accounting for darker areas. These variations are acceptable . . . they are inherent in the method. The wall drawing is perceived first as a light tonal mass, light enough to preserve the integrity of the wall plane—and then as a collection of lines. Neither the wall drawing, this drawing in ink or the photographic record of the wall drawing, are definitive but all are of equal importance. This wall drawing is temporary and will be removed at the discretion of the Paula Cooper Gallery. Sol LeWitt, May 20, 1969.[47]

In 1970, he presented a fairly lengthy statement in *Arts* on how he thought about wall drawings. He wrote about the need for the drawings to be as two-dimensional as possible—that is, to be organically part of the wall, not something placed on the wall—and commented that "different kinds of walls make for different kinds of drawings. The world had too many objects, so why not eliminate the need for an intermediary support, such as paper or canvas, and work directly on the wall? The physical properties of the wall: height, length, color, material and architectural conditions and intrusions, are a necessary part of the wall drawings."[48]

He pointed out that walls are different from canvases in other ways —"most walls have holes, cracks, bumps, grease marks, are not level or square, and have various architectural eccentricities, and the handicap in using walls is that the artist is at the mercy of the architect."[49] Even so, he chose to use walls, and more than 1,200 wall drawings testify to the marriage of wall and art.

The idea of a seamless (if physically rough) connection between image and wall was influenced, LeWitt later said, by a seminal exhibit in the late 1960s in Rome. Jannis Kounellis produced an exhibit directed by Fabio Sargentini at the L'Attico Gallery that included the presence of a dozen live horses. The animals were not controlled and were therefore occasionally threatening to viewers, turning a usually staid art gallery into something else entirely, altering its meaning as a place to experience art, and blurring the distinction between the art and the place for which it was created. LeWitt had seen the show, and it affected the way he would think from then on about space and exhibits.

The influence of the Italians convinced LeWitt that using the whole space as part of the art was a natural step both forward and backward. In his final interview before his death, he looked back on this step:

> The idea of using the total space of the gallery or whatever
> architecture, was something that the Italians were involved
> in. None of the Americans [were doing it. For them] it was all
> object based. . . . Yes, the whole space, and it was so obvious, you
> know, one step after the other, that's what I mean by an organic
> development. Even before we moved [to Italy], I used to go there

every year and see all the frescoes and there was a movement in New York to get away from easel-painting. So before easel-painting there were the frescoes. Easel-painting came in in the late 1400s, you know, from Belgium, when they started to use canvas.[50]

The fresco, or mural, idea had reappeared with Diego Rivera and other Mexican artists, and the murals commissioned by the federal Works Progress Administration during the Great Depression. LeWitt's practice of using the whole space rather than a small area, as in his first Cooper drawing, evolved over time.

At Fischer's gallery in Düsseldorf LeWitt's work changed in two ways. For *Wall Drawing 3*, completed in 1969, he created a title that was also the instructions for its installation: *A 40" (100 cm) band of vertical and both sets of diagonal lines superimposed, centered top to bottom, running the length of the wall.*

Wall Drawing 4: A square divided horizontally and vertically in four equal parts, each with a different direction of lines was the first to be composed in direct relationship to the size of the wall that it would cover. Unlike what came before it—drawings largely based on traditional painterly dimensions that would reflect the size of a canvas, the surface now extended beyond that familiar field. In short, LeWitt's thinking had leaped over traditional boundaries.

The idea of having assistants grew out of tradition and necessity. LeWitt recounted in a 1999 interview: "Once you start working on a wall you start thinking in terms of the whole wall, the whole room, the whole building. You can't do all of this yourself, but it is a very traditional idea in art that artists have assistants and craftsman who are very good, sometimes even better than the artist."[51]

He made a distinction between the assistants who could draw lines and those who could bring something deeper to the projects:

When I started to do the wall drawings, I had the idea that if you can pass on the instructions from one person to another that they can draw a line or a group of lines or different kinds of lines, arcs, etc., and it is still true. But although anyone can do the kinds of lines that are very precise, only a very few people can do them very well. Perhaps your ten-year-old child can play a Mozart piano sonata, but you wouldn't pay money to hear it played. If a great pianist were playing it, then you would. There are very sublime ways of making these wall drawings that even I would never have imagined when I first started. I have assistants who are so good at it that I am completely amazed and in awe of the result.[52]

The final comment in his 1970 *Arts* piece introduced some readers, however, to the way that LeWitt's mind could sometimes be playful and contradictory, and the mystical nature of the wall drawing: "The wall drawing is a permanent installation, until destroyed. Once something is done, it cannot be undone."[53]

A point to consider in all of this is LeWitt's 1967 reference in "Paragraphs on Conceptual Art" to the "perfunctory affair," in that all of the serious work on the piece is done before a brush or pencil or piece of wood is ever handled.

This presumes, of course, that the "perfunctory" part is carried out by someone who can make it perfunctory. But that word took on a different meaning as time went on, and as LeWitt's work became more complex and required the work of many people. For example, *Wall Drawing 57*, installed at the Pasadena Art Museum, required a crew of fifty-nine artists. There is nothing that can be perfunctory when that many people (artists, to boot) have a hand in something. Videos of LeWitt installations, some of them set to lively music, show the complexity of the process.[54]

In the case of a symphony, of course a great number of people are involved. So it's easy to understand that a work by Mozart was not complete when it was composed. It had to be played before it existed as a commodity. Is the playing of Mozart perfunctory? If it were, then there would need to be only one recording of each piece. As we know, different interpretations of Mozart's work have produced a variety of approaches, emphases, and tempos depending on who performs it.

More to the point, it is helpful to consider a description by the artist Chris Cobb, written in 2008 while Cobb was working on the wall drawing retrospective at the Massachusetts Museum of Contemporary Art about recreating *Wall Drawing 343*, the instructions for which reads, simply: "On a black wall, nine geometric figures (including right triangle, cross, X) in squares. The backgrounds are filled in solid white."

In his essay wryly titled "A Perfunctory Affair," Cobb writes:

I am in the middle of a fifty-seven (and three-quarters-of-an-inch) wall, which itself is situated in the middle of a maze of walls on the second floor of Building 7. I am working alongside my apprentice Julia. . . . By "working on," I mean that I am attempting to recreate from a brief page of written instructions, a work of conceptual art. The instructions, written by LeWitt in 1980 and first drawn by Jo Watanabe at Larry Gagosian's gallery in Venice that same year, read like a Zen koan or a secret code comprising equal part precision and mystery. Yet we are only the most recent people to follow these instructions — over the past twenty years or so, #343 and variations of it have been installed at galleries from Rome to Los Angeles. Some variants have the drawing as being black on white, or colored shapes on a white background. . . . At the moment, we're using watercolor soluble crayon pastels that have the consistency of frozen butter; if held in the hand long enough, they will indeed begin to melt. We are supposed to scribble in random directions until our hands hurt and the layers of lines look almost opaque. If our hands don't hurt, according to one of LeWitt's most senior assistants, we're not doing a good job.[55]

Clearly, "perfunctory" doesn't cover the task, as LeWitt would acknowledge whenever he talked about the surprising differences between what was intended and what actually emerged. Playwrights like Beckett or even Neil Simon may well imagine, in their crafting of a play, what a character will sound like or how an actor will interpret that character, but they are often surprised (and sometimes delighted) by the unexpected dimensions actors can bring to a performance.

LeWitt used helpers in 1969 for *Wall Drawing 12, Black Pencil*, at a seminal show in Bern, Switzerland, that for the first time brought together artists (including Hesse, Ryman, Flavin, Weiner, Barry, and many others in the LeWitt circle) whose work was part of art's new revolution. "This was the show that changed everything," according to Dibbets. "It was the place where all the broader ideas of change put everything together."[56] Curated by Harald Szeemann and titled *Live in Your Head: When Attitudes Become Form*, the show included works by artists with no picture frames and no reference to traditional form. Though it ran for only a few weeks and was held in what was hardly an arts capital, it became iconic. Nearly half a century later, it was reprised in Venice. For that occasion the *New York Times* published an article on the original show:

Puzzlement was understandable. The work, by almost 70 artists, jammed into two floors and a nearby annex, wasn't quite sculpture and certainly wasn't painting. Its mediums included ice, fire, broken glass, lead, leather, felt, fluorescent tubing, peas, charcoal and margarine. Ropes snaked through rooms; electric wires wound down a staircase. Nothing was framed or on pedestals or behind stanchions, and visitors trampled on work, though it was hard to tell where the art ended and the damage began.[57]

The conservative Swiss public did not react well to the show. There was mockery in cartoons, and manure was dumped at the entrance to the Kunsthalle. Despite positive reviews, the museum cancelled Szeemann's planned Joseph Beuys show. He resigned as director.

But writing forty years after the original show opened, the British curator Barry Barker considered the context of the time, and the lasting impact:

> This was a time when many artists, writers and gallery directors, whether working within an institutional or private context, found themselves in a world in which their vocation and even their aspirations no longer fit happily within a traditional definition of art or culture. There appeared to be a chasm between language, ideas and the world. Protests against the Vietnam War were at their height both in America and Europe. Lacking a fixed cultural order in equilibrium with the past, artists found themselves in a place of disenchantment. In a positive sense, however, it was also a time of discussion, idea exchange and information. The world was becoming a smaller place; every artist and thinker felt that there were many ideas and places to explore, yet they in turn had something to contribute to the cultural life of a global environment. It was in this spirit that Szeemann researched and brought to light artistic developments of a younger generation.[58]

When considering the rise of LeWitt internationally, and his refusal to submit to the customary rites of celebrity, this 1969 show reveals much. That is, the show and its notoriety attracted attention to his work and that of other artists who refused to pay celebrity games. LeWitt played the insider's game and played it well, as demonstrated by the preparation for his first solo museum show, at the Gemeentemuseum in The Hague in 1970.

LeWitt visited the museum briefly on the way to Germany, where another exhibit of his work was about to open. He inspected the space available—the walls and the floors—and then spent most of his time consulting on the nature of the catalogue, for it was the catalogue that reflected his view that books were the best vehicle for showing art. But there was a difference between what his catalogue would show and what other artists would include in their own. LeWitt asked the museum to include comments on and interpretations of his work by as many other people as possible—artists, critics, gallery owners, and so on. This would include material considered unfavorable. He told Enno Develing, a curator at the museum: "I know a lot of people dislike my work and they should have some say in the catalogue. If there are any other unfavorable reviews you know about and want to use it's OK with me."[59]

In the annals of art and ego, this was an astounding pronouncement. But LeWitt knew what he was doing—calling attention to the work, not the person who creates it. In fact, in his instructions for the catalogue in one of the many letters he wrote to people at the museum, he makes this clear: "I think you should write to the people for my catalogue and ask them to write something on my work (not my personality)."[60]

LeWitt took a strong hand in the design of the catalogue. He wanted nine photographs on each page—reflecting his longtime emphasis on grids and what would a decade later be reflected in his *Autobiography*, and "in this way many photos could be shown, and one would not appear to be superior because of a large size. Therefore, there would be space for more pages of writing." All of the photographs should be "about the same size." And he gave this contradictory instruction: "The large pieces should be as small as possible." He also wrote that the catalogue should have as much documentation and information as possible, and he commented that "I am interested in making the catalogue important (but not expensive)."[61] He wanted to publicize his drawings in an authoritative but not elite manner, involving as many people as possible—who in turn would help get out the word about the work being shown. This effort signaled his larger effort to sidestep the normal practices of getting work known—celebrity profiles—by working from the inside out and recognizing other artists and gallery or museum staff members along the way. It became LeWitt's practice to know the names of everyone involved in his projects and to leave gifts for each in addition to paychecks. His was a grass-roots campaign that in time covered a lot of territory.

■ All of LeWitt's preliminary instructions for the show at the Gemeentemuseum were carried out. Then, on June 2, 1970, LeWitt, having received the devastating news of Hesse's death, wrote again to Develing. LeWitt was doing a wall drawing in Hesse's memory in the Galerie Yvon Lambert, and he said he would like it to be on the first right-hand page after the dedication page in the catalogue. He noted that "the drawing is in black lead and free hand (no straight lines) vertical lines, very many."[62]

There were some works that could not be painted over, and some things that lingered as the years passed. Though LeWitt and Hesse had not been as close as they once were, they had kept in touch. He had taken her, in a wheelchair, to her openings. He had taken her to dinner for her thirty-fourth birthday. And they knew of each other's struggles, particularly Hesse's cruel burden — the certainty that she would die before reaching the age of thirty-five. Her death, from brain cancer, occurred on May 29, 1970.

LeWitt wrote home:

> Dear Mother,
> Eva Hesse died a couple of days ago. It is something that was expected. I received a telegraph from her sister when we arrived from Düsseldorf on Saturday. It makes me very sad because she was a good friend for many years and in many ways we were very close, probably like sister and brother. She was also a great artist and at the height of her creativity.[63]

At Hesse's memorial service, her sister, Helen Hecht Charash, said: "My feeling today is, with all her ambivalence and all her problems, the positive force was always the art. Sol, as an artist, understood this, and understood how great she was, and that she just needed to push through."[64]

In one of her last gestures toward LeWitt, Hesse wrote him a poem:

> Sol LeWitt,
>
> I have seen your work.
> I have seen your work change.
> I have seen your work grow.
> I have seen your work.
>
> Now it's there, where you put it.
> Now it extends itself unto us.
> Now we have grown to see it.[65]

LeWitt wrote in his notebook:

This morning would be a splendid morning if yesterday's morning
had not been an utter fiasco.

The past is galloping away. The trench widens.

Tomorrow is further off than it was yesterday because yesterday's
horse has run wild and men with leaden shoes cannot catch up with
him.

Between the good of the morning and morning itself, there is
a line of pus which blows a stench over yesterday and poisons
tomorrow.

This is a morning so confused that if it were only an old umbrella
the slightest sneeze would blow it inside out.[66]

In 1977, his entry about Hesse's death was more prosaic:

Some of the problems of women in our art system were made clear
to me by my friendship with Eva Hesse. This young woman's work
was unquestionably of great importance. She was, if not totally
ignorant, relegated to a [unintelligible] position by critics, journals,
etc. Fortunately many of her friends and admirers voiced objections
to this treatment. However it wasn't until she died (or only weeks
before) that the critics or journals tried to rectify this error. Now she
is well known for her work and an inspiration to other women who
would not have had the courage to defy the male-dominated art
system. Many if not most of the better artists now are women. But
the system is still the same and it is still difficult for a woman to have
her work conceded to be superior to that of her male counterparts.
It is only when a woman achieves this superiority that she is denied
that recognition.[67]

When Develing's catalogue for The Hague show was published, it
contained an artist's statement by LeWitt that reveals his frustration,
sense of loss, and rage at the time. It ranges from race relations to the
Vietnam War and no doubt is a statement about Hesse's place in a male-
dominated world. It makes bold assertions about the nature of art and
its ownership, rejecting the forces of elitism. And it presages the causes
he would fight for in the years to come. It represents the first time he
made an overtly political statement about his work:

As an American, I protest the immoral, unjust and illegal use of
American power to make war on people who are no threat to the

United States, to kill these people indiscriminately, destroy their
homes and crops, and deny them the right to determine their
own political and social order. The use of American political and
economical power throughout the world to further this aggressive,
inhuman and racist policy; the suppression of dissent, and the
harassment, imprisonment, exile and murder of dissenters; the
use of police and military power to deny the rights of the black
racial minority in the U.S., and the systematic murder of its leaders;
the intimidation and control of the press and news media by the
government and the growing division in the country fostered by
those in power which if continued will end in a police state or in
civil warfare.

As an artist I believe that art cannot be owned by individuals or
institutions, but is held in trust by them for all people. The art of the
past is the heritage of all and no one should be denied free access
to it. If there are decisions to be made concerning the purchase or
exhibition of contemporary art by public or private institutions, the
artists of the community should have a voice in these decisions.
A public museum has the obligation to encourage, support and
exhibit the work of artists in its own community. It should be a
matter of pride for them to do this. The artist should be regarded as
a valuable member of society, through whose talents the values of
the community are tested, preserved or destroyed. . . .

I would like to dedicate this exhibit to my friend and fellow artist
Eva Hesse, who just died.[68]

TEN

SEPARATIONS

FROM HESTER STREET TO THE WORLD

Highlights from Sol LeWitt's International Emergence, 1969–1971

1969
Galerie Konrad Fischer, Düsseldorf, Germany
Galleria L'Attico, Rome, Italy
Galerie Ernst, Hanover, Germany
Dwan Gallery, New York, New York
Museum Haus Lange, Krefeld, Germany
Galerie Bischofberger, Zürich, Switzerland

1970
Art & Project, Amsterdam, Netherlands
Wisconsin State University, River Falls, Wisconsin
Galerie Yvon Lambert, Paris, France
Galleria Sperone, Turin, Italy
Dwan Gallery, New York, New York
Lisson Gallery, London, England
Gemeentemuseum, The Hague, Netherlands
Galerie Heiner Friederich, Münich, Germany
Pasadena Art Museum, Pasadena, California

1971
Protetch-Rivkin Gallery, Washington, D.C.
Dwan Gallery, New York, New York
Lisson Gallery, London, England
Galerie Stampa, Basel, Switzerland
Galleria Toselli, Milan, Italy
Informations-Raum 3, Basel, Switzerland
Galerie Konrad Fischer, Düsseldorf, Germany
Art & Project, Amsterdam, Netherlands

John Weber Gallery, New York, New York
Dunkelmann Gallery, Toronto, Canada
Galerie Ernst, Hanover, Germany[1]

By the summer of 1970, LeWitt's financial status had changed considerably for the better in a couple of ways. First, he had had an unexpected windfall. LeWitt was one of twenty US artists who had each been given a $7,500 grant from the National Council on the Arts, the forerunner of the National Endowment for the Arts.

And after about fifteen years in New York, much of it spent on the outside looking in, LeWitt found that he was suddenly in demand in foreign countries, where there was a growing interest in his work among collectors. He traveled nearly everywhere his drawings were installed. Indeed, many artists in his circle demanded that as part of the deal for exhibitions, the institution pick up the airline fare. As Lawrence Weiner put it, "We all said, 'No tickee no showee.'"[2]

LeWitt's heavy travel schedule was bound to affect any new romantic relationship, and it certainly did after his time with Mary Peacock ended and, in 1969, he took up with another staffer at *Harper's Bazaar*: twenty-two-year-old Mimi Wheeler, who had just joined the literary department.

The match of the artist and the staffer seemed odd in some ways. For one thing, there was an eighteen-year age difference. Though both were natives of Connecticut, their geographic similarity ended there. In terms of class structure, LeWitt's New Britain is worlds away from Wheeler's Easton, in the heart of Fairfield County—one of the richest areas in the nation. The Wheeler family property (her father was a high-profile Bridgeport lawyer) covered a hundred acres, with plenty of space for the family's horses to graze and run. In addition, LeWitt's and Wheeler's educations were hardly similar—Wheeler had gone from an elite boarding school to a variety of campuses (one in Switzerland). But their personalities and interests were in sync.

Both loved great writing and history. Though untrained in art, Wheeler developed a deep interest in it and had a keen eye for new talent. Decades later this gift would be described by her friend Alice Weiner: "Mimi can go into a little shitty gallery and find an artist who has star quality."[3] But she also brought some inherent problems to her relationship with LeWitt.

Growing up, she had felt invisible in her "Anglo childhood,"[4] and she and her sister Joan (she had two older siblings out of the house by then) were not very close to their parents. For example, they were required to eat dinner before their parents did and rarely spent time with them. Their supervision was largely left to two household employees, a husband and wife team.

Recalling the LeWitt-Wheeler courtship, Alice Weiner thought that the qualities and intense nature of the romance and the age difference was "something out of a [Vladimir] Nabokov novel."[5] But Wheeler became the first of LeWitt's lovers to immerse herself in his work and become his muse. By 1969, only a few months after they met, the two were living together on Hester Street.

Wheeler recalled that LeWitt used the front of the apartment as a studio.[6] The bed was in the back, and then he moved it to the front. In 2013, she still could picture many other elements of their living quarters, some of which didn't make it into LeWitt's *Autobiography*: a garbage can from her parents' house in Easton, Sophie LeWitt's embroidery, a beautiful Persian carpet purchased from a cowboy selling rugs, an Eva Hesse table, couches LeWitt made with cubes on the bottom, a Jackie Windsor sculpture, a Brionvega radio, and drawings by Ethan Ryman (son of Lucy Lippard and Robert Ryman). It was a sparse space, but there were things of interest in it. There were Mies van der Rohe chairs, palm trees, an art deco lamp, and tons of bookcases. She also remembered LeWitt's routine:

> Sol got up every morning at 5:00 to get the [*New York*] *Times*, and then start to work.
>
> During the day he listened to radio station WINZ—their slogan: "Give us ten minutes and we'll give you the world." Otherwise, he listened to WBIA, which carried alternative programming, including discussions on contemporary issues. He'd have eggs for lunch, but by then his workday was over. In the early days, he did no exercise, but he had a health scare. He really wasn't fit. He smoked little cigars in a blue tin. After [the artist Alighiero] Boetti had a health scare, Sol started swimming laps at the Y[MCA][7].

Boetti and LeWitt had met in 1969, when both had works on display at the Kunsthalle exhibit, and became friends.

LeWitt and Wheeler's social life wasn't glamorous but was related to the art happenings of the time. Wheeler recalled:

People were out on Fridays looking at Fifty-Seventh Street galleries and those downtown. We saw Lucy [Lippard] or Eva [Hesse] often, but we didn't host many dinners. In those days I wasn't really a cook.

We'd go often to Max's Kansas City. Sol knew Mickey well. We sat a table with Dan Flavin and Sonia [Severdija, Flavin's wife]. We had early dinner, near the front. . . . [Andy] Warhol was there. [Robert] Rauschenberg. Joseph Kosuth. Lawrence Weiner. . . . One day Mickey Ruskin was at the front door, and a blonde woman wanted to come in but he told her it was too crowded. The blonde woman, the artists later told him, was Catherine Deneuve.[8]

However, there were weeks and even months during which there was no chance to go to Max's or any other favorite hangout. LeWitt's spreading reputation as a hot artist meant that he was traveling to disparate locations around the globe.

In 1969 alone he had work exhibited, with the help of a growing number of assistants, not only in New York but also in Düsseldorf, Zurich, Rome, Vancouver, Amsterdam, London, Seattle, Munich, Antwerp, and more than a dozen other locations. This meant that there were long periods when he and Wheeler were apart, which caused frustrations —though on many occasions the two traveled together. (Wheeler was fluent in Italian, which helped LeWitt a great deal on his trips to Bari and Spoleto.)

More than that, as time passed, there were two phenomena that competed for LeWitt's attention: not only was his career taking off internationally, but at the very time he was beginning to receive global recognition and the financial stability that resulted, he was obsessed with and worried about Mimi. Unable to sleep, she had taken Quaaludes, medication that LeWitt had secured from a physician friend. Quaaludes were considered safe and were regularly prescribed for insomnia. But it turned out that they were not safe for Wheeler, who "was on the floor" after taking them, and the effects lasted and proliferated for months: "I was hopelessly psychotic." She couldn't navigate daily life, remembering that "I lost touch with myself."[9] LeWitt drove her to New Britain to seek his mother's counsel. Sophie LeWitt was sympathetic—she liked Wheeler—but said that the issues were so profound that Wheeler's family needed to handle them. Though always courteous to Wheeler,

Sophie still hoped that her son would become involved with someone of the Jewish faith. Her choice was Susan Ginsburg, a New York friend of her son who eventually earned a PhD in art history and who qualified as a marital choice, Ginsburg remembered, "simply on the basis that I was Jewish."[10] But her relationship with LeWitt never became romantic.

The effort to find a solution for Wheeler landed her in High Point, a private psychiatric hospital in Port Chester, New York. The many letters and postcards sent over a period of a few years by LeWitt to Wheeler serve as a record of the two competing forces on LeWitt. They also provide insights into his balancing of an increasingly complex schedule of far-flung commitments and are a record of how he viewed some of them. In particular, they highlight the importance of Konrad Fischer and his Düsseldorf gallery during this period. Fischer was a rare gallery owner whose taste in art defied the provincialism of postwar Germany. He was a significant champion of the works of the LeWitt circle, exhibiting pieces by Carl Andre, Hanne Darboven, Richard Long, Bruce Nauman, and others.

The LeWitt-Wheeler correspondence also discusses relationships among the emerging artists. Lawrence Weiner, for example, refers in interviews to disagreements with LeWitt and their occasionally uncomfortable relationship. Decades later, Weiner's view of this was expressed clearly in the documentary film *Sol LeWitt*: "Sol was not a friendly human being."[11] In his letters, LeWitt also commented on his often unharmonious friendship with Andre, who decades later would recall that after walking through a revolving door in Kyoto his old friend greeted him with a kick in the shins. However, Andre admits to his own dramatically bad behavior.[12] LeWitt also occasionally complained about Seth Siegelaub, the writer, gallery owner, promoter, and producer, but in other correspondence he praised Siegelaub for his work on behalf of many fellow artists and the work he did on *Xerox*, one of the most innovative and revered books for artists ever published. *Xerox* was an exhibition in the form of a book, containing the work of seven artists that, in contrast to tradition, was not to be seen in a gallery. LeWitt's work was included, occupying twenty-five pages of the book, and similar amounts of space were devoted to Andre, Robert Barry, Joseph Kosuth, Douglas Heubler, Robert Morris, and Weiner. Moreover, it got LeWitt thinking about books as a primary way to deliver great art to readers, which in turn led him to start Printed Matter, a company devoted to this effort, in 1976.

LeWitt's letters and postcards to Wheeler testify to the way he spent his time and to the inspiration he found, for example, in great books. In addition to what he mentioned in the correspondence that follows, he also read volumes on the Holocaust, most prominently William Manchester's *The Arms of Krupp*, which describes how a huge family-owned manufacturing business produced much of Hitler's war materiel. Several decades later LeWitt's work would address this dark period in history.

In early April 1969, at the Konrad Fischer Gallery, he made his first surviving comment on the work of his assistants: "My helpers are quite good, so I won't have to do very much."[13] Later that month, he wrote Wheeler from Rome, where he was preparing for his first Italian show, at Fabio Sargentini's L'Attico Gallery. By October he was back in Düsseldorf, where he saw Jan Dibbets, Siegelaub, and Weiner.

In the spring of 1970, LeWitt and Andre were invited to be part of the Tenth Biennale, *Between Man and Matter*, at the Tokyo Metropolitan Art Museum. LeWitt wrote several letters to Wheeler during the period when his work was being installed. These letters reflect his championing of female artists, his renewed fascination with Japanese culture and art, and the way he had to improvise when certain materials were unavailable.

During some of this time, Wheeler was in London, waiting to meet LeWitt and for his show to open at the Lisson Gallery. At other times, she was in New York, taking courses at the New School in Russian literature and basic design. One letter refers to camel riding. Wheeler and Ginsburg also traveled to various Middle East destinations.

LeWitt wrote from Kyoto that "the most impressive place (and it is one of the most impressive places I've ever seen)" is the RYOGEN-IN Temple — a series of temples with "fantastic rock gardens, shrines, temples, all in a single compound. Each place there is more beautiful than the next." He also said he was having difficulty getting along with Andre: "We clash in terms of personality and get on one another's nerves." And he noted that he was having trouble working on one wall at the exhibit because it was perforated: "So I am having them roll small pieces of paper and put them into the holes. White on the first wall, white and yellow on the 2nd, white, yellow, red on the 3rd, and white, yellow, red, and blue on the 4th. All the holes are used and the colors are placed randomly. Today I shall have to buy the paper." He then sent a postcard to Wheeler in which he applied his penchant for pattern and twists in personal correspondence, writing "I love you" thirty-seven times but signing the card, "Your friend, Sol."[14]

The following year the letters became darker, as Wheeler's mental health began to deteriorate and as she learned that "my body produced too much dopamine."[15] Wheeler was back at High Point, where — at the age of twenty-four — she was one of the oldest patients: "So many kids were having acid flashbacks." Many letters and postcards from that time indicate the difficulties that LeWitt had in arranging to see Wheeler. There were strict visitation rules, and it took many weeks before LeWitt was granted permission to come to the hospital.

In June 1972, Wheeler released herself from the hospital, though it was against the wishes of her doctor. "I couldn't stand it anymore," she recalled.[16] She went to her parents' house in Easton, but it turned out that this was not helpful:

> I was sleeping all day, reading all night. I took a real dive. I called a girl I'd been at High Point with, and then decided to do something drastic. I went to a doctor's office, took a prescription pad, and wrote a prescription for myself for thirty barbiturates. I didn't say I wanted to die, but it just welled up inside me. It took over inside. I took the pills in Easton. Waverly [one of her parents' employees] tried to wake me up the next day. He took me to the hospital and told them, "You'd better help her. She's Mr. Wheeler's daughter."[17]

When she recovered from the effects of her suicide attempt, Wheeler decided to go to Colorado, where her sister was living. "I had a great feeling of shame," she recalled. "I couldn't stay. This is how shame manifested. This guy [LeWitt] I absolutely adored. But I was uncomfortable. I couldn't figure it out. No reflection on Sol. His attitude was, 'It's all right, Mimi.'"[18]

She took a job near Denver in a stable, taking care of two horses, and also worked at an art gallery. She did not inform LeWitt of her decision to move west. At the beginning of the summer LeWitt, though still thinking of Wheeler, discovered other romantic opportunities though, not surprisingly, there is no mention of this in his letters to her. One other aspect of the letters begs for some interpretation. LeWitt wrote that if Wheeler had doubts about their relationship, she was free to find what she needed elsewhere. This would certainly seem, on its face, to be a generous point of view, and no doubt it fit with LeWitt's character. However, Wheeler didn't know at the time that he may have expressed this view in part for his own convenience, as he had apparently moved on romantically.

Nevertheless, Wheeler would remain a part of LeWitt's professional life for many years, and his presence and spirit would always linger with Wheeler. In 2015 she wrote:

> It is finally so obvious to me; it has to be said. There is much I buried and never processed around Sol for many reasons. I never felt so rightly or deeply connected to anyone again for such a long time or enjoyed the emotional life love provided or even felt at home at Beach Street for many, many years either. It wasn't all conscious. Part of it was burying the pain and along with it the pleasures and memories. Also, I was often struck dumb [by the fact that] such a guy loved me so well. It was not a desire for things to have been different or a longing to be with him — there was the truth of the necessity of a more developed self.[19]

■ Petra de Jong, LeWitt's new romantic interest, was in her early twenties in 1970, and something of a rebel. She had grown up in Holland as one of six children and had pursued an interest in art, against her parents' wishes. The conflict became so heated that she was expelled from the house and, without financial help from her parents, had to rely on scholarships at art school.

Enno Develing, the curator at the Gemeentamuseum in The Hague, asked de Jong to head the crew that was to install LeWitt's wall drawing as part of the artist's first solo museum show. She and her colleagues worked for three weeks to complete the drawing. During that time and afterward, she and LeWitt spoke, but there was no romantic involvement — though evidence shows LeWitt was clearly taken by the tall, blonde de Jong. Two years later, LeWitt asked Develing for her address, and he wrote her that he wanted to see her during his next trip to Holland.

De Jong recalled that the combination of Hesse's death and Wheeler's illness had driven LeWitt to a point of near despair: "He felt lost. He said he wanted to be away from the world, from people, from everything. Could I suggest a place where he could be together with me alone?"[20] She thought of Schiermonnikoog, a remote Dutch island that had only one hotel and only a few hundred permanent residents.

There, the two walked for many miles, and over dinners LeWitt talked of his distress. He talked about Hesse's enormous talent and short life, and how what had happened to Wheeler grieved him. His frustration showed up in his behavior. At an island restaurant he ordered a fish entrée, and when he was informed that the kitchen was out of it, de Jong said, "He became really angry."[21]

Otherwise, they talked about their families, books, and architecture. De Jong had very little say about her childhood. She didn't even mention that when she was eleven or twelve years old, she was so good at art that neighbors bought her drawings to put on their walls. LeWitt told her about his mother and the fact that she was forty-two years old when she had him, at that time a very late age to become a mother.

He told her that *Alice in Wonderland* was his favorite book and that architecture had inspired much of his work. For de Jong this was a revelation, as she was becoming interested in how to integrate art in architecture.

After their time together on the island, they spent a week in Brussels working together on one of his wall drawings.

Though she spoke English as well as Dutch and French, de Jong felt unsure about certain subtleties of English, so LeWitt became her teacher. Even decades later, she kept notes he had made for her. For example, he made two lists to show the difference between words (in the left-hand column) that show specifics and those (in the right-hand column) that are more general in nature.

FEW / LITTLE
MANY / MUCH
NUMBER / AMOUNT
FRANCS / MONEY[22]

Over the next few years, the two carried on their relationship in Paris and Brussels. "Sol was in love with me," she recalled. "And I guess I was in love with him."[23] But she recognized that the age difference between her and LeWitt was a problem. In addition, he was an established artist, and she still wanted to explore her own possibilities. In time she did, and her curriculum vitae lists many public art projects. De Jong married a Turkish economist, but apparently LeWitt was not convinced that the relationship would last. He kept sending her notes asking, "Are you still married?"[24] And during a trip to the Middle East, he photographed every sign he could find that had the word Petra in it and sent the pictures to her.

They were reunited professionally in 2003, when they had a joint exhibition at the Livingston Gallery in The Hague. As she recalled, "He told me he will always love me."[25]

As for Wheeler, she recovered and went on to a variety of professional pursuits. No longer lovers, she and LeWitt became dear friends and colleagues.

Wheeler was pursued romantically by the Italian artist Alighiero Boetti, who wanted to take her to off to foreign lands (including Guatamala), but he was unsuccessful. Boetti would later become involved with Alessandra Bonomo, but he would die prematurely in 1994.

In 1999, Wheeler married a former oil executive, Jim Aird, who took her to Thailand for their wedding and bought a place in the south of France and started writing poetry. She has lived there every summer while retaining her fifth-floor walk-up rent-controlled apartment ($600 a month in 2015) in lower Manhattan.

She had been under the impression for decades that it was her well-to-do parents who had paid for her very expensive stay at High Point. It was only when she got back in touch with others in the LeWitt circle that she learned the truth: LeWitt had quietly paid, a fact he never intended to divulge to her.

ELEVEN

CIAO, ITALY

In 2005, in the heart of Spoleto, Italy, a maître d' welcomed two American guests at 7:00 P.M. They were the only diners in the old and well-appointed Ristorante Apollinare, since the dinner crowd, as is customary in Italy, wouldn't arrive for an hour or two. As a result, the guests, inquisitive types, had time to ask about the history of the restaurant. The maître d' responded, "We have had famous people come here. Two of them come often—the actress Sophia Loren and the artist Sol LeWitt."[1]

The actress, of course, had been born in Rome. The artist had become an adopted son of Italy, though the process had taken a long time. He first had visited Italy during his shoestring European tour in 1950 with his Syracuse University pals, and he had been fascinated by the work of the Italian Renaissance masters. In 1969 he had returned as a professional artist, with a show at Fabio Sargentini's L'Attico Gallery in Rome. The following year, he had had a show at the Sperone Gallery in Turin that featured *Wall Drawing 51, Blue Snap Lines* (also known by its more direct title, *Lines Connecting Architectural Points*), the piece that made dramatic use of the wall's impediments. And in 1971 at the Galleria Toselli in Milan, he employed colored pencils to expand what was becoming his signature design—lines in four directions. As his European successes proliferated, Italy became their focus and a natural draw for LeWitt because of its art, natural beauty, and welcoming inhabitants. Italy warmed to him quickly and more demonstratively than his native country had. But his route to Spoleto, where he would buy a small house just outside the city and later a studio in the heart of it, followed an unusual path—not via the art capitals of Rome, Venice, and Florence, but via Bari, a city on the Adriatic known instead for its seaport, its universities, and being stuck artistically well in the past.

■ Marilena Bonomo could be considered the Paula Cooper of Bari, the biggest city in the region of Puglia but one that hardly qualified as

170

a destination for art lovers. By 1971, she and her husband, Lorenzo, a physician and medical school professor, had put together an impressive private collection. It included works by Italian artists but also, as the Bonomos traveled internationally, by those of other countries. The couple had spent a considerable amount of time in the United States, where Lorenzo had continued his studies in immunology in Dallas, Texas.

In the summer of 1971, Marilena, having learned the art of curating during her brief association with the Dallas Museum of Art, decided to open her own gallery in Bari. If Cooper had been questioned about the wisdom of starting a gallery in lower Manhattan, Marilena Bonomo faced similar astonishment at her decision. "But where is Bari?" became part of the foreign artists' response when she contacted them, as she pointed out, like a perpetual joke hovering over the gallery (indeed, she published a book many years later titled *But, Where Is Bari?*).[2] The city was where it had always been, of course, in the heart of Puglia, but it is often overlooked by tourists even though it offers some stunning sites, including the twelfth-century Castello Normanno-Svevo built by a Norman king. Bari took much pride in its history, and its art museum seemed to reflect the notion that history was more important than innovation. It contained fine works from the nineteenth and early twentieth centuries but seemed to have no room for anything produced after that. In this, the city reflected attitudes common in Italy. As Marilena would later recall, "In those years there were scarcely any avant-garde galleries in Italy."[3]

She knew of LeWitt's work because she had seen it in the United States and because it was becoming known in Italy. As early as 1968, Maurizio Calvesi wrote in the influential magazine *Cartabianca*: "With Sol LeWitt, primary structures assert their cultural direction, their disdainful contempt for the all-American immediacy of Pop Art, their ambition to be redeemed even through the election of a European and French culture."[4] He went on to insist on the relevance and importance of the work at a time when the public was skeptical, to say the least, about minimalism and conceptualism.

Marilena remembered that "Sol first came to Bari with Mimi Wheeler. . . . He knew of our family by name as collectors."[5]

No doubt LeWitt was mightily impressed by the Bonomos' villa, with its large, high-ceilinged rooms; lavish appointments; and formal garden in the back that featured a fountain, walkways, and a great variety of plantings.

Marilena recalled: "It was August, and we were leaving the next day for Spoleto [where the Bonomos had their summer home, a former Franciscan hermitage at Monteluco, above Spoleto with a view overlooking the city]. Sol asked me, 'Can we come with you?'"[6]

It is not known why he did this or what accounted for his boldness, but the Bonomos agreed. Marilena clearly had something at stake: within a few months after their summer meeting, she would open her new gallery. She needed LeWitt, whose work she had seen and admired —and just as important, the work of other members of the LeWitt circle —to mount a high-caliber show that would focus attention on the gallery and Bari as innovative places.

As Marilena recalled, LeWitt and Wheeler stayed a month in Spoleto and "Sol fell in love with Umbria."[7] The first thing to see was, of course, the great Spoleto festival, begun in 1958 by Gian-Carlo Menotti and Thomas Schippers. That summer the festival featured an array of arts and artists, including the Dance Theater of Harlem and the Duna Ensemble (which performed Hungarian songs and czardas and "Bread, Love and a Cello"by Elena Doni). LeWitt, who was quite familiar with New York's cultural opportunities, was impressed that such a mass of creative people could be gathered in one relatively small community.

In Spoleto, LeWitt saw Filippo Lippi's *Life of the Virgin* frescoes in the cathedral and Bennozzo Gozzoli's *Procession of the Magi* in the Medici palace. He was also introduced to a contemporary movement that would eventually be called Arte Povera, of which Alighiero Boetti, a friend of the Bonomos, was a leading practitioner. Shortly after meeting LeWitt, Boetti invited him to stay for a week at his house in the Cinque Terre on the Tuscan coast, the kind of gesture that deepened LeWitt's affection for Italy.

Arte Povera, begun around the same time as LeWitt developed his conceptual ideas, was related in many ways to the downtown New York art revolution. It rejected traditional ideas of art and returned to simple objects and messages, as well as exploring matters of space and language—radical departures from the art of the time. LeWitt made many friends in this school—Boetti, Jannis Kounellis, Mario Merz, and Giulio Paolini among them. He liked all of their work but was particularly intrigued by Paolini's use of metaphysics in his work "in a way," LeWitt later said, "that made it look classical,"[8] though it certainly had a contemporary feel. Paolini's work for the 1969 Venice Biennale was a plaster cast replicating an eye of Michelangelo's *David* but with a fragment of a mirror replacing the pupil. Paolini, then twenty-nine, became associated with Arte Povera and the avant-garde though, as in so many cases, formal categories were limited in accommodating an artist's thought processes or the elements of his or her work.

"These kinds of ideas," LeWitt would recall, "have to do with juxta-position of form and this is one of the ideas that grow into irony. You compare one thing to another and there is an ironic difference."[9]

As the days in Spoleto went on, LeWitt discovered other treasures. Marilena drove him to nearby Assisi, the birthplace of Saint Francis, where churches displayed masterpieces including frescoes by Cimabue, Lorenzetti, and Giotto. There was also Spoleto's natural beauty, with its old piazzas and stunning architecture, surrounded by the foothills of the Appenines.

In a 1998 essay, the art historian Antonio Carlo Ponti wrote:

> Spoleto gets straight to Sol's heart. In 1972 he buys an unpretentious little house a solitary cube on the Monteluco cliffs, overlooking the Ponte dell Torri, opposite the Rocca, formerly Lucrezia Borgia's abode. . . . Sol becomes a "citizen of Spoleto," he gets to the heart of matters in the splendid ducal town, he spends part of the year and works here. . . . Sol is very American in his formation and nationality, but he is also Italiana, Umbrian. His analytic—almost analogic—rationality finds itself at home in the rough waters—stagnation, according to some—of Italian contradictions, of our ethical and ideological chaos, always hovering between God and the devil. The classificatory logistics of his art, at first sign attached to technology more than to theology, actually finds subtle—and profound—connections in the mystical climate of the Umbrian nature, in the chastity and poverty of the Franciscan tradition and legend, in the essential linearity of Umbrian features.[10]

By all accounts including his own, LeWitt felt right at home, though he had trouble picking up Italian during his Spoleto years, in part because his hearing had continued to decline. Marilena recalled: "He tried all the time to learn Italian, but he didn't speak so much. Just enough to survive."[11] He had been a man of few words in English, and that didn't change when he spoke Italian. He could order *il formaggio* in a cheese shop or *del vino rosso* in a restaurant, but that initially represented a hefty portion of his vocabulary. In time, he prided himself on improv-ing, but became furious, according to Marilena, when he tried to speak Italian but the responses from Italians came in English.

Every morning, he walked to the city center to pick up a copy of *La Repubblica*, a newspaper he would read for the rest of his life, and he learned, as the Italians would say, *piano, piano* (little by little) to understand the language as the years passed. In the 1970s he violated his own rule about not owning real estate (rooted in his father's bankruptcy, which had been related to his real estate holdings) by purchasing a house across the aqueduct from Spoleto.

"When we first met Sol," Marilena said, "he was not well known in Italy." But by five years later, "all the art world came to Spoleto to visit him. I think he became so famous because he was so different from other artists. The work he did appeared to be so simple everybody understood it—a line, a point, a circle—people were attracted by its simplicity. But to arrive at such simplicity you have to have a big understanding. People don't like simple men, because they are not interesting people. But to reach simplicity from a more complex state of mind, that's different, and that's something that does interest people."[12]

Her comment that "everybody understood it" may be an exaggeration. In the early 1970s, his work was inspiring a variety of comments, some of which mirrored convoluted and nearly impossible to understand arguments of American critics. Here, for example, is part of what Filberto Menna wrote in *Data* in May 1972, a one-sentence example of erudition mixed with, it might appear, self-parody—an indication why LeWitt often said, "Reading art criticism is like chewing glass":[13]

> A certain ambiguity can be seen also in the interpretation [LeWitt]
> gives to his particular, heterodox declination of "conceptual art":
> if, on one hand, he poses the problem of a system of painting,
> seeking a meeting point between conceptual art and naturalism,
> on the other the exercise of concentration within a purely mental
> dimension and the strong suspicion shown toward the physical
> components of art-making overflow into initiatory territories
> where conceptualization links up the experience of absence and
> of emptiness, of the emptiness-fullness of Oriental thought.[14]

Other Italian commentators proved more direct. Carlo Ponti wrote: "Sol LeWitt, like a rock climber, marked out his lines on open walls, or on the domestic walls of friendly houses. Lines that remain as such, mirror-beings, or optical grids, or even anagrams, geometrical acrostics: what is important is the aim without an object, the fidelity to the precept, to the rules against the terrain vague of feature. Sol is next to the axiom: Beauty consists of greatness and order."[15]

LeWitt was never comfortable trying to explain in interviews why he was so popular in Italy—more revered there than anywhere else, including the United States. Such questions made him uncomfortable and violated his sense of modesty. But he did speak often about his reverence for Italian art, particularly in the context of the way American and even European critics seemed to ignore the contributions of Arte Povera, futurism, and other contributions of these artists. In his final interview, LeWitt reflected on this point:

> I think that mainly it had to do with the art scene in New York, which I think was immediately taken over by the French Academy and one thing they hated most of all was Italian art. I mean, that's why in *Art Since 1900* by Rosalind Krauss and Benjamin Buchloh, you have three pages in a thousand-page book to do with Italian art. . . . Everyone goes through Paris and the Russians, you know, they barely acknowledged the Italians. They wouldn't even be acknowledged at all because it didn't fit into the intellectual skin that they were so interested in. . . . I think [Italian art] is much better but if you ask young American artists to name twenty non-American artists, in the list there would be no Italian artist.[16]

Italians, of course, were grateful for the attention LeWitt brought them, and no doubt that was a factor in his fame. But that measure of fame wouldn't have been predicted in the early 1970s, given LeWitt's reluctance then to grant an interview.

When the first interview request arrived from an Italian magazine he declined. But Marilena talked him into it, saying that if he wanted his work to be well known he had to submit to the interview process, and "it's important to be polite to these people."[17] LeWitt said fine, but he wanted to have the questions in advance and then write the answers without having to sit with the interviewer. In time, LeWitt realized the importance of such interviews and reluctantly granted them, though he never expanded on personal issues. He would later begin such an interview with a general statement of his views on the process and result:

> First, I would like to say something about the general nature of interviews, which I generally resist for several reasons: I think that the interview is itself an art form which some people do very

well and some don't. For those who do them very well, they speak for themselves, but for those who don't, interviews make them sound foolish. . . . I have never felt that words were my medium — if they were, I would have been a writer. Nor am I a talker — I don't think quickly enough to answer questions well. Words spoken in conversation do not translate well to the printed page without a good deal of editing. [Indeed, LeWitt always insisted on editing interviews as a condition to sitting for them.] People want to interview artists because they think that they will explain their work — the work explains the artist. Those who want to understand the artist should look at the work. To a question such as "Why did you do this at that time?" or "Why did you not do this at another time?" the answer always has to be very subjective and based on what you think now and not on what you thought then. If you want to ask me questions, I'll be glad to answer them, but with these qualifications. Also, I remember that Robert Smithson once told me that when he was interviewed he never told the truth. Maybe that's why he was such a good interviewee.[18]

LeWitt's demanding work schedule in Italy during the years he visited the country and lived there mirrored what he had done in New York. He began at 7:00 A.M. and finished at noon. Much of the work at first was creating wall drawings at the Bonomos' hermitage on walls that would also, in time, include works by Boetti, Richard Tuttle, Mel Bochner, and David Tremlett.

Lorenzo Bonomo recalled in 2012:

After his work hours he took long walks in the Umbrian hills that still offered views like Renaissance landscapes by Ambrogio Lorenzetti or Perugino. He walked down to Spoleto or went to a trattoria near the ancient abbey of San Giuliano, midway up the ascent to the summit of Monteluco, at an altitude of 800 meters. The atmosphere was simple and friendly, the food excellent, a delicious Umbrian home cuisine with tagliatelle, game, mushrooms, simple genuine wines . . . Anna Maria, a beautiful young Umbrian waitress with a generous physique, accompanied the fine food with a smile and a jest. . . . His long stays in Italy had turned Sol into a gourmet, an expert in wine and truffles. He did not talk a lot but enjoyed the company of friends and relatives from America or Europe who often came to visit him.[19]

Tremlett, a frequent visitor, recalled LeWitt's daily swimming ritual at the city's Olympic-size pool, reflective of his studio work: "In Spoleto, we would swim lap after lap. Sol would have worked out a method, rhythm, and particular number of laps to be done, and I generally watched the last few from the sidelines."[20]

The pool also became a venue for recruitment. The photographer and artist Carol Heubner Venezia recalled this conversation she had with LeWitt one afternoon after lounging in the late summer sun, when LeWitt began with a question:

"Would you do a project with me?"
"What?"
"Photograph a cube."
"How?
"A white cube with lights directed on each corner and each face, every possible combination."
"How many photographs would that be?"
"I guess about 100."
"OK."[21]

The directness and clarity of the exchange was typical of LeWitt.

In Spoleto he had become a familiar and highly respected figure. He seemed to revel in the atmosphere. He would say to visitors, "This is not the end of he world. But you can see the end of the world from our house."[22]

LeWitt never seemed to grow older. He always had the same spirit and sense of humor. The move to Umbria inspired him to change his work and the materials he used. Instead of pencil, crayon, and chalk for wall drawings, he began to use ink washes. Color became more important, particularly the earth tones so evident in the Italian frescoes of the fourteenth and fifteenth centuries created in the Umbrian hills. He also expanded his use of geometric forms, employing isometric ideas so the viewer could see several sides of the form at once.

There was another, literally more concrete, change in his work: he began to use concrete blocks. He had been influenced by Arte Povera figures such as Merz, Giuseppe Penone, and others who used unexpected materials for their work. LeWitt considered these works to be "lyrically operatic or mystically metaphysical."[23] He also knew of Carl Andre's and Donald Judd's work in concrete, and he decided that this no-frills material—basic to construction and architecture—could combine ordinary elements with an artistic vision. In addition, he said, the advantage to these blocks was that "you could build fat and large, and it had kind of a grungy presence so it was the opposite of a refined material. It had this kind of ruggedness that I liked . . . because it's such a basic material it has an inherent ugliness that's objected to, but it also has a presence."

LeWitt's interest in architecture was reflected in this work, which seemed to be an extension of his earlier thinking. In 1966, for example, he had written about "ziggurat buildings" in midtown Manhattan, structures with multiple setbacks.[24]

■ Once LeWitt secured his downtown studio, just a two-minute walk from the piazza where he bought his coffee and copy of *La Repubblica*, his work proliferated. The studio was actually much more than that. The workspace, decorated by posters from his shows and those of his friends, was a room on the ground floor just off the entrance hall and another room that would serve for many years as a guest bedroom. Up the wooden staircase were more comfortable living quarters, where eventually a modest kitchen was installed.

As time passed, LeWitt drew old friends to Italy. Though the women he brought to Bari and Spoleto varied according to his love interest at the time, LeWitt became close to the Bonomo family, a relationship that would last until his death.

Alessandra Bonomo—one of the daughters of Marilena and Lorenzo and, for a time, Boetti's girlfriend—remembered: "For me Sol was like somebody in my family, and more than a friend, because he was a person I relied on for many years for many different things, not only for art. When I met him, he was very young, but like somebody I've known forever. There were times I was not decided in life—didn't want to work in a gallery, or in art at all. He always gave me good advice."[25] He also introduced her to the music of Billie Holiday and Ella Fitzgerald.

One summer after the end of his relationship with Wheeler, LeWitt brought another younger woman—she was then twenty-three—who was fascinated by the world of art and trying to enter it.

Beatrice Conrad-Eybesfeld had spent a lot of time in New York galleries, and she had met some of LeWitt's contemporaries (she recalled: "Mel Bochner was not nice to me. Lawrence Weiner was."[26]). She had seen LeWitt's work but had never met him. However, in the summer of 1972 they met on a beach. Conrad-Eybesfeld was living in Paris but spending the summer in the south of France, "looking for my way in life—I didn't know if I wanted to be an artist or historian, and I was still fighting with my mother." She recalled that she and LeWitt "talked and talked," then they swam toward a nearby island. They were out in the sun so long that "we were red like lobsters." By midnight, they were still walking on the beach, "talking and talking." She told him about her struggles in her native Argentina and about losing her father when she was thirteen years old—on that point they had much in common. She said that according to family tradition and expectations, she was supposed to marry an ambassador. But the family had lost all of its money, and she was staying in a cheap apartment without a bathroom. She was technically the owner of one-quarter of a castle in Austria, near Gratz, but that was only on paper. There was no money to claim it or live there.

That first night she and LeWitt slept together in the same small bed. The next morning, he gave her a rose and small drawing and said: "What are you doing this summer? Would you like to come with me to Italy?" They went to Siena, Milan and Spoleto: "We stayed in very little hotels, the cheapest hotels. I was a feminist. I didn't want him to pay for me." Later on, she tried to get her mother to like LeWitt, but her mother complained that he was too old for her and "not what she envisioned for me. She knew nothing about contemporary art." But the affection grew between Conrad-Eybesfeld and LeWitt: "We talked day and night, sometimes until the sun came up. He was very left in his politics. He loved food. And at the time, we drank whatever was red."

"I think Sol loved me very much," she said. "And I adored him. He was the nicest person I met in my whole life. He wanted a serious relationship, but I didn't. By this time everything was in the open. Sex, too. I was searching [for] my path. I got involved with being a Maoist, I thought I had the answer for everything."

She was raising money for *La Liberation*, taken as she was by the protest movement and by the idea for the newspaper itself (it had been founded in Paris by Jean-Paul Sartre, among others), subscribing to the idea that even its pay structure reflected its radical ideas. For example, each employee from the janitor to the editor in chief received the same salary (a policy eventually abandoned). And it had a strict advertising policy—no ads were accepted, at least at first. The paper aligned itself with no political party but put forward its own ideas in the later 1960s, following turbulent general strikes and unrest in France.

Conrad-Eybesfeld persuaded LeWitt to donate some of his own works, and ask his artist friends to do the same, to help raise the 100,000 francs needed at the time to cover the newspaper's operating costs—funds that in typical publishing situations would come largely from selling ads.

Though LeWitt complied with her request, the love affair ended as quickly as it had begun. Conrad-Eybesfeld met another man and then told LeWitt that she wouldn't have him as her husband: "Sol was very sad and very hurt." Even so, she later asked him to be the godfather of her first child, a son named Alexander. He agreed. When Alexander was four years old, he was hit and killed by a truck in front of the family house. LeWitt tried to comfort his former lover, and this was something she never forgot: "I never met anyone nicer, more genuine, more authentic. I think it was his warmth, his gentleness, his understanding of the feminine side of women. He treated women equally [with men]."

■ In the autumn of 2013, the prominent and innovative Italian collector Giuliano Gori opened his private museum to show a biographer what LeWitt's work meant to Italy, and specifically to his own view of contemporary art and how it relates to nature.

It was in the early 1970s when Gori, an industrialist who had amassed a large private collection, moved from Prato to a seventeenth-century villa and farm in the little town of Santomato—just outside of Pistoia, in the heart of the Tuscan hill country. Gori's fifty-eight acre property, open by appointment to visitors from mid-April to the end of September, looks out over Leonardo's hometown of Vinci and across rolling fields. It was here that Gori established the only museum of site-specific sculpture in Italy, and one of the few in the world. The land, still a working farm, contains scores of works that have been commissioned by Gori to relate specifically to the stunning landscape. Over the years, he has invited artists from around the world to create artwork for him both in the gardens and open spaces and in the property's many outbuildings. Richard Serra's *Open Field Vertical Elevations* are on a hillside of their own. *Melancholia II*, "a fused metal space" with a backdrop of bamboo, was conceived of and installed by Robert Morris and Claudio Parmagiani.[27] With *Utsorohi*, the Japanese sculptor Aiko Miyawaki provided the wind, in a sense, using metal in linear forms to refer to the path of circling winds and the flight of birds. LeWitt's work is all over—throughout the sculpture park and in the outbuildings. In a way, these works represent both the artist's growth over time and his contribution to Italian culture.

There are diagrams for structures and wall drawings, specifically numbers 445 and 495. The drawings are carried out in a variety of colors in farm buildings, one of them meant to complement Richard Long's floor sculpture of rocks discovered on the property and arranged in a circle. On the eastern side of the property is LeWitt's *Cube without a Cube*, made from modular cement blacks and surrounded by a ring of chestnut trees. His *1-2-3-2-1* structure of aluminum, placed in front of one of the property's historic buildings, recalls the artist's modular adventures in the 1960s.

After a tour of the grounds and buildings, Gori offered the biographer lunch prepared by his cook, with a variety of courses — including a desert of *kaki*, fruit plucked from the property's many persimmon trees. During the meal Gori talked of his relationship with LeWitt and about the artist's time in Italy.

Gori had become known for his independent taste. He said, "I buy art with my eyes, not my ears."[28] That is, he cares not what others say but trusts his own instincts. One of his instincts many decades earlier was to commission work from LeWitt: "I had seen his work and desperately wanted to meet him." Unfortunately, Gori's English was rudimentary, and LeWitt's Italian worse. "But Sol and I spent many hours together and never had any trouble understanding each other," Gori said. "Our friendship was never interrupted over thirty years."

Gori recalled his private moments with LeWitt. He thought of the artist as apart from others who had *tanto fuomo ma poco a rosto* — the Italian idiom meaning lots of smoke but no roast meat. In the Gori family, he said, "Sol is a kind of a myth. Sol never tried to make his gifts a weight to other people. Sol is Sol, and most artists don't come up to his ankle height in terms of greatness."

As an example of LeWitt's largesse, Gori mentioned Long's floor sculpture. When LeWitt saw that work, he felt compelled to provide an homage to it in a way that would complement the work — thus, he created his wall drawing. In essence, this combination is a metaphor for the entire Gori farm, which has married nature and art.

When Gori was asked to be the curator of the public library in the northern city of Reggio Emilia when it was being remodeled, he did not hesitate. It was an opportunity to create new art for the new space. He contacted LeWitt, who created his first wall drawing as a ceiling drawing in the library's reading room. Over the course of two months, a dozen installers (including nine young Italian artists) worked on the ceiling and finished the sixty-six-centimeter-square drawing of scores of connecting bands of color 8.5 centimeters wide. LeWitt titled the piece *Whirls and Twirls*. Gori referred to his 2005 work as "LeWitt's Sistine Chapel."

Gori said that Reggio Emilia had been the beneficiary of a contemporary art ethic born in Spoleto: "Sol fell in love with Spoleto at the time when the city was presenting sculpture in open air—the biographies of the town and the artist almost collided. The city seemed to stimulate him. I can only speak for myself. In my life as an art lover, the best thing that can happen is a fine artist who is a great human being. You can't have more than this."

■ The "great human being" tag stuck with LeWitt, certainly in regard to his generosity to other artists, causes, and friends. However, some artists have suggested that it is not apt, saying that LeWitt had stolen ideas from others.

Though she never expressed this view publicly, Rosemarie Castoro agreed with it.

Castoro privately seethed when she saw LeWitt's early wall drawings: "He had looked at a pad of drawings I made. Then I saw *my* drawing on the wall at MoMA. I got pissed off at him."[29] Castoro presented her argument in the context of the sexist culture of art: "I'm a woman, it's very easy to piss off a woman." She said that women's ideas were stolen all the time, and that there was very little they could do to set the record straight in a male-dominated art world. As a result of what had happened, she recalled, "I didn't want Sol in my studio anymore."

Castoro's work has been honored in recent decades, and a recent catalogue shows the wide range of ideas she has put forward. Her early work, from the late 1960s, looks similar to some of LeWitt's wall drawings—though unlike LeWitt's, her ideas were not carried out on plaster or wallboard. In 1966, *ARTnews* ran a review of a group show that said: "Rosemarie Castoro, the most interesting of the group, shows large canvases penciled with diagonal lines that make faintly tinted, overlapping bands, pleasing to the eye with their all-at-onceness and their bouncing delicacy."[30]

Tuttle also had issues with LeWitt, though not about his old colleague purloining his own ideas. He made his feelings public in a 1981 letter to Andrea Miller-Keller at the Wadsworth Atheneum, who was soliciting tributes to LeWitt for an upcoming exhibition.

Miller-Keller's entreaties to fellow artists produced a great variety of tributes to LeWitt's innovations. Andre wrote about "Sol's invention in his wall drawings of an utterly new form. We are only beginning to grasp the vast possibilities which he has opened to us."[31] The muralist Richard Haas wrote about the LeWitt wall drawings that "there was nothing like them." Channa Horwitz, an artist specialized in linear progressions, wrote that "Sol LeWitt's wall drawings give a new meaning to dimensionality." She went on to articulate the difference between producing a traditional commodity—that is, a work of art, usually three-dimensional, that is composed entirely of the object—and creating a work that becomes part of wall, even if not permanently: "The power of this double aspect of the wall and the motif honoring flatness reinforces the meaning of two dimensionality and causes the need to redefine the meaning of what dimension art is. If a drawing or painting is hung on a wall, the work displaces the wall. The wall is intruded on. What protrudes on the wall becomes three-dimensional. This can only be felt after viewing the strength of a LeWitt wall drawing."

Tuttle, though, wasn't convinced. Ignoring the issue of dimensionality, he focused on LeWitt's images: "In all, I've always felt [that LeWitt] ripped off my friend, Agnes Martin, and although I know his work is different—though not better—he has never acknowledged Agnes and even criticized her."[32] This is not accurate. Bernice Rose's piece for the 1978 MoMA retrospective includes LeWitt's tribute to Martin as an important influence on his drawing.[33]

Martin's early work had been abstract expressionist, but by 1959, while LeWitt was still struggling as an artist, she developed her first painted grids (they were not on walls) and had an exhibit of them at the Solomon R. Guggenheim Museum in 1966—two years before LeWitt's first wall drawing. However, what Tuttle didn't point out in his letter to Miller-Keller was that LeWitt had spoken about Martin's work and his being influenced by it, and that when he first met her, LeWitt recalled that he had said, "Thank you for the grid."[34] LeWitt pointed out that the grid wasn't a form that even Martin—as innovative as she was—had invented, but "she was the best artist to use it."

Lawrence Alloway wrote in 1973: "Sol LeWitt's pencil drawings on the wall, which started in 1968, may be an extrapolation of Martin's incorporation of the pencil into painting. The combination of the grid image and the promotion of the pencil to major usage suggest such a link. Martin is, I think, unique for her use of direct pencil marks within full-bodied painting. The variable interpretation of LeWitt's instructions for his delegated drawings functions in a way comparable to the varieties of manual pressure in Martin's work."[35]

The question of influence or, to use a darker term, purloining was to become a much more public issue while LeWitt was at work in Milan. In 1973, *Flash Art*, an influential international art journal, published an ad that charged LeWitt with stealing ideas. The ad was produced and paid for by Galerie m in Bochum, Germany. It featured photographs of three works of art that had similarities and the obviously accusatory boldface text: "Which works of what European artist of the sphere of Neue Konkrete Kunst will be taken next for a copy of his newest works—which will be propagated with much publicity as his own innovation?"[36]

The ad compared the work of LeWitt with that Jan Schoonoven, François Morellet, and Oskar Holwek. Persuasive or not, the ad would not have appeared, of course, had LeWitt's fame not been growing. That fame—even though it was the artist and not a celebrity who was famous—sparked lavish praise and negative criticism of LeWitt. These were not in equal amounts, but to have such an ad appear in an influential magazine clearly affected the artist.

In a May 1973 letter to Conrad-Eybesfeld from Milan, LeWitt addressed the issue and his thinking about how to respond. He wrote:

> My mind is still composing an answer to the [Flash Art] ad. . . .
> I don't think it is necessary to defend myself against nebulous
> charges of "copying" other artists. All artists see what other artists
> do. It becomes part of their intelligence; anyone who sees art and
> understands it as a language can understand its vocabulary and
> syntax. It is not a secret, but truly an international language, we all
> use each other's ideas. Ideas are only good if they can be passed
> on. It depends what one says with this language—not who invents
> words but what is said with these words. We cannot sit on ideas
> —they are the property of all who understand them. To say I copy
> ideas is not true but if they become part of my mentality they are
> mine also. It depends how much one says with them or how deeply
> one goes into them—that is what is important. Well—I have to
> work out my statement along those lines.[37]

His published (and toned-down) answer to the *Flash Art* ad appeared in a later issue of the magazine and argued that similarities between works are irrelevant:

I would like to address the more interesting part of the ad:
the accusation that I "copy" other artists' work and that I claim
"innovation." There are many works of art that superficially
resemble the works of other artists. This has been true throughout
history. Single works can always be shown to be similar to other
single works. Unless one compares the total work of each artist
one cannot say the work is the same. Comparisons have been
made between Manzoni and Ryman because they both made
white paintings, between Beuys and Morris because they both
used felt; between Lurich and Bochner because they both
used measurements, and many others. Those that make such
comparisons do not know the work of these artists and operate on
the level of petty gossips. They are not to be taken seriously. It is a
pathetically outworn romantic notion that "real artists" emerge fully
formed, having no traceable antecedents. The absurdity of this idea
is apparent, and yet there are artists who claim this for themselves.

I believe that ideas, once expressed, become the common
property of all. They are invalid if not used; they can only be given
away and cannot be stolen. Ideas of art become the vocabulary of
art and are used by other artists to form their own ideas (even if
unconsciously).

I hope this will be the last hate ad to be published in *Flash Art*,
which has become a real forum for artists. One can always find
interesting items in *Flash Art* because the texts are mostly by artists
and not by art critics who would place their ideas between those
of the artist and the reader. I want to thank [the editor] for the
opportunity to answer this vicious and stupid attack.[38]

In time, many artists expanded on these points, writing persuasively
about the contributions of LeWitt as an artist who, rather than copying,
was a source of inspiration.

The artist Lucio Pozzi wrote a particularly colorful letter to Andrea
Miller-Keller:

Prominent in that encyclopedic time, Sol LeWitt developed
innumerable observations, each focus[ing] on one or another facet
of the artist[ic] enterprise. The parameters of his work are so many
that they form a web as intricate as one of his drawings. It's difficult
for other artists to avoid touching on at least some of the things he
has done. . . .

He might be obsessed with the search for the Holy Grail,
the Blue Beard Key which opens all doors, the Faustian secret of
eternal life, like I am. For sure, the majority of people diseased with
"classificationitis" would never see any connection between my
apparently dispersed activities and his apparently rigorous one[s].
This is a riddle I'd love them to confront.[39]

The Israeli artist Pinchas Cohen Gan lists three specific contributions
made by LeWitt: "1. The wall paintings have released the spectator from
the classic approach to the object in art. 2. They have reduced the level
of involvement of the artist and his creation. 3. They have combined political elements (Arte Povera) with mathematical elements."[40]

The artist Michael Kirby put the essence of LeWitt's wall drawing oeuvre in more poetic terms: "Several years ago, a painting was discovered
on the wall of an old apartment in Paris. It had been done some time
around the first World War as a wedding present for the couple who
had lived there ever since. Apparently the artist couldn't afford a more
traditional gift. He was Pablo Picasso. The building was torn down; the
painting was preserved. What methods of painting can be used so that
the art only lasts as long as the wall that it's on? Of course, the idea for
one of Sol LeWitt's pieces is not on the wall."[41]

Lawrence Weiner put it more briefly:

THAT WHICH CAN BE

CARRIED OUT

COVERED OVER

BUT NOT

REMOVED.[42]

Two years after the *Flash Art* controversy another one contributed
to the awareness of LeWitt's work. This one played out over several issues of *Art in America* and was an argument between art experts about
LeWitt's work. It fit very well with the artist's idea that a certain kind of
publicity involving critical assessment, positive or negative, can be as
effective as celebrity-driven material.

Donald Kuspit published a nuanced piece titled "The Look of
Thought" in the September–October 1975 issue of *Art in America*, in
which he asserted that LeWitt's structures "barely generate any sensuous intensity, and instead seem to demand an intellectual response."[43]
They seem "like a cold bath, at once repressive and exhilarating, instinct-

denying and at the same time creating a sense of drummed up energy." His point, he said, is that "LeWitt's modular consistency illustrates the idea of art as a realm of essential order." Furthermore, "LeWitt pushes art onto philosophical ground." The piece became iconic, in part because it seemed to dive into the essence of the eternal question, "What is art?" and to ask whether beauty, as defined through the ages, is even relevant to the discussion. Kuspit was critical of Lucy Lippard's assessment that LeWitt's work had an inherent beauty.

In response, the art historian Joseph Masheck wrote a piece for the same publication titled "Kuspit's LeWitt: Has He Got Style?" He said: "The notion that LeWitt sculptures somehow do without style strikes me as so mistaken that I'm not sure where to begin."[44] Masheck is in Lippard's camp, arguing that LeWitt's work "generates pure beauty." Much of Masheck's essay focused on LeWitt's *Incomplete Open Cubes*. Mocking Kuspit's analysis, Masheck wrote, "How often will he need actually to behold a work of art in order to stay out there in his 'higher realm'?"[45]

Then it was Kuspit's turn again. He wrote a letter to the editor of *Art in America* that defended his stance. It was published in the January–February 1977 issue,[46] and Masheck took up the renewed challenge in the March–April issue, accusing Kuspit of simplifying Masheck's argument: "I was pointing up Kuspit's readiness to dissolve the bodily—and human—concreteness of art into purely philosophical transactions, as though philosophy, happily, were the universal solvent."[47]

One price of emerging fame, of course, is that the artist opens himself or herself to second-guessing on the part of others and to a certain amount of envy. LeWitt's reaction to criticism generally could be characterized as indifferent, but that wouldn't tell the whole story. He was pleased that critics discussed his work, even if the results were not entirely laudatory. It all fit in with the idea of getting the word out. He never commented directly on, for example, a 1982 review in the *Daily Telegraph* about his work in the exhibit *A Century at the British Museum*, but it's entirely possible that the review amused him. He had mistaken, the critic said, LeWitt's *Straight Lines in Four Directions* for an unfinished plasterboard wall. He wrote: "These things have a legitimate place in a collection representing modern drawings. This should not confuse anyone into imagining they have aesthetic merit."[48]

LeWitt was not one to wear his emotions on his sleeve or to complain bitterly about others as a way to feel better about himself. But there were a few exceptions.

In a letter dated only April 22 (no year was given, and it is unclear whether the letter was ever sent or just written to blow off steam) to James Fitzsimmons, a critic and the editor of *Art International*, Le Witt displayed his capacity for sarcasm and more than a little wit:

> In a recent card to [arts writer] John Chandler (which he saw no harm in showing me), you commented, more or less, that you found my work arid and that what I needed was a good piece of tail. I only want to thank you for your solicitude. Indeed, who doesn't need a good piece of tail and the more the better? If you have any addresses of young, accommodating girls in or around New York, please sent them on — I will be forever grateful.
>
> But I wonder about you. Just what kind of art excites you? Do you salivate over the lush modulations of Rubens or [is it] the fleshy invocations of [Jules] Olitski's latter paintings that give you erections? . . . I wonder what kind of art you really like, I mean what really leads you to a grand climax, or secret bouts of masturbation.
>
> As for me, I prefer to use women as my sexual outlet (or inlet). They are softer than most art. (Maybe some of John Chamberlain's foam rubber pieces would suit you best.) But as I say, I would prefer women and would advise you also to look into this area of sexual gratification. In that way you may be better able to clear your fevered brain and see art a little more objectively, as art, and keep your prick in your pants. So thanks again for your concern. If I have been able to straighten you out I am very glad.
>
> Sincerely, Sol LeWitt.[49]

■ During the 1970s, LeWitt split his time between New York and Spoleto. And when he went to Italy it was often with his female companion at the time. The first to follow Wheeler and Conrad-Eybesfeld was a young artist (again, much younger than LeWitt).

Karen Gunderson — like Gene Beery, a native of Racine, Wisconsin — had earned a master's degree at the University of Iowa and was teaching at Ohio State University (OSU), in Columbus, when she met LeWitt. Her classes included intermedia (she was a pioneer scholar in this new field), art history, and sculpture. As she recalled in an interview in 2014, "It was me and forty men at OSU. I got patted on top of my head or on my ass every day."[50]

Gunderson took a studio in downtown Columbus, where she could drive in her 1964 Porsche 356C. The studio had no heating, but it gave her a place to do her own work—which at the time involved, among other things, spray painting. "At the time I was painting graffiti paintings of the clouds," she recalled.

She met LeWitt when he did a structure for OSU's School of Fine Arts: "I got there when [his assistants] were making the piece, blue lines on a white wall. He was standing there, telling people what to do." It was just about finished when she said to him, "I think it's beautiful," and he said, "Thanks." Then she said, "Let's go have a beer." And he said, "Let's do it."

As it turned out, the two members of the crew came with them to a tavern with a pool table on High Street. Teams for pool were chosen, and LeWitt and Gunderson formed one and the crewmembers the other. Gunderson recalled:

> Sol and I won—and we bet the other guys. He was good at it. It must
> have been his instinctive geometry. Then we went up to my place.
> I had this incredible house on a ravine, built like a New England
> home. I'm short, so everything fit in it—it was built for short people.
> Sol stayed with me for a couple of days, and then he went back to
> New York. I would visit him from time to time. I had just gotten
> out of a nine-year relationship with a neurophysiologist. He was
> in Iowa, but he would follow me. And when he came to Ohio he'd
> make me [into] a basket case, and then he'd leave.

Gunderson decided to leave Columbus for New York, where she rented a loft in Tribeca. She wanted to live alone because she "really wanted to be independent and [was] tired of being taken over by strong men." She fought sexism from anyone, saying, "I'm an artist, not a model." LeWitt was what she needed, for the moment: "He was supportive to women."

Their dating routine was not much different from what others experienced with LeWitt:

> I remember the first time he took me to Umberto's Clam House in
> Little Italy and told me about the mobster [Joseph Gallo] who had
> been shot there.
>
> We went to the movies, too, but mostly we went to dinner. I
> remember having dinner with Phil Glass and other couples that
> were artists. They always tried to draw Sol out, but he didn't respond

often. These were never big parties, usually just dinners with four people.

LeWitt took Gunderson to the cities in Europe where he had by then become a hot commodity. In 1973 and 1974 he had shows in Rome, London, Bari, Milan, Brussels, Amsterdam, Turin, Liege, Belgium, and Münster, and he spent time in Spoleto, where he introduced her to his new friends.

But this time it was LeWitt who did the leaving. Gunderson recalled: "A roommate of my college roommate—Michelle Calvez—worked for the French government's tourist bureau and American Express. She was very pretty and had a great accent, a nice figure, and a good sense of humor. I introduced [her] to Sol. They got together." He said to Gunderson, "I saw Michelle." She replied, "Ooh la la." Reflecting on this later, Gunderson said, "How could you be critical? It was the '70s, after all."

LeWitt's romantic French connection, his second in a fairly brief span, was just as short-lived as the first, and he was soon introducing Spoleto to another younger female artist.

As for Gunderson, she went on to have a formidable career as artist and teacher. She stayed in touch with LeWitt for the rest of his life, eventually becoming the first artist to have a show at the synagogue in Chester, Connecticut, that he and the architect Stephen Lloyd designed. And after LeWitt died, she produced an homage to him, *Water Edges #1*, a charcoal wall drawing, in Denmark.

She has many detailed memories of LeWitt, including recollections of what envious male artists said to her while she was dating him—mostly put-downs: "They said, 'He's an old queen.' I replied, 'It was the best sexual experience I'd had in years.' Though this was a slight exaggeration."

TWELVE

ART AND TRUST

An editorial on a LeWitt exhibit at the Joslyn Museum in Omaha, Nebraska, appeared in the *Omaha Herald* in January 1977:

> We hereby nominate Sol LeWitt for the 1977 Nobel Prize in Art. Out of his fertile imagination has come a concept, infinite in possibility, which can revolutionize the world of visual art by making any ordinary citizen capable of creating masterpieces of painting and sculpture. . . .
>
> Think of it. You too can be among the creative elite. Just conceptualize your masterpiece, write the instructions, and get someone else to execute it.
>
> We have a concept, as a matter fact. Here are the directions:
>
> To one fresco painting of a reclining Adam, add one picture of a reclining God, touching index fingers. Add angels, cherubs, clouds and rocks to taste. Cover with a good grade of antiquing glaze (not included.) The result should be suitable for basement ceiling, rec room, parsonage or friendly neighborhood art museum.[1]

According to a reporter for the UK newspaper *Independent*, at the opening of the LeWitt exhibit at the Lisson Gallery in London, in 1971, one person remarked about a piece featuring white cubes: "It's just a stack of wine bottle racks."[2] In contrast, Caroline Tisdall's review in the *Guardian* argued: "This is the most refreshing work to show in London for some time. . . . It is the objective of the artist who is concerned with conceptual art to make his work *mentally* interesting to the spectator, and therefore he would want it to become emotionally dry."[3]

Chrissie Isles, exhibitions coordinator at Modern Art Oxford, said: "LeWitt didn't want an association of meanings. . . . This was the idea of art being more democratic, a reductive, almost impersonal rationalization of artwork as pure form free from descriptive or subjective expression. . . . Anyone could make it."[4]

But not everyone did make it. It takes an eye, a heart, a steady hand, a great deal of patience, and in many instances a strong body and will.

The question of how LeWitt recruited younger artists to carry out his ideas naturally arises. On one level the answer is obvious: They needed the work and were pleased that an artist of LeWitt's stature thought them skilled enough to rely upon. But there was something else, too, that was related to his deep interest in the work and lives of others.

Michael Harvey never became an official member of a LeWitt crew, but he did complete some work for his benefactor, and his recollections reveal how LeWitt related to younger artists.

Harvey, who eventually became a prominent painter and filmmaker, devoted a section of his memoir, *South of Houston: Sketches from the Art World in Pen and Youth*, to his encounters with LeWitt. In a particularly telling passage, he described the time in the early 1970s when he arrived at 117 Hester Street in a state of near self-loathing, his girlfriend having left him. He had taken on odd jobs to make a living:

Sol looked surprised when he opened his heavy metal door, though we'd agreed to meet. It was just his manner, shy unassuming, a stay-at-home guy who didn't care for the bars or openings. He'd send a postcard if he wanted to stay in touch.

"C'mon in."

He was a friendly, avuncular figure on the edge of success. He was already well known to other artists and within a few years he would achieve international recognition. His place was small compared to the giant Soho lofts. An old rundown, Lower East Side building: cramped iron gates over the street windows, low ceilings, a wood stove. It was easy to imagine an overcrowded sweatshop of dressmakers stitching calico, or milliners braiding straw hats, their eyes straining under oil lamps.

The front room, overlooking the street, was his workplace. A long table ran the length of the wall under the windows. He had a drawing board angled on it, with his pens and pencils laid out neatly beside it. The stove, its chimney disappearing into the blackened wall, sat in the corner with a lot of old wood.

"I used to carry bags of coal up those stairs when I was your age."

He wasn't old, early forties, with a solid, barrel-chested build.

Two of his sculptures sat in the middle of the room. But the biggest

     SOL LEWITT

thing in there was a double bed. I knew he lived with his girlfriend, Mimi, but there was no sign of her, no imprint anywhere. He threw my pea coat across it and we went back to the kitchen-hallway.

"This breaking up your day?" I was deferential, him being older and successful.

"My day's over," he said. "Want an espresso? Sit down." He gestured to the table in the back room. "I was in the Quartermaster Corps when I served in Korea." He stayed at the kitchen counter to fix the coffee. "We had to get up at five every morning. I never got over it."

The back room was crowded but not cluttered — three tables, a couch, numerous chairs, and several bookcases. For a minimalist, Sol had a lot of stuff. But organized. . . .

The room was an homage, of sorts, to the European styles of the Bauhaus and De Stijl. Tables and chairs aligned and squared. Much of the furniture had been built by him, with his signature spare rectangular frame designs, painted white. The only signs of his newfound success were the expensive Reitveld and van der Rohe chairs he had. The first things on his wish list — more beautiful to look at than sit in.

I've never met anyone more dedicated to art. Its history, its making, the people who made it. He lived totally immersed in it. He was easy to talk to. His reluctance to hold court, to dominate the conversation, made him singular in the art business, almost enigmatic.

"You ever read the Beckett novel *Molloy*?" he said. "The section with the sucking stones?"

"Oh, yes." . . . Molloy, on a beach, his sixteen pebbles arranged equally in four pockets. His ritual is to suck each stone in turn. Determined never to suck a stone out of order, he transfers the pebbles from pocket to pocket with mathematical precision to ensure their exact circulation.

How perfect. The orderly nature of the room was the same: methodical, precise, respectful. His art was a love for systems, organizing algorithms.

"Of course the outcome's important. I don't know what it's going to look like. I want it to be a surprise." His love of music made me think his systems were annotations, like musical compositions for canons and fugues.

"Yeah, true . . . same piece of music can be played on a church organ, or by a marching band. . . ."

As I was leaving he asked how I was surviving. I told him I'd just finished a job. I had to find something new. He paused.

"Could you make something like that?" He pointed to one of his complicated sculptures, made up of opened-frame cubes, on the table. I hesitated. The craftsmanship was excellent. I needed the work but wasn't confident I had the skill. By now I felt sure that Sol's orderly life style was not simply self-imposed discipline but, in fact, the very thing that kept him running. It was anything out of order that gave him fits. I wasn't sure I was up to snuff, but it looked like more fun than sanding floors.

"I dunno. . . . It's very well done."

"Why not try one? See how it goes."[5]

Here is a very different story of recruitment: In 1971, a twenty-seven-year-old native of Japan arrived in New York with a duffel bag and the dream of becoming an artist. When he got to the Lower East Side, Jo Watanabe climbed five flights of stairs at 117 Hester Street. But when he knocked on the door there was no answer. The telegram with flight details he had sent to his brother, whom he hadn't seen in seven years, had apparently never arrived. Not knowing what to do, he left his duffel bag in the hallway and walked around the neighborhood to kill time until his brother got home. He looked at all the shop signs, not knowing how to read them, and, on the street he didn't understand any overheard conversations. He wondered how he might make it as an artist in the United States with at least two striking handicaps: not knowing how to say anything but hello, and having a curriculum vitae that mentioned extensive training in dance but not in art.

When he returned, his brother was still not there, so he knocked on the door of a fourth-floor apartment. Adrian Piper came to the door and saw a stranger, who could say only his name. Piper assumed correctly that he was related to her neighbor upstairs and so let him keep his duffel bag there while he waited for his brother to return from work. There was a good deal of activity in the hallway, with sheetrock and plywood being carried up and down. And in the chaos Watanabe saw a man who was called Sol LeWitt.

Soon thereafter Watanabe found lodging on Avenue A, a place where he had roommates who could help him learn English. At first he lived only on canned food, which was all he could afford. He had a hard time making a living: "I was doing carpentry work, which I didn't know anything about. But what I built never broke down, and so I developed a reputation, going to people's apartments. When people hired somebody like me, cheap, they didn't expect too much. I made sure the place was cleaner than when I started, and that impressed people more than anything."[6] His reputation spread by word of mouth, and he soon had many clients on the Upper West Side. LeWitt hired him to do some work on Hester Street, but he soon saw that this meticulous young man could be valuable in other ways.

Watanabe's arrival in the United States coincided with LeWitt's increasing need for reliable people to execute his wall drawing concepts —even people like Watanabe, who clearly lacked a formal art education. Over time LeWitt discovered a few others on whom he relied for years. One was another immigrant from Japan, Kazuko Miyamoto, who arrived before Watanabe.

Unlike Watanabe in that she was trained in art, Miyamoto had also taken a studio at 117 Hester Street, which is how she met LeWitt. The two were outside the building during a fire alarm when they began talking. She said that she had seen one of his shows and liked it, and he asked her to make models for him. The fact that he had recruited two Japanese artists early on to lead crews around the world may be traced to the respect he had had for Japanese culture and art since his army days. He admired the work ethic, the fact that they could accommodate tedium, as well as the sense of taste of the people, and their ability to solve unforeseen problems. In the case of LeWitt's walls, which required many days to finish, there were always such issues. The real difference between conceiving art in a studio, LeWitt's job, and the installer's task is considerable. The crew must deal with the inconsistencies of the plaster and wallboard, the intrusions of electrical outlets and fire extinguishers, and walls that don't square up. All this requires group huddles without having to wait for the artist responsible for the general plan to come to the rescue. Indeed, LeWitt often remarked on the collaborative nature of the work and said that he needed, and fully appreciated, the talents that crew members brought to the process.

Watanabe and Miyamoto were employed in this work for many decades while they made their own independent ways—in her case, as a painter, sculptor, and gallery founder; and in his case as one of New York's finest art printers and makers of maquettes for a variety of artists.

He had tried his hand at doing cubes, influenced as he was by the man he worked for, "but I figured the world is better off with just one Sol Le-Witt."[7] So he opened a series of studios in Brooklyn to make prints for customers including high-profile museums, such as MoMA.

In the summer of 2014, then seventy-one and suffering from serious illness, he reflected on that experience: "In my lifetime the greatest thing that happened in art is Sol LeWitt, not Jasper Johns, [Andy] Warhol, [Roy] Lichtenstein, in terms of history. I didn't care about them before, and the future I don't care about—I won't be here. What Sol did was more than other people. Sol hit the jackpot. He had a brilliant mind and instinct. His work is simple and complex at the time."[8] Many of those who headed LeWitt's crews over the years shared this view.

Miyamoto wrote in a 1981 letter to Andrea Miller-Keller:

> I have been executing Sol LeWitt's wall drawings since 1971, the first at the [Solomon R.] Guggenheim Museum. Since then facing the huge, bare walls before labor starts is a constant challenge and excitement as if the wall is my stage.
>
> I have done one of his most strenuous drawings over and over again on different wall surfaces. However I enjoyed every execution. . . . The repetitiousness, evenness, the sound of the pencil running on the wall has a deep calming effect on me. . . . Sol said I should train my dogs and cats to do the wall drawing. If I could, my entire family would travel all over Europe together.[9]

Over the years there have been thousands of young artists who served on one or more of LeWitt's wall drawing crews. One of them was Maria Schiavelli, who pointed out in her recollection of the work a dimension that few others talk about: that artists, who by nature and profession assume they will work alone, do not do so when working on a LeWitt wall drawing, and that doing so teaches them to be part of a team, not only literally but metaphorically. This point is evident in the arc of LeWitt's career. Part of the way he promoted his art was through an impressively broad network of personal relationships and by employing so many artists in his work, emphasizing the collaborative nature of what had always been a profession of people working alone.

Among those who began working with Watanabe and Miyamoto was a highly educated artist named Anthony Sansotta, who had come to New York after earning a master's degree in painting at Cornell University. He had a job in John Weber's gallery, though on his off hours he was polishing a series of works that he described in a 2012 interview as "abstract works that were amorphous, in terms of imagery and that evolved into something that was a bit more concrete in terms of abstraction. After some exposure to someone like Robert Ryman, I was interested in how painting appeared on a wall, so they took a three-dimensional aspect to them. Sometimes they leaned on the wall and protruded."[10]

Working in a gallery gave Sansotta the opportunity to meet a variety of artists and, as he put, "be constantly exposed to their work." These included Robert and Sylvia Mangold; Robert Ryman; Carl Andre; Stephen Antonakos and his wife, Naomi Spector; and Dan Flavin. After Virginia Dwan's New York gallery closed, Weber continued Dwan's tradition of showing minimal and conceptual artists. Sansotta recalled "that people didn't know what to make of Carl Andre's sculpture. During a Robert Ryman exhibit—all white on canvas—someone said, 'What is he going to paint the paintings?'"

Sansotta met LeWitt at Weber's gallery:

He just appeared one day, a mild-mannered man. I knew who he was. He was not wildly popular at the moment but a well-respected figure. After a month he had me do this installation, a series of five cube structures in various configurations, for the Dag Hammarskjold Plaza near the United Nations building. It was a piece made of steel and interlocking pieces, like an Erector Set. We painted it white and made the cubes in different configurations (as the instructions directed). I assisted artists with putting up the installations and also dismantling them. I did shipping and inventory work. I just wanted to survive.

Sansotta was the crew chief many years later on LeWitt's "Sistine Chapel" in Reggio Emilia. The plan for *Swirls and Twirls* for the library's reading room hung on the wall of LeWitt's studio for many months. Typically, it was drawn in pencil on a flat piece of paper, with indications for the colors marked in the bands.

The transition from plan to finished product illustrates the difficulties involved in applying an idea physically, particularly when it involves something other than a wall. "The ceiling was a bit different than anticipated," recalled Sansotta. "The curvature was not predicted from the flat plan. There was an area more curved [than anticipated] on the side, so we had to play around a little with positioning it. The other problem was the physical discomfort, standing on a scaffolding, working with your hands above your head."

Many of the problems also come before the painting. Though LeWitt never considered the natural shapes and presence of functional aspects of a wall (such as electrical outlets and inconsistencies of dimension) to be impediments, he did insist that his crews prepare the walls properly.

In 1999, Sachiko Cho, the crew chief, explained to the *New York Times* the process that the crew undertook while transforming a maquette into an enormous finished piece. First the walls were sanded carefully. Then she made measurements and taped the design in place, marking each area with numbers indicating the colors to be applied. The colors were applied seven times, as was customary, and after each time the wall was sanded smooth and covered with varnish.[11]

John Hogan, a long-time associate of LeWitt who described himself as the "mixologist," prepared the paint. It came from Switzerland and had to reach a certain consistency before it was ready to use, just as in a complicated recipe. He typically added retarders to slow the drying process and used distilled water as a binder.

Hogan, who led many crews over the years, articulated the sometimes hard to define line between artist and crewmember: "Essential to the idea, the ability to share understanding of the drawings with the others involved, the draft person's execution is a visualization of their understanding of the drawing/idea/plan. . . . The wall drawing is the artist's art as long as the plan is not violated, if it is then the draftsman becomes the artist and the drawing would be his work of art, but art that is a parody of the original concept.[12]

Cho put it this way:

"Do not do anything that would be a disservice to Sol and his art," is
what I always try to keep in mind as a draftsman. When he sent me
to places to make wall drawings, he would often say, with a smile,
"Don't work too hard." That was his way of saying, "Keep it simple,
use your common sense, and don't distort the idea by thinking too
much." . . . Even though Sol also said, "It is difficult to bungle a good
idea," erroneous decisions in the process of implementation can,
in fact, lead to disastrous results that do not do justice to Sol's art.
A wall drawing should never be seen or executed as just a pretty
interior design or, at worst, a parody of the original concept. One
of the most difficult problems is to avoid overworking a drawing to

a point at which the work becomes sterile through its mechanical execution. On the other hand, a simple line or color can express complex thoughts and inspire a deeper understanding of all the possibilities of universal beauty.[13]

LeWitt predicted the variations between the original instructions and the finished product and accommodated them. He said: "I always equate it to a musical performance. Every time you hear the same Bach piano or harpsichord thing it's different even with the same person. Even if Wanda Landowska plays it in March and then in April, it would sound different. If Ralph Kirkpatrick plays it, it will be different. Whoever does it will leave their mark on it. In a way it's good that the draftsman has a part in it, and it's not just the artist doing it. It's a collaboration."[14]

◼ In a 2012 interview, the artist Pat Steir recalled days when the execution of a wall drawing was a much simpler process—because when LeWitt had just begun to work on this concept, he did the drawings himself. "It was a nightmare to watch him [up on a ladder]," Steir said. "I'd shout 'Don't fall!'"[15]

Steir was at first a casual friend. She had come to know LeWitt when, as a neighbor, he chased away a man from her door who wanted to trade fresh fish for art.

In those first days, Steir told LeWitt that though she was still in her mid-twenties, she had much experience in encountering the obstacles of art and gender.

Born in Newark, New Jersey, Steir was the daughter of a man who had gone to art school but who never pursued art professionally because, in his view, it was too hard to make a living that way. He offered Steir a certain amount of encouragement in terms of her ability, telling her when she was eight years old, "If you can learn to write you can learn to draw." Yet when she announced she would like to go to art school, he tried to dissuade her: "He told me, 'If a man can't make it, how can a girl?'" When she mentioned to him that she was also interested in poetry, he said: "Be a poet—you'll earn more money." Her teachers in high school also tried to persuade her to pick other fields: "They said I was too smart to be an artist." But that's what she wanted to do, so she enrolled at the Pratt Institute and, after completing her studies there, earned a master's degree in fine arts at the Boston University College of Fine Arts.

She had some early success. The year that she got her diploma, she was included in a group show in Atlanta, Georgia. Two years later her drawings were in a group show at MoMA, and around the same time she had her first solo exhibition in New York. Even so, she found it hard to navigate a sea of male domination. "You had to wear army boots and deny femininity to get anywhere, to be taken seriously," she said. One solution was to get a nine-to-five job in a related field, so she became an art director at Harper & Row, during which time she designed a book on Eva Hesse's work. Then she went out to make it on her own.

It was during this time that her stalker, the fishmonger, appeared. And reappeared. He wouldn't give up his quest to exchange fillets for paintings until LeWitt solved the problem by shooing him away for good.

As she and LeWitt got to know each other, their relationship became intimate. Steir was drawn to the man "who lived in a humble way, never splashy," though by then he had a lot more money than all of the artists she knew at the time. She was also impressed by his general attitude, which was: "Nobody can tell me what to do with my life, what to do with my work." Steir said, "He could have a show in the biggest gallery in New York City, or in a telephone booth, or on a public wall." He didn't express a sense of hierarchy or need or status. And at a time when every other successful artist worked with an agent, LeWitt worked alone. Yet this wasn't to save money.

"Sol was a socialist at heart," she said. "He gave a lot of artists money. He felt that he was lucky and he should share." The luck, however, didn't come out of the blue: "The gift of Sol was that he believed in himself. He stuck with his conviction." This is what, in Steir's view, allowed his work to become known even as he shied away from the requirements of celebrity: "He said, 'Be true to your work and it will be true to you.' He just kept working, moving ahead, just like an animal building a nest, with purpose and without doubt. Sol acted on his political beliefs. He knew the feminist movement was starting. He knew it was harder for women. He had a lot of women friends." And he demonstrated to them what it took—the slow but persistent plodding; the belief necessary to sustain effort; and, to overcome negativity, the need not to plot a career but to simply move ahead, piece by piece. "He was a Napoleon of art," Steir said, "going everywhere at once. It wasn't a plan to conquer Europe. It just happened. I would ask him, 'How many shows do you have there?' He'd say, 'I have five.' I'd say, 'Is that all?' He'd respond, 'When I'm dead I'll do more.'"

As he had done with other women, LeWitt asked Steir to accompany him on trips to Europe. The flights there were always those with the cheapest tickets possible, which required a long stay. She remembered that they covered a lot of ground on the Continent, much of by car, and "the trouble with Sol was that he didn't drive, and so I had to drive everywhere. He was, though, a terrible backseat driver, telling me somebody is going to cross the street, the light is going to change, to start, to stop."

It is widely believed that Sol never got behind the wheel himself. But once in Italy with Steir he decided to drive. He couldn't figure out how to stop the car and, according to Steir, brought it to a halt the only way he could devise at the moment, "by rolling it slowly into a building." (In a recollection published in 2009, Bernice Rose also referred to his driving in Italy.[16])

Steir also recalled another moment that didn't go according to plan but turned out to have a reasonably happy ending. This one occurred during dinner with Charles Saatchi, cofounder with his brother of the advertising agency in London that became the largest in the world. In 2009, Saatchi published a book titled *My Name Is Charles Saatchi and I Am an Artaholic.* In it, he discussed building one of the most dramatic collections of postmodern and classic art in the world and on his work as an art dealer. In the early 1970s, he had no such art of his own, but he became a patron of the Lisson Gallery, where LeWitt's work was displayed. Saatchi described his philosophy of buying: "For me and for people with good eyes who actually enjoy looking at good art, nothing is as uplifting as standing before a great painting, whether it was painted in 1505 or last Tuesday."[17] Over time, he purchased twenty-one works by LeWitt, eleven by Donald Judd, seventeen by Warhol, twenty-three by Julian Schnabel, and hundreds of others. But his first purchase made for a memorable tale about the art of not getting too excited about a big sale.

Steir recalled: "We were having dinner in London with Saatchi when he first started collecting. His first piece, he hoped, would be one by Sol though he hadn't yet paid for it. Over dinner, we were waiting for him to say, 'Here's the check,' but he never did. During the dinner conversation, Sol fell asleep. I didn't know what to say to Saatchi. Well, I wasn't Sol's wife, just his girlfriend."[18] Nevertheless, the payment was eventually made.

Steir became attached to LeWitt's mother during her final days. He took Steir to New Britain to visit, and she recalled: "Sophie was very proud of him. She knew her son was a genius, because she was a Jewish mother. She was teeny and strong, living in an apartment with a tiny bedroom, a living room that had a couch that opened into a bed, a spinet piano. And unlike many children of his generation, Sol did not reject his mother. He adored her."[19] She lived just long enough, reaching the age of eighty-eight, to know that her genius son was being celebrated his first retrospective, at MoMA — the temple of contemporary art — in 1978.

Steir went on to become a prominent painter and printmaker whose work is displayed at the Metropolitan Museum of Art, MoMA, the National Gallery of Art, and many museums in Europe.

Her relationship with LeWitt endured until he met yet another young woman, the one who would become his second wife — though the exact date of Steir's breakup with LeWitt is not clear. There was, it appears, a bit of an overlap. In any case, Steir said, "Sol and I had different calendars for when we started and when we ended our relationship."[20]

■ LeWitt's retrospective at MoMA came just before he turned fifty. Alicia Legg, who had started in 1949 as an assistant in the museum's library and worked her way up to curator, had developed the plan for this major exhibit. When LeWitt was working as a receptionist at the museum, the two had become friends, and, in the late 1970s when she was appointed an associate curator, she became a champion of LeWitt's work. "She was wonderful. She was very precise and very understanding," he recalled in 1993. "At that time Mr. [William] Rubin was the director, and he called me and asked me if I would do it [the show]. He said, 'Either you do it now, or the Museum is closing in '79 or so for renovation and then it would be years and years,' so I said I might as well do it."[21]

By that time, LeWitt had an enormous amount of work to consider for the exhibit but nothing to wear to it. He had had nearly half a century to purchase a sport coat or suit for such an affair. Nevertheless, as the opening night loomed, he had nothing appropriate in his closet. It was left to his cousin, Bernard LeWitt, who had come in for the show from Connecticut with various other relatives, to take him shopping to purchase a suede jacket.[22]

Whatever his shortcomings in attire, LeWitt had worked tirelessly to prepare the exhibit. It consisted of modular structures; serial structures; serial drawings; incomplete open cubes; and concepts for arcs,

     SOL LEWITT

circles, and grids, photographs, and other forms of art. Before he conceived more adventurous names such as *Swirls and Twirls* and *Loopy Doopies*, LeWitt stuck to a regimen of titling his wall drawings instructively. This show, for example, featured *Lines from the Midpoint of the Left Side of Two Facing Walls to Points on a Grid, Red, Yellow and Blue Lines from Sides, Corners and Center of the Wall to Points on a Grid*, and many other titles that will never compete with Botticelli's *The Birth of Venus* or Vermeer's *Girl with a Pearl Earing* for dramatic effect. But what they lacked in lyricism and allure, they compensated for in clarity.

In a *New York Times* article about the show titled "Jungle Gym for the Mind," Grace Glueck referred to a few prominent commentaries about LeWitt's work, both favorable and otherwise. For example, she quoted Kuspit's "The Look of Thought" essay. The works, she said, "seem to transcend the compulsion to create objects. . . . One spots their convergence toward an ideal meaning and one contemplates that."[23] The educator and critic Robert Rosenblum called the work "stunningly beautiful . . . with a logical rigor that implies the tonic, intellectual clarity of a Euclidean theorem."[24]

In his review of the show, the *New York Times* critic John Russell began with a certain degree of astonishment and incredulity:

> When *Cezanne: The Late Work* was nearing the end of its run at the Museum of Modern Art we wondered what on earth could take its place. Those rooms seemed stamped forever by that particular vespertinal genius. Cezanne had made them his own; to send in another artist after only a week or two would be like putting the place at Mycenae on the market when the walls were still streaked with the blood of Clytemnestra.
>
> The only solution was to make over the rooms to a kind of art that in no way sought comparison with Cezanne and yet conducted itself with a consistent dignity. Someone had to come forward and suggest not only that art had turned a new page but that it was "well worth our while to read on."
>
> This task (duty, honor, privilege — call it what you will) fell to Sol LeWitt. . . . As it is, he already — and on two quite separate counts — has his place in the history of art.[25]

Later in the review Russell compared LeWitt's intentions to those of Matisse, given that Matisse seldom did what was expected of him, moving on to new thinking and new directions even as critics and fans yearned for familiar approaches: "Above all, the wall drawings of Sol Le-Witt have solved all over again the problem of how to animate an entire room without falling back on the blandishments of personality."[26] And he ends the review with three words about the show that even an artist who is critical of critics must have welcomed: "Don't miss it."

In *New York* Thomas B. Hess wrote: "The whole system explodes in sunbursts of poetic intuition—or self-indulgent mush, depending on your preferences. Think of an equation, something binomial perhaps, or quadratic. Now substitute for one of the terms the archangel Michael, complete with fiery sword and peacock's wings. What began as a system for deductive reasoning becomes a work of art. An act of faith."[27]

Many of LeWitt's friends from earlier years didn't miss the show, and some were astonished to see how far their buddy had come. A dentist in West Hartford, Connecticut, Harold C. Richman, wrote the artist: "You may or may not remember me, but we grew up together in New Britain. I visited the Museum of Modern Art last week and was very excited to see that you have become one of America's foremost artists. . . . I would like to add my small praise to all the international acclaim you have already received. My wife always chides me about having come from New Britain, and doesn't believe that the two of us came out of the same melting pot."[28]

As it is now, it was then the custom of MoMA to ask artists to give lectures during the course of their exhibits. Though LeWitt by then was a veteran of the classroom, having taught occasionally at a variety of places under the kind of duress that accompanies a shy teacher who doesn't like to hear himself talk, he agreed to MoMA's wishes on the condition that his "lecture" be in the form of answering questions from the audience. As a result, audience members wrote down questions that were passed to the moderator, Bernice Rose. What is particularly notable in this brief excerpt from the transcript is that the questions asked seem quite different in nature from those art historians asked LeWitt. This prompted answers that LeWitt had not previously given:

Q: With all of the heavy thinking behind your work, is it all right if some of it just turns out beautiful?

SL: Oh, it's not so heavy and it's not so beautiful. I don't mind it. . . . If you think something is beautiful, somebody else may think it's banal. Those kinds of words don't really mean anything except to the person who uses them.

Q: [Can you ask] whether Mr. LeWitt drew on the walls when he
was younger, while growing up, and whether there was there any
correlation between his drawings and the kinds of graffiti that
one finds on public walls?

SL: I suppose I made a few passes at the wall with crayons when I
was a kid. Actually, I think if you live in New York City, you are in
a really great, rich area of art. When you look at the walls in the
city start with the subway cars — those are really beautiful. . . . The
graffiti on the walls of the city are really interesting. Because they
tell exactly what the people in the neighborhood are thinking. . . .

Q: [*The questioner wonders whether Mr. LeWitt would like it if
someone whistled and sang while Mr. LeWitt spoke*], because that
would be rather like people going to public walls and drawing or
painting on them when it might not be what he especially wanted
to see on the wall?

SL: Well, I don't know if it's a very good analogy. I don't take you
and march you up and put your nose up to a wall. The walls in
the city you can ignore them if you want, you don't have to study
them, you can walk by them, they're there. If you whistle, maybe
it will improve the performance here, I don't know. I wouldn't
want to limit your expressiveness. If you want to whistle go
right ahead.[29]

The catalogue for the MoMA show featured, of course, images of
LeWitt's work, and essays on his work (by Lippard, Rosenblum, and
Rose), as well as elements unusual for such a publication, including the
charge that LeWitt had stolen art leveled by the *Flash Art* ad and Le-
Witt's defense against it. The catalogue also reprinted what may seem
like an impertinent argument that had been presented nine years earlier, in which LeWitt had offered his own idea of a mission statement for
MoMA — which he thought had become too much of a repository of art
and was not active enough in helping create it.

As it turned out, the show and LeWitt's reputation benefited not only
from the customary forms of getting the word out but also from a very
different kind of exposure — the fertile mind of Woody Allen, or perhaps
the fertile memory of Diane Keaton.

In the early part of Allen's 1978 classic film, *Manhattan*, four characters — including those played by Allen and Keaton — are walking down
a street when the subject of the MoMA exhibit comes up. At this point,

Keaton is playing Mary, who is married to a man named Yale. Allen, playing Ike, is dating Tracy, a high-school student played by Mariel Hemingway.

> YALE (*to Ike*): You wanna go see the Sol LeWitts?
>
> IKE: Sure, that'd be fun. (*to Tracy*) You wanna see the Sol LeWitts too?
>
> MARY: (*overlapping*) You know, he's having an opening at the Modern soon. I was gonna, uh, do a piece on Sol for *Insights*. Do you know that magazine? It's a—you know, it's one of those little magazines. I mean, they're such schmucks up there. (*chuckling*) Really mired in thirties radicalism. (*looking at Tracy*) What do you do, Tracy?
>
> TRACY: I go to high school.
>
> MARY: (*chuckling and nodding*) Oh, really, really, hmm. (*aside, to Yale*) Somewhere Nabokov is smiling, if you know what I mean.
>
> YALE: (*laughing, to Ike*) I think LeWitt's overrated. In fact, I think he may be a candidate for the old Academy.
>
> MARY: (*interrupting*) Do you? Oh, really? (*laughing*) Oh, that's right, *we*—
>
> YALE: (*interrupting*) Mary and I have invented the, uh, Academy of the Overrated—
>
> MARY: (*interrupting*) That's right. (*she laughs*)
>
> YALE: —for, uh, such notables as . . .
>
> MARY: (*overlapping*) Such people as, uh . . .
>
> YALE: (*laughing*) Gustav Mahler.
>
> MARY: And Isak Dinesen and Carl Jung . . .
>
> YALE: . . . Scott Fitzgerald and . . . (*chuckling*) uh—
>
> MARY: (*interrupting*) Lenny Bruce. We can't forget Lenny Bruce—now, can we?
>
> YALE: (*laughing*) Lenny Bruce.
>
> MARY: And how about Norman Mailer and Walt Whitman and—
>
> IKE: (*interrupting*) I think those people are all terrific, everyone that you mentioned.[30]

A moviegoer at the time, particularly one who lived in the provinces, might have wondered at this conversation. And it is sometimes a mystery how dialogue ends up in Allen's films. He writes the basic dialogue but often it is trumped by actors who are encouraged to ad lib conversations that he often decides to retain in the final version. So what was the source of this scene? Allen might have known about the MoMA show, and so might Keaton. In the period after the exhibit, when LeWitt met the young woman who would become his second wife, he told her that he'd had two dates with Keaton.

LeWitt's friend Susan Ginsburg, who knew Keaton well, recalled that in the years before she made her mark as Annie Hall, Keaton was a constant presence in the circle of contemporary artists, and that "they all wanted her."[31] She was, Ginsburg said, hilarious at dinner parties and genuinely interested in what was happening in art: "She was an original — kind, cordial, compassionate. She was self-deprecating, too. She took the buses and subways, like all of us." But further details about whatever relationship Keaton had with LeWitt were never forthcoming from either of them.[32]

■   Of course, LeWitt's show at MoMA attracted his fellow artists, but the list went beyond those who were merely curious about his work. It included artists whose work had been championed by LeWitt in one or more ways. One of those ways was his idea that art should be accessible to all without having to fly to New York or pay the prices boosted by healthy (and necessary) commissions of gallery owners. It is for that reason that, along with Lippard and a few others, he had helped found Printed Matter, a nonprofit company established in 1976 that still distributes books containing the works of artists with the intention of promoting these artists and widening their audiences to people who can appreciate the work in the comfort of their homes.

In an interview in December 2006, Lippard said:

> My first vivid memory of Printed Matter is sitting in my loft with Sol LeWitt (in front of the coffee table he made me years ago, piled with a mess of books; he always remarked on it) and he came up with the idea of publishing artists' books. . . . Printed Matter was triggered by Sol's involvement in making artists' books which got no respect; dealers used them as freebies — bait to draw in collectors to buy the big stuff. We both took them more seriously and wanted them to become a real option for artists. (This was also a point in my own life when I couldn't sit down at a table with people without starting an organization. . . .)[33]

The first catalogue promoted works by, among others, Andre, Laurie Anderson, Ad Reinhart, Edward Ruscha, John Baldessari, Lawrence

Weiner, and LeWitt. Most of the books were available for as little as two dollars. At the time, the only books that contained the work of such artists were those published as exhibit catalogues — merely edited inventories of what the visitor sees — and available only to those able to make the trip to the exhibit.

As a result of the Printed Matter effort, artists began to think of books not only as a repository for their work, but to create a kind of "book art," work that is conceived to be displayed on pages rather than museum walls.

In 1976 in *Art-Rite* LeWitt wrote:

Artists' books are, like any other medium, a means of conveying art ideas from the artist to the viewer/reader, unlike most other media they are available to all at a low cost. They do not need a special place to be seen. They are not valuable except for the ideas they contain. They contain the material in a sequence which is determined by the artist. (The reader/viewer can read the material in any order but the artist presents it as s/he thinks it should be.) Art shows come and go but books stay around for years. They are works themselves, not reproductions of works. Books are the best medium for many artists working today. The material seen on the walls of galleries in many cases cannot be easily read/seen on walls but can be more easily read at home under less intimidating conditions. It is the desire of artists that their ideas be understood by as many people as possible. Books make it easier to accomplish this.[34]

Looking back on Printed Matter's early years, Ingrid Sischy said in a 2015 interview, "Sol LeWitt was the person I was waiting for all my life."[35]

By 1977, Sischy had seemed to lose her way professionally. She had grown up in South Africa and Scotland, and she had arrived in New York just as interest grew in feminism and gay rights. She had "a politically idealistic" education at Sarah Lawrence, after which she learned quickly the hard realities of making a living in the business of art: "It was as if I was shot out of cannon into the world. The first jobs I got were typical, get-your-feet-wet art-world jobs, but I would say disappointing."

She worked for a time in the subscription department of a company that printed newsletters for collectors. Her interest in writing, though, led to her taking a job in the public relations department at the Guggenheim Museum. "It was a bust," she recalled. "I stayed only a few weeks. The day I left I was very disappointed, and wondered, 'What am I going to do now?' I went home and the phone rang, and it was Sol LeWitt. He said, 'We're looking for a director of Printed Matter. Would you be interested?'"

At the time LeWitt was helping install his MoMA retrospective, so they met at the museum: "Sol was up on a ladder, and he came down and shook my hand." The two then went to the staff dining room, where "we had a great conversation." LeWitt told Sischy that the organization needed to have a nonprofit statement, and Sischy said she could help with that. He told her she would have to meet with the board, which she did. She was hired, though at a salary that was hardly up to New York standards, and she recalled, "Sometimes it was a big deal if [Printed Matter] made thirty bucks for the week." The paltry salary of the director was an issue that LeWitt addressed.

Sischy recalled: "One day I arrived at work and found a check on my chair, a personal check from Sol for $5,000. I called him and said, 'What is this?" He said, 'Listen, I know your salary is really low and I don't want you to struggle.' I tried to refuse the money, but he said if I did, he'd find my bank account and put it in anyway. I tried to pay him back later, but he never would accept it."

Under Sischy's leadership, Printed Matter attained nonprofit status, and the business grew and thrived. During her second year, however, she got a call from MoMA, offering her a curatorial fellowship. When she told LeWitt about it, he said, "That's great. You gotta take it." Then he added, "And you'll just have to run Printed Matter at night."

That is what she did—at night and on weekends, too. It was a back-breaking schedule, but she managed to keep it in part because of Le-Witt's example: "Sol knew that a human being can accomplish a lot." Indeed, Sischy took a good deal away from the experience with Le-Witt when she finally left Printed Matter to become the new editor of *Artforum.*

Her first issue was directly affected by her tenure at Printed Matter and the idea of getting the work of artists directly to art lovers without the viewers having to pay anything but a magazine's subscription price. "Sol was the first artist I thought of," she said. She asked him to produce a calendar for the back page, which he did, and she also gave four to six pages each to artists to fill however they chose to do so. This was a clear break from the previous *Artforum* formula, and it raised the magazine's profile even as it caught the attention of readers and drew the ire of traditionalists.

After working at *Artforum*, Sischy became editor in chief of Warhol's *Interview*, a magazine she stayed at for eighteen years. Then she became an international editor for Condé Nast, coeditor of the Italian and German versions of *Vanity Fair*, and a writer of wide influence. But even then, she said that LeWitt's influence had made all the difference: "His fundamental ideas about what art is, why it exists, why it matters to us allowed me to have faith in art. Sol was very humble but extremely ambitious in his pledge of allegiance and lifelong commitment to art. He set an example for me as a writer every day."

An exhibit at the 80WSE Gallery in Greenwich Village in 2014–15, titled *Learning to Read Art*, presented an overview of the history of Printed Matter and some telling details, though it certainly couldn't include everything because of the volume of materials. One element that it might have highlighted was the way that artists' egos manifested themselves even there. Lisa Liebman, who at the age of twenty-three came to work there under Sischy's tutelage, recalled a heated argument among artists over the order of listings in the index.[36]

By 1981, after Sischy's tenure had ended, the Printed Matter catalogue listed and promoted the work of more than a thousand artists, from (according to the alphabet, not any hierarchy) Martine Aballea, of Joinville, Le Pont, France; to Richard Zybert, of San Francisco, California. The books were usually priced from $1 to $5.95.

This is not to say that the business model was as well thought out as the images in the books were. Mike Glier, an artist who worked at Printed Matter in the early days, recalled: "There was not a strong business plan. It was all done out of love, not realism. We accept all artists' books [for distribution]. Quality was not an issue. Materials not an issue. Price not an issue. It was all part of Sol's vision for this. A lovely, inspiring idea, but as a business model it was bad."[37] Private money had to be found, and a lot of it came from LeWitt. Nancy Linn, who came to Printed Matter four years after it began, remembered that LeWitt gave $10,000 at one time, which was "quite a bit of money at the time." She said, "Fund-raising was the hardest project at Printed Matter."[38]

The place provided work for artists such as Glier and Linn, and also for those who wanted to pick up $100 by producing the window displays in the shop on Lispenard Street, in what eventually became known as Tribeca. These displays, as might be imagined, were individual creations that were not subject to change by the group, except on one occasion—after passersby and others objected to the clear image in the window of a swastika.

The boost that Printed Matter and LeWitt's support in general gave artists often went undocumented, but there are exceptions. After the 1997 death of Kathy Acker, a writer who used visual elements in her work (maps, Persian and Arabic script, and so on), Peter Wollen wrote in the *London Review of Books* that at one low point Acker sent her work to anyone who asked for it, at no charge.[39]

When she arrived back in New York toward the end of the 1970s, Acker quickly abandoned the world of the St. Mark's Poetry Project, her first port of call, for the downtown art world. It turned out that her mail art writings were already known to artists in New York and this, in turn, led to her first true publications, the chapbook editions of her Black Tarantula writings and *The Adult Life of Toulouse Lautrec*, with drawings by William Wegman.

Both publications were subsidized by LeWitt, who had them printed by a small artist's press in association with Printed Matter, the leading outlet for conceptual book art.[40]

Acker said:

> Sol went to Ted Castle and Leandro Katz—Ted is an art critic and Leandro a filmmaker—and he said he wanted to print these texts as real books. He basically became my patron. I didn't know who Ted and Leandro were—I thought they were part of the St. Mark's poetry scene—so I came back to New York and lo and behold it wasn't that scene at all. They had a party for my book and Joseph Kosuth and Keith Sonnier were there. I was absolutely flabbergasted 'cause I'd been reading *Artforum* regularly and worshipped these people. I don't think I could open my mouth all evening [a startling confession on Acker's part]. From then on I was just in the art world.[41]

LeWitt's own artist's books contain some familiar images, but they were tailored for the page. The books also include elements that haven't been seen on any museum wall or floor, including photographs, posters (such as *Sunrise & Sunset at Praiano*), and variations on the work of other artists as a way to pay tribute to them. And the books contain images from his life, as a sort of biography—even though the new person who came into view is not pictured.

Those artists whose careers were boosted by books or by LeWitt's personal interest (and investment) in their work never forgot his generosity, and over the years many would try to repay it.

In the late 1970s Philip Glass, whose early scores had been purchased by LeWitt, was working with Lucinda Childs on a new piece for her dance company. The two had previously collaborated on *Einstein on the Beach*, which had debuted in 1976. Now they had a new idea, a piece simply and audaciously titled *Dance*. That title represented Childs's preference for a particular kind of dance, one reliant more on form and design than on the traditional form that audiences had been accustomed to seeing and adoring. Of course, Childs was not trying to disappoint audiences; she hoped, as any choreographer would, that her work would be successful by any measure, including how it was received. But as a disciple of Merce Cunningham, she had pushed beyond boundaries to the point where her dancers often performed with no music at all and in unusual places, such as on rooftops or in church basements. *Dance*, however, would have music by Glass and would certainly be performed on traditional stages, first in Europe and then in the United States, with its American premiere at the Brooklyn Academy of Music. Childs and Glass hoped that LeWitt could provide the set design.

The two came to see him on Hester Street, where he was watching a football game on television. During the conversation, LeWitt occasionally consulted the screen to see what the score was. He wasn't interested in being a set designer, he said: "What would be the point of my involvement? Wouldn't a visual artist be redundant?" The point of a dance, he said, is for the audience to focus on the dancers. As Childs recalled the meeting, "He was firing himself from the job."[42]

A few weeks later, Childs had the idea of making a film of the dance as part of the overall performance, though she had no specific ideas about what to do or how to do it. She and Glass mentioned this to LeWitt, who responded that he would like to produce and direct the film. "Lucinda and I were completely surprised," Glass said. "He'd never made a film before. So there was a moment of silence. We thought he'd want to do the lights, or the props, but not this."[43] Even so, Glass considered Childs to be a "structuralist," a choreographer who had the ability to display the essence of dance simply and directly, so it made sense to engage someone who had done that in another art form.

LeWitt's idea of how to do the film was to project the dancers, whose action had been recorded in rehearsal, on a scrim as they danced live

on stage, to create a double image. Lacking the experience of directing
without help, he hired a filmmaker, Lisa Rinzler, who shot the dance
action during rehearsals, and then the two of them edited the film so
that it could be projected. LeWitt at first thought it might work best if
the projection, showing the dancers large, appeared on panels next to
or above the stage. But Childs had a better idea, using a scrim through
which the live action could be seen while the projected images mirrored what was happening on stage.

LeWitt told Childs: "I was not interested in doing the sets or décor
but wanted to do something of equal status with music and dance. I
had never done work with film before but had an idea of simultaneous
images from different viewpoints."[44] It was something, he said, like the
idea of televised sporting events, where different views of the same play
would be shown.

Though LeWitt had no experience with film, he had shown the ability a decade earlier to understand and break down stage action. In 1969,
when he was doing a lot of work for *Harper's Bazaar*, he created a visual
interpretation of a three-minute play by Samuel Beckett, *Come and Go*,
which had a modicum of action and a great deal of silence (not uncommon in Beckett's work).

LeWitt recalled: "The major problem came with the musicians. In
order for the film shots (overhead, from left, right and center) to work
they had to coordinate with the action on the stage exactly. Even a small
deviation would not work. The dancers would be doing different things
on stage and on the scrim. They had to be an exact replica of each other.
With live music this would not be possible. The musicians objected to
using 'canned' music. We compromised by doing three dances with the
scrim and two without."[45]

LeWitt's letter praised Glass and Childs as being easy to work with. He
wrote of Childs, "At some point in the piece I wanted to show Lucinda
as a personality. I doubt if I have ever seen a more beautiful woman and
wanted everyone to be aware of her. That is why I showed her, still, for
as long as possible (18 seconds)."[46]

At the time, Judy Padow had been dancing for Childs' company for
six years in addition to doing choreography with her own company. She
shared Childs's determination to expand the idea of dance, just as Glass
was doing with music and LeWitt with visual art. In her view, "Lucinda
made demands on the audience. She was concerned not with story, which
audiences love, but geometric patterns and special relationships."[47]

Elements of the work, without the film, were first staged in Europe, where the reception in the large cities was respectful—even at times enthusiastic. "Europeans were hungry for American art at that point," Padow said. "They understand going out on a limb."[48] Or as Glass put it, "pretty edgy stuff."[49] But some in the audiences of Europe had no interest in being on the edge. In France, one woman said, in a huff, "This is not music and this is not dance."[50] The most hostile response, though, was yet to come.

At the curtain call of the American premiere of *Dance*, the creators of the piece, including LeWitt, took a bow on the stage and were greeted by some enthusiastic applause and some eggs, hurled by unknown dissenters in the seats. LeWitt said, "Wow, *Sacre du printemps!*"[51] He, Childs, and Glass were not hit, but Danny McCusker, a young dancer, was directly in the line of fire and looked down to see a big splotch of yellow on his costume. "It was arts politics," Glass said in a 2015 interview.[52] In short, it indicated the passions involved whenever change—which is of course the essence of art—is perceived as a threat.[53]

A more objective observer, the *New York Times* critic John Rockwell, had a mixed reaction to *Dance*. He wrote: "To this taste, the work is a failure. But it is a fascinating failure, full of wonderful things, and the reasons that it fails are revelatory in a way that superficial successes sometimes are not."[54]

But when the show was performed later in the nation's capital, nothing but huzzahs were hurled at the creators. In a review in the *Washington Post*, Alan M. Kriegsman wrote, "a few times, at most, in the course of a decade a work of art comes along that makes a genuine breakthrough, defining for us new modes of perception and feeling and clearly belonging as much to the future as to the present. Such a work is *Dance*."[55]

At the end of the Brooklyn Academy of Music's five-performance run, each dancer was left with lasting memories and an original framed work by LeWitt. As invariably happened during his career, he had made drawings for his collaborators. So each person in the Childs company took home a different view, drawn in graphite, of dance floor patterns.

However, LeWitt never made another film or became involved in another live performance. Many years later he was asked to design a stage set for a Glimmerglass Opera production. He turned it down without even asking a question. When asked why, he said, "When I was doing *Dance* I learned I am not a team player."[56]

■ The woman who accompanied LeWitt to the premiere of *Dance* was, as she always liked to refer to herself, exactly what the artist was looking for in a partner: "An Italian girl with a driver's license."[57]

Carol Androccio was born in New Jersey, but she came from hardy Italian stock. Her grandmother owned the family's ancestral home in the town of Praiano on the Amalfi Coast, just a few miles from the much more famous tourist destination of Positano. Androccio had wanted to go to art school, but "my mother said 'no way.'" Instead she chose to attend the new Ramapo College in Mahwah, New Jersey, in part because of the "rebel priests" who taught there—Daniel and Philip Berrigan, anti–Vietnam War activists—and because of another member of the faculty, Carol Duncan, who was a scholar of feminist history.[58]

After she graduated, she got a job as an assistant to Chuck Close, whom she immediately impressed. He recalled, "Though she was wet behind the ears, she could get more done in two days than most people in a month." He also referred to her as "the single most competent person I've ever met."[59]

In the mid-1970s, Androccio had an internship at Artists Space, and it was during that period that LeWitt came to an opening there. He was still involved with Steir at the time. The day after the opening, he brought Androccio a drawing.

After Close lent Androccio's services to Robert Feldman—the owner of Parasol Press, a publisher of prints by artists—she visited LeWitt to arrange a printing and was intrigued by the man if not his living conditions. "I expected him to have a simple, minimal monastic kind of space," she said. "It was instead like the Collyer brothers [notorious hoarders in the 1940s]. He saved anything: old Con-Ed bills—anything that interested him, from Barnett Newman's obit to his friends' exhibit announcements, would get stapled to the wall. The bathroom was still the old factory bathroom, so the old the porcelain was gone."[60] Later on, when the two became close, she took it upon herself to replace the sink while LeWitt was away at an exhibit. On his return, he was incredulous. "Why'd you do that?" he said. "The sink was holding water just fine."

Androccio quickly learned that her new beau was not one to be impressed by appearances or inclined to be a consumer, except for his hunger to buy and trade for art, a passion she soon came to share.

The two went to Italy together, first stopping in Praiano to see her grandmother, Letizia Fusco, and to introduce her new beau. The age disparity between LeWitt and his newest girlfriend—twenty-eight years

—was so apparent that Androccio's grandmother asked her, "And so what does your father do?"[61]

Later, in the summer of 1979, Androccio spent time alone with her grandmother in Praiano. She had also fallen in love with the ancestral home and its tiers of gardens. The process of transferring the title to the property to her proved arduous, as reflected by a letter she wrote to LeWitt from Praiano on June 28, 1979, a letter that also points out LeWitt's financial support in this effort.

> Hi Sol–
>
> I got your card the other day. It was good to hear from the real world about real things like the Mets. It's very isolated here. You can't even buy the [*New York Herald-*] *Tribune*. So I have no idea what's going on, but if it is as usual, all the better. I also keep forgetting to wind my watch and clock, so I really don't know the time either. It is quite a novel way to live, but it suits me very well.
>
> The money arrived yesterday. Now I must wait for the lawyers to come. Unfortunately they won't tell me when so I get stuck here every day just waiting. Living with my grandmother is one step above camping, only dirtier! I don't feel I can say anything about how she has chosen to live . . .
>
> You know how much this house means to me. Right now I only have you to thank for it. Perhaps you'll get to share my happiness here. . . .
>
> To my surprise I'm getting along with my grandmother. Her health varies day to day, but the last few days she's been in bed. I wish there was something I could do, but there just isn't. She's an independent, tough character — wants things her way and her way only. I have much of that in me, too. Occasionally, we knock heads (mostly over my working in the gardens — she finds it intolerable). One thing I've gotten from her clearly is a strong, addictive love for this place.[62]

Family and friends noticed the way Carol Androccio affected LeWitt. His older cousin, Celeste LeWitt, reflecting on this in 2012, said: "There was a great personality change. . . . He seemed much happier, a joyous person, more communicative."[63]

Carol and Sol were married in 1982 in an ecumenical ceremony under a makeshift chuppah in the chapel at the United Nations, and held their reception in the Delegates Dining Room.

By then they had established what they thought might be their permanent home in Spoleto. New York had become too much, both in terms of socializing for LeWitt's taste and in terms of graduate students pummeling him for information they could use in their theses on contemporary art. Life, he said, was unmanageable in Manhattan. And he craved to live in a place where he couldn't speak the language. He would later say, "Leaving New York was for me at that time a good move because I thought that the American artistic scene was very narrow, and what I found in Italy was something much larger and bigger. . . . [The American scene] was narrow in its kind of ideology that had a lot of Calvinism [underlying it]. . . . It was moralistic."[64]

He later explained his decision in an interview with Gary Garrels:

There were two sets of reasons: one negative and one positive. The negative one was that when I traveled throughout the States and Europe people were very kind to me and eventually they all ended up being in New York. I could never say no to them, so my social life was a wreck and unmanageable. The positive is I managed to buy a small farmhouse in Italy, was in the process of renovating it, and got together with a young woman who became my wife later. We decided the best thing to do would be to move to Italy and live in that house, which we did.[65]

Even there, the private collection he was building, now with the help of Carol, expanded exponentially. Carol later recalled in an interview: "Sometimes he would buy things that we couldn't afford. He would just find a way to make it work. I remember he saw a Richter show of candle paintings at Sperone Westwater Fischer in the 1980s, and if he could then he would have bought the whole show. He did buy a painting. It was $10,000 at the time and a tremendous amount of money for us. But an incredible investment now if you look at it. But I'm sure that's not what he was thinking. That never would have occurred to him."[66]

The collection continued to be diverse. As Carol explained, "Sol was the great proletarian collector, everything from young people, artists that had little recognition, little value. None of that ever mattered to him."

There was always, in the back of his mind, and even considering his passion for Italy, the alternative of returning to Connecticut, but by 1981 the state, and particularly his hometown, had turned him away.

THIRTEEN

HOMETOWN BLUES

Andrea Miller-Keller, the mother of two small children, was finishing a master's degree in art history at Columbia University when, in 1974, James Elliott, the director of Hartford's Wadsworth Atheneum asked her to come to work at the museum. "You can do one of three things," Elliott told Miller-Keller in his pitch. "You can be the person in charge of renovations, or public relations, or work with the collection."[1] As it turned out, she would create a spot for herself that helped restore the museum's edge.

Miller-Keller recalled the time of her hiring: "My assignment when I first went there was to make checklists about English, French and Spanish paintings, and to run a seminar for Yale [University] grad students," with a work schedule flexible enough to allow for adequate child care.[2] She also wrote grant applications and was involved in a variety of other projects, including one that intersected over long periods with LeWitt, as she became one of his primary champions and, often, his defender.

Since the departure under duress of Chick Austin in 1945, the Atheneum had reverted to its old conservative ways. This view was verified when the sculptor Tony Smith, who knew Elliott from his days in California, visited Hartford. Sitting in Elliott's office, and looking at the artwork on the walls, Smith said, "I don't want to insult you. But your office is more interesting than your galleries."[3]

The effort that followed to give the museum more modern content resulted in Miller-Keller's writing a grant to start the Atheneum's new MATRIX Gallery, which would be devoted to the kind of art outside the comfortable traditions of staid Hartford. She asked LeWitt to design a poster for the MATRIX as a place of changing exhibits of contemporary art. The poster caused something of a stir. It was unlike the typical promotional poster, and "you couldn't see the message instantly," Miller-Keller recalled.[4] In addition, some people in the museum's hierarchy who didn't think much of LeWitt's wall drawings objected to his art in any case: "They said it must not be worth much if it gets painted out."

But it would be a few years yet before the real controversy began and LeWitt felt the sting of rejection — at which point Miller-Keller, who by her own estimation had started at the Atheneum "green,"[5] would step up as the curatorial champion of the artist whose wisdom and influence spread everywhere with the notable exception of his hometown.

■ In the early spring of 2015, construction had begun in Hartford to make part of its downtown more walkable by straightening Gold Street. In this effort, construction workers marked the route of electrical and utility lines below the ground with the use of bright orange spray paint. So the city woke up one morning with one of the country's most controversial installations of conceptual art defaced, the latest of a long list of insults. This was not an installation of LeWitt's, but it was one that would cost him dearly. If he had once kicked Carl Andre in the shins, Andre had unintentionally returned the favor.

Stone Field Sculpture, as it was formally called, and "The Rocks" as it would be popularly (or unpopularly) known, was a 1977 work by Andre, who had a large body of installations that made use of natural rather than man-made materials. The Hartford Foundation for Public Giving, as a birthday gift to itself and the city, had commissioned the sculpture for Hartford.

The foundation's first choice had been to commission a work by Richard Serra. However, he had turned down the offer because the site — a triangular piece of land adjacent to the Ancient Burying Ground and across from Bushnell Park, the oldest designed public parks in the United States — was too small for his taste. Andre was chosen next. He decided to build on the legacy of the adjacent ancient cemetery by creating a work in ancient stone. He used a total of thirty-six boulders, most dug out of a quarry in the nearby city of Bristol, arranged to point toward the park.

Though no public tax money was used to pay the artist's $87,000 fee for the sculpture, that didn't stop the public outrage over it, led by Mayor George Athanson. At the time the mayor was still angry about the previous installation on the Burr Mall between City Hall and the art museum, Alexander Calder's *Stegosaurus*, an enormous red abstract steel sculpture that suggested the basic shape of an extinct reptile but to Athanson was an eyesore. He permanently closed the blinds over his office window so he wouldn't have to look at it. Then, after Andre had finished his *Stone Field Sculpture*, the mayor declared it "just a bunch of rocks," and said that "little kids could do it."[6] Members of the public who felt that they had been taken joined him in this view. The brouhaha became so intense that payment for the work was held up for a time, until lawyers got involved and sorted everything out.

The legacy of this installation had a major effect on LeWitt shortly thereafter when the Hartford Civic Center, which contained shops and an arena that hosted professional hockey and basketball games, was being restored in 1980 after the arena's roof had collapsed under the weight of heavy snow. (Though the damage was major, no one was hurt because the incident occurred after midnight.)

Despite the lingering outcry about Andre's rocks, in reasonably short order the Hartford City Council approved taking $40,000 from the Civic Center reconstruction fund to use as part of an announced $100,000 fee for new art. Half of the commission was to come from the National Endowment for the Arts (NEA), and the balance from Connecticut's art commission—though as it turned out that contribution had to be augmented by a $10,000 pledge from the developer David Chase.

The plan was to install a large mural on a prominent wall of the new construction. The NEA organized the search for the right artist, and it quickly came up with the obvious choice—a wall drawing pioneer who happened to be a native of the city.

LeWitt agreed to provide a mock-up of the work for consideration. It emphasized three primary shapes (a triangle, circle, and square) in the three primary colors.

But as soon as his name was divulged by the commission, objections were raised by the editorial board of the *Hartford Courant*, the most influential newspaper in the state (founded in 1764, it still refers to itself as "the oldest continuously published newspaper in the United States").

Editorials ignored the international standing and innovations of a native son and railed against LeWitt's idea. (Indeed, some of the editorials referred to him as a New York artist and ignored his Hartford roots.) The plan was "a costly and inappropriate way to decorate the Civic Center," the board said. "Mr. LeWitt is not doing the city any favor by designing . . . a circle, a square, a triangle and two four-sided figures. Intellectual obscure art is fine for a museum or a public building or space where one has time to contemplate, but not for Hartford's hive of physical activity, its Civic Center Coliseum."[7]

In the summer of 1980, the newspaper published some of the nearly three hundred letters to the editor that it had received, most of them agreeing with the *Courant*'s stance.

Kathleen Fleming Reed, of Simsbury, wrote in part: "Art should reflect something about the people of the age, and in this case the murals will say it all—vanity, selfish arrogance, pride, and shameless waste of money and resources, in a time when many are struggling to keep a roof over their heads."[8]

As Hartford officials were feeling the heat from the public and the media, Paul Germaine-Brown, the city's arts coordinator, told the *Hartford Courant*, "We're getting the bargain of the century and people want to screw around with it."[9] Neverthless, the Hartford City Council, proposed an alternative plan and asked LeWitt to make one of his structures in the shopping area instead. The artist refused and pulled out of the project.

In a letter to the *Courant*, Germaine-Brown wrote, "I hold *The Courant* directly responsible. Sol saw those editorials. He was deeply hurt by those editorials," which the arts coordinator called "vicious—absolutely vicious."[10]

LeWitt said nothing publicly. He let his new business agent, Susanna Singer, issue a statement instead. It said in part: "Sol is not angry at anybody. He just doesn't want his work to make people angry."[11]

However, those who knew him well at the time and even many years later had no doubt that the anger was there. He was simply determined to reveal it to no one but intimates.

Miller-Keller, who by then had worked often with LeWitt and who promoted his work tirelessly, said, "He quietly and with characteristic dignity walked out on these clowns."[12]

Perhaps it was fortunate that LeWitt wasn't in the Darling Room of the Wadsworth Atheneum in the fall of 1980, when the museum was considering the purchase and installation of its first LeWitt wall drawing. One of museum's curators, William Hosley, attended the meeting of the collections committee. Sage Goodwin, one of the city's patriarchs who was both on the committee and a member of the board, exemplified the kind of conservative attitudes so common in the Insurance City, which made its fortune on minimizing risk.

"I remember that Andrea Miller-Keller made her presentation," Hosley said in 2013:

By then Sol was already famous, and so she didn't have to go into that. My impression was, though, that Sage Goodwin had a sense of entitlement, [as] the scion of an illustrious family. He was unflinching in his objection to this acquisition. It had nothing to do with content. It had everything to do with form. If it had been a Cleve Gray color field picture, when you got tired of it, you could sell it. But the fact that you were buying these instructions was something he couldn't grasp.[13]

Indeed, Goodwin felt so strongly about it that when the committee decided to buy the drawing in spite of his opposition, he resigned from the board.

Miller-Keller would spearhead the museum's retrospective of LeWitt, a show that would prove his critics wrong. In September 1981, when LeWitt's first retrospective outside of New York opened in Hartford, the *New York Times* sent a reporter, Ann Barry, with a calculator. Barry wrote that the installation of LeWitt's work at the museum required 2,000 worker hours (more than eighty days of labor), 2,000 pencil leads, and 1,000 crayons. One drawing alone, the plans of which were borrowed from London's Tate, required 54,000 lines of various lengths to be drawn, an equivalent of fifty-one linear miles.[14]

To prepare for the show, Miller-Keller wrote dozens of artists asking for comments to include in the catalogue, a measure that could help provide a proper welcome for the man who had been rejected by Hartford just a year earlier. The responses arrived quickly and were generous. Stephen Antonakos said that "Sol's wall drawings can go on forever." Andre commented, "but more important to me is the ravishing beauty which Sol so often attains." And Gene Beery asked, "Is this the beauty of science or the science of beauty?"[15]

Miller-Keller felt that the 1981 retrospective represented a breakthrough for LeWitt, "an incredible departure" from past practices: "Everything until then had been flat. Here, he had a three-dimensional cube on the wall" and a burst of color.[16]

But the show also demonstrated that when installing work by LeWitt, the usual practices in the business of art were seldom involved. Of course, museums need to get sponsors for such large exhibits, and these have typically been local corporations that want to attach their names to cultural events and thereby enhance their brands.

In Hartford, one of the biggest sponsors of cultural events was United

Technologies (UTC), one of the country's leading manufacturer in the aerospace and related industries. The Fortune 500 company gave a great deal of money over the years to support the arts in the city. And in the case of LeWitt's retrospective, it was eager to participate and provide much-needed cash.

When Tracy Atkinson, then the director of the Wadsworth Atheneum, told Miller-Killer the happy news about UTC, she replied, "I don't think Sol's going to like that."[17] She said this because a significant portion of the company's business was producing weapons and war materiel.

Atkinson was in a squeeze, obviously. He spoke with LeWitt—who, as Miller-Keller had anticipated, had a negative reaction. She recalled: "Then Tracy tried to argue that only 18 percent of UTC's output is armaments. Sol replied, 'That's 18 percent too much for me.'"[18] Atkinson had to look elsewhere for the funding.

This was just one of the times when Miller-Keller ran up against LeWitt's unbending opinions. A decade after the retrospective, for example, the Atheneum's MATRIX Gallery was planning an exhibit of works by Ian Hamilton Finley, a British poet, artist, and garden designer. LeWitt had some of Finley's work in his collection but objected to Miller-Keller's plans. Finley had been commissioned to do a sculpture for the gardens at Versailles, but a French magazine published a piece about the artist's use of Nazi symbols in his work, and the French press picked up the story. For a 1982 project in the garden at Spandau Prison, Finley had corresponded with Albert Speer, Hitler's architect,[19] and had produced work for his *Third Reich Revisited* series. His intent was not to pay homage to the Nazi era and its horrors, but simply to use a piece of iconography to make a point, as artists are wont to do. LeWitt, an artist who clearly believed in artistic freedom, apparently could draw a definitive line. He urged Miller-Keller and her colleague in the MATRIX project, John B. Ravenal, to cancel the exhibit. "Sol was adamant," Miller-Keller recalled. "And, in general, there was a lot of accusatory stuff going around. People were riled up. They got Sol riled up."[20] When she visited him in Spoleto, he told her, "I don't want you to do that show." Finley had obviously run up against what other artists, playwrights, filmmakers, and writers had: the view that art is art and should be seen and experienced as that, unless it evoked horrors of the Holocaust, in which case it became deeply insulting and even, in the view of many people, potentially dangerous, fanning the lingering flames of anti-Semitism. Miller-Keller, herself Jewish, was not indifferent to this argument, yet she told LeWitt, "I have to do it." In spite of that, she re-membered "being up in the middle of the night, looking out of a win-dow and seeing a storm, and thinking, 'How can I not listen to Sol?'" Nevertheless, she produced the show, which contained no Nazi sym-bols. And Miller-Keller and LeWitt maintained their deep friendship, LeWitt deferring to her strong sense of principles.

One of the staff members at the Atheneum at the time was Mark Rosenthal, who would later hold positions at the Guggenheim and the National Gallery of Art and who, like Miller-Keller, would have to deal with LeWitt's ethics.

Rosenthal was involved in the 1990s plans for a LeWitt work, a con-crete brick structure for the Guggenheim's abstraction retrospective. Rosenthal had seen LeWitt's work in concrete for the first time and "was overwhelmed by it," he said in a 2012 interview.[21] He thought a piece by LeWitt would be ideal for the Guggenheim show, and in time the ar-rangement was made to give the resulting piece a very prominent spot —in front of the museum. Everyone coming in would see it. And every-thing seemed to be going well: "Sol was excited. I was thrilled." But, as testing was being done to see if the sidewalk could withstand the weight of the concrete, the matter of who would pay for the exhibit came to the fore.

Rosenthal recalled: "Philip Morris came through with an immense grant that made the show possible."[22] The cigarette company, with other tobacco firms under attack because of the deleterious health effects of its products, had become a major funding source for such projects as it tried to upgrade its image. But it was also a major funder of Senator Jesse Helms, not only a vocal enemy of the NEA but also a man who had clung to his anti–civil rights stance, earning the nickname "Senator No."

"We were all of us over the top, feeling great," Rosenthal recalled, be-cause with the grant there was no doubt that the show could be mounted. "But then somebody told me I should speak to Sol. I told him [about the Philip Morris funding], and he had a stricken look on his face. He had once before pulled out of a show because he learned that the cigarette company had been a sponsor, and so [he] said, 'I withdrew once and I don't see how in good conscience I can not withdraw again.' He didn't make a decision then and there."[23] There were, of course, a lot of things to consider. One of them was the prestigious spot he'd been offered, on the sidewalk of Fifth Avenue. Another was the damage he might do to the show itself and to artists who were depending on it. "But," Rosenthal said, "Sol called me back a couple of days later and said, 'I just can't do it.'" Rosenthal tried to argue with LeWitt, talking about the realities of funding and even acknowledging that it was blood money, or guilt money—but money all the same. LeWitt was not moved and held to his decision to withdraw.

That episode was far from the only time that LeWitt turned down significant money because of his convictions. In the early 1980s, Chase Manhattan Bank, whose CEO was David Rockefeller, wanted to commission a LeWitt wall drawing for its main office. According to Singer, LeWitt said he wouldn't sell anything to Rockefeller because of Chase's loans to South Africa's apartheid government. Singer argued that Rockefeller "really loves your work." To which LeWitt replied, "I didn't say he was stupid."[24]

■ For many years by then, LeWitt had been able to rely on the wiles and business skills of Singer, whom he usually spoke to at least five times a day—but she had never imagined herself in such a position.

Singer had been hired in 1975 at the age of twenty-three to be a secretary at John Weber's gallery. When she asked for a raise, Weber asked if she would like to be the gallery director. She said, "I'm not qualified."[25] He replied, "I'll help you." Nevertheless, Singer considered herself too shy and felt that she "knew nothing."

Eventually she took the job and ended up forging a close relationship with LeWitt. Before that, she'd become a fan of his. "People told me I'd love Sol, but I didn't expect to like him."[26] When she did meet him, "he treated me the same, as a secretary, as he treated the director." When she became the director, he sent her a postcard that said, "Congratulations on your new job. Let me know if I become a pain in the ass." Singer became, in effect, LeWitt's firewall: "He worked alone in his studio. I managed everybody else so he could be alone."

When LeWitt was installing the Museum of Modern Art (MoMA) exhibit, Singer recalled, "I made him call me every afternoon to tell me how the day went."[27] In the years after the show, Singer said, people thought that LeWitt had seemed very confident and self-assured. But she recalls his sense of vulnerability during that period: "He wasn't as secure as people think." But then, when the show opened, Singer recalled, "People were shocked at how spectacularly beautiful it was."

In 1980, Singer went for a time to her parents' house in the Berkshires. LeWitt called her there. His business affairs had become increasingly complicated, particularly since the attention the MoMA show had attracted. Singer told him that he needed to find the right person to set the prices for his art, arrange logistics, and so on. She recalled: "I told him I'd think about it [who the right person would be]. He said, 'No, that's you.'"[28] So from 1980 to the end of LeWitt's life, Singer was the person he talked to most often every day, generally more often than he did to members of his own family.

The two of them worked out a way to market his work that departed from the usual. That is, normally the physical work of art and the documentation that authenticates it and its sale become the elements of a transaction. But in the case of a LeWitt wall drawing, for example, the only element of value, technically and in reality, is the documentation. If a wall drawing lasts for a century, it is only because the owner has not sold the certificate to someone else and had his or her own work destroyed.

Without the documentation, the drawing is worthless, even if a buyer has paid a lot of money for it — a circumstance that would lead to court cases even after the artist's death.

■   For Sol and Carol LeWitt, life in Spoleto held many charms. Sol was treated well by the local populace, and his commissions proliferated. Carol, too, seemed to thrive. She started a business with her friend Alessandra Bonomo, opening a wine shop called Vino, and she would also begin with Carol Venezia a business called Ceramica, which marketed the products of local artisans. The LeWitts' first child, Sofia, was born in Spoleto in 1983, and their second, Eva, was born two years later in the same city. The names were a nod to history, family, and other loved ones. Sol's mother, though called Sophie, was originally named Sofia. And he had a cousin named Eva — though of course by giving his second child that name, he would also be honoring the memory of Eva Hesse.

The time in Italy was tranquil and productive for Sol and Carol both at work and at home. Sol had had a professional breakthrough. He told Gary Garrels in 2000: "I had reached a turning point in my art thinking. I decided I would make wall drawings with ink, and then with colored ink. My crew invented a technique of painting the wall with water-based paint and having the ink be absorbed by this paint. I could cover a large wall in a short time. That was about the time I was moving to Italy and had been exposed to large great paintings on the wall. It was a confluence of ideas and the nature of my life."[29]

Sol and Carol followed much the same routines as they had in the States. Sol worked his usual hours, and Carol, as always, threw herself headlong into her own enterprises.

During the summertime, the LeWitts swam daily at the public pool in nearby Terni during the hours it was available, after 7:00 P.M. — a time that annoyed the artist, who preferred afternoon exercise. In the winter, he was able to keep to his preferred schedule, swimming after working hours at the pool in Feligno and then having lunch with their friends, Afranio and Ann Wood Metelli.

Up until the birth of Sofia, the LeWitts had had few, if any, discussions about religion. Sol didn't appear to be interested; he remained a secular Jew, as had most of his extended New Britain family. And though Carol's background was Italian Baptist and she had grown up in the church, she was no longer interested in it. After the birth of Sofia, however, something changed. The LeWitts' housekeeper kept asking where and when her baptism would take place. At that point Sol sent a telegram to New Britain and asked his relatives to go to one of the local jewelry stores and purchase a small Star of David necklace. When it arrived in Spoleto, he put it around Sofia's neck. There would be no doubt that his children would be raised Jewish, and Carol had no objection.

The photographer Vera Lutter was a frequent guest during the LeWitts' years in Spoleto, and she recalled LeWitt's passion for the environs of the city: "He and Leila [his dog] would walk over the aqueduct to town. Italy's heating systems weren't so great, and in the fall he loved the smell of the wood fire in the cold air. He often talked about that. And it was the exact same thing for me. You're outside in the dark. It's both lonely and connected."[30]

As Sofia and Eva grew, Sol took them on walks. On one occasion with Eva (who was not yet three years old), he applied his artistic thinking (theme and variations) to parenting. When she began to run in the woods, he said, "Don't run." When she didn't heed him, he said, "And if you run, don't fall." Still, the girl seemed to have a mind of her own. He said, "And if you run and if you fall, don't hurt yourself." Eva wasn't listening. He said finally, "And if you run and if you fall and if you hurt yourself, don't come crying to me."[31]

During the time the family was in Italy, LeWitt responded in detail to letters and questions from his Hartford curator, Miller-Keller. LeWitt found the exchanges difficult. On November 6, 1983, he wrote: "I've battled your questions. My answers I hope are not too terse. It's hard to remember what I thought years ago. Try to keep my mind on what I'm doing now. That is why I don't like to do shows that include old work."[32]

The letters have served as effectively as any of LeWitt's formal interviews over the years to clarify his thinking about his work, and how it developed.

For example, Miller-Keller asked about the origin of the wall drawings, and whether LeWitt thought they would be marketable commodities. He responded: "I didn't think about selling them, but it wasn't a 'gesture' as an anti-market ploy either. I never think about selling a work while doing it. Afterwards it was just another 'thing.' Anyway, no one knows what will sell or not."[33]

Many of Miller-Keller's questions drew LeWitt out about his decisions on the use of color, which at the time was becoming more and more important to the artist. She wrote: "Your introduction of secondary colors in the Florida (Miami-Dade) wall drawing (#344) was a surprise. Was this a spontaneous decision or one given much prior consideration? What led you to introduce orange, purple and green in this direct way?"[34]

LeWitt's answer: "It is logical to use six colors with six figures. The circle, the square and the triangle, are to me more basic than the rectangle, trapezoid and parallelogram, and red, yellow and blue more basic than orange, purple and green."[35]

In Italy, the LeWitts expanded their art collection in ways other collectors couldn't because many excellent European artists at the time (Hanne Darboven, Shirazeh Houshiary, and Giulio Paolini among them) did not have much exposure in the United States.

Conducting the business of art in Italy, however, was more difficult than it was back home. Sophie Clark, who handled administration, shipping, and correspondence for LeWitt in Spoleto, recalled in a 2015 interview:

I tried to do what I could to help out, though I had no experience in this. He knew it was a difficult situation in Italy, but he wasn't the sort of person who got upset at problems. Italians don't respect time lines. They're inevitably doing things thirty seconds before they need to be done. Sol was never that kind of person. He was very methodical. So [the] interface between two aspects of reality could be difficult. There were other difficult aspects, too. One time there was a collector who negotiated with Sol to have a large wooden cube built on his property. The man wound up wanting to pay only 80 percent of the price. The cube was supposed to be five meters by five meters. So Sol said, "OK, I'll make it four by four."[36]

Clark remembered that above all LeWitt was very practical: "When artists were sitting around complaining about the world and collectors, he would say, 'You shouldn't criticize them too much because [instead of collecting art] they could be collecting tin soldiers.'"[37] She also recalled conversations that involved Carol, who, she said, "wanted Sol to put everything in the hands of a large international gallery, the best way to have dealings all over the world." But he always maintained his independence, working with a variety of galleries and making no exclusive deal. To Clark, LeWitt seemed very secure.

During his time in Spoleto, LeWitt continued to support artists. In one case at least, he also inspired someone to paint a portrait in a new way. Robin Heidi Kennedy, who moved there in 1982, recalled: "Sofia had this little white dress that she loved. She wore it for a photograph, and [her parents] showed me the picture, and I said it would be great to do a portrait of her."[38] But the work didn't turn out as she hoped. "Kids have a tendency to look like cemetery statuary," she said. "Then I thought, wait a minute, Sol was always saying do what you can do, not what you can't do. He was always giving me freedom. The dress was fantastic, even if the rest of portrait wasn't working. So I chopped off the arms and legs and head. Suddenly [the portrait] was just beautiful. They hung the portrait in the house. Sofia was relieved she didn't have to look at herself."

Kennedy also recalled that although LeWitt found a great measure of comfort in Italy, he didn't alter his social habits to acknowledge this: "Sol walked everywhere in Spoleto and always took his dog, Lilla. Sometimes we'd walk together, along with my dog, Booboo. One time Sol was in a show in Perugia, and he didn't want to go. I said, 'Don't worry. I'll go and I'll take your dog.' So I did that. I told them Sol couldn't come, but his dog was free to do so."[39]

■ The time the LeWitts spent in Italy, however productive and comfortable, would also be a time of grieving and suspicion, inaugurated by a phone call from New York to Spoleto in the late summer of 1985.

Seven months earlier, the LeWitts had attended the wedding of Andre and Ana Mendieta. It was his third marriage and her first. Ana had become close to Carol, who liked the spunk, warmth, and the artistic talent of the Cuban immigrant. Mendieta had become one of her dearest friends. Carol admired her strength and her fiery Latin spirit. Alhough she didn't have children of her own, Mendieta charmed Sofia and Eva. Lucy Lippard said of Mendieta, "She was a little fireball, and a little bit neurotic."[40] Lippard said that when Mendieta was about to go to Cuba to visit her family, she knocked on Lippard's door "and she gave me a shopping bag, and said, 'Take care of my revolutionary soul. And be nice to Carl—he'll be lonely.'" Inside the bag was a clay piece that featured a hammer and sickle.

In a short time—Mendieta was only in her mid-thirties—she had won two grants from the NEA and the Guggenheim Museum, and her work was being celebrated around New York to the point where Lippard asked her, "Aren't you going to save anything for your old age?"[41] It was a question that later seemed prescient.

Andre and his new bride took up residence in an apartment on the thirty-fourth floor of a building on Mercer Street. They were described by friends as a couple very much in love, but their passion sometimes turned rowdy and drunken, and seemed to be on the edge of violence. In 1980 in Seattle, both were arrested for public intoxication. In New York, patrons of a New York pizzeria witnessed a scene in which Andre threatened Mendieta. In early September 1985, the relationship became more heated and troubled. Then on Sunday, September 8, the police department received a phone call at 5:29 A.M.:

OPERATOR: Police. Where's the emergency?
CALLER: Yes. My wife has committed suicide.
OPERATOR: Say again.
CALLER: My wife has committed suicide.
OPERATOR: Where are you calling me from, ma'am [*sic*]?
CALLER: I'm calling from 300 Mercer Street, apartment 34E.
OPERATOR: 34E?
CALLER: Yes,
OPERATOR: What floor are you on?
CALLER: Thirty-four.
OPERATOR: On the thirty-fourth floor?
CALLER: Yes.
OPERATOR: OK, and what's the telephone number you're calling
    from?

    SOL LEWITT

CALLER: 533–2609.

OPERATOR: OK. Uh, what happened exactly?

CALLER: What happened was we had — my wife is an artist and I'm an artist, and we had a quarrel about the fact that I was more, uh, exposed to the public than she was and she went to the bedroom and I went after her and she went out of the window.

OPERATOR: She jumped out of the window. How long ago did this happen?

CALLER: Oh, I don't know, I don't know, I don't know. It was — I don't know.[42]

The investigation that followed was intense. Police and prosecutors learned about incidents in which the couple had been demonstrably cruel to each other and came to the conclusion that Mendieta had not jumped but had been pushed. They brought a charge of second-degree murder against Andre. There was a media frenzy, not only because of the gruesomeness of Mendieta's death but also because the case provided a rare glimpse into the intimate lives of artists — particularly artists who were a part of a new and controversial movement. Andre made the cover of *New York*, though it was against his wishes, and the photo that was used had been taken on the street by a photographer who had violated LeWitt's and Andre's view that personal publicity was to be avoided for an artist. But of course when an artist is charged with a heinous crime, he gives up the right to privacy.

In Spoleto, the night of the death coincided with the birth of the LeWitts' second child, Eva. The news from Mercer Street seemed to turn the world upside down. "Sol was out of his mind," recalled Marilena Bonomo.[43] The LeWitts wondered aloud to each other about Andre's culpability, and in the months that followed the art world was split between those who supported Andre's story and those who felt that he had committed murder.

The memorial service for Mendieta was held at the Latin American Center in Manhattan. Some of the mourners, including Lippard, were surprised that Andre was there. Some greeted him, offering condolences, and some stayed away from him, keeping to the back rows.

Before the trial began, Andre became an outcast in the US art world. No gallery or museum in the United States would schedule an exhibit of his work, but in Europe it was a different story. In 1987, he had three museum shows in Italy and the Netherlands and group shows in Germany and Switzerland. The German show also included work by LeWitt and set up something of a confrontation.

According to Robert Katz, author of *Naked by the Window: The Fatal Marriage of Carl Andre and Ana Mendieta*, Andre was pleased to be back with part of his old crowd—Konrad Fischer and his wife, Dorothee, were there, too—and he had lunch or dinner with the LeWitts during the days they were all in Münster. Katz wrote: "Carol, however, found it hard going, growing very upset at being with Carl and the Fischers, everyone, including herself, avoiding mention of Ana. . . . It was bad enough to pretend that she had never existed, but, thought Carol, it was presumptuous, even a presumption of guilt, to act as if Carl wasn't suffering."[44] When the group went to a farewell dinner in Düsseldorf, Carol became direct, as was her general mode of operation. Katz wrote:

> Both Sol and Carol had strong feelings about how passions might have gone haywire that night, but the feelings, and their love for Ana, came with compassion for Carl and refusal to sit in judgment. Carol had always been uncomfortable with Carl, afraid of him, finding him intimidating, but when toward the end of the meal she could bear all the make-believe no longer, she worked up the courage to bring it out in the open.
>
> "You know, Carl," she said while the table fell silent, "it's so hard for me to be with you, just because I miss Ana so much, and I really am looking forward for this to be over so we can mourn her." To Carol, it seemed that Carl almost cried as he said, "I really need to do that." She believed him, and she believed that he truly had loved Ana.[45]

When the murder trial began, the media frenzy resumed. Andre's lawyer, the savvy Jack Hoffinger, knew little about art and museums but had for a very long time been working in criminal courtrooms. He urged Andre to waive his right to trial by jury and instead have the matter decided only by a judge. A jury, no doubt, would be much affected by the sympathetic portrait prosecutors would paint of Mendieta, standing no more than four feet ten inches tall and being a warm, if temperamental, artist making her way in the world. In contrast the judge, Alvin Schlesinger, would focus much more on matters of law, and on the state's meeting its burden of proving guilt—not merely suggesting it from the evidence. This turned out to be a winning strategy, and in February 1988, Andre was acquitted of murder.

■ By the time of Andre's trial, the LeWitts had decided that Spoleto would become a refuge, once again—a place to go to but not to live permanently. Sol had once said to Carol, "I'll live the rest of my days in Italy," but he'd changed his mind.[46] "Sol didn't want his children to have a provincial Italian education, "Carol recalled in 2015. So they made plans to move back to the United States, though they kept both the house on the hill and the studio in town, places they would return to often.

"I had wanted to move to Rome, or to the Upper West Side in New York—that was my solution. But for Sol, Connecticut was always home. There was no question but that we'd move there, though we didn't know where," Carol recalled.[47] "Connecticut, at the time, had a real estate boom. We started in Litchfield County [a rural retreat where many of Sol's friends from the city had purchased homes]. When I told [the real estate agent] our budget, he said, 'Don't bother, Madam, there's nothing for you.'"

The LeWitts were invited to lunch in Durham by John Paoletti, an art history professor at Wesleyan University. "At that time, Chester had been voted Connecticut Town of the Year," Carol recalled, "but John was knocking Chester and said, 'Who'd want to live in a town with a French restaurant?'[48] He was pitching Durham, but that's where big farms had been turned into housing developments. That's the kind of town I grew up in in New Jersey. I said, 'I'm not going to move to this place. Let's go look at Chester.'"[49]

Chester's geography is different from that of most Connecticut towns. Its downtown, a modest but cozy array of storefronts with apartments over them, is unusual in that it is not situated on a state highway but nested between two of them, so in many ways it looked like it had decades earlier. Back then, it was referred to derisively as "Dogtown" by residents of other nearby communities, who considered it a dowdy place compared particularly to nearby Essex, where captains of industry and yachts ruled every summer. But that image has slowly changed.

When urban development was the rage in the 1960s, Chester turned down grants that would have required the razing some of its downtown, so the character of the neighborhood never changed and chain stores were not invited in.

Because of that and of its French restaurant, Restaurant du Village, it was becoming a hotter location, particularly for writers and artists, as well as a tourist destination. To be sure, the town had residents who had descended from people who long before had settled the community, which was incorporated in 1636. But in the 1960s, new families from New York City and other places began to move in. Barbara Delaney, former managing editor of *Antiques*, and her husband, Edmund, a prominent Manhattan lawyer, started the local historical society and a series of classical music concerts. Peter Good and his wife, Janet Cummings Good, established a graphic design business. The artist Richard Ziemann, who had taught at Yale and whose elaborate etchings of trees were in the collections of such institutions as the Art Institute of Chicago, had a house on Maple Street. Jack and Sosse Baker had opened the Chester Gallery on Main Street. David Hays, a retired Broadway set and lighting designer and founder of the National Theatre of the Deaf, lived in the town's small center with his wife, Leonora, who had been a prominent modern dancer in New York. Max Showalter, an actor who had first come to Chester in 1958 to make the film *It Happened to Jane* with Doris Day and Jack Lemmon, had stayed because of the Chester's charm. Constance Baker Motley, known for her pioneering work on civil rights, had a home there. William L. Schaefer established a company that specialized in vintage photographs — including the work of Berenice Abbott, Ansel Adams, Margaret Bourke-White, Dorothea Lange, and Walker Evans, among many others. Morley Safer, a correspondent for *60 Minutes*, was a weekend resident, a fact that would create something of an impediment to LeWitt's sense of well-being in Chester.

The Lunch Box cafe was open for coffee and political discussion at 5:30 each morning. It was true that Chester, compared to its ritzier neighbors, could have been seen as an odd choice for the LeWitts, but they loved the feel of the town, its residents' pride in the place, and even the wryness shown in the semi-official town slogan, seen on many bumper stickers: "Chester, CT: We Know Where It Is."

The intimate village atmosphere was perfect for the LeWitts because, since Sol didn't drive, he needed to live close enough to the center of a community (as he had in Spoleto) to walk there in the mornings. In rejecting other communities, he had told Carol, "I can't raise our girls in a town where you can't buy a magazine." Chester had a grocery store, a bank, and a pharmacy. Carol recalled in 2015, "If we had moved to Killingworth [an adjacent town without that kind of center], he would have been pacing at my bedside waiting for me to drive him to get the *New York Times*."[50]

The LeWitts found a large old colonial house on Pratt Street that was "a mess," Carol recalled.[51] Formerly the parish house for St. Joseph Church, it had been situated on the Middlesex Turnpike before being moved to the lot on Pratt Street by the previous owner years before. Despite its condition, it had many advantages over other houses available in Chester. For one thing, the 1820 structure retained touches of the period in which it was built, including twelve-over-twelve windows, eight hand-carved fireplaces, a large spider-web window directly above the door with its original glass (with a gold-leaf eagle in the center of the web), and was large, with high ceilings and rooms big enough for receptions and similar gatherings.

The LeWitts renovated the interior not long after they moved in. One of the first things they did was cover the white or light gray paint on the walls throughout the house. Carol recalled: "Sol started by painting the central hallway of this federal house a kind of brown. I remember his once saying, 'Brown is not exactly a fashion color. I don't know about that.' He looked at me and said, 'I'm one of the great colorists of the century, and I think this is the color!' It went on and on: We had a kitchen that was electric yellow that went into a chartreuse room with a red door. It was very personal and very eccentric."[52] As Gabriella de Ferrari, a long-time family friend, pointed out, the contradictions in LeWitt's life showed up even here, with his penchant for both Josef Hoffmann furniture and a wardrobe that could easily be bought at Marshalls.[53]

The house is nestled in a secluded plot of land, heavily treed, where a studio could be built, and where plenty of outdoor sculptures from the LeWitt collection could be displayed. And from the property, it took just five minutes to walk to town. In short, the LeWitts had discovered a stateside version of Spoleto.

Carol began to contribute to the community almost immediately. She purchased downtown retail space and opened a local outlet for Ceramica, her business of ceramic imports from Italy (she also had stores in New York City, and other locations). Her husband formed connections with the Bakers' Chester Gallery and could often be found with friends in a booth at the Restaurant du Village's bar, where he liked to pour the wine himself—often out of bottles with labels that he had designed for the Benzinger winery.[54] He tipped lavishly and in the Christmas season, he gave gifts of gouaches to waiters and waitresses as well as sending many to close friends.

Sol's daily routine reflected the same patterns displayed earlier in his life, which by now had become ingrained, almost invariable. "An extremely poor sleeper," according to Carol, he was usually up by 4:00 A.M. and then read books until he could get the *Times*. He would have read every page of the newspaper by 7:00 A.M., and then he would work from 8:30 to noon in the studio that he had had built according to his design. After lunch, a driver took him to the YMCA in Middletown, about twenty miles away, for an hour of swimming. Afterward, he read or watched films (for example, something by Ingmar Bergman), listened to his music tapes, or watched videos of operas. After dinner, he often continued his reading. Throughout the day, he also spent time with the children. Eva had showed a deep interest in art from a very early age, and she came to the studio almost every day to be with her father and watch what he was doing.

Sofia and Eva were enrolled in local schools. When Eva was not yet five years old, she described her parents in an exercise at the Jack & Jill Cooperative Nursery School. In the exercise, the teacher used a form to ask children questions and write the answers down:

MY MOMMY, BY EVA

My Mommy's name is . . . Carol. I call her Mommy.

She works . . . at Ceramica stores. She sells the Ceramica things. At home she opens mail—she always gets lots of mail because all the friends of hers send her mail.

She does special things for me . . . We always plant the plants. We keep gloves on. She lets us have gum. She runs around the garden with us—we have a race.

She likes . . . Chicken—I love chicken but only plain. She likes to watch the news with my Daddy. . . .

She doesn't like . . . butter because it's not good for you. She doesn't like cartoons. She didn't like when thieves stole the radio from the car.

A description of my Mom . . . . . . She has curly hair. She's 35. She wears skirts. She wears good shoes in the rain and snow.

MY DAD, by EVA

His name is . . . Sol LeWitt. I call him Daddy. Mommy calls him Sol.

At home he . . . cooks. He put this big sculpture up.

He works . . . at the warehouse. He paints. When he was only 10 he made a picture of a building with a chimney.

Sometimes we do special things together . . . We like to cook pasta

—spaghetti. I like cheese and butter on it. Daddy likes sauce and black olives on it. We go to get the newspaper together.

He likes to . . . cook. He likes to watch baseball. He likes root beer soda—sometimes orange. He likes movie shows on TV. He likes to talk with Mommy at night.

A description of my Dad: He always wears glasses. He doesn't have bangs or hair on top. He wears pants. He only gets dressed up to go to meetings.[55]

What Eva could have said, if she had been asked and had mastered metaphors at a young age, was that since the she had learned to walk she had been her father's shadow.

Looking back on her childhood in a 2015 interview, Eva remembered being drawn to making art at an early age: "I used to wake up, like him, really early, and follow him to his studio. He wasn't waiting around for me, so I had to be ready. Either I was coming or not. In the studio, he set me up with a little station to do my work." He also showed her the rituals of being an artist—washing brushes, sharpening pencils, and so on. As a result of this closeness, the LeWitts' younger daughter "grew up thinking that mailman, artist, doctor, lawyer—they were all viable professions."[56]

Later, however, when she attended a private school in Connecticut, she found that even gifted children didn't know much about art: "I went to a school that had a high premium on athletics, not on the arts. They knew my father was well known but wouldn't have understood him at all. Conceptualism is really hard to explain to sixteen-year-old jocks. My closest friends who got to see him and his work in person maybe understood it better. Some of them now are in the arts, and now they understand."[57]

Because of her early interest in her father's work and her own natural talent, it surprised no one when she took up art as her vocation. By the age of thirty, she had exhibited in, among other places, Los Angeles, Oslo, and New York.

■ The first people the LeWitts had met in town were Sosse and Jack Baker, owners of the relatively new Chester Gallery. Jack recalled: "I told Sol, 'Let's have a party for friends and neighbors.' He said sure. It was a rainy Sunday, but everyone came."[58] Sosse recalled, "We had ninety people and served fabulous deli sandwiches, meats, and blanched asparagus made by Jack's mother."[59]

Very quickly the Bakers, who had been dealing primarily with local artists, had a new world of art opened to them through the LeWitt connection. "It became very much an education for us," Jack recalled. LeWitt gave the Bakers, who also had the town's only framing business, a lot of work, including pieces by Chuck Close, Hanne Darboven, and Pat Steir. "It was a different level of art, something we never would have encountered otherwise," Jack said. Not only that, but there was a buzz about the place, "and so many different artists wanted to show here." But it was five years before they had a LeWitt exhibit. Jack had been afraid to make the request, but after he had done so, LeWitt said, "All you had to do was ask." Baker replied, "We're not the Whitney." LeWitt replied, "What does that matter?"[60] This exhibit, it turned out, "changed everything for us," Sosse recalled. "He did twenty-six gouaches, and every painting sold. Plus he was willing to do more. On opening night, we were nearly sold out."[61]

The Bakers obviously benefited from LeWitt's influence and participation. In turn, LeWitt found them to be just the sort of supportive gallery owners that he had come to rely on over the years. The LeWitts and Bakers became good friends, and occasionally the Bakers served as escape artists. In 1989, there was a show of LeWitt's work at nearby Wesleyan University, one that he couldn't avoid attending. "When we walked into the gallery," Sosse recalled, "there were so many people standing around Sol we thought, 'We see him very day, let's just look at the art.' So we looked at everything. Their girls were very young then, and they were climbing all over his sculpture. He didn't mind. What he minded was that people were smothering him. Sol came up to us, put his hand on Jack's shoulder, and said, 'Do you guys want to go out for a pizza?'"[62] So the four of them evaded the crowd the rest of the night.

LeWitt, who made an art form of crowd evasion, also avoided the Bakers' regular cocktail parties for the Democratic Town Committee. "He never came to the event," Jack recalled, "but he always sent in his money," and he'd say, "Well, the important thing is that I buy a ticket."[63]

The Bakers were among those who quickly learned the impossibility of returning LeWitt's favors. "You could never give that man anything," Sosse said, echoing the views of many other people.[64]

Patricia Klindienst, who at the time taught a course titled "What Was Modernism?" at Yale, also lived in town. She recalled that during her very difficult pregnancy, during which she was often bedridden, both Sol and Carol LeWitt went out of their way to help: "Carol brought me homemade soup and sat on the edge of my bed, and we talked. At the time, one of her best friends was dying of AIDS, and my brother was dying of cancer, so it was helpful to both of us. Sol would come to the apartment and ask for a grocery list. Then the nanny would drive him to the store, and he'd return with the food. That he would do it himself—not just send the nanny—made a great impression on me."[65]

He gave her other gifts, as well—tapes from his music collection that related to some of her writing projects, such as his tapes of the Benjamin Britten opera *The Rape of Lucretia* when she working on a related essay, and of Richard Wagner's *Parsifal* when she was writing about Virginia Woolf, whose work was influenced in particular by that opera.

Klindienst also consulted LeWitt when her marriage disintegrated. "I was hoping to save the marriage, to go with my husband to counseling," she recalled.[66] "Carol said to me, 'You should talk to Sol. He's very wise.' We sat in his music library in those Bauhaus chairs. He listened as I went on, and then he looked me, and said slowly, 'You know, sometimes it's best to do nothing.' Even here, he was the minimalist. Unfortunately, I didn't take his advice."

LeWitt made several other friends in Chester, including the graphic designer Peter Good, considered one of the people at the top of his field yet still eager to learn. Good was particularly affected by LeWitt's use of typography: "It was uncontrived, unutilized, just the way he would pick out plumbing for his bathroom. He was never pretentious. He had an aversion to slick things. He was anti-trend. I remember asking him about how he decides to do something. He said, 'Whenever everyone goes to the right, I go to the left.' I think he had a sophisticated, intellectual approach to art, balanced by a childlike ability to perceive simple things. I also asked him, 'Why did you never do an opera set for the Met[ropolitan Opera]?' He replied, 'Because I'm not a team player.'"[67]

LeWitt asked Good to design his letterhead—but only up to a point. Good recalled: "He picked the typeface—Cheltenham, a folksy face. But then the next time it was Beton Bold condensed—a face of simplicity and geometry."[68] However, LeWitt sometimes relied more heavily on local expertise.

William L. Schaeffer's shop, open by appointment only, features rare photographs. Schaeffer's clientele is international, and sometimes buyers pay considerable amounts for the rarest and most beautiful of images. While he lived in Chester, LeWitt expanded his interest in photography and relied on Schaeffer to help him establish a new collection.

Moreover, he often sought Schaeffer's counsel when buying gifts for his many assistants and members of his family. In fact Carol told Schaeffer, "I've got to keep him away from your place—it's very dangerous for Sol."[69]

As it turned out, LeWitt's own work would be affected by what he bought. For example, he took a particular interest in images made by Clarence John Laughlin, a New Orleans photographer whose 1930s work focused on technology. LeWitt bought a black-and-white print titled *Light on the Cylinders*. Schaeffer recalled: "Sol loved that picture, bought it and took it right over [across the street] to Jack's [the Chester Gallery] for framing."[70] Many years later, LeWitt worked on a series of black-and-white drawings that featured cylindrical shapes, obviously influenced by Laughlin as he had once been influenced by Muybridge.

Schaeffer had the feeling that his shop was useful to LeWitt in other ways: "Sol would come here with curators in tow on his way to lunch at the River Tavern. It's almost as if [the visit here] was a litmus test. These curators all wanted something from him. If they weren't willing to be patient while he stopped here for five or ten minutes, he'd know their motives were not up to snuff. It seemed like it was a little test."[71]

The Schaeffers, the Goods, and others often joined the LeWitts at the corner table in the bar at Restaurant du Village. Foodies Charles van Over and Priscilla Martel had started the business in 1979, at great risk. No one knew, particularly them, whether fine dining would work in "Dogtown." Van Over thought that "Main Street was in the doldrums, but the surrounding area was filled with interesting people."[72] Van Over and Martel decided that they would strive for authenticity and not seek to accommodate traditional American tastes. They offered lamb cooked with garlic and rosemary; porterhouse steak with tarragon and red wine; duck with red peppercorns and raspberry vinegar; sweetbreads with tongue; and roast chicken with prosciutto, tarragon, and sage under the skin with mushroom sauce on top. LeWitt loved to hold court there or let others do so while he poured the wine.

Though not a natural storyteller, he did have an array of tales to tell over lemon tart, some of them involving local people. For example, one day he told his wife that he had just gotten a call from Ravi Shankar, who had asked him to design a cover for a new book of poetry. He was surprised that the Indian composer and sitar player also wrote poetry, but he was happy to do the cover for him. It was only later that LeWitt discovered that the Ravi Shankar who had called him was not the musician but a poet who lived in Chester. Nevertheless, he followed through on the request.

Marilyn Buel, who lived near Chester, recalled the sense of intimidation she felt when she met the world-class artist. She boned up on her contemporary art and over dinner at the LeWitt house said, "Sol, I have to ask you—was Josef Albers an influence on your work, his squares in particular?" LeWitt said, "Well, the square has been around for a long time." Six months later, she recalled: "He took me aside and said, 'I was a little glib with you,' referring to his square remark. It was a very sweet thing. Then I said to him, 'I like the sculpture you did in the living room.' He said, 'What sculpture? I don't have one there. That's a stereo speaker.'"[73]

As time went on, Buel learned that LeWitt demystified art, as happened when she was in charge of a fund-raiser at a local school and asked him to donate prints for an auction. He complied. When she wondered aloud whether the work should be hung horizontally or vertically —it wasn't obvious from the content—he told her, "You buy them, you hang them however you want."[74]

LeWitt's massage therapist, Deb Paulson, had been similarly intimidated but nonetheless decided to ask him to take a look at some of her work:

> I showed him one of my watercolors—two pears and an apple in a bowl, the best thing I'd ever done. He's looking at it carefully and said, "I like it . . . what are you going to with the background?" I said, "I already did it." He said, "You have to think about the background" —but he said it like he was taking me really seriously. It wasn't patronizing—very succinct. And about one drawing I did in India ink that I had on the wall, he said, "I like that." I was too shy to ask why. One day he came by the studio and said, "Here's a little gift for the holiday." I said, "Should I open it now?" He said, "Why don't you wait?"[75]

It was one of his gouaches—a sign, to his massage therapist, of acknowledgment and acceptance.

There were times, too, when his stature as God was literal. For the first night of Passover each year, the LeWitts invited about twenty-five guests to their home, including many who had never been to a seder. The Haggadah that was often used was homemade. For it, a small group of residents of Chester had completely rewritten the text—the story of the exodus from Egypt—as a play, with parts for Moses, Aaron, Miriam, and even an imagined character, the slave on the street. There was also a part for God. Invariably, LeWitt was cast (actually, typecast) in the role of the Supreme Being. This did nothing, however, to enhance his assessment of the script, which he thought inane.

Even so, little Chester, it turned out, was just what the artist had sought—close enough to New York City (two and half hours by car or train) and small enough to provide the feeling of sanctuary. On occasion, however, the outside world intruded, as in the early 1990s, when another resident of town became infamous in art circles.

■   Morley Safer and his wife, Jane, had come to Chester a few years before the LeWitts arrived. Most of the key staff members of CBS's breakthrough television magazine *60 Minutes* bought weekend houses in the Hamptons or Fairfield County. But Safer and one of the program's producers, Philip Scheffler, found the charms of the Connecticut Valley irresistible. Scheffler and his wife, Linda, moved to Essex, and the Safers bought the old Burr homestead off the Middlesex Turnpike, where Morley could spend his weekends gardening. The Safer, Scheffler, and LeWitt families were all members of Congregation Beth Shalom, then holding its services in a small converted church in the adjacent town of Deep River.

Safer, a native of Canada, had long been a star on CBS. He had first gained national attention with his reports from the battlefields of Vietnam, particularly one that showed US Marines setting a small village aflame. The reports had had such an effect, casting doubt on official public pronouncements from the Pentagon, that President Lyndon Johnson had tried to get Safer fired.

In the years that followed, there was no doubt that Safer, like his colleagues Mike Wallace and others, were not afraid to dig into difficult reporting tasks—even the task of reporting on the world of contemporary art.

In 1988, Safer, who described himself as "a Sunday painter" and who chiefly created landscapes, did a segment on contemporary art and used his gift for ridicule to describe the art of Robert Gober and Robert Ryman.

But his 1993 report on an auction of contemporary art at Sotheby's that raised $20 million for its sellers dripped with sarcasm, including, for example, the master showman P. T. Barnum's quote, "There's a sucker born every minute" and calling the art "worthless junk." LeWitt's work was not included in the auction featured in the Safer report, but that of his long-time friends Ryman and Jan Dibbets were, both of whom were skewered by Safer. Many other artists were taken to task in the report — most prominently Jeff Koons, who no doubt did not help matters by trying to explain in artspeak why his three basketballs in a fish tank constituted art ("It has the integrity of birth"), while Safer commented on it, "This 'art' gives new meaning to 'slam dunk.'" Safer also said: "This one, a canvas of scrawls done with the wrong end of a paint brush, bears the imaginative title of *Untitled*. It is by Cy Twombly and was sold for $2,145,000. And that's dollars, not Twomblys." Safer took on not only the artists but also critics for their obfuscations and attempts to sound important without actually saying anything. What, he wondered, do "a discourse reduced to the irreducible" or "Installations function as utopian and dystopian examples of taste "actually mean? Safer said, "This [exhibit catalogue] might as well have been written in Sanskrit." The end of the report featured Hilton Kramer, who as a critic had followed Clement Greenberg in his disdain for prominent schools of contemporary art. Kramer said: "Artists live in great dread of waking up one morning that someone blew the whistle and they're not going to be important."[76]

In the next issue of the *Village Voice*, Peter Schjeldahl took the CBS correspondent to task, rather harshly: "Morley Safer's art-stupid, television-smart, emperor's new clothes number on '60 Minutes' has almost everyone in the art world upset. . . . Of course almost everyone in the art world was upset already. These are hard times." To be sure, Schjeldahl had his own measure of healthy skepticism: "Am I to pretend that the art world is free of hustler's and idiots?" But he argued that Safer had gone way too far: "He is a moron about art in the way I am a moron about nuclear physics. He does not grasp that art is to be looked at with active curiosity, suspending prejudice, or to be left alone."[77]

LeWitt and his friends were also furious. In their view, Safer had fallen on his face — taking all of the art out of context, ignoring the lessons of the history of art, and committing dozens of other reportorial felonies.

The following week, *60 Minutes* broadcast responses — including a letter from Marc Glimsher of the Pace Gallery, which represented LeWitt, in which he said that the Safer segment "stank of anti-intellectualism." In addition, Andre Emmerich, the owner of the Andre Emmerich Gallery, said that "the broadcast's smug, smiling, Philistine approach was appalling." And the artist Ellsworth Kelly said, "I am disappointed that a group of people like [the staff of] '60 Minutes' who are generally respected have slipped up so completely that none of them are more sophisticated about the arts."[78]

In a small town like Chester, it was inevitable that the *60 Minutes* reporter and the contemporary artist would meet. The center of town, home not only to shops but also to Memorial Day parades, the Fourth of July road race, a winter carnival, and many nights of "Chester Homecomings," offered ample opportunities for unintentional encounters.

Four years after the broadcast aired, the consequences of it were still obvious, even in public. One day in 1997, Safer was buying bread at the Mad Hatter, a small shop in the center of town. He turned to leave and passed LeWitt coming in. As they walked by each other, an observer could not see either man acknowledge the other but could hear, a few seconds later, LeWitt's own tidy review: "Asshole."[79]

By that summer, however, LeWitt's own view of sophistication and what constitutes art had been challenged not by a television reporter but by no less than one of the country's most prominent museum directors.

FOURTEEN

TOUCHING NERVES

In his work as a conceptual artist, LeWitt grew accustomed to controversy. In most cases, it resulted from the usual suspicion that arises when long-held traditions are ignored. Generally, the artist was inured to such a reaction and even welcomed it as a way for his work to be noticed and to be talked about. A rare exception was the agony and sense of betrayal he felt when his hometown of Hartford rejected him, a blow that affected him deeply. On other occasions, controversy simply came with the expanding territory. But once it carried with it a strong sense of irony.

In the summer of 1991, the National Museum of American Art, a part of the Smithsonian Institution, opened an exhibit titled *Eadweard Muybridge and Contemporary American Photography*. The show was imported from Massachusetts, where the Addison Gallery of American Art at the Phillips Academy had originally produced it. It showed how Muybridge's photographic ideas had influenced artists. The original exhibit contained pieces by thirty-five living artists, including Le-Witt — who was represented by *Muybridge 1*, a piece he had completed twenty-seven years earlier, before he did his wall drawings, cubes, or concrete structures.

The work was complicated: a black box about a foot tall, a foot deep, and eight feet long, in which LeWitt had drilled ten tiny holes. To see the whole work, the viewer had to look sequentially through the holes to see images (by the photographer Barbara Brown) of a nude woman's body. The model came progressively closer to the viewer, from far away to very close — with the last image focusing on the model's navel. At the time he did the work, LeWitt was trying to build on Muybridge's ideas of sequence and progression, something that eventually led to LeWitt's reliance on permutation as a basic idea on which to build his oeuvre.

When *Muybridge 1* was on display at the Addison, the piece drew curiosity but no public objections. But when the show was exported to

Washington, it became a part of an intensifying debate over what is appropriate to exhibit in a publicly supported museum.

Elizabeth Broun, director of the National Museum of American Art, pulled the work from the exhibit. She wrote to Jock Reynolds, director of the Addison—who with James Sheldon, the gallery's curator of photography, had brought the Muybridge pieces together. Broun said that *Muybridge 1* was a "peep show" that might be seen in an arcade and that "focusing increasingly on the pubic region invokes unequivocal references to a degrading pornographic experience."[1] Her decision was also influenced by logistics. One of her curators, Merry Forefpa, had brought to Broun's attention the fact that the original Addison show had been augmented by twenty-two additional pieces, and there wasn't room for everything. One of the cuts, then, would be the work by LeWitt.

Not surprisingly, Broun's decision caught the attention of the media, including the *New York Times*, which published several pieces and letters to the editor about it over the next few days. Broun told a *Times* reporter that LeWitt's work was "so far afield from the purpose of the exhibition that it does not enhance the show. . . . I have no doubt that LeWitt intended the piece as a serious reflection on Muybridge, but he made this piece in 1963 and since that time we have had more than two decades of examination of issues involving the representation of women. It would be impossible for me to present this in 1991 without some aspect of this heightened public consciousness entering into the viewer's experience."[2] Broun's judgment that LeWitt's work, as seen in a contemporary light, was degrading to women carried irony with it.

Lovers, colleagues, and friends described LeWitt as an oddity in the art world in terms of his attitudes about gender, reporting that he had supported and helped market the work of female artists long before the women's movement. But Broun was trying to address what exhibitors must deal with—what visitors actually see—not the deeper context of where a piece fits in the development of the artist's work or the artist's attitudes about gender. That's the thing about visual art. LeWitt said, famously, that it's not too important what a work of art looks like. But of course to the viewer, the look is almost everything.

What the viewer doesn't see is the context playing out behind the show. Broun had been in her first year as director when an exhibition about the American West opened, causing a political furor.[3] Senators Ted Stevens of Alaska and Slade Gorton of Washington had threatened to lead a campaign to cut off funding based on the museum's "politically correct" and "leftist" interpretation of history that depicted the brutal treatment of Native Americans.[4] This, too, was in line with a general crackdown in Congress over what was seen as obscene art, particularly in the instances of exhibits of the work of Robert Mapplethorpe and Andres Serrano. In response, the art community fought back.

For Reynolds, Broun's action was nothing but censorship. The Addison director wrote to the Smithsonian and requested that its exhibit on Muybridge be closed. To add a measure of solidarity to the effort to call attention to Broun's actions, twenty of the artists whose work was on display, including LeWitt's old friend Mel Bochner, insisted that their pieces be withdrawn. Reynolds told the *Times*: "We want to protect the integrity of the artist and the issues of freedom of expression. . . . [Broun] sees this as a boy-girl thing, that we as men don't understand. Betsy keeps representing the piece as if it were a crotch shot, but in actuality it is the image of an advancing nude woman that comes so close to the viewer's eye that you focus on her bellybutton. To treat it as a pariah and decontextualizing the work and making it something separate, focuses her own individual problems with the piece before anyone has had a chance to see it or think about it. There is a much larger principle at stake here. Once you contract for an exhibit, have viewed it by slides, hung it on the wall, you can't edit it for content restrictions."[5] Reynolds told the *Times* that he had called LeWitt in Rome and that the artist was "very troubled and unhappy." Even so, Broun was impressed that LeWitt stayed on the sidelines in the debate. "Sol was not fanning the flames," she recalled in a 2015 interview.[6] But others were.

LeWitt's champion in Hartford, Andrea Miller-Keller, told the *Times*: "I think I am a pretty strong-minded feminist and I respect that Ms. Broun has a strong opinion, but I disagree [with her action]. She is quite focused on the peephole aspect of the piece, but that is the basis of most optometric investigations for centuries. It is the basis for most photographic processes, but she's taken a very narrow reading on this. It is an image of a woman striding forward very aggressively. She is aware of this exchange. She is not a woman as victim." Miller-Keller added, "This is not a time in our history when museums should attempt to universalize the personal views of individual administrators."[7] Michael Kimmelman seconded the motion when he wrote in the *Times*: "Removing a key work by the artist whose relationship to Muybridge is fundamental to the show's concept undermines the integrity of the exhibition's argument. It then becomes [Broun's] show, not Mr. Reynolds's and Mr. Sheldon's."[8]

Jamie James wrote to the *Times* in response to Kimmelman's piece, "The idea that Mr. LeWitt's *Muybridge I* was an acceptable work of art in 1964 ('so long ago,' says Ms. Broun) but is now unacceptable because it is 'a degrading pornographic experience' is precisely the same line of reasoning that Victorian prudes used when they pasted fig leafs over the naughty bits of classical statues."[9]

However, this view was not universally held. A letter to the *Times* from another reader, Thomasine Bradford, reaffirmed the political touchiness of the situation: "Change the category from sex to race. If Mr. LeWitt had made a degrading image of a black person, everyone would understand Ms. Broun's action, even if they disagreed with her methods. . . . Women finally see the connection between 'artistic' objectification of their bodies and the near state of war being waged against them. Yes, a powerful, unconscious connection exists between Mr. LeWitt's 'artwork' and the rape and murder of women."[10]

But soon after after the controversy began, Broun changed her mind and restored LeWitt's piece to the exhibit. She said, "As this artwork has become the centerpiece of a public debate, we believe that the public is best served by including LeWitt's work in the exhibition so everybody can discuss the issues after having seen it."[11]

Recalling that time nearly twenty-five years later, Broun said that the episode "taught me an important lesson about the press. They love to champion freedom of speech, but they like to do it on someone else's issue."[12] It was telling to her that the *Times* and other newspapers were happy to rail about apparent Smithsonian censorship but wouldn't publish the images themselves. More frustrating to Broun was the fact that Muybridge's nudes, in effect, hadn't really been censored in the show. For example, a large and full-length image of a nude greeted visitors near the entrance, but no press accounts mentioned this.

Looking back on the controversies over Muybridge and the West shows, Broun made no distinction between political forces on the left or the right. She was battered from both sides and considered the outrage over the Muybridge show as a highly selective campaign. She also thought it both odd and telling that the organizers of the exhibit made no effort to restore the twenty-one other pieces that had been cut: "What had begun as a space issue turned into a censorship issue."[13]

However, she certainly had a role in causing that, considering her "peep show" comment.

For LeWitt the brouhaha resulted in a victory of principle. Moreover, if one examines the way LeWitt's name became increasingly prominent though he never submitted to personality interviews, this episode explains a good deal. The debate over the work informed many, and certainly contributed to the fame of the LeWitt brand.

With certain rare exceptions, LeWitt seemed to thrive on controversy. That crowd-gathering element made it unnecessary for him to grant personality interviews. As for the final irony of the exhibit, about a third of the money to mount the original Addison Gallery show had been in the form of a grant from the Robert Mapplethorpe Foundation.

In the case of *Muybridge 1*, LeWitt had unintentionally walked through the minefields of politics. But though he generally made it a point to keep his art free of such associations, it wasn't always possible. And there were certain situations in which controversy was inherent in the work itself.

He certainly knew that in 1987, when he produced his first piece directly related to the Holocaust. It wouldn't be on safe ground as an American city's memorial—those would come later—but directly on the spot where Nazism had flourished and reduced most of European Jewry to ashes.

LeWitt had very little personal connection with the Holocaust, but by the late 1980s, coinciding with his move to Chester and after he had joined Congregation Beth Shalom, he had a reawakened interest in Judaism and the legacy of the Jewish people.

As the influence of the original circle of minimalists and conceptualists expanded, so did the context of their work—which sometimes venturing into dark history. Steve Reich, for example, composed music as a commentary on the Holocaust. His parents had descended from Eastern European and German Jews, just the sorts of families whose members were rounded up and sent off to their deaths. It was a legacy that affected Reich deeply and that showed in *Different Trains*, a piece that features voices of Pullman porters and Holocaust survivors as well as the mournful sounds of a string quartet.

Bochner's *Via Tasso* project was installed in a former Nazi prison in Rome. Made of burned cooks' matchsticks, his three sculptures are arranged on the ground of the cells, the remnants of which still exist. The matchsticks make six-pointed stars. Much earlier, in 1951, the painter

Morris Louis (born Maurice Bernstein) had created a series called *Charred Journal: Firewritten*.

Frank Stella, who had influenced LeWitt greatly, was also affected deeply by what had happened in Europe. His friend Richard Meier, an architect, had given him a copy of *Wooden Synagogues*—a book written by Maria and Kazimierz Piechotka and published in Warsaw. It was illustrated with line drawings of seventy-one synagogues destroyed by the Nazis and their sympathizers. This book inspired not only Stella's *Polish Villages* but would lead LeWitt many years later to work on his only public architectural project—the new building for his own congregation. However, LeWitt's first work drawn from the Holocaust was the one that involved a major measure of controversy and irony.

LeWitt was invited to participate in *Skulptur Projekte 87* in Münster, Germany. He created two pieces. The first was a white pyramid. The second, a rectangular shape in pitch black, was the one that drew all of the media attention.

LeWitt was the only artist who had been asked to address a particularly compelling site, one of the few buildings of consequence that had not been substantially damaged in the city during the World War II bombing raids—the eighteenth-century baroque castle that had become the home of Münster's prominent university. The location for a piece of art there would be in the front of the building, where there had been a statue of Kaiser Wilhelm II until the British army destroyed it in 1945. LeWitt recalled in 2006: "They said, 'You can have a space in front of the Schloss and you can have one in the back,' and I said, 'Well, I'll do both.' I did the pyramid in the back and the rectangular block structure in the front."[14]

During a site visit to Müunster, Sol and Carol LeWitt visited a nearly completed installation by the German sculptor Rebecca Horn, which specifically referred to the horrors of war. The piece, *Concert in Reverse*, features in the artist's words "a miniature wilderness."[15] Her example caused LeWitt to give to his work what was for him an unusually provocative title. Before World War II, Münster had been home to more than 500 Jewish families. By the end of the war, only a few Jews alive. LeWitt titled the black rectangular shape, composed of painted concrete block, *Black Form: Dedicated to the Missing Jews of Munster*. He explained: "I wanted to make a piece that was completely different from the lacy architecture behind it so I made it in a sort of ungainly block. I wanted it to be hard to swallow in terms of form and completely antithetical to its site. Then I decided to make it even more antithetical by painting it black. Once that was done, I thought, well, I'll take another step and give it a title that will make it even more unpalatable."[16]

It was, obviously, a stark and bold commentary set in extreme juxtaposition to the elaborate architecture behind it that carried the weight of an ugly history. In *The Texture of Memory: Holocaust Memorials and Meaning*, the historian James E. Young writes, "It sat like an abandoned coffin amid the soaring mock-Baroque façade and gas lamps, a black blight squatting in the center of a sunny and graceful university center."[17]

The historian Sergieusz Michalski writes in *Public Monuments: Art and Political Bondage*: "The sheer incongruity of the cubic shape evoked the break in civilization caused by the Nazi genocide, the black colour constituting an obvious symbol of mass death, of the disappearance of the figure into nothingness. For LeWitt, the idea of the piece was to signify that for this town (and others) it was the end of a certain history; there were no Jewish children in town, and so the monument signified the end of generations."[18]

But the piece was soon covered in graffiti and political slogans, including some anti-Semitic messages that naturally brought to mind the smears of Jews that had been pasted on shop windows and in a variety of other public places in the Third Reich. Some members of the German public took a different approach, complaining that the work was ugly —which of course it was meant to be. University officials, clearly not wanting to seem insensitive to overwhelming historical issues, focused their complaints on disrupted traffic patterns, as if this was an ordinary planning and zoning dispute in a small town. And over LeWitt's objections and those of the sculpture project's officials, jackhammers were taken to the site and the piece was reduced to rubble and carted off to the dump.

Several months later, the chastened city council asked LeWitt to come back. He agreed, thinking it was possible to reconstruct the black shape, but the controversy was reignited. The result was that LeWitt rebuilt the piece not in Münster but in front of the town hall of Altona, part of the Hamburg metropolitan area. In a way, as unanticipated as it had been, this move brought a sense of familiarity and perhaps a sense of comfort. Hamburg had been home to several of LeWitt's colleagues and friends, including Hanne Darboven and most significantly Eva Hesse, who had escaped the Holocaust.

LeWitt produced his last Holocaust commentary on German soil many years later. This work did not attract a lot of attention or controversy, but it had a quiet eloquence that deeply affected those who worked on it and those who saw it.

A tiny stone synagogue (twenty-nine feet by twenty-two feet) in the town of Stommeln, Germany, had been built in 1882—during an era when German Jews had flourished and that had been characterized generally by their assimilation into the country's rich culture. It was here that LeWitt created a work, titled *Lost Voices*, that nearly twenty years after the Münster piece proved to be a powerful commentary on genocide and also provided a clear definition of conceptual art—demonstrating why the idea is more important than the execution of the piece or, more specifically, the aesthetic outcome. Much of the physical manifestation of *Lost Voices* is a brick wall, one that closely matches the brick walls of the synagogue. How, a cynic may easily ask, can an ordinary brick wall be art?

LeWitt's idea was to create something to illustrate the gulf between Jews and those who were determined to murder them, as well as the legacy of hate and genocide. Many artists have addressed this subject, of course, in a variety of ways. What makes this wall both interesting and conceptual is that it demonstrates, as much as any LeWitt work does, its idea on its very face, and any viewer (in this case, also any listener) can see why the carrying out of the piece is, as LeWitt so often said, "perfunctory." That is, a brick wall is a brick wall. But in this case the wall bars visitors from entering the sanctuary. And the whole becomes an art installation when recorded voices are heard behind that brick wall, reciting and singing the liturgy of the Jewish High Holy Days—a sound that, presumably, live Jewish voices will never again produce in Stommeln. Peter Friese, a German art historian and curator, wrote in the catalogue:

> At issue here is . . . the physical experience of confinement, the
> feeling of being locked in or locked out. . . . Those who once filled
> this place with religious life are no longer there, and that which they
> once represented as an element of what was once a vivacious Jewish
> culture in Stommeln can only emerge out of the distance within the
> framework of memory fragments in the present.
>
> What Sol LeWitt is doing in his space-sound installation is not
> reconstructing something, but rather performing an exemplary
> deconstruction of history and thus also critically questioning the

way we are accustomed to recalling past events. It deals with an experience of loss conveyed spatially and acoustically, with making reference to something that is simply no longer there, and with the associated consequences for the present.[19]

LeWitt had a much different idea when he was approached in the late 1980s to contribute a piece to the US Holocaust Memorial Museum, then being planned in Washington.

Nancy Rosen, an independent curator who met LeWitt in the mid-1970s while he was still working and living on Hester Street, recruited him for the job. "Even as a student," she recalled in 2014, "I was interested in the intersection of art and architecture, and I went to see him to talk about this. As the years passed, and I was given projects to work on, there were times when I thought Sol would be a good candidate for certain sites, and certainly [one of those was] the Holocaust Museum," whose planners gave Rosen responsibility for arranging art commissions.[20] However, there were certain hurdles to overcome.

First and foremost was a question of what art could do in a setting in which such horror would be documented: the rise of Nazism, the growing intensity of anti-Semitism, the concentration camps, and the executions of millions of people—not only Jews but also Catholics, gypsies, homosexuals, the mentally ill, and others not deemed to conform to Aryan models of citizenship. "To write poetry after Auschwitz is barbaric," said the German philosopher Theodor Adorno[21] (a view not shared by the writers Primo Levi, Nellie Sachs, and others). The founders of the museum decided that art could contribute to the experience in some ways, though they had certain expectations for that art.

Rosen recalled: "Some of the main board members expressed the need for figurative art. But the building itself had such a material presence and specificity (for example, intimate portraits and piles of shoes collected from victims), it needed contrast. And this is what an artist can bring. The work of the artist wouldn't be confused with the specificity of the exhibits, wouldn't be misunderstood as evidence."[22] There was, not surprisingly, a great deal of competition for the few commissions open, and eventually it was decided that only American artists would be considered. As it turned out, the museum would install pieces by Serra, Joel Shapiro, Ellsworth Kelly, and LeWitt.

However, LeWitt's first proposal was rejected. It called for "a wall-like sculpture with an irregular ('broken') top edge, made of black, concrete blocks to be stacked along the long diagonal wall of the rooms."[23] In *Abstraction and the Holocaust*, Mark Godfrey speculates that "LeWitt's initial proposal suggests that his first inclination was towards a symbolic use of both colour and shape . . . it does seem to relate to his earlier use of black concrete blocks [in Münster]."[24]

Instead of withdrawing from the competition after having an idea rejected, as he had done in Hartford, LeWitt offered a second idea, this time presenting models for a work he titled *Progression of Colored Squares*, five square paintings in different hues (muddy red, purple, mustard, blue, or orange), each of which had a square at the center of smokestack (or perhaps Auschwitz) gray. The jury accepted this proposal, though it changed the title of the work to *Consequences*—a decision explained in part by its position in the museum.

Visitors see the work only after they have passed over a bridge that replicates a Lodz ghetto structure, walked through a cattle car and a field of human hair, and seen photographs of the doomed citizens of Eishishok—where an ss killing squad destroyed the community and its population. There was a need, then, for a sense of contemplation. The LeWitt installation was intended to provide just that.

Of the work, LeWitt said the intent was to keep the squares within the squares all the same, using gray "to keep the area in a calm and not very aggressive mode. I thought it would be more apt to have the same figure in each one [the gray field]—which is a square within the square —then just change the color from square to square."[25] Godfrey writes, "Certainly, compared to other contemporaneous wall drawings by the artist, *Consequences* establishes a sombre rather than joyous mood."[26]

Susan Morganstein, the museum's director of special exhibitions, said: "Coming where [the work] does in the exhibition, it's almost like the smoke has poured out. If that was LeWitt's intention, and it may easily be inferred, he never expressed it directly. It certainly departs in that regard from any other of his more than 1,200 wall drawings, none of which suggest concrete references to phenomena or history."[27] In that way, it was the drawing equivalent of the structure *Black Form*. Yet that is where the literal nature of the work ends.

Godfrey argues that the museum erred in changing the name of the work:

The repetition of LeWitt's forms resist the narrative progress of
the exhibition. In this respect, it is important to recall that LeWitt

preferred the title *Progression of Coloured Squares* over the museum's *Consequences*. The latter title superimposes on the work the idea of a sequences of causes and effects such as those where for instance the Final Solution is a consequence of Nazi anti-Semitism. But the work actually holds off the idea of narrative. The artist's own progression of colored squares implies no sense of movement or of causality.[28]

LeWitt's work on Holocaust projects coincided with his growing interest in his religion and family heritage, which had never been central to his thoughts until the birth of his children. He and his wife sent their two girls twice a week to the Hebrew school of Congregation Beth Shalom, in Deep River. The school was physically apart from the sanctuary, occupying rented space above a laundry and a wine store in Chester.

The congregation at the time was a small one, consisting of fewer than a hundred families spread out over about twenty towns in an area that had once been home to many Jewish farmers. Thus, its facilities had never been lavish, and the congregation had made do with an old church for several decades. However, the shortcomings of this arrangement became clear on many occasions. One of them was the bat mitzvah of Eva LeWitt in 1998.

Eva prepared for the ceremony (held two years after her sister's) in a way that reflected her father's independent spirit. His bar mitzvah speech had seemed rote, a fill-in-the-blanks routine. Since that time, the ritual had changed in most synagogues. It has long been the custom for bar mitzvahs—and then for bat mitzvahs (the congregation celebrated its first in 1955)—for the young person to preach a lesson extracted from that week's portion of Torah. Though Eva chose to do so, she didn't preach it so much as show it. An artist herself, Eva delivered her sermon with the aid of paintings she had made for the occasion. The congregation and guests were engaged by this unusual presentation until a rude interruption occurred.

The sanctuary was a small one, and there was no entrance hallway, which meant that anyone could walk into it from the sidewalk at any time. In the midst of Eva's interpretation of her Torah portion, a man dressed in a white T-shirt and work pants entered and shouted, "Would the owner of a black Volvo please move your car—I can't turn my truck."[29] It didn't seem to occur to him that he was interrupting anything, much less a significant rite of passage.

The incident itself wasn't mentioned as a factor in the decision to design and build a proper home for a congregation, but there is no doubt that it contributed to the feeling that the time had come to invest in such a place.

Over a period of several months, members of the board of directors and an ad hoc committee considered ways to address what they well knew would be a great challenge for a small community, particularly since in the mid-1990s the synagogue's treasurer, Stefan Marmon, had appropriated funds for his own use, which had left the congregation nearly bankrupt (Marmon, would be sentenced to prison for his crime). From the outside, the loss of the money seemed as if it might be the death knell for a congregation that had never had a strong financial base.

Thus, the idea to build a new synagogue raised many eyebrows and provided a challenge that was uncommon even in a religious tradition in which congregations are responsible for raising every dime spent on a sanctuary and for hiring a rabbi and staff. And in this case, it was estimated that to provide a proper place would require a surfeit of dimes. As it turned out, it cost about $3.6 million to pay for the land, preparation of the site, and construction of the building.

Some members of the board of directors, seeing the challenge for what it was, felt that something bold should be planned. Others wanted to play it safe and persuaded the board as a whole to hire an architect who had designed many suburban synagogues, one of a handful of finalists who had proposed ideas. But his presentation of preliminary sketches fell flat, as they seemed to be cookie-cutter stuff. Besides, this congregation was in the exurbs, not the suburbs, and it needed a solution that fit its small-town environment. The land was next to the historic Warner house, a Greek Revival colonial that stood at the corner of Route 154 and East King's Highway, and the architectural context had to be honored.

It was then that LeWitt entered the picture. He had become interested in the legacy of the old wooden synagogues of Eastern Europe and in the way that the architect Louis Kahn had built on that legacy for a Chappaqua, New York, congregation. In the summer of 1996, LeWitt traveled through Europe to see what remained of the wooden synagogues, and when he returned to Chester, he began to imagine designing one of his own.

He and Carol made a trip to Kahn's Chappaqua synagogue. There he saw the copy of *Wooden Synagogues* that had so inspired Louis Kahn. He put it under his arm and took it without telling anyone.

Later, he made a few sketches and then gave one of them to an assistant who built a model. He wrote notes to two board members, inviting them to his studio to see it. He then asked Carol to drive him from Chester to Chappaqua so he could return the book as quietly as he had taken it.

In selling his ideas to his congregation, an anticipated problem quickly arose. Except for a few in the synagogue community who followed the art world, the name Sol LeWitt merely signified a shy but affable fellow who showed up on occasion for Shabbat services. Though the congregation included many professionals and highly educated people, most members had no idea they were worshiping alongside a man who was revered in dozens of countries. He was always polite, even though his brand of politeness was not always obvious.

The president of the synagogue's board at this time of big change was Donna Moran, and she helped get LeWitt's design for a new building approved in spite of skeptics who asked why the board should engage an artist whose resume didn't include designing a public building. To be sure, the effort would have the advantage of expertise in such work, since Stephen Lloyd, a local architect with an excellent reputation, had agreed to translate LeWitt's basic plan into technical drawings with specifications that could be easily followed by a competent builder. In addition, Moran's husband, George Amarant, an experienced builder, would become a major resource and would identify materials from old factory buildings, for example, that could be used in the building process.

As Lloyd recalled, the work that he and LeWitt undertook at first was to "explore design ideas from a broader range of history and culture. The exploration was influenced by two precedents. Sol had previously prepared a proposal that featured an octagonal sanctuary and east-facing courtyard. He was intrigued by the wonderful wooden synagogues of Eastern Europe. Perhaps the most handsome of the wooden synagogues was an early eighteenth-century synagogue in Wolpa, Poland, which featured an expressive tiered roof and a dramatic central worship space. We studied it."[30] Out of this process came a modified preliminary plan.

The task of selling all of this to the congregation as a whole presented its own challenges. Like most Jewish congregations, this one had no shortage of opinions. But at a general meeting called to determine a response to the basic idea, Lloyd was equal to the task, listening to each idea—no matter how impractical or outside the boundaries of what he and LeWitt were trying to do—and responding with variations of "That's something, certainly, to think about," or "Thank you so much for pointing that out."[31] Once the congregation's members felt that they had been heard, the building's planners in effect were free to do what they wanted. It had all worked because neither Lloyd nor LeWitt ever gave the impression of considering themselves to be geniuses and above the congregation.

However, other decisions had to be made, including one that required a little arm twisting between the building's designers. Lloyd recalled:

> Near the end of the project Sol asked me to meet him at the synagogue. He walked up to the center of the panels at the back of the sanctuary. He had an idea for a design which might be used there. He showed me a Star of David inscribed in a circle . . . fractured into segments rendered in bright colors. It was spectacular. "No, Sol," I said. "Not on the back wall. This belongs on the ark"—the holiest spot in the building, where the Torah scrolls are stored. Sol asked me to present the idea to the design committee and, doing so, I was more nervous than at any time in the whole process. That is, here was a non-Jew advising a very opinionated group of Jews about how to create the focal point of a new synagogue. What if I could not convince them to employ this wonderful piece of art in the heart of the building? But I needn't have worried. The committee loved Sol's design. And since, it has become a symbol of the congregation.[32]

LeWitt's artistic legacy is honored in a variety of ways in the building that opened in Chester in October 2001, not only through his work but also through that of an array of artists whose work has been on display in the synagogue's gallery in changing exhibits. The first of these artists was Karen Gunderson, with whom LeWitt had carried on a brief romantic relationship in the 1970s. Gunderson's exhibit illustrated a dramatically different perspective on the Holocaust years than LeWitt's *Lost Voices* or *Black Form*, as indicated by its title—*Moral Courage During World War II: Denmark and Bulgaria*. In paintings and drawings, Gunderson portrayed scenes of people—both those in high places and ordinary people—who risked their lives to save Jews. Of course, LeWitt had a major hand in arranging the exhibit, but it was officially organized by the synagogue's ailing art curator, Liz Gwillim. LeWitt wrote a tribute to her in the catalogue: "Liz believed that the synagogue's walls could be used to speak to a diverse audience, and was enthused by the prospect of bringing these dramatic works to Chester. Though very ill with cancer, Liz met with the artist to make the arrangements. A few days after that meeting, she died. The exhibit is dedicated to her memory and to her generous spirit."[33]

■ LeWitt's low-profile role in the building of the synagogue—he let Lloyd be the spokesperson for the creative team—was typical. He avoided personal adulation, as opposed to adulation for his work, even at events that were all about him.

Just before he conceived of his first proposed design for the new synagogue, Sol and Carol traveled to São Paulo, Brazil, for the twenty-third Art Bienal in 1996. The regular show is considered the most prestigious art event in the Western Hemisphere, drawing half a million visitors over a three-month period. Of the 140 artists from seventy countries chosen for the exhibit in 1996, LeWitt was given the prime space in the enormous exhibition hall for his *Stars with Three, Four, Five, Six, Seven, Eight and Nine Points, within Bands of Color Ink Washes Superimposed*. The chief curator, Nelson Aguilera, had secured this high-visibility space for LeWitt and said that if he could have his way, LeWitt's work would be streamed throughout the museum: "I said there will be no limits at all in the Bienal for Sol LeWitt. I couldn't give a limit to him because for a conceptual artist there are no limits. It is something that happens in his mind. There is infinity. It is the idea of art."[34]

But if LeWitt was the star of the show, he was largely a no-show in terms of crowd adulation. In the days before the Bienal opening, he avoided many of the rituals of the event. For example, he missed a photo shoot while touring Oro Preto, a historic colonial city. Joel Lang reported in the *Hartford Courant* from São Paulo:

People in the Atheneum delegation wondered nervously whether he'd show up for a reception that evening at the U.S. consulate. "Sol is like a shooting star, you catch him when you can," said Andrea Miller-Keller, who had also traveled to Brazil for the show on behalf of LeWitt and the Wadsworth Atheneum.

LeWitt, in the end, did show up for the formal reception, wearing an open-collared shirt, a blazer, and hiking sneakers. . . . While white-jacketed waiters served hors d'oeuvres and Chivas Regal, LeWitt was besieged politely by the diplomatic and business elite of Sao Paolo.[35]

Later that year, he also showed up when his hometown finally celebrated him—fifteen years after deeply insulting him. Sol and Carol donated *Wall Drawing 763C* to the Atheneum, which desperately needed to change its "dark, dingy, dismal" lobby, according to the acting director at the time, Kristin Mortimer.[36] The wall drawing was an enormous four-sided work, forty-five feet high, that lit the Helen and Harry Gray Court. A visitor to the museum could easily conclude that LeWitt was at peace with his hometown. That, however, would be too easy a deduction.

■ In late 1998, the Wadsworth hired a new young curator of contemporary art. Nicholas Baume, a native of Sydney, was lured from Australia to succeed Miller-Keller, who retired. For Baume, though it meant living far from home, it was a natural move.

When he was a child, Baume and his family lived next door to John Kaldor, a prominent collector who owned a great deal of LeWitt's work. Baume was fascinated by what he saw, and in 1977, when Baume was twelve years old, LeWitt came to Sydney. Even at that age, Baume wanted to speak to the artist, but, as he recalled, "The message I got back is Sol is a private, quiet chap, and doesn't like to be interrupted when he's working."[37]

Many years later, in his work as a curator, he came to Chester to interview LeWitt for a show he was mounting of the artist's work in Australia: "I had been warned. Sol was not a chatty, small-talk kind of guy and not that given to doing interviews. The whole experience was sort of forced from my point of view, as an inexperienced young curator. He was nice, but I don't think I managed to elicit any profound insights from that encounter; [I was] simply honored he agreed to do the interview. I think it was a measure of his fondness for John Kaldor."

Three years later, Baume produced another LeWitt exhibit, and this came as news spread of the job opening in Hartford. Applying for the position seemed obvious to Baume. He had produced shows of contemporary American art, including work by Andy Warhol, Robert Mapplethorpe, and Jeff Koons. But he had seemed to reach a dead end in his work in Australia, as there was no clear path for promotion at the Museum of New South Wales — and he recalled wondering "what was I going to do, go to Perth or Adelaide?" Besides, he was free to travel. The long-term romantic relationship he had been in had ended, so he had no ties. In addition, his father had become the Australian consul general in New York City. And he recalled "I would have a chance to work with one of the greatest artists of our period," referring to Sol LeWitt. But when he applied for the job in Hartford, Carol LeWitt, who was on the board of the Atheneum, gave him a sober view of what lay ahead: "Carol wanted me to be under no illusion about what Hartford was like. I was coming from Sydney, which is a very vibrant city, and she wanted me to know what I was getting myself into. She told me about the history of Hartford, and that it once had great wealth, and then the decline of industry, and the challenges that arose from the urban point of view." She also told him about the city's conservative views on art, which had only intermittently been challenged by visionaries like Chick Austin.

After some time at the Atheneum, Baume concluded that its director at the time, Peter Sutton, was not a strong champion of contemporary art. However, as Baume pointed out, Sutton did support the idea of blockbuster shows, which his new curator produced. Among them were exhibits of Warhol's work and, coinciding with LeWitt's huge retrospective at the Whitney, a show of the artist's incomplete open cubes. In that exhibit, Baume had created a new concept: the space for exhibiting contemporary art at the Atheneum is limited, so he came up with the idea of spreading the LeWitt structures throughout the museum rather than restricting them, as is customary in such exhibits, to one gallery or group of galleries. He had worried about LeWitt's reaction to the plan, and there had been resistance to it at the Atheneum:

> Other people at the museum weren't so thrilled. But when I asked
> Sol, he said, "It's your concept, so you can do whatever you want."
> I came away from the meeting scratching my head. Most artists
> are control freaks, concerned about every detail of how the work is
> presented. I couldn't believe that this major artist, on an important
> body of work, would say to me, a young curator, "Do whatever
> you want." I kept thinking that right before the deadline for the
> catalogue, he'd say, "I think it'd be better if you did this or that,"
> but he never did. He was generous and trusting.

LeWitt liked the way Baume tried to feature the many pieces of the LeWitt Collection that the museum housed. To be sure, most of these pieces were stored in inadequate below-ground facilities. However, Baume was able to put together themed shows. One of them was based on the Venus statue in the midst of the museum's Avery Court—an exhibit that included the work of many artists from the LeWitt Collection and showed how they related to that piece in various ways, which was a very creative undertaking.

But in time the LeWitt Collection's presence at the museum became a sore point for the artist. Despite Baume's efforts, it didn't seem to LeWitt that the collection as a whole was being cared for or exhibited in a way that he felt was appropriate. As the years passed, the collection was moved to Chester and other locations, including the New Britain Museum of American Art.

■ In 2014, João Leonardo, a native of Portugal, recounted the story of what happened to him in Australia. He was just one of an untold number of young artists who had benefited from LeWitt in some way, and though he never met the artist, he credited him for having saved him from ruin.

In 2001, Leonardo was living in a luxury apartment in Sydney. He returned home one day from his job of designing logos for corporations. He said to himself, "Commercial art means bullshit. I should be doing real art, what I was trained for."[38] That night he was eager to begin his routine indulgence in too much whiskey and maybe some crystal meth, even though his boyfriend—a wealthy architect who made the good life possible for Leonardo—increasingly disapproved of this behavior.

During his ride upward in one of the apartment building's glass elevators, Leonardo saw workers on a scaffolding in the lobby who were completing a very tall wall drawing in stripes of red, blue, yellow, and green. Leonardo concluded that it must be the work of Stella or LeWitt. He was annoyed that he didn't know which artist was the right one. He thought back on his art education in Portugal, where he had been taught art history that covered only the period from ancient Egypt to the 1950s—as if art had died the day when Jackson Pollock, in a drunken stupor, drove his Oldsmobile 88 into an oak tree.

Leonardo knew only that what was being made on that enormous wall in the lobby, both simple and complex, was part of a revolution in art. He asked himself: "What is painting? It is decision making. First one decides the surface, the location, shape, texture, medium; then decides the color, the mixture or absence of color; then again one decide [*sic*] which brush (or non-brush) to use, decide [*sic*] the direction of the stroke, its purpose, its personality, character, impression, its impulse. . . . To decide. To paint it's to decide."[39]

In time, he discovered that the work was indeed LeWitt's, though the artist himself was not there to oversee its creation.

Leonardo said: "I see the sun in the art of Sol LeWitt. I see pure beauty, organization, abstract thinking, refined humor, and generosity."[40] On the occasion of LeWitt's death, Leonardo wrote a tribute in his blog:

> One day, after many bottles of whiskey and beer, I had to leave the apartment tower that had the Sol LeWitt in the lobby. I took my belongings with me, and these were slowly changed in those cash-advanced stores, where addicts often exchange stolen goods for money to buy the dose of the day. . . . In this chosen path of self-indulgence and self-destruction, I was selling or losing everything, and shortly after losing my job, I found myself on the street, with the catalog of Sol LeWitt on [*sic*] my hands. It was all I had. In the catalog, there was a letter he had written to Eva Hesse in 1965. I read this text once and then realized I had hit rock bottom, that life is a transformation process and that's the challenge: change. And then, in fact I did [change] and I am here to tell the story.[41]

Leonardo also recalled: "I felt as if the letter to Eva Hesse was written personally to me. It was [LeWitt's] embrace to all of us. He was saying do whatever you want. But do it."[42]

To Leonardo, LeWitt seemed to have all the right answers. But the young artist was at the time ignorant of LeWitt's formative years and his own decade of doubt.

Nevertheless Leonardo understood LeWitt's powerful message and changed his life and fortunes. He went back to Portugal, and his recent art has been exhibited in the United States as well as Germany, Iceland, Iran, Spain, Sweden, Turkey, and Uruguay.

FIFTEEN

COLLECTING LEWITT

The collecting of LeWitt's work required that it be measured in a way not usually emphasized in art transactions. That is, a buyer of a wall drawing was, in effect, purchasing not a physical work but a LeWitt idea. The physical manifestation would appear later, during the "perfunctory" stage—when the buyer would pay for the time and expenses of the people who would install the drawing.

Throughout art history, of course, the object was the point. Even Marcel Duchamp's revolutionary urinal turned upside down into *Fountain* was still a physical object that could be carted from a bathroom to a gallery to a private home. Like all other works of art up to that point, it could be mounted on a wall, placed in a corner, positioned as piece of sculpture in a garden, or stored in the cellar. In a way, of course, a LeWitt work had the same possibilities, but the work, its value, and its physical manifestation are defined differently. For example, Julia Halperin reported in May 2012:

What is the essence of a Sol LeWitt wall drawing? What makes these works—which famously exist as a series of instructions, executable by anyone who owns them—authentic LeWitts and not just some lines on a wall? This metaphysical quandary is about to be played out in a lawsuit filed by disgruntled collector and dealer Roderic Steinkamp against Chicago's Rhona Hoffman Gallery.

On May 22, Steinkamp sued Hoffman and her eponymous gallery for a total of $1.4 million, alleging that she lost a certificate of authenticity for a Sol LeWitt drawing he consigned to her in 2008. (The lawsuit was first reported by *Courthouse News*.) "Since the wall drawings do not constitute freestanding, portable works of art like a framed canvas or a sculpture on a podium, documentation of the work is key to transmitting it or selling it to a collector or institution," says the complaint, filed in New York County Supreme

Court. "The unique nature of Sol LeWitt's wall drawings renders their accompanying certificates of authenticity critical to such works' value."[1]

The arts writer Daniel Grant commented in the *Huffington Post*:

[Steinkamp] had entrusted to her a certificate of authenticity and a diagram for a Sol LeWitt (1928–2007) wall drawing, not the wall drawing itself, and she somehow lost this paperwork. Big deal: You ask the Sol LeWitt estate for a duplicate certificate and diagram, which it certainly has, maybe paying a certain fee for the trouble, just as you would if you lost the deed to your house or to your car. However, the LeWitt estate said no. It is the view of the estate that the certificate of authenticity and especially the diagram are the actual work of art; the paperwork is the art, rather than an installation of the wall drawing, and in this instance no installation appears not [*sic*] to have taken place.[2]

However, the refusal to give duplicate certificates that emerged in the marketing of LeWitt's work seemed to counter an earlier idea that LeWitt had expressed about the process of marketing to Andrea Miller-Keller in the early 1980s:

ANDREA MILLER-KELLER: When you sell a wall drawing to a private collector of a museum, what is it that you think you are selling? The idea? The plan?

SOL LEWITT: Both are inseparable, but the plan can be used without it being bought. The idea that may be comprehended by anyone seeing the plan.

AMK: Are you selling the right to use an idea that is still yours (because authorship cannot be transferred)?

SL: Ideas cannot be owned. They belong to whoever understands them. The piece takes a physical form and becomes an object. This object may be possessed. "A work of art," says Gertrude Stein, "is either priceless or worthless."[3]

Later, Miller-Keller pressed LeWitt on the question of how the ideas of others can be used:

AMK: You are very often traveling in order to share your work with anyone who is genuinely interested in it. You certainly had not reserved the enjoyment of wall drawings for only wealthy

collectors and museums. Your drawings have been done in
many prestigious institutions but also in tiny towns and small
universities across the United States, Canada and Europe.
To whom do you give permission to do your drawings?

SL: Anyone who would follow the plan is eligible to try (in good
faith, I would hope).

AMK: How would you feel if someone executed a wall drawing of
yours without permission but with care to follow the instructions
in an appropriate site?

SL: OK.

AMK: Would you consider this an "authentic" LeWitt wall drawing?

SL: Yes, it would be authentic.

AMK: Would you consider such an unauthorized use of wall drawing
instructions unethical?

SL: No. It would be a compliment.[4]

In a certain way, LeWitt never changed his mind. That is, anyone
could duplicate a drawing of his. But unless a certificate came with the
drawing, it couldn't be sold to someone else.

In time, the issue of copying became nearly moot because the wall
drawings were made site-specific and thus tailored to the unique character of the installation wall. Moreover, the long and straightforward titles that would indicate in themselves how to do a wall drawing were
replaced by less specific titles and instructions that required interpretation by experienced crew chiefs.

The hard line on replacing the document of sale was drawn after an
unsatisfactory episode in a French court after the owner of a structure
of cubes had lost his certificate. LeWitt replaced it, but then the original
was found, and the integrity of the process of sale was threatened. The
case proved costly in terms of legal fees, and after that he and Susanna
Singer decided to stop replacing certificates.

Certificates of ownership, of course, have always been central to art
marketing, but the dramatic extension of their meaning in LeWitt's case
was demonstrated in 1987 when Christie's sold an idea rather than a
physical piece. At that point, the Gilman Paper Company owned the
certificate for the 1971 wall drawing titled *Ten Thousand Lines About 10
Inches (25 cm.) Long, Covering a Wall Evenly*. The company was selling
its collection of contemporary art.

"This is the first time we will auction a work of art that cannot be taken away in a truck or under the buyer's arm," Martha Baer, the head of Christie's contemporary art department, told a *New York Times* reporter. "We are selling the right of the buyer to have the drawing recreated on his or her wall."[5]

Even *People* crawled into the weeds of contemporary art, publishing the results of the auction:

> An art sale was about to take place at the respected Christie's auction house . . . only something seemed to be missing—namely, a piece of art. . . . The auctioneer pointed at a wall. . . . Even from the front one could make out only faint, crisscrossing lines. But this was no time for finicky carping, let alone raising a hand for a question. About 80 seconds into the bidding, art dealer David McKee had it for $26,400—though just what it was he had, to Philistines in such matters, was less than clear.
>
> The only immediate visual reward for McKee's money was a typed certificate that indicated that the work be drawn in "black pencil" and bearing the instructions: McKee had, in effect, paid about $2,000 per word. But to LeWitt's growing legions of fans, such numbers were considered to be bargains.[6]

Though owning a LeWitt, obviously, requires attentiveness to paperwork, it also brings with it a certain advantage. John Weber, LeWitt's dealer at the time of Christie's auction, said of the wall drawings: "Museums love them—when they are not on view, they present no storage problems. The artwork consists in terms of instructions in a drawer."[7]

■ In 2003, Henry McNeil bought a 13,000-square-foot neo-Georgian mansion on Philadelphia's posh Rittenhouse Square. Though he couldn't refurbish the outside due to historic district restrictions, the Tylenol heir completely reconstructed what was behind the red brick façade. He turned what had been law offices into an open contemporary space that came to house the most dramatic private display of minimalist art in the United States, with fourteen LeWitt wall drawings, an equal number of sculptures by Donald Judd, and works by Carl Andre, Dan Flavin, and Richard Tuttle.

McNeil would not have predicted such an outcome when he first started collecting art in the 1970s. In an interview in 2013, he said:

I had this really marvelous girlfriend who worked for John Weber while Sol's work was showing there. She also had a framed note [from LeWitt] that said "Anytime you want to bring your sleeping bag over . . ." I said, "Who the hell is this, and why are you framing a note from your next boyfriend?" What I didn't know was Sol had a tradition of giving little drawings to all who work on his exhibits, and my marvelous girlfriend was one of those people.

I was collecting different art at the time, work by Julian Schnabel and Cindy Sherman. That period became so hot for those particular artists. My much more informed girlfriend said, "You know, that's not going to be as important as minimalism." It had been around, but wasn't getting much attention.[8]

McNeil began to buy minimalist works, but he worried: "I'm buying this piece of paper for thousands of dollars." At the time, Charles Saatchi was trading much of his collection for tax purposes. McNeil traded all he had accumulated to that point for LeWitts, Flavins, and Judds.

Soon after he purchased the plans (hence, the certificate) for a particular LeWitt wall drawing, a dealer offered him "a gigantic amount of money for the piece. I didn't want to jeopardize our friendship. I wrote Sol and asked, 'What would you think of me selling this?' He wrote back a two-page letter, and he said, 'You'd be a moron to sell it. It's one of the most important pieces I ever did.'"[9]

McNeil abandoned any idea of selling and began to collect more, even going after the plans for LeWitt's very first wall drawing that the artist had completed himself at the Paula Cooper Gallery, but McNeil was outbid.

Even so, McNeil became a dominant collector and an intimate part of the contemporary art circle. He knew the names of the pet dogs of every artist, mostly because—in his recollection anyway—they were all called Giotto.

However, the relationship between LeWitt and McNeil turned frosty in the 1990s. The collector wanted to create a sculpture garden of Le-Witt's structures on his New Jersey property. LeWitt responded, "Why would you want to do this? You can see one in Paris, one in Minneapolis, one in New York, and so on." The conversations continued, and Mc-Neil invited LeWitt and Singer to the proposed site of the collection. As Singer recalled, the location "seemed like a garbage dump, a ridiculous quarry. Hank's idea was to charge admission, and give Sol the opportunity of a lifetime — a Marfa-like set up [in that Texas city, Donald Judd's work has been collected]."[10] LeWitt and Singer rejected the idea.

McNeil recalled: "I told him I wanted to bring together all periods of his work. He was miffed. Neither of us felt very good about this."[11] The two men were reconciled a few years later.

LeWitt's informal accounting notebook records other sales to private collectors over the years. For example, a 1971 wall drawing sold at Lisson Gallery earned $15,000 for the artist. In 1981, David Bellman of Toronto bought a variety of pieces, including wall drawings, for about $200,000. Entries from around that time show similarly large sales to Yvon Lambert of Paris.

But private collectors were just a part of the marketplace. For example, corporations wanted to buy art not only make to office spaces more interesting to work in, but also to enhance their images.

In the mid-1980s, AXA Equitable Life Insurance Company commissioned LeWitt to provide art for a dramatic new atrium space in its new headquarters on Avenue of the Americas. The company hoped to present a cutting-edge image and a celebration of Manhattan's vibrancy, and thus it arranged to acquire very large works by LeWitt and Roy Lichtenstein. LeWitt's was the wall drawing *Bands of Lines of Colors in Four Directions*, which suggested the grid pattern of the city's streets. The commission fee was high — about $500,000, with 70 percent going to the artist and the other 30 percent to the commissioning gallery, as was typical in such an arrangement. Equitable had to pay the installation fee on top of that. Other corporate commissions, some nearly as grand and expensive, followed.

In the late 1990s, Microsoft hired the art consultant Michael Klein as its first chief curator to help the corporation build an art collection.

Klein had begun his rise to prominence in the contemporary art world after earning a graduate degree in art history at Williams College at a time when, as he recalled in a 2014 interview, the number of minority students were limited, "gay was a lyric in a Cole Porter song, and contemporary art was certainly not a subject deemed worthy of discussion, let alone a full semester's course."[12] In 1983, Klein opened his own gallery in New York City. After it closed in 1997, he became an independent curator.

He had met LeWitt in 1980: "I was always a great fan, but didn't know him." Pat Steir introduced the two. That meeting loomed large years later when Bill Gates gave Klein the task of making the Microsoft headquarters reflect the company's innovative character. Or as the company would put it to employees and prospective clients, the idea of building an art collection "reflects the Microsoft's standards of innovation and creativity. It represents the diverse and global community of Microsoft employees and our customers, and humanizes and energizes the work environment."[13]

Over time, the company would buy about 4,500 pieces by hundreds of artists. But the LeWitt work provided one of the biggest challenges.

"I was presented with a problem," Klein recalled. "There was a new complex in Redmond [Washington, near Seattle]. The place had a cafeteria which had a very large wall, 20 feet deep and 50 feet wide, and the architect wanted to do a wood treatment on the wall." Klein wanted instead to offer the space for a commission to either Ellsworth Kelly or LeWitt.

Kelly's prices would have busted the Microsoft budget, but LeWitt could do a work that would make use of the entire wall at a cost of $400,000 plus expenses. *Wall Drawing No. 1,000* would be one of the most colorful and dramatic, if the deal could be arranged. Klein recalled:

> To make the sale, I had to get the buy-in from the architects. I felt it was very important to have the architects on my side, even though I was the decision maker. Art people are thought of as crazy, and architects are thought of as people who know what they're doing. So I wanted them to understand and to work in conjunction with the artist with what they had designed. They really got it. They understood that Seattle in winter is very gray and cloudy, and there are great shifts of light. The brilliant hues of LeWitt's drawing could be a counterpoint, could bring a great uplifting sense to the place. Also, the work would be integrated in Microsoft's daily life. The employees are working with technology — they could write codes morning, noon and night, but they hadn't necessarily seen things. The architects said, "Let's do it."

When Klein put the plan for the wall on the desk of Bill Gates, the founder of Microsoft told his curator, "This is beautiful."[14] Of course, that was enough to allow Klein to proceed.

The work was scheduled to start on September 11, 2001. "That morning," Klein remembered, "my mother-in-law called from New York and told me the horrible news." As all flights were canceled for several days, no work could begin. But Klein used that time to start introducing LeWitt's process to Microsoft employees:

I wanted employees to understand how [the work] was done, so
we documented it, putting it on the website. For me it was a big risk.
Microsoft had never done a work like this. I thought big murals,
though, were more cost efficient, a dramatic statement. At night
you can see it from the street, pretty spectacular.

I spent the next couple of weeks after the installation was
finished having lunch to hear what employees thought of it. The
average employee was twenty-some years old and I was in my fifties.
I felt like Grandpa. But the reaction was very positive. A girl said,
"My god, look at this." They all got it. One employee called it "the
wall that lights up." One woman said she had just been to a museum
and had seen a LeWitt, and "now we've got one, too. What a cool
company."

If Microsoft was the symbol of American innovation, Christie's and
Sotheby's auction houses on the other coast were the ultimate pur-
veyors of worth and of how image affects worth, as determined by the
amounts of hard cash that sales generate.

In 1998 when Christie's was planning its new American headquarters, at 20 Rockefeller Center, it contacted the Pace Wildenstein Gallery
—which represented LeWitt, though not exclusively. The auction house
hoped to make a bold artistic statement in its lobby and to do so by
commissioning the first mural in the Rockefeller Center complex since
1946. (A mural by Diego Rivera in the RCA building had been removed
when he refused to paint out an image that gloried Lenin.)

After arrangements were made and the work had begun, LeWitt told
Carol Vogel, an arts writer for the *New York Times*, that it wasn't the
Rockefeller Center space as a whole that he had considered but merely
the large lobby space. "Rockefeller Center is a work of art in itself," he
said. "It resonates with history." LeWitt told Vogel that he had thought
of the work by imagining a giant panel (nearly thirty feet high and eighteen feet wide) as a fifteenth-century gesso painting: "I thought of it as
the world's largest miniature. It's like a big box in which I had to figure
out how to visually enter the space and move around in it. It had to be
bright, shiny, intense, because the area is so compressed."[15]

The work to do that took more time than anticipated, and it was further complicated by something that had never happened in the course
of more than three decades of painting LeWitt's wall drawings. The
painters' union required that each member of the eight-person crew

join the union before any work could proceed. LeWitt, always supportive of labor, had no objection, and hence the work proceeded.

The crew for that project was led by Sachiko Cho, who with remarkable ease applied the features of a maquette to a wall fifteen times its
size. She measured and taped the design in place and, following the
usual practice, assigned a number to each area to indicate the colors.
After each of the seven coats of paint was applied, the wall was sanded
smooth, and a coat of varnish applied.

Cho said, "Sol doesn't mind a bit of handiwork showing. That way it
doesn't look as if the paint has been sprayed."[16] The secret to making
the colors pop, she said, was the labor-intensive layering technique.

When asked by Vogel if the wall drawing would fade over time, Le-
Witt replied, "Come back in 100 years. That's the only way to tell."[17]

Here was the unusual and effective kind of publicity that LeWitt
sought, a kind of playfulness and contemplation, matters that critics
and feature writers were eager to seize upon. And because he was able
to do create this kind of media stir, he could avoid the traps of the celebrity culture.

■ A few years later a Connecticut collector had a different idea for a
collection in one place — bringing together old friends to celebrate Le-
Witt's seventieth birthday in the Avery Court, a dramatic and historic
space in the Wadsworth Atheneum. Micky Cartin, s major collector and
longtime Connecticut friend of Sol who organized the effort, knew that
if the artist learned about the celebration in advance he would likely
cancel it. Still, Cartin persisted, and brought Carol LeWitt in on the
planning. Scores of people who had been important to the artist were
invited with instructions to stay mum, knowing the effort — with its lavish catering and other costs — would go for naught if LeWitt found out
about it ahead of time.

The planning process for the September 9, 1998, event went well. A
bus was chartered in Manhattan to bring a variety of old friends to Connecticut. There were many local guests as well who dusted off festive
evening wear. But something went awry in Chester.

During breakfast on September 9 at the LeWitt house, the artist's
daughter Eva, who was also born on that date, complained that her
special day was ruined because she wasn't permitted to come to the
party that night. LeWitt, of course, asked her to identify the party she
was referring to. Her answer, not surprisingly, put him in a foul mood.

He understood, however, that some people were coming from far away, so he reluctantly agreed to go. That night Carol drove him the thirty-five miles from Chester to Hartford, at least relieved that the event would occur—though as it turned out, not in the way anyone imagined it might since the guest of honor, never loquacious in public, forcefully delivered a minimalist sentence limited to two words.

In contrast to expectations, LeWitt came in with a smile on his face, greeting old friends and seeming to enjoy everything. In the crowd were Martin and Mickey Friedman, Chuck Close, Carl Andre, Singer, Robert and Sylvia Mangold, Steir, and many others who had known LeWitt in his formative years.[18]

The guests, finally relaxed, sat at round tables and enjoyed a meal catered by Au Musee, the upscale restaurant in the building. Just before the strawberry dessert was served, however, the mood changed—at first, to one of curious delight and then to one of disbelief. Singer, angry about what happened, told LeWitt later that he had misbehaved.

What happened was this: Peter Sutton, who was director of the Atheneum at the time, strode to the podium to begin a formal program to honor LeWitt. Sutton, a tall and distinguished man, offered some introductory remarks, including the view that Hartford had produced two world-class artists over two centuries, Frederick Church in the nineteenth century and LeWitt in the twentieth. Sutton had barely gotten through this brief tribute when LeWitt, sitting the table directly in front of the podium, shouted, "No speeches!" Apparently thinking this was simply the expression of a notoriously modest man, Sutton continued, saying there were a few people who had prepared remarks. But LeWitt would have none of it. "No speeches," he repeated, this time with a clear edge of determination in his voice. And he said again, "No speeches." Sutton, however, persisted, "But Sol, there are people who have prepared . . ." The artist interrupted again with his two-word demand. "At least, if you would, let Andrea talk," Sutton said. Andrea Miller-Keller then stood up at the table next to LeWitt's and began to walk to the podium. She carried with her the text of a brief tribute that she intended to deliver. She had planned to say: "I have felt privileged to watch your life unfold over the past few decades, from Hester to Chester. There were the pre-Carol days, when less was more. And then there was the remarkable blossoming (and major expansions) of the Carol days— the burst of color in your work, enduring love, home, daughters, animals, nannies, properties, bat mitzvahs, philanthropy. There was even, arranged by you, the man who doesn't drive, the very touching arrival of a BMW sedan in your driveway the morning of Carol's fortieth birthday."[19]

There was more as well, but she never got to say any of it. "Come here," LeWitt said. "Let me see it," referring to her speech. He took it and put it in the pocket of his sport coat. "I'll read it later," he said.

Sutton, a man unaccustomed to such impertinence at celebratory affairs, was momentarily speechless. Then, from a back table a voice boomed. Carl Andre said, "Well, I'll speak." He did so from his chair, saying, "No other artist in the world has done so much for other artists as Sol LeWitt." As he said this, he used his hands for emphasis, and at one point guests at tables closer to the podium could see that on the far wall, behind his hands, was a painting by Ana Mendieta, his late wife, whose mysterious death had led to a murder charge against him.

LeWitt responded to Andre's remarks with his only lengthy public sentence of the evening, deflecting praise toward a colleague and thus proving Andre's point. "This man," LeWitt said, referring to the creator of Hartford's notorious rocks project, "created 500 yards from this museum the greatest public art installation in America."

The intended formal part of the evening ended there, and guests—particularly those who had to travel back to Manhattan on the chartered bus—said their goodbyes. Trying to part on a light note, Martin Friedman, the retired director of the Walker Art Center, shook LeWitt's hand and said, "Welcome to my side of the decade," referring to the fact that he had turned seventy a few years earlier. Friedman recalled that "Sol's steely eyes focused on me and [he] was still in combat mode. He said, 'It doesn't seem to have done much for you.'"[20]

Friedman recalled after LeWitt's death:

On the late-night bus ride back to Manhattan . . . the quiet was palpable. In some ways, it was a continuation of the silence that LeWitt demanded of those who sought to praise him. Now and then it was broken with wry observations from a few of the exhausted passengers. For many of those aboard, the wreckage of the party was not entirely surprising. After all, they reasoned in retrospect, Sol was an artist who always wanted the focus to be on his art. His behavior in the face of all those attempted encomiums was, alas, all too predictable. That was the consensus, and many of us nodded reflectively. Eight years later, the invitation . . . [to contribute to] this catalogue brought back pungent memories of that surreal evening. My talks with the artists who were there made clear that even if Sol denied them [the] opportunity to express themselves then, their respect and admiration for him and his accomplishments remain undiminished.[21]

LeWitt's efforts at dodging the limelight proved only partly successful. He continued to be in demand at openings, and he grudgingly acceded to the wishes of party planners. This, of course, was necessary when the largest and most dramatic of his exhibits to date occurred in 2000 with a retrospective featuring four decades of his work—an exhibit that traveled from San Francisco to Chicago and then to New York over a period of about fifteen months.

The monumental show, including more than 400 pieces, was organized by Gary Garrels of the San Francisco Museum of Modern Art. Garrels wrote that this was an attempt to do something that had not been done before and was not limited to the great volume of LeWitt's work: "This exhibit and book attempt to give a larger perspective and to reveal the inner coherence of Sol LeWitt's art as well as clarify its development and the diversity of his achievement."[22] A tall order, indeed.

Garrels's essay managed to identify a few of the artist's defining moments, including the one in 1998 that had led to LeWitt's wall drawings —his putting aside the muted tones that had been featured in his earlier work and beginning to use color boldly.

LeWitt told Garrels:

Sometimes inadvertent and casual things can set my ideas into another direction. I was asked to do a poster for Lincoln Center. I decided to do something that was completely different, a one-time thing. Perhaps I felt, since it was an unusual kind of work, that that made it easier to cut loose. I started using curved lines and bright colors, everything that was completely different than what I was doing then. I thought I would do things differently for that one time only. But I liked the way the poster came out, so I kept after it. That turned into what I'm doing now and a new way of thinking.[23]

Christopher Knight, an art critic at the *Los Angeles Times*, wrote: "The amazing thing is this: However abstruse, clotted and mind-numbing the instructions for LeWitt's wall drawings can be, that's exactly how simple, refreshing and deeply soul-satisfying the drawings themselves always turn out to be. LeWitt, like some latter-day Rumplestiltskin, spins straw into shimmering strands of gold."[24]

Arthur Lazere observed that in this show LeWitt had gone beyond the idea of the marriage of wall and image to tackle the much more complicated task of reflecting the character of a museum's historic atrium space:

> With the opening of the Sol LeWitt retrospective, the first survey of his work in over two decades arrives in the atrium not like an invader but like a triumphant ally taking a seat at the victory table. The museum commissioned LeWitt to create two new wall drawings specifically for this space. *Arcs in Four Directions* and *Bands in Four Directions* flank either side of the stairwell, high above the floor of the atrium. Bright washes of green, yellow, orange, red, and blue, in precise stripings, are arrayed in curves in the former, vertical, horizontal, and diagonal bands in the later. What is especially remarkable is that the drawings—monumental in size and vibrant in color—do not conflict with the understated elegance of the atrium and, indeed, are remarkably sensitive to it, as if engaging in dialogue the pre-existing elements.[25]

When the exhibit moved to a slightly smaller space at the Museum of Contemporary Art Chicago, a few of the drawings had to be scaled down, and other adjustments needed to be made, but the character of the show stayed intact.

LeWitt's reputation in Chicago had been built with the considerable help of the owner of the Rhona Hoffman Gallery. In 1975 Hoffman and her partner at the time, Donald Young, asked LeWitt to come to the city and offered to create a show for him, the first of more than a dozen the gallery produced over the years. The first was of prints for Parasol Press, and it was in the process of producing the show that Hoffman met Carol Androccio. Hoffman recalled in 2015:

> Sol never liked to stay overnight in Chicago if he could help it and when he had to he preferred the Allerton Hotel. It had a swimming pool. (Once I put him home at the Standard Club which he did not like so much.) . . . I asked him to spend another night in Chicago once and he declined but when I told him I had box seats on the left side of Orchestra Hall with Daniel Barenboim playing all the Beethoven Sonatas, he stayed happily.

Sol's favorite place to have dinner was Gene and Georgetti's
... one of the oldest restaurants in the city, [which] started as a
speakeasy during Prohibition and that remains in the possession
of the same Italian families. They served huge portions of liver
slathered in onions, huge steaks, chicken Vesuvio, and [it] was,
and remains, a place for the pols to hang out.[26]

Hoffman also recalled LeWitt's stubbornness and willingness to take
a monetary hit for the sake of artistic integrity. When Hoffman produced an exhibit of seventy-two of his gouaches at her gallery in 1998,
the Museum of Contemporary Art (MCA) wanted to buy some of them.
"But Sol would not break them up," Hoffman recalled. "At $10,000 each
it was obviously more money than the MCA could or would spend. So
Sol lowered the price to $1,000 each, or $72,000 total — a 90 percent dis-
count, and the museum raised the money from members of the board.
Then Sol made a print with Joe Watanabe and gave one to each donor.
The only demand Sol made was to have them make a little book of the
gouaches, which they did, and which was beautiful."[27]

In Chicago, LeWitt also had to maneuver between the world of art
and the workaday world, and sometimes, as in the following case, both
benefitted. Hoffman recalled:

In 1997 I had a huge space and we decided to do a big concrete
block structure in it to play off a Fred Sandback sculpture in another
adjacent space. I realized that if I used union bricklayers it would
cost me a fortune so I called the union and asked if they had
apprentices who would like a unique experience. They came and
they learned how to make a concrete block sculpture perfectly. I
stood by to curate and in the beginning the work was a bit sloppy.
I would make them clean it better and in the end it turned out
amazingly.

I told Sol about what I had done and, though he usually didn't
come to openings, he made an exception. He decided to have a pre-
opening for the apprentices and the other bricklayers who wished
to attend. It turned out the [International Union of Bricklayers and
Allied Craftworkers] was in Chicago for an annual meeting. A lot
of them attended. We took photos of the apprentices with Sol and
it showed up in the [union's magazine]. What fun. Everyone got
something out of the experience.[28]

The 2000 exhibit was a huge affair in the Windy City, drawing thousands of attendees. At the opening, the director of the museum stood at the podium as Sutton had at the Wadsworth Atheneum two years earlier, but this speaker was able to finish his remarks, paying tribute to LeWitt in a lavish way though mispronouncing his first name as "Sole." LeWitt made no speech himself that day—not surprisingly—but did participate in a question-and-answer session in which he offered low-key explanations of his work but, characteristically, nothing in the way of anecdotes.

The arrival of the exhibit in Manhattan, where by then LeWitt had created nearly twenty public projects, created a stir, as anticipated. Celestine Bohlen, a reporter for the *New York Times*, wrote:

> How many people does it take to put together a Sol LeWitt exhibition? For the Whitney Museum of American Art, where a full-scale retrospective of this conceptual artist's work opens on Thursday, the correct answer is 30, most of them artists themselves. Their job was to sand, tape and paint surfaces as high as 17 feet, applying as many as seven layers of paint and penciling in tens of thousands of lines as they reproduced Mr. LeWitt's diagrams directly on the gallery walls.
>
> The work lasted a month, with only Thanksgiving off. The museum's lobby and fourth-floor galleries resembled building sites, with scaffolding, buckets of paint, spools of tape, rolls of calculator paper and rags and brushes: the clutter needed to produce works known for their simplicity.
>
> The installation of a LeWitt exhibition has become a science. The artist, who supervises every step, pronouncing whether the greens are deep enough or the purples too pale, produces new diagrams for each show. He adjusts his drawings—he doesn't like the term painting—to the wall space available. He has a team of about 15 regulars; for this exhibition, the Whitney hired almost as many more, culled from 300 applicants.[29]

When the show came to New York, both the *Times* and the *New Yorker* were effusive in their praise. In the *Times*, Michael Kimmelman wrote: "Hands down, this is the most beautiful exhibition by a living artist in a New York museum in a long time, an antidote to the nonsense on view in several other museums around town, a rebuttal to soreheads saying there's never serious contemporary art around anymore, and also a digestible, brightly colored package just in time for the holidays. The perfect gift for the city that has everything except enough shows like this one."[30]

Peter Schjeldahl wrote in the *New Yorker*: "Like the Old Masters of classical music — Bach, especially — LeWitt illuminates the workings of his mind. He structures large understandings of perception and thought. If his art is without apparent emotion, that just leaves an inviting vacuum. Love rushes in.... LeWitt's wall drawings belong in a hall of fame for parsimonious, incredibly potent inventions, like the lever and the wheel."[31]

However, the praise was not universal. LeWitt's old college acquaintance, Hilton Kramer, wrote in the *Observer*:

> On another subject, however, Mr. LeWitt's claim that there is
> no reason to suppose "that the conceptual artist is out to bore
> the viewer" — something more needs to be said. For there is an
> immense quantity of work in this retrospective — rooms and
> rooms of it — that this viewer found to be almost unendurably
> boring. I am not suggesting that Mr. LeWitt has set out to bore us,
> but a large measure of boredom is built into his depersonalized
> method. When "the plan" designs "the work" and "the execution
> is a perfunctory affair," then boredom awaits us, whether or not
> the artist intends it.[32]

Regardless of the impression left by Kramer, writing with authority and insight about LeWitt's wall drawings is a more complex issue than the vocabulary of art allowed at the time. Six years before the retrospective, that point had been made in another kind of collection — one of words rather than visuals, a book published in Rome titled *Sol LeWitt Critical Texts*. The book's editor, Adachiara Zevi, compiled dozens of essays written over the years about his work, including LeWitt's own pieces and those of, for example, Rosalind Krauss, Ira Licht, Filiberto Menna, Lucy Lippard, Robert Rosenblum, Rudi Fuchs, Michael Kirby, and Miller-Keller. *Sol LeWitt Critical Texts* also serves as a fine compilation of other quotable quotes from the artist. Among them are:

> From "Paragraphs on Conceptual Art": "New materials are one
>   of the great afflictions of contemporary art. Some artists confuse
>   new materials with new ideas." And "Conceptual art is good only
>   when the idea is good."[33]
> From "Sentences on Conceptual Art": "One usually understands

the art of the past by applying the convention of the present, thus misunderstanding the art of the past." And "Successful art changes our understanding of the conventions by altering our perceptions."[34]

From LeWitt's response to the 1973 *Flash Art* ad that accused him of plagiarism: "Those who understand art only by what it looks like often do not understand very much at all." And "And it cannot be said that what looks alike is alike."[35]

From the interview at Oxford in 1993, a commentary on a simple truth about art and what it depicts, and why there is a certain authenticity in his work that is missing from representational artists: "Obviously a drawing of a person is not a real person, but a drawing of a line is a real line."[36]

Sol LeWitt Critical Texts is a bible for understanding LeWitt's work, though it contains very little in the way of anecdote (Michael Kirby's delightful essay, "I've Known Sol LeWitt," is an exception) and sometimes relies heavily on what LeWitt despised—artspeak—to such an extent that a casual reader would require the services of a translator.

For example, Tracy Atkinson (who later became director of the Wadsworth Atheneum) wrote in 1970 that LeWitt's "wall drawings can be seen to exhibit the characteristic LeWittian 'anaesthetizing' of baroque operationalism."[37]

LeWitt's own words and the interpretation of them have been of great interest to the arts writer and college professor George Stolz, who is compiling and interpreting them in a book to be released by Yale University Press.

However, Stolz went well beyond mere words in a previous publication, *Sol LeWitt: Fotografia*, a compilation of LeWitt's photographs taken over many years. In it, Stolz honored the formula LeWitt established in his 1980 *Autobiography*, arranging the photographs in grids without captions. Indeed, the book's first element (there are no chapters indicated) consists of photographs from *Autobiography*, though with thirty-six images on each page as opposed to the original nine. When a viewer looks at the inventory of LeWitt's Hester Street life through this lens and after considering his oeuvre, it becomes a revealing study of influences. For example, a simple colander hung on a kitchen hook can be seen as an inspiration, because of the design of its drainage holes, of LeWitt's wall drawings featuring six-pointed stars.

The second element of the book features LeWitt's 1982 photographs of Renaissance sculptures that he has altered simply by imposing a variety of hues on a black-and-white images. This certainly can be seen as a metaphor for the artist's attempt to honor and yet build on the ideas of the past.

His 1977 photographs of a brick wall presage the work he would do a quarter of a century later in a German synagogue, though in the photographs the wall is just a wall, not a symbol of oppression.

Perhaps most surprising is LeWitt's enthusiasm for graffiti, as documented by nearly seven hundred square photographs of images on walls—mostly in Manhattan, specifically the Lower East Side. The impression here is one of generous regard for all wall drawings, even those done in frustration, not artfully, or obscenely. LeWitt also seemed taken by contemporary and historical signage. The book includes signs for Sol Stein Jeweler, Abe's Fashion Place, Lien Fok Grocery, KCF Produce, Get Sun: Shoes ReNew, and "Close Monday." Slogans for causes are present throughout, such as "Avenge Attica," "Free Rachel McGee," and "Stop Nuclear Power." But mostly Le Witt seemed fascinated by the designs of the wording, elements so despised by residents who rightfully lament the proliferation of graffiti on urban streets, walls, and subways.

Stolz includes in this collection a detailed presentation of the photographs that caused the 1991 stir at the Smithsonian's National Museum of American Art (the sequential nude portraits as seen in a box); LeWitt's studies of cubes; the vistas from the balcony of his wife's ancestral home in Praiano, Italy; and an impressive section on grids not meant as art, such as common fans, sewer covers, elevator doors, and wrought-iron fences—a commentary, it would seem, on the relationship between ordinary life and what might be seen in a gallery that interprets that life.

In his commentary at the end of the book, Stolz writes, "Photography was at the source of LeWitt's incorporating of narrative into his art, and was thus at the very source of all seriality a conceptual art."[38]

Stolz's book, then, provides a kind of visual summary of LeWitt's thinking. And it was published, it turned out, as something of a coda—just as LeWitt contracted the disease that would prove fatal.

SIXTEEN

THE WORK OF A LIFETIME

Nearly sixty years after he first came to the Syracuse University campus, Sol LeWitt returned as an honored guest. In February 2004, a fellow Syracuse alumnus sent his private jet to pick up the artist and an assistant, Jeremy Ziemann, at the tiny airport in Chester, Connecticut. When the plane landed forty-five minutes and one bottle of champagne later, its two passengers were driven to the office of the university's new chancellor.

Nancy Cantor hoped to celebrate her own installation as head of Syracuse with an installation of sculpture by engaging the most celebrated artist among the school's graduates. She was careful, however, not to say "sculpture" in her conversation, as that word was not in the LeWitt lexicon. "Structure" was the term he preferred, a term that evoked the architectural nature of his pieces and was less laden with historical baggage, mental images, elitism, and artistic limitations.

In working on the Syracuse project, which would be a series of undulating cement block walls, LeWitt showed his disdain for pomp and circumstance. One day the official delegations—hydraulic engineers, structural engineers, and construction foremen—awaited his instructions and the details. But all they heard was LeWitt telling Ziemann, while gesturing with his arms, "I want the pieces to curve like this on the hill." He handed his assistant the general plan, and told the group, "Jeremy will answer the rest of your questions." On their way home, LeWitt told his assistant that when "you finish this project, you'll have a degree in block."[1]

Undulating Walls consisted of six twelve-foot-high walls made of concrete block. The juxtaposition of the most basic construction materials not generally associated with sensual curves eventually earned the campus work much praise,[2] but in the manner of much contemporary art, the work sometimes draws unimagined response: on autumn Saturday afternoons it has also served as an outdoor latrine for inebriated football fans.

In the later 1990s and early 2000s, LeWitt continued to be productive. He saw no reason to slow down or to stray from his disciplined daily routine. Indeed, his energy seemed to increase as his colors and dimensions grew bolder. In 2000 alone, the year that his dramatic retrospective drew tens of thousands of admirers across the country into museums, he also had work on display in Austin, Berkeley, Boise, Boston, New Haven, Philadelphia, and Santa Fe in the United States, as well as in Avignon, Barcelona, Bilbao, Luxembourg, and Rome. The following year he exhibited in fifteen cities. As Jan Dibbets put it, "This monk, this recluse, started to cook in his head, and it started to boil, and there was creation that couldn't stop, like [that of] the late [Henri] Matisse."[3]

In 2002, writing a comprehensive survey of modern movements and artists, Dorothy Valakos wrote of LeWitt's wall drawings, "Subversive and sublime, calculated and random, vibrantly sensual and rooted in the objective here-and-now, the expressive range of these . . . wall drawings testifies to the seemingly endless inventiveness and intellectual rigor with which LeWitt fashions complex variations from a simplicity of means."[4]

LeWitt traveled, as always — but now not without incident or portent. He had a hard time walking when he was working in Naples in 2002. That was the first time he'd ever experienced such a problem. After his return flight to the United States, he felt groggy and planned to catch an Amtrak train from Penn Station in New York to Connecticut, where Carol would pick him up.

Carol drove to New Haven's Union Station in time for the scheduled arrival, but Sol didn't get off the train. She waited for the next one, and when he was not on that either and not answering his cellphone, she called Susanna Singer. But Singer hadn't heard from Sol either.

It was only when a nurse called Carol from St. Vincent's Hospital did she learn that her husband had collapsed at Penn Station. Carol called Singer, who could get to St. Vincent's quickly from her Upper West Side apartment, while Carol drove to the city from Connecticut. On the way, she was of course alarmed, but she also knew that her husband had taken care of himself. He exercised every day, had yearly physicals, and made medical appointments whenever he noticed any problem. "He was a model citizen in that regard," his wife said.[5] The one thing he hadn't done was have a colonoscopy — which seemed odd to Carol, as Sol's father and several other relatives had had colon cancer. LeWitt's primary care physician, in fact, had recommended against a colonoscopy, Carol recalled, saying that the benefits were unclear.

But tests administered after LeWitt's collapse revealed that he had a cancerous tumor in his colon that had to be removed immediately. For this he was transferred to Yale–New Haven Hospital, where emergency surgery was performed.

As Carol recalled the aftermath, the surgeon said he had removed all of the cancer from the colon, but the pathologist's report was not so optimistic, indicating that the cancer had spread to the lymph nodes. This meant, of course, that monitoring LeWitt's health would become even more important as time passed. Moreover, tests indicated that he had an aggressive form of cancer, so no one was under the impression that he had been cured.

LeWitt's response was moving on by continuing to work, but he and the family knew that the prognosis for people with this condition was not promising. Statistics showed that the great majority of patients died within five years.

LeWitt focused on his legacy. He expressed the desire to create a place that could serve as a repository for his work and a long-term home for his archive. He needed some system in place that would ensure quality control, historic preservation, and curatorial oversight, be a repository for scholarship, and show a significant body of work. In short, he needed an institutional partner. Yale was an obvious choice. His relationship with the university and Jock Reynolds, the Henry J. Heinz II director of the Yale Art Gallery, was long and strong. As it turned out, Yale was eager to accommodate some of LeWitt's needs, but there was no way it could devote the display space necessary to his work. A different solution would have to be found.

In the late 1980s, Williams College had a large problem to solve. Work had been completed on the school's art museum, a beautiful building, but it wasn't large enough to exhibit whole bodies of work, let alone more than a fraction of the nearly 14,000 works that it owned. The museum's director, Thomas Krens, led a quest to purchase, if possible, a cheap mill in nearby North Adams, Massachusetts.

That city had suffered hard times. As manufacturers had closed or moved away, what was once a thriving factory-driven community had lost its tax base, as the unemployment rate climbed to 18 percent. Attempting to lure cutting-edge manufacturers to buildings like the old Sprague Electric complex, a vast array of twenty-six buildings with a combined total of 800,000 square feet, proved impractical. Manufacturers needed state-of-the-art facilities. Desperate to fill these buildings with something that would put the city on a sound financial footing, Mayor John Barrett III asked Krens and his colleagues from Williams to consider them as a solution to the university's display problem.

The collaboration eventually proved fruitful, though like any large project, it required great patience. Funding initially appeared certain to come from the state but then was pulled away—and in time restored. The Massachusetts Museum of Contemporary Art (MASSMoCA) finally opened in 1999.

Reynolds was well aware of the emergence of North Adams as an extension of Williams College's art influence and had a vision for increasing it. He also shared LeWitt's desire to create a permanent center. "I always felt," Reynolds said, "that Sol deserved a place where people could get an overview of his work, as in the case of Donald Judd."[6] In Marfa, Texas, the Judd Foundation maintains the artist's residence, art studio, library, archives, and a large body of his work, and it draws a substantial number of tourists. The idea had come from Judd himself, who said in 1977: "The installation and context for the art being done now is poor and unsuitable. The correction is a permanent installation of a good portion of the work of each of the best artists. . . . The main reason for this is to be able to live with the work and think about it, and also to see the work placed as it should be."[7]

Reynolds became the matchmaker between LeWitt and MASSMoCA. He spoke with Joseph C. Thompson, the museum's director, about the need for a center for LeWitt's work. As Thompson recalled in a 2015 interview, LeWitt took a three-hour tour of the museum in 2003. LeWitt wasn't interested, though, in the part of the complex that had already been renovated. Thompson recalled: "Though Sol was sick, he seemed spry to me. He looked through the pigeon-infested buildings. The visit required some ladder climbing and leaping across holes in the floor. He said, 'I'm thinking of building 7.' I responded, 'Which part of building 7 are you thinking of?' He didn't blink and said, 'Oh, I'm thinking of it in its entirety. If you would make it available for a significant show for a significant amount of time I'll make an exhibition that you'll really like.'"[8]

Several months later LeWitt sent a plan for the exhibit that would require the building of walls to display 105 wall drawings over a space of 27,000 square feet, a remarkable amount of real estate for one artist's work. The idea would be to borrow the works (that is, the right to reinstall them) chosen from among the more than 1,200 wall drawings from their owners and to show the progression of LeWitt's work from his first self-installed lines on the walls of Paula Cooper's gallery, through the huge installations that were many yards wide and deep, to the new directions his work might yet take. Thompson said:

> At the time Sol came to us, we were known for changing exhibitions and for new commissions, teaming up with mid-scale artists. The exhibitions might be displayed for ten months, and then everything changed. When we sat down with Sol we talked duration. We thought, "Well, if we're going to do this let's make it generational, but maybe not permanent. Let's leave it to the next generation to cast a referendum about what to do with it. If it doesn't want to keep it, this still will become the world's longest temporary exhibition." I threw out twenty-five years. Jock said, "Yes, let's leave it long enough to make it count." So the deal is simple. The exhibit runs from 2008 to 2033. Two years before the end, the director of MASSMoCA, [the director of] the Yale [University] Art Gallery, and Sol's family are supposed to have tea, and if all those parties look each other in the eye and say "Let's keep it up," we'll do it. If any one of them says twenty-five years is long enough, it'll come down.
>
> I had become a believer [in the idea] that change is good. We were not a collecting institution. But I also believed that institutions with permanent collections are stronger than those without. Sol, a modern master, could introduce a beautiful core to MASSMoCA. He was very clever in choosing building 7. I said to him during lunch that it's a little bit to the side [meaning on the periphery of the complex]. He said, "For now it is."[9]

■ During the years he was ill LeWitt continued to support the careers and welfare of others. One of those who took advantage of the latter was Vera Lutter, a photographer and native of Germany who exhibited black-and-white negatives rather than prints. Her subjects were often of urban sites such as abandoned factories and transit centers. In 2004, she was invited to do an installation on the third floor of Austria's GrazMuseum. LeWitt had an installation — a wavy wall of concrete blocks — on the second floor, and to everyone's surprise he came to see Lutter's exhibit. "We became friends," Lutter said in a 2015 interview. "It was the first trip he took after his illness [was diagnosed]. . . . There were a few people he wanted to see."[10] He knew it would likely be his last trip to Europe.

The two artists discovered that they agreed on the ugliness of art openings. As it turned out, LeWitt didn't go to the opening night party, as customary. "I had to weather it myself," Lutter said. "Everybody hates [openings]. However, I feel I can't say no. Galleries get very angry. But you have to talk to people who don't understand anything, and shake hands with the mayor and the city council." Even so, she endured, and at other times she had chances to speak with LeWitt, who with Carol — Lutter remembered them as being "amazingly generous people" — invited her to come to Chester.

"As soon as I visited in Chester," Lutter recalled, Sol "gave me a beautiful Italian book from a Milanese publishing house about Umbria and the art of Umbria, and he wanted me to go to his house in Spoleto." He also wanted Lutter to work in his studio, as so many artists had done over the years:

> He was still — even at that point in his life — eager to promote my work. There was a dealer he was friendly with, and he said, "Let me connect you." When he talked, Sol wasn't making air bubbles. Certain people say they'll do this and that, and it turns out they don't even remember your name the next day. Sol was different. We felt like old friends even though we weren't.
>
> I felt art history consisted of powerful and overwhelming acts of painting or sculpture [but LeWitt's contribution was different]. You could develop a concept for a piece. You could walk it backwards. It's entirely based on intelligent thinking, something a young artist who wants to be a good artist can understand. You can't think about how to be a genius. You are one or you aren't. . . . Especially as a woman artist how am I supposed to be an artist based on that — have an eruption of genius?
>
> Of all the fabulously intelligent and gifted women I studied with [in art school painting and sculpture classes], only two had minor careers. It was very discouraging for women. They wouldn't be taken seriously and always heard condescending remarks: "If you're that pretty you can't be a good artist. We want to fuck you and have fun with you." I was dating a painter — a good painter, a very smart man. He was also a good cook and was going to prepare dinner in his studio. He was already represented by a gallery. . . . [She asked if he could introduce her to someone there.] "No," he said. "You have such pretty legs — look at you, don't even try to be an artist, it would be a waste of your good looks."

LeWitt—who did nothing but encourage Lutter—thought exactly the opposite. And his ideas about art resonate today. Lutter said: "Breaking the mind down into conceptual thinking is something I could understand. In looking at the work you can see the concept. That is something incredibly compelling and truly encouraging. If you believe in your mind then you have all that it takes to succeed."

■ By 2005, LeWitt's own work had taken another startling direction, one that could easily have been perceived, considering his circumstances, as a commentary on his outlook at that point. He abandoned his bold explorations of color and returned after many decades to black and white, but in a way that was different than anything he had done before. The new wall drawings, rendered in graphite only, were explorations of light and dark. The dark, in various shadings, seemed to dominate, but then the viewer would notice that the dark isn't the point.

LeWitt's precarious health seemed to fuel his single-mindedness.

In 2005, the art historian and curator Gabriella de Ferrari arranged for two wall drawings for the Thirteenth Street lobby at Manhattan's New School, an installation that tested LeWitt's tolerance for obstinacy and ignorance. De Ferrari's association with LeWitt had begun in the late 1970s when, as a young curator for the Fogg Museum at Harvard University, she had pushed a reluctant administration to embrace new art. Part of what drove her was what she had learned as a Harvard graduate student from Professor John P. Coolidge (eldest son of President Calvin Coolidge)—that it's not possible to understand the art of the past until one understands the art of the present.

As the years passed, she provided the same service—producing exhibits of contemporary art in spite of difficult odds—at other places, including Colby College, where she served as president of the board of trustees. In that case, LeWitt responded to her request by proposing a concrete block structure, an idea that met with great skepticism in the conservative academic community. A board meeting was scheduled and, according to de Ferrari in a 2015 interview, the museum director "was so scared he didn't go. The board members couldn't understand why we would need to hire a construction company to install the piece. They didn't want to understand it."[11]

By 2005, of course, as LeWitt's illness was entering its critical stage, he had become used to such objections and confusion and, according to de Ferrari, welcomed it as a way to bring attention to the work. But in the case of the New School, LeWitt blew his top.

Bob Kerrey, a Vietnam War veteran and a former US Senator, had become president of the New School in 2001. He was credited with beefing up the endowment and other significant achievements, but in 2010 he resigned under great pressure. For LeWitt, apparently, Kerrey's tenure was five years too long.

According to de Ferrari, Kerrey didn't like LeWitt's preliminary drawings. If they were going to accept the work as a gift from LeWitt, Kerrey wanted to place it somewhere other than the lobby. "He didn't understand it was site-specific work," de Ferrari said:

> He didn't even understand what site-specific art is. He said, "I want to talk to Mr. LeWitt."
>
> Sol knew how angry I was, and I was surprised when he agreed to go to the school to accommodate Kerrey's request. He said to me, "I've got to meet this jerk." The meeting was confrontational. Kerrey held firm that he didn't want the wall drawings for the lobby, and LeWitt said, "They're mine. If you don't like them I'll take them back," and started to walk out of the office. Kerrey, though, asked him to stay, and eventually there was agreement, and the drawings were installed where intended.[12]

De Ferrari witnessed LeWitt's outrage on one other occasion in a touchy circumstance involving his hometown. In the early 2000s the Wadsworth Atheneum was planning its first major expansion in a century, and the Dutch architect Ben van Berkel had been chosen from five finalists to complete the final design. The usual Hartford outcry ensued. Critics complained about everything from the unworthiness of foreign intruders to a design that looked to various people like a dustbuster or a stealth bomber. De Ferrari, who had been a driving force behind the hiring of van Berkel, heard from LeWitt. He was not concerned about the overall design—he thought that was very good—but he had deep reservations about certain aspects of it and felt so strongly that he came to New York specifically to see de Ferrari and complain in a fashion that stunned her by its fervor.

■ Meanwhile LeWitt's health was worsening. In 2005, he accompanied his wife to a doctor's office. Carol thought she had pneumonia and was advised to have a chest x-ray, which was negative. But the doctor advised Sol to have other tests as well, as a precaution. The results stunned them. He had new tumors.

Sol was scheduled for more surgery, including a colostomy. His spirits surprised Carol: "He told me how much he loved me, and what a beautiful life he had, and how beautiful the nurse was."[13]

The follow-up treatment, though, included the powerful chemotherapy Avastin, and his body couldn't tolerate it. "He should never have had chemo," Carol reflected later: "His best defense was his immune system."[14] Not only did the treatment make him weak and violently ill, but it didn't work.

By then he had lost his appetite for red wine, which he had always adored, even if he still craved it. But he sometimes ate borscht, prepared by friends who knew that it was a dish that had a spiritual meaning for him. There was one other food, though, he had retained a taste for.

He was still scheduling massages with Deb Paulson, and she recalled that one day "he had this little thing wrapped up. He said, 'This is for you.' As he was leaving I said, 'What is it?' he said, 'It's a brownie.' I said, 'What kind of brownie?' He said, 'It's a special brownie, a magic brownie.' I heard later they busted him in the hospital for the brownies he had with him."[15] Steve Henry, of the Paula Cooper Gallery, offered similar testimony: "Once, when he had been diagnosed with cancer and [was] under treatment, he was ingesting marijuana to help his appetite. . . . I walked him out to the car—Carol was driving . . . he took out some Tupperware, and there were brownies in it. It was in the morning. I'm talking to him, he says, 'It would be a nice breakfast brownie.' I didn't know [what it was]. I ate that brownie, and I was stoned all day —he smiled and giggled. I couldn't even speak."[16]

LeWitt also remained a consummate reader. One of the family friends, Sukey Howard, was a book reviewer and had advance access to books she thought he would like. "We'd go through the publishers' lists of books that were forthcoming, and he'd pick," she said. "I gave him Ian McEwan and a lot of heavy-duty history and [the theological explorations] by Karen Armstrong."[17]

During this time LeWittt served as an informal cancer counselor. His old friend Seth Siegelaub had also been diagnosed with colon cancer. LeWitt wanted to talk with Siegelaub but didn't have contact information for his friend, so he called Robert Barry, who provided it. LeWitt then called Siegelaub at his home in Amsterdam and told him in detail what to expect from surgeries and treatment—conversations that, according to Siegelaub's wife, Marja Bloem, proved comforting.[18] During this time generally, he seemed to others at peace.

In 2004, the artist Adrian Piper visited Chester from Germany. She later wrote:

[He] looked well and rested. He was surrounded by his books, his music, his art, his friends, and his family. He was blissfully happy. I felt healed and warmed by being near him. We visited his archive, which housed not only his own work but his collection. I saw his studio, full of images and memories I remembered from Hester St., and noted that among his snapshots he kept a photo of my mother, because, he said, she was beautiful. I saw how happy Carol had made him. I saw how happy it made him to banter with Eva, and marveled at his ability to regard both her and Sofie [*sic*] with both fatherly love and respect for their budding independence. I saw that this was a man who genuinely liked and respected women.[19]

Also that year, LeWitt apparently got into the marriage-saving business. The artist William Anthony recalled in 2008:

I was feeling long in the tooth and thinking often about the big studio in the sky. I felt the overwhelming desire to display a *memento mori*—a human skull, in the manner of St. Jerome—in our humble one-room apartment. My wife, Norma, was having none if it and was planning to kick my buns out onto the street, along with the aforementioned egregious object, a dire prospect.

Then, right at that time, Sol came on the scene. We traded art. And I came into possession of three of Sol's gouaches, composed of exquisite, wavelike horizontal lines. They were, for me, a river of life and death, a metaphor that Baba Ram Dass had implanted in my brain back in the 1960s. No longer did I need a skull to contemplate; I had these wonderful paintings. I was happy. Norma was happy. And our marriage was saved.

That is the power of Sol's art.[20]

As time went on, however, LeWitt's condition deteriorated so badly that it looked as if the only option would be for him to go into a nursing home. But then the LeWitts' old friend Martin Friedman—who with his wife, Mickey, had retired to New York—made a call to an artist, Ursula von Rydingsvard. Her husband, Paul Greengard, winner of the Nobel

Prize in Medicine, owned an apartment near his lab in the complex of Rockefeller University. The Greengards offered the place to the LeWitts for as long as they needed it.

There they resumed what Carol referred to as something of a normal life. Though weak, Sol continued his work, doing sketches and planning far into the future. He refused the services of a nurse, and Carol was obliged, in effect, to become one.

Occasionally they went out to meet friends. The artist William Anastasi recalled a lunch in New York with the LeWitts; Virginia Dwan; and Anastasi's partner, Dove Bradshaw:

> Sol told us he and Carol would not be going to Italy that summer, and that it would be a shame to have his studio in Spoleto unoccupied. Then he added, "Why don't you and Dove use it?" Virginia shouted, "Pounce! It's an incredible place!" We did, and it was. Our first evening there, Sol called from Chester to ask how we found everything. Then he said, "Bill, do you see that stack of drawing paper in the studio?" He meant a stack of 22 by 30 inch hot-pressed Fabriano [white watercolor paper] on the floor next to his drawing table — it went from the floor up at least to my knee. Sol continued, "Well, I don't want any of that paper left by the time you leave."[21]

Together at night the LeWitts watched old movies on television. "It was a very reduced existence," Carol said in 2015, "but it was fine. I'd go exercise in the morning. Sol talked to Susanna [Singer] every day, as always. My cousin Tony [Florio] was a rock."[22] Florio helped do the enormous amount of cleaning necessary and with the logistics involved in caring for a desperately ill patient. It was during this time, too, that the LeWitts' seventeen-year-old Italian mutt, Lilla, had to be put down. Lilla, the only dog that the artist had ever owned, had walked with him every day.

However, Mark Pecker, the physician in charge of the case thought something extraordinary was happening — not in terms of a miracle cure but in terms of the patient's burst of creativity and endurance. Pecker, who had been recommended to the LeWitts by Chuck Close, said: "The two of you are remarkable. You know when to hold and when to fold."[23] Or as Carol said, "Sol was not ready to die. He said, 'I can't die. I have a big show at Pace in September, scribble drawings, light and darkness.'"[24] He was also thinking about the following year's planned opening at MASSMoCA and kept in touch with assistants on that project's progress. He wanted to talk about work, "but," he said, "I don't want to talk about fucking cancer." Many friends came by to say their goodbyes.

Close said that LeWitt "couldn't take all the attention. He was so self-effacing, even then. He wouldn't go, of course, to his own openings, and he didn't want to go to his own death. He was very uncomfortable, but he didn't want sympathy and didn't want to be cheered up. But he also looked at me as someone who had spent eight months in a hospital [a blood clot in his spine had left him temporarily paralyzed]. Sol said to me, 'I don't know how you did it.'"[25]

Lutter recalled: "The last time I saw him—I didn't realize it would be the last time—he had lost a lot of weight, and didn't look well. It was just before Christmas, and I came late. The buses were full, and streets were crowded. It was a little formal. We just sat and talked. Carol gave me this long and deep look—that's when I understood. I was upset that I had come late on that particular day. I've thought about it so many times."[26]

Some visitors half expected LeWitt to do what he'd done so often in the past in social situations: remove himself from the circle and, without explanation, go off to listen to music. But of course everything had changed.

Even so, he worked until the end. Singer said: "The very last thing I said to him was, 'We have to figure out the scribble drawings for MASS-MoCA.' He said, 'We have time for that.'"[27]

A few hours later, just before he fell into his final coma, he said to Carol, "If anyone asks, tell them my best work is still ahead."[28]

He died that day, April 7, 2007. Singer was in the room, as were Carol, Sofia, Eva, and Florio.

Close recalled the immediate aftermath: "When Sol died, Dr. Pecker said to me, 'I have no idea how he lived this long, because there wasn't anything in his body that wasn't malfunctioning. His will to live was the amazing thing.'" Close said, "How he managed to function—the pain and lack of control must have killed him."[29]

The timing provided an eloquent juxtaposition. As word of the artist's death spread around the world, the bells of Easter Sunday rang out.

EPILOGUE

Artists everywhere called each other with the news of LeWitt's passing. In Atlanta, where the public art project *54 Columns* had once caused a public protest, a group of art lovers met and offered an impromptu toast to the creator of the work.

Others posted comments on a website devoted to eulogies. A Virginia man said, simply, "Note to Sol, thanks again for turning the art world on its ear."[1] Others, though, observed that the art world—including some critics—still did not know what to make of LeWitt's legacy.

One of those critics, presumably, was Roger Kimball, a cultural critic in the United Kingdom, who wrote that he wanted to offer "a counterweight to some of the hagiographic drivel about [LeWitt] that is filling the obituary pages."[2] He was referring to pieces such as Michael Kimmelman's in the *New York Times*, in which Kimmelman called LeWitt a "lodestar of American art."[3] Kimball wrote:

> "*De mortuis,*" your mother probably told you, "*nil nisi bonum dicendum est.*" About the dead you should say nothing but good things. I admire the spirit of reverence that motivates the advice but cannot agree with the policy of transforming all posthumous commentary into eulogy. Take the "conceptual artist" Sol LeWitt, who died on Easter at 78. If I were to have sat down on Saturday to write something about LeWitt, it would have been critical, not to say dismissive, since in my view he is interesting chiefly as a specimen in the history of the corruption of art rather than as an artist. Why should I write otherwise just because I write two days after his death rather than the day before?[4]

Had the artist been able to read this, he might have had a different reaction than his survivors and friends did—who of course found such commentary offensive. LeWitt might only have lamented that Kimball's piece should have been longer.

To be sure, Kimball was distinctly in the minority when it came to addressing LeWitt's oeuvre. And when it came to LeWitt's character, there could be no dispute.

The Chester graphic designer Peter Good wrote: "Many speak of Sol LeWitt's artistic genius and his profound effect on generations of artists and art lovers, but to me, it was his unpretentiousness, intelligence, wit, generosity and high ethical standards that defined his total being. He was an American original, the antithesis of the romantic, self-possessed artist. He lived his life like he practiced his art, without focus on himself."[5]

■ In the weeks before he died, Sol had given instructions to Carol about his funeral. There would be no memorial service in Manhattan of the kind produced in theaters or, perhaps in his case, at a large museum. The man who for most of his life had been a secular Jew but had at the end of it found comfort in Judaism's rituals and teachings insisted on a service back in Chester, Connecticut, in the synagogue he had designed.

There, an ad hoc committee prepared for the service with such vigor and attention to detail that Carol would later refer to the effort, in awe, as "producing a state funeral."[6] As with most such events at Congregation Beth Shalom Rodfe Zedek, there was no way to predict the size of the crowd, but it was instantly clear that this event could attract the congregation's biggest gathering ever and test the physical limits of the synagogue. Artists from New York were coming by chartered bus. Artists, gallery owners, and old friends from around the world were on their way, too.

A large tent was erected behind the building to accommodate people who might not find a seat in the sanctuary or social hall. A local bus service was hired to ferry attendees from an off-site parking lot at St. Joseph's Church, a mile away. But the planners couldn't anticipate how Mother Nature might weigh in. As it turned out, the funeral coincided with the stormiest spring day in many years, as a nor'easter pounded the Connecticut shoreline, ripping down trees and in many places, though not Chester, cutting off power. Nevertheless, an estimated six hundred people attended the service.

After Rabbi Ilene Bogosian and the cantorial soloist Belinda Brennan offered Hebrew prayers, and the pianist Meg Gister played selections from Bach on the Mason & Hamlin grand piano, old colleagues and friends of LeWitt were called to the bema to address his legacy.

Speakers that day included the curator Andrea Miller-Keller, Jock Reynolds, Mel Bochner, Chuck Close, and Adam D. Weinberg.

The first eulogist, however, was Rabbi Douglas Sagal, who many years earlier had been the spiritual leader of the congregation and remained a much-loved figure locally. He compared LeWitt to the most storied of all Jewish artists—not Chagall, Pisarro, or Modigliani, but Bezalel, the chief artist of the ancient Tabernacle. "Sol," Sagal said, "was the modern world's Bezalel."[7]

He also said that, "many years ago Carol told me it was her belief that her husband would be recognized as having one of the truly great minds of our time." But it wasn't just LeWitt's mind that the rabbi praised that day:

> Much will be said of Sol's humility and self-effacing nature. But that was only in regard to himself. When it came to his family he took delight in their accomplishments. He was never more animated than when he was speaking of his daughters. He loved Sofia and Eva unabashedly and completely. Carol and Sol not only loved one another, but had a genuine admiration and respect for one another. Carol admired Sol's genius and generosity. Sol admired Carol's intelligence and business acumen, as well as her gifts as a mother. And this community. Sol was instrumental in designing not only this beautiful building but, along with Carol, was instrumental, while demonstrating his creativity and generosity and commitment, in designing the soul of our congregation.

Then Chuck Close jacked his wheelchair up to its highest level to enhance the sight lines and commented on the beauty of the LeWitt-designed building: "Every time you walk into this place you're walking into a work of art."[8] He told a revealing story about LeWitt's tenacity in promoting the work of others. Over the years, Close said, LeWitt had nominated many people for Guggenheim Foundation fellowships. For most of that time, none of his nominees received a fellowship: "So Sol wrote a letter to the Guggenheim Foundation. He had kept track of everything. He always kept track of everything. He had list of the people who won Guggenheims over that time and a list of people he'd nominated who didn't win [but who went on to do great things]. And Sol asked them, 'Tell me. Who has the better list?'"

Mel Bochner observed that LeWitt's legacy, though supported by persuasive testimony from fellow artists and (most) critics, was still evolving: "When Manet died, Degas said, 'He was much greater than we thought.' And the same is true of Sol LeWitt."[9]

But the most eloquent tribute came from thousands of miles away via the internet. Adrian Piper, who had benefited from the artist's largesse and promotion of her work since the mid-1960s, posted a tribute on her website from Berlin:

Now that the sun has gone down permanently, it's time for those who knew him to bask reflectively in the memory of its rays, as Sol never allowed us to do it while he was alive, so that others who were not thus privileged will understand what we all have lost. . . . Maybe if all of his friends [describe the loss], we will gradually, collaboratively sculpt a complete picture of him out of all our partial ones, a celebration of all the known permutations of Solhood. And maybe Sol would be okay with this, if he understood it as an expression not only of our love but of our grief. He was above all a compassionate man. . . .

I always wanted to be just like Sol—a real gentleman: strong, calm, kind, modest, soft-spoken; unassuming but unflappable, generous, honest, forthright, good through and through. He was not just lucky, but blessed, for his kindness to others was repaid with love, and that enabled him to be who he was, fully, for all of us who were privileged to circle in his orbit. One of the reasons he was so averse to all the encomia his friends tried to arrange or publish during his lifetime was his personal modesty: He did not want it suggested he had an orbit, or that we were drawing light and inspiration from his presence. But we were; and in that we, too, were blessed.[10]

One year later, a crew of sixty-five artists completed LeWitt's massive wall drawing retrospective, covering over 27,000 square feet and three floors at MASSMoCA, starting with the first drawing—which was initially installed at Paula Cooper's galley in 1968.

The exhibit, which opened in the spring of 2008, turned out to do exactly what its organizers hoped it would: it increased attendance by about 30,000 visitors a year, or 20 percent of the total. Three of the attendees at the opening were Guiliano Gori, the Italian collector, and two of his grandchildren.

Gori had also been invited to visit Storm King Art Center, the outdoor sculpture park in upstate New York, but he canceled those plans (causing some consternation at the center) because of the amount of time he needed to spend in North Adams, Massachusetts. He recalled: "To see all that work together in one place—the sense of the spiritual path, to see this amazing work. I felt I was on a spiritual procession and went through the show with an amazing amount of emotion that haunted me for weeks afterward. I felt as I had been to Lourdes, or some other spiritual place."[11]

As a companion to the exhibit, the museum published an ambitious catalogue titled *Sol LeWitt: 100 Views* that consisted of commentary and recollections of a hundred colleagues of LeWitt.

One of the most compelling and inventive tributes was that of the independent curator Nancy Rosen, who assigned one or more personal or professional LeWitt reference to each letter of the alphabet, a kind of *Autobiography* in words only:

Aharon Appelfield, Altona, Androccio, arc, Bach, Bauhaus, Benozzo Gozzoli, Beth Shalom, *casella postale*, Chinatown, circle, Cleveland Indians, Consequence (WD [wall drawing] 720), cube, Davenport, Deep River, Deruta, Eva, Fabriano, Ficciones, Gemeentemuseum, Giotto, gouache, graphite, grappa, Holocaust, ink, Isozaki (WD #667), James Ingo Freed, Joyce Carol Oates, Korean War, Las Cruces, Lippi (father and son), Lower East Side, Monteluco, Muybridge, Nabokov, NBA, New York Cultural Center, Oskar Schlemmer, Pinturiccio, postcards, Printed Matter, pyramid, Quirinale, relatives, Richard Strauss, Scribbles, Sofia, sphere, square, *stangozzi*, swimming, tee shirt, triangle, typeface, Umbria, Villa Celle, Wadsworth Atheneum, Wiener Werkstatte, working drawings X (WD #1247), Yiddish Book Center, zigzag.[12]

The media and public response to the exhibit was everything museum officials had hoped. Reviews in newspapers and magazines were rapturous, including one by Christopher Knight in the *Los Angeles Times*, who seemed to challenge Gori's view about which LeWitt installation could be compared to that of Michelangelo's at the Vatican: "This may be the most perfect union of contemporary art and architecture in the United States. It's our Sistine."[13]

By the summer of 2018, a decade after the exhibit opened, more than two million people from forty-four countries had seen it. And millions of others have seen it digitally through Facebook and Instagram posts of their friends taking selfies in front of various wall drawings.

Joseph C. Thompson, director of the museum, said: "Everyone who visits LeWitt has some revelatory experience with the art. We are lucky too that visual and performing artists who come to MASSMoCA to make new work frequently draw inspiration from LeWitt—from Caroline Shaw, who wrote her Pulitzer Prize-winning 'Partita for 8 Voices,' to Mike Gordon of Phish, whose 2014 solo album was written in the galleries."[14]

LeWitt's effect on artists, then, continues. And more than that, there is this revelation that extends beyond the boundaries of everything we know about art and life. Two years after the opening, Chuck Close came to visit MASSMoCA. Accompanied by Thompson, he stopped his wheelchair in front of one drawing, and said, "Goddammit, Joe."

"What's the matter?" Thompson asked.

Close said, "Sol was always so much smarter than all of us. Look at this. This drawing is dated 2009. You see, he's still figuring out how to make art after he's dead."[15]

ACKNOWLEDGMENTS

The writing of a biography is a daunting and complicated task, and its outcome depends on the help of many people. In that regard, I have been blessed over and over again. Overwhelmingly, those who knew Sol LeWitt (including peers, gallery owners, curators, friends, relatives, and young artists who worked on his projects) were eager to pass along anecdotes and observations about a man who had affected their lives. Of the more than a hundred potential interviewees I approached, all but three were happy to meet me or talk to me by phone, and two of the holdouts referred me to their writings on LeWitt. I also benefitted from enthusiasm and help locally.

Sol and his wife, Carol, lived in Chester, Connecticut, and we attended the same synagogue and became friends. For Sol's funeral in 2007, Carol asked me to speak about his private life in Chester. Some months afterward, I suggested to Carol the idea of writing a biography, one that would have the advantage of access to family and personal files. "Well," she said, "someone is going to do it." I had a certain advantage because I had known Sol during the last twenty years of his life and had already published a profile and essay about him in my former work as a Sunday magazine editor and columnist. Carol also was aware that over the years I had conceived of and fostered many public art and culture projects.

From time to time Carol suggested I interview someone about Sol before it was too late. Many relatives and colleagues were in fragile states of health, so I conducted a few key early interviews—some of them in Italy, where the LeWitts had lived many years, and in other parts of Europe. These interviews gave me a wealth of intimate recollections.

I had the enduring support of a variety of friends and relations. Chief among these was my wife, the poet Suzanne Levine, who over the years has been a partner in many professional pursuits.

In 2013 and 2014, along with the novelist Wally Lamb, Suzanne and I had taught writing at a retreat at Carol's ancestral home in Praiano, Italy, where Sol had conceived several wall drawings. Having also known and befriended Carol LeWitt in this way, Suzanne read each draft of the biography, focusing not only on the specific content but also on overall matters of fairness and objectivity.

Jon Joslow, a supporter of many of my projects over the years, weighed in often with ideas and sound advice. Stephen Davis offered rich perspective and guidance throughout.

Steve Metcalf, dean of the President's College at the University of Hartford, invited me to teach a course on LeWitt. As it turned out, the course was quickly filled (the President's College draws its students from the community at large). I used this teaching opportunity as a lab, mixing the personal and professional LeWitt as a way to test and sharpen my view of the pertinence of examining them together. The enthusiastic reaction of the students was heartening.

In the end, the book has evolved considerably from early drafts. The primary reason it changed and became more authoritative can be traced to the work of Suzanna Tamminen, director and editor in chief of Wesleyan University Press. When I found myself in need of a home for the project, I offered the manuscript to Wesleyan, and Suzanna responded immediately and enthusiastically. Over time, she asked four readers with considerable knowledge of the contemporary art world to review the manuscript and offer assessments and suggestions. At this point I have no idea who the four were (such reviews are confidential), with one exception: Kirsten Swenson, an art professor and author of *Irrational Judgments: Eva Hesse, Sol LeWitt, and 1960s New York*, outed herself in a note to me. I owe much gratitude to Swenson and my three anonymous benefactors, at least two of whom provided a long list of elements that in their view required attention, alteration, deletions, or additions. I also owe thanks to the staff and associates of the Wesleyan University Press.

■   I would also like to acknowledge the work of Lorin Rees, owner of the Rees Literary Agency in Boston, who provided much counsel and encouragement.

Major contributors to the effort included employees of the LeWitt Collection during the time before the family withdrew its support for the book. These included in particular Janet Passehl, the director, and John Lavertu. I also received counsel from the curator and author Veronica Roberts and the scholar Erica DiBenedetto. The retired curator Andrea Miller-Keller, who may well have known Sol LeWitt better than anyone else in the museum world, was particularly helpful in the early stages of my research. Mimi Wheeler, who had a romantic relationship with LeWitt in the late 1960s and early 1970s, invited me into her New York City apartment to examine correspondence that she had received from the artist over the years and to offer her assessment of his life and work.

Early on, LeWitt's eldest daughter, Sofia, provided excellent family background, as she is particularly adept at tracing origins. Her sister, Eva, an artist herself, recalled for me her early memories and said that she would be particularly interested in reading the book because, even though she considered herself her father's shadow, "There is so much about him that I don't know."

Susanna Singer was particularly helpful in recounting the business practices that she and LeWitt devised and that made his approach to marketing different that of any other artist, and in explaining how the delicate business of wall drawings is handled. Dane Kostin and Jo-Ann Price put me in touch with former high-school and college classmates of the artist. Joseph C. Thompson, director of the Massachusetts Museum of Contemporary Art, spent a good deal of time helping me reconstruct the monumental effort on the part of many people to exhibit 105 LeWitt wall drawings for a period of twenty-five years.

Other key contributors include: Carl Andre, Robert Barry, Cecile Gray Bazelon, Marcie Begleiter, Robert Benson, Marja Bloem, Alessandra Bonomo, Lorenzo Bonomo, Marilena Bonomo, Tenley Brainard, Elizabeth Broun, Marilyn Buel, Rosemary Castoro, Beatrice Conrad-Eybesfeld, Sophie Clarke, Chuck Close, Amy Bloom Coleman, Max Coleman, Molly Coleman, Paula Cooper, Gabrielle de Ferrara, Petra de Jong, Jan Dibbets, Tom Doyle, Deborah Faerber Evans, Walter Friedenberg, Martin Friedman, Rudi Fuchs, Eugene Gaddis, Susan Ginsburg, Janet Cummings Good, Peter Good, Jesse Good, Philip Glass, Giuliano Gori, Martin Greenberg, Beatrice Gross, Karen Gunderson, Michael Harvey, Rhona Hoffman, Ethelyn Honig, William Hosley, Douglas Hyland, Nalini Jones, Peter Kagan, Mort Kaish, Franz Keiser, Heidi Robin Kennedy, Michael Klein, Patricia Klindienst, João Leonardo, Celeste LeWitt, Michael LeWitt, Peter LeWitt, Stephen Lloyd, Vera Lutter, Robert Mangold, Saul Ostrow, Sylvia Plimack Mangold, Priscilla Martel, Henry McNeil, Mary Peacock, Deb Paulson, Jane Rainwater, Steve Reich, Judith Rosenkrantz, Rabbi Doug Sagal, Anthony Sansotta, William L. Schaeffer, Pat Steir, Naomi Bragman Stern, Marjorie Strider, Nancy Strider, Scott Timberg, Charles van Over, Herbert Vogel, Dorothy Vogel, Grace Wapner, Jo Watanabe, Alice Weiner, Lawrence Weiner, Bryan Wolf, Jeremy Ziemann, Joan Ziemann, Kurt Ziemann, and Richard Ziemann.

NOTES

INTRODUCTION

1. Ingrid Sischy (1952–2015) edited *Interview Magazine* from 1989 to 2008 and then became coeditor of European editions of *Vanity Fair*. Her view of LeWitt was informed in part by her work for him in the 1970s at Printed Matter, a distributor of books that featured the work of specific artists. See chapter 12.

2. Ingrid Sischy, "Spotlight: Sol's Patch," *Vanity Fair*, June 2011, 122.

3. Comment by Carol LeWitt to the author following the artist's seventieth birthday party, the Wadsworth Atheneum Museum of Art, Hartford, Connecticut, September 9, 1998.

4. Author interview of Marilena Bonomo, Bari, Italy, February 22, 2012.

5. Author telephone interview of Robin Heidi Kennedy, August 16, 2014.

6. Christopher Knight, "Sol LeWitt; Sculptor and Muralist Changed Art," *Los Angeles Times*, April 10, 2007.

7. Peter Schjeldahl, "Less Is Beautiful," *New Yorker*, March 13, 2000, 98.

8. Sol LeWitt, "Paragraphs on Conceptual Art," *Artforum*, April 1967, 61.

9. Ibid., 79.

10. LeWitt expanded on this point in a March 27, 1977, interview in Sydney with Hazel de Berg, produced by the National Library of Australia. A sound recording is available from the library online (https://catalogue.nla.gov.au/Record/1479762).

11. Gary Garrels, "Sol LeWitt: An Introduction," in Garrels, *Sol LeWitt: A Retrospective*, 23.

12. This was an element in early paintings of Pablo Picasso and other Cubists.

13. Quoted in Art Institute of Chicago, "On Art and Artists," Video Data Bank (1992), 1991.

14. Michael Kimmelman, "Sol LeWitt, Master of Conceptualism, Dies," *New York Times*, April 9, 2007.

15. "Sol LeWitt, American Artist, Dies at 78." *Pravda*, April 9, 2007.

16. Michael McNay, "Sol LeWitt: American Artist Whose Forms and Treatments Defied Critical Analysis." *Guardian*, April 11, 2007.

17. Sol LeWitt, "Paragraphs on Conceptual Art," *Artforum*, April 1967, 61.

18. Paul Cummings, "Oral History Interview with Sol LeWitt," July 15, 1974,

https://www.aaa.si.edu/collections/interviews/oral-history-interview-sol-lewitt
-12701#transcript.

19. Andrea Miller-Keller, "Excerpts from a Correspondence, 1981–1983," in Zevi, *Sol LeWitt Critical Texts*, 109.

20. Quoted in Sharon Butler, "The Wall Drawing Is Permanent, Until Destroyed," *Two Coats of Paint*, December 7, 2008, http://www.twocoatsofpaint.com/2008/12 /wall-drawing-is-permanent-installation.html; quoted in Saul Ostrow, "Sol LeWitt," *Bomb*, October 1, 2003.

21. Quoted in Susan Rand Brown, "The LeWitt Riddle," *Hartford Courant* Sunday magazine, October 23, 1981.

22. LeWitt, "Paragraphs on Conceptual Art," 61.

23. Rachel Barnes, "The Idea That Counts," *Guardian*, August 16, 1993.

24. LeWitt, interview with de Berg.

25. Quoted in Ostrow, "Sol LeWitt," 43.

26. Sol LeWitt, instructions for *Wall Drawing #211*, installed in 1973 in the Portland (Oregon) Center for Visual Arts.

27. See chapter 1.

28. Quoted in Enno Develing, "The Minimal Art," in Develing, 47.

29. Peter Schjeldahl, "Less Is Beautiful," *New Yorker*, March 13, 2000, 98.

30. Quoted in "Sol LeWitt," *Daily Telegraph*, April 10, 2007.

31. LeWitt worked with the architect Stephen Lloyd. The details can be found in chapter 13.

32. Even here, contradiction rules. LeWitt's studio was behind the family house in Chester. Though the yard featured a great number of artworks, mostly sculpture by other artists, his studio had only one permanent display, the image of Chief Wahoo, the mascot of the Cleveland Indians. LeWitt, known for his social justice campaigns, dismissed complaints about the stereotypical image that was eventually retired by Major League Baseball.

33. *Whirls and Twirls* is *Wall Drawing #1126*. It was commissioned by the Marimotti family, owners of the exclusive clothing chain, Max Mara. Christina Passariello refers to the piece as "colorful lines that look like psychedelic spaghetti" ("The Culture of Understatement," *Wall Street Journal*, December 1, 2011).

34. After this, he became acutely ill. When he saw the finished work, he was impressed by the interpretive work of the crew. He was often surprised by what he saw when he looked at finished work. Michael Kirby wrote, "Words or a sketch or a model may have the same concept as the show, but the results, in terms of experience, are vastly different. I think it's very important to Sol's work that the experience can't be predicted, even by himself" ("I've Known Sol LeWitt," in Zevi, *Sol LeWitt Critical Texts*, 177). This, of course, invites a conversation about whether all decisions, or just all major decisions, can be made beforehand. Crews faced small decisions in nearly every installation. They had to adjust plans to fit specific site is-

sues, such walls that didn't square up and elements (such as electrical plugs or fire extinguishers) that became part of the art.

35. Author interview of Giuliano Gori, Pistoia, Italy, November 14, 2014.

36. Quoted in Ostrow, "Sol LeWitt," 47.

37. Miller-Keller, "Excerpts from a Correspondence," 102.

38. LeWitt wasn't the first to do this. Most historians point to the prominent work of Marcel Duchamp—particularly "Fountain," a "readymade" piece. This was a urinal removed from its usual place in the men's room and put on display upside-down. Though considered to be "conceptual," this work was quite apart from LeWitt's idea of conceptualism, which deemphasized the idea of object.

39. Quoted in author interview of Carol LeWitt, February 22, 2012, Bari, Italy.

40. Actually quite a sketch, so to speak. See Armstrong, "Learn to Say F**k You."

41. Benedict Cumberbatch, "Sol LeWitt to Eva Hesse."

42. Author interview of Susanna Singer, New York City, May 14, 2014.

43. Chris Teerink, *Sol LeWitt*. The film has no narrator and relies heavily on interviews with people who worked with LeWitt. The artist's own voice is a very small part of the film, explaining certain works. When the film opened in New York in 2014, A. O. Scott wrote, "The on-camera absence of its subject and its overall indifference to matters of biography make 'Sol LeWitt' a welcome departure from most documentaries about artists, as well as a fitting and serious tribute to his art" ("An Artist Who Let His Ideas (And Others) Do the Work," *New York Times*, May 6, 2014).

44. Stoppard, *Travesties*, 29.

45. LeWitt letter to Mimi Wheeler, June 7, 1970. Wheeler allowed the author to read her collection of letters, stored in her New York City apartment.

46. Robert Rosenblum, "Notes on Sol LeWitt," in Alicia Legg, *Sol LeWitt*, 15. The catalogue, edited by Legg, was designed by LeWitt. The featured essays are by Lucy R. Lippard, Rosenblum, and Bernice Rose.

1. THE LIFE OF STUFF

1. LeWitt, *Autobiography*.

2. Most of the Nouveau Roman were French novelists who departed from tradition by experimenting with form, and whose work LeWitt admired. Among them were Michel Butor, Alain Robbe-Grillet, and Marguerite Duras.

3. Carol LeWitt, interview by author, Chester, Connecticut, August 12, 2012.

4. Sol LeWitt, "Paragraphs on Conceptual Art," *Artforum*, April 1967, 79.

2. SOLLY

1. The card is among the materials stored in an unnumbered box in the LeWitt Collection, Chester, Connecticut. The LeWitt Collection is the central location for materials relating to the artist, and for management of exhibiting his work.

2. Quoted in George Plimpton, "The Art of the Matter," *New Yorker*, June 10, 2002, https://www.newyorker.com/magazine/2002/06/10/the-art-of-the-matter.

3. Directed by John Houseman, the opera had its premiere on February 7, 1934. According to Celeste LeWitt, family members were in attendance (interview by author, Farmington, Connecticut, October 20, 2008). Carol LeWitt identified these relatives as Bella and Nellie LeWitt, Sol's older cousins (interview by author, Chester, Connecticut, June 2, 2013). Thirteen days after the opera's premiere in Hartford, it opened on Broadway. For more details on this and other stories of Chick Austin's years in Hartford, see Gaddis, *Magician of the Modern*.

4. The house is one of the few original houses still existing on Hartford's Main Street. It is just a few blocks from the location of the old Mount Sinai Hospital.

5. Abraham LeWitt birth certificate, unnumbered box, LeWitt Collection.

6. "Certificate of the Exalted Ottoman State, Minister of Interior Affairs," unnumbered box, LeWitt Collection.

7. Abraham LeWitt schooling material, unnumbered box, LeWitt Collection.

8. "Four in France from One Family in New Britain," *Hartford Daily Courant*, December 22, 1918.

9. LeWitt Collection.

10. Carol LeWitt, interview by author, Chester, Connecticut, August, 12, 2012.

11. Ibid.

12. The 1914 compilation of registered automobiles published by the Connecticut Department of Transportation lists only 23,305 cars in the state.

13. Abraham LeWitt's essay on the dangers of driving and his short story in which the protagonist is Doctor Hamlin are stored in a box of memorabilia in the LeWitt collection.

14. Abraham LeWitt's funeral was mentioned in "Funeral of Doctor LeWitt," *Hartford Courant*, April 13, 1934. The newspaper indicated that among the among the pallbearers was Herman P. Kopplemann, who represented the Hartford area in the House of Representatives.

15. Carol LeWitt, interview by author, Chester, Connecticut, April 16, 2014.

16. Some of the details in the text are from family accounts, including those of Celeste LeWitt and the family historian, Liz Bernstein. These are stored in boxes of memorabilia in the LeWitt Collection.

17. Douglas Hyland, interview by author, New Britain, Connecticut, February 27, 2013. Hyland was the longtime director of the New Britain Museum of American Art.

18. Paul Cummings, "Oral History Interview with Sol LeWitt," July 15, 1974, https://www.aaa.si.edu/collections/interviews/oral-history-interview-sol-lewitt -12701#transcript.

19. Quoted in Thibodeau, *New Britain: The City of Invention*, 22.

20. Ibid., 23.

21. Dewey Van Cott, letter to the *New Britain Herald*, May 19, 1929.

22. Quoted in Ronald Abbe, "NBMAA Has Its Own Armory Show," September 26, 2013, https://nbmaa.wordpress.com/2013/09/26/nbmaa-has-its-own-armory-show/.

23. Gaddis tells the story of the purchase of the Caravaggio, the only such painting available for sale in the United States. The original asking price was $50,000 (*Magician of the Modern*, 336).

24. Anna Foberg's comment is among the memorabilia stored in unnumbered boxes in the LeWitt Collection.

25. Miss Brown's comment is among the memorabilia stored in unnumbered boxes in the LeWitt Collection.

26. Walter Friedenberg, telephone interview by author, March 17, 2014.

27. Celeste LeWitt, interview by author, Farmington, Connecticut, August 9, 2008.

28. Friedenberg interview by author.

29. Sol LeWitt, bar mitzvah speech, stored in unnumbered box of memorabilia, LeWitt Collection.

30. Copy of Sol LeWitt letter to Reverend H. G. C. Hallock, 1941, LeWitt Collection.

31. The portraits are in the LeWitt Collection.

32. Mort Jaffe, author telephone interview, April 9, 2013.

33. Ibid.

34. Walter Friedenberg letter to author, April 10, 2014. During my first conversation with Friedenberg, I asked if he could write down his memories rather than trying to recall them in an interview. A few weeks later, he sent me this detailed account and one of the Korean War, discussed in chapter 4.

35. The academic records are stored in boxes of memorabilia in the LeWitt Collection.

36. Ibid.

37. Mort Jaffe, telephone interview.

38. Ibid.

39. Cummings, "Oral History Interview with Sol LeWitt."

40. *Red and Gold Review*, May 29, 1945, 3.

41. Ibid.

42. Cummings, "Oral History Interview with Sol LeWitt." In 2000, with the advantage of reflection and experience, LeWitt said, "Being an artist seemed to be a way of rebellion, an assertion of individuality, a chance to deal with the world in more radical ways" (quoted in Jeffrey Kastner, "A Playful Geometer Makes the Complex Seem So Simple," *New York Times*, December 3, 2000).

43. *Hartford Courant*, July 14, 1936.

44. Cummings, "Oral History Interview with Sol LeWitt."

45. Sol LeWitt, "Ode to New Britain," stored in an unnumbered box in the LeWitt Collection.

3. THE BOY FROM SYRACUSE

1. Martin Greenberg, telephone interview by author, July 21, 2013.

2. Alan Nevas, interview by author, Westport, Connecticut, July 19, 2013

3. Ibid.

4. Paul Cummings, "Oral History Interview with Sol LeWitt," July 15, 1974, https://www.aaa.si.edu/collections/interviews/oral-history-interview-sol-lewitt-12701#transcript.

5. Naomi Bragman Stern, interview by author, New York City, August 8, 2013.

6. Cecile Gray Bazelon, interview by author, New York City, February 2, 2014.

7. Morton Kaish, telephone interview by author, December 10, 2013.

8. Unada Gliewe, telephone interview by author, December 10, 2013.

9. Kaish, telephone interview by author, December 3, 2013.

10. Bazelon, interview by author.

11. Ibid.

12. Andrea Miller-Keller, "Excerpts from a Correspondence, 1981–1983," in Zevi, *Sol LeWitt Critical Texts*, 118.

13. LeWitt's college grades are available in the Academic Records Department at Syracuse University.

14. A graduate of Syracuse, Tolley was named its chancellor in 1942 and served for twenty-seven years, overseeing a great expansion of the university's physical size and the improvement of its academic prowess.

15. Kaish, telephone interview by author.

16. Ibid.

17. Cummings, "Oral History Interview with Sol LeWitt."

18. Ibid.

19. Bazelon, interview by author.

20. Cummings, "Oral History Interview with Sol LeWitt."

21. Bazelon, interview by author.

22. Stern, interview by author.

23. Ibid.

24. Ibid.

25. Ibid.

26. Ibid.

4. THE ART OF WAR

1. Paul Cummings, "Oral History Interview with Sol LeWitt," July 15, 1974, https://www.aaa.si.edu/collections/interviews/oral-history-interview-sol-lewitt-12701#transcript.

2. Ibid.

3. Alan Nevas, interview by author, Westport, Connecticut, July 19, 2013.

4. Ibid.

5. Sol LeWitt, European sketchbook, unnumbered box, LeWitt Collection.

6. Nevas, interview by author.

7. Ibid.

8. Quoted in James M. Lindsey, "The History of the Cold War in 40 Quotes," November 7, 2014, https://www.cfr.org/blog/history-cold-war-40-quotes. The domino theory was drawn from the Truman Doctrine, developed after World War II and articulated most prominently by Truman's successor, President Dwight D. Eisenhower, and then by various public figures involved in making decisions about the Korean and Vietnam Wars.

9. Nevas, interview by author.

10. Ibid.

11. At the Uffizi Gallery, LeWitt would have seen among other masterpieces, Leonardo's *The Annunciation* (circa 1472–75) Botticelli's *Spring* and *The Birth of Venus* (circa 1485) Caravaggio's *Medusa* (1596), and most significantly (because of its sense of order) Fra Angelica's *Coronation of the Virgin* (1533–34).

12. Nevas, interview by author.

13. Andrew Wilson, "Sol LeWitt Interviewed," *Art Monthly*, March 1993, 152.

14. Nevas, interview by author.

15. Walter Friedenberg, letter to author, April 12, 2014.

16. All the letters from LeWitt quoted here are in a box of assorted material at the LeWitt Collection.

17. Issues of the *Breckenridge* newsletter are stored at the LeWitt Collection.

18. Cummings, "Oral History Interview with Sol LeWitt."

19. Sol LeWitt letter to Mimi Wheeler, April 18, 1970, LeWitt Collection.

5. LOST IN THE CITY

1. In the early 1950s, New York City was full of work by artists such as Jackson Pollock, Mark Rothko, Barnett Newman, Robert Motherwell, and Helen Frankenthaler. Though it is difficult, and perhaps foolish, to lump them together as abstract expressionists, it is safe to say that painting in this style typically used fields of color and abstract forms.

2. The term was popularized in the United States by the art historian and critic Barbara Rose. The movement featured the use of popular images, modern materials, and absurdist juxtapositions. Artists associated with the movement included Jim Dine, John Chamberlain, and Yves Klein.

3. Paul Cummings, "Oral History Interview with Sol LeWitt," July 15, 1974, https://www.aaa.si.edu/collections/interviews/oral-history-interview-sol-lewitt-12701#transcript.

4. When it opened in 1947, the Cartoonist and Illustrators School had three faculty members and thirty-five students, most of them men on the GI Bill. The name was changed to the School of Visual Arts, and today it offers eleven undergraduate and twenty-two graduate programs.

5. Cummings, "Oral History Interview with Sol LeWitt."

6. Sol LeWitt, interview by Hazel de Berg, March 27, 1977. A sound recording is available from the library online (https://catalogue.nla.gov.au/Record/1479762). At the time of the interview, LeWitt had just completed a wall drawing that had been done by six Australian students. The wall was 100 by 13 feet, and the drawing featured arcs, angles, and lines. "It's a temporary piece," he said in the interview. "It's owned by another person, so it can't be permanent unless he wants to." Asked if he believed in the permanence of work, he said, "I don't think anything is permanent."

7. Martin Greenberg, telephone interview by author, July 21, 2013.

8. Deborah Faerber Evans, telephone interview by author, September 16, 2013. She also provided me with a copy of the drawings made for her by LeWitt before her European journey.

9. Ibid.

10. Ibid.

11. Evans sent a copy of the letter from LeWitt to the author.

12. Evans, telephone interview by author, March 12, 2014.

13. Ibid.

14. Evans letter to Sol LeWitt, September 3, 1954, stored with other letters to the artist at the LeWitt Collection.

15. McCarthy, *On the Contrary*, 42.

16. Ashbery, *Reported Sightings*, 47.

17. Cummings, "Oral History Interview with Sol LeWitt."

18. Ibid.

19. Gary Garrels, "A Conversation with Sol LeWitt," *Open*, Winter–Spring 2000, 35.

20. Veronica Roberts, "Eva Hesse, Sol LeWitt, and Seventeen Magazine," Blanton Museum of Art, February 10. 2014, https://blantonmuseum.org/2014/02/eva-hesse-sol-lewitt-and-seventeen/. Roberts was the curator for the 2014 exhibit and the author of the book of the same title, *Converging Lines: Eva Hesse and Sol LeWitt*.

21. Cummings, "Oral History Interview with Sol LeWitt."

22. Ibid.

23. Charles "Don" Page (1917–2007) was a prominent architect and interior and graphic designer.

24. Cummings, "Oral History Interview with Sol LeWitt."

25. Ibid.

26. The complex was built on land that had included the airstrip from which Charles Lindbergh departed on his historic solo flight to Paris.

27. Cummings, "Oral History Interview with Sol LeWitt."

28. Greenberg, interview by author.

29. Tony Candido, interview by Veronica Roberts, New York City, July 18, 2013. Roberts emailed her notes on the interview to the author.

30. Cummings, "Oral History Interview with Sol LeWitt."

31. Tom Doyle, interview by author, Roxbury, Connecticut, July 12, 2012.

32. Quoted in Maurice R. Berube, "The Greatest Paintings Produce a 'Spiritual Calm'—One That Jackson Pollock Was Never Able to Share," *Chronicle of Higher Education*, January 15, 1999.

33. Perl, *New Art City*, 45.

34. Katz, *Naked by the Window*, 97.

35. Tony Candido, telephone interview by author, August 17, 2014.

36. Quoted in Perl, *New Art City*, 171.

37. Quoted in ibid., 172.

38. Cummings, "Oral History Interview with Sol LeWitt."

39. Butor and Graham, *Conversation*, 6.

40. Cummings, "Oral History Interview with Sol LeWitt."

41. Ibid.

42. Ibid.

43. Janson, *A Basic History of Art*, 86.

44. Candido, interview by author.

45. Vera Lutter, telephone interview by author, January 29, 2013.

46. Quoted by Jeremy Ziemann, interview by author, Chester, Connecticut, September 14, 2014.

47. Charles W. North promotion material, LeWitt Collection.

48. Among the pioneering artists who lived in the area south of Houston Street (SoHo) were Carl Andre, Stephen Antonakos, Christo, Dan Graham, Al Held, Ethelyn Honig, Jasper Johns, Lee Lozano, Robert Mangold, Sylvia Plimack Mangold, Brice Marden, Louise Nevelson, Yoko Ono, Dorothea Rockburne, Mark Rothko, and Naomi Spector (Roberts, *Converging Lines*).

49. Marjorie Strider, telephone interview by author, March 14, 2013.

50. Nancy Strider, telephone interview by author, March 18, 2013. The following quotes from Strider are also from this interview.

6. STIRRINGS

1. In addition to works by Frank Stella, the exhibition featured pieces by Jay DeFeo, Wally Hedrick, James Jarvaise, Jasper Johns, Ellsworth Kelly, Alfred Leslie, Landes Lewitin, Robert Lytle, Robert Mallary, Louise Nevelson, Robert Rauschenberg, Julius Schmidt, Richard Stankiewicz, Albert Urban, and Jack Youngerman.

2. Quoted in Cohen-Solal, *Leo and His Circle*, 266.

3. Paul Cummings, "Oral History Interview with Sol LeWitt," July 15, 1974, https://www.aaa.si.edu/collections/interviews/oral-history-interview-sol-lewitt-12701#transcript.

4. Perl, *New Art City*, 35.

5. Quoted in ibid., 420. A leading critic and academic, Rosenblum published eighteen books.

6. Quoted in ibid. Ashton was an art critic for the *New York Times* and was at

odds with John Canaday, the lead critic, who was disdainful of contemporary art. This comment was unusual for Ashton, who was known as a champion of contemporary art. Her stay at the *Times* was brief; she was fired in 1960.

7. Cummings, "Oral History Interview with Sol LeWitt."

8. Jasper Johns, "Artist's Statement," in *16 Americans*, edited by Dorothy C. Miller (New York: Museum of Modern Art, 1959), https://www.moma.org/documents /moma_catalogue_2877_300062200.pdf.

9. Ibid.

10. For more on Muybridge, see Hendricks, *Eadweard Muybridge: Father of the Motion Picture*.

11. Sol LeWitt, "Interview by Gary Garrels," *New Art Examiner*, December 2000–January 2001, 13.

12. Cummings, "Oral History Interview with Sol LeWitt."

13. Andrea Miller-Keller, "Excerpts from a Correspondence, 1981–1983," in Zevi, *Sol LeWitt Critical Texts*, 102.

14. LeWitt, "Interview by Gary Garrels."

15. Cummings, "Oral History Interview with Sol LeWitt."

16. Blackwood, "Scene from *Sol LeWitt*."

17. Cummings, "Oral History Interview with Sol LeWitt."

18. Sol LeWitt, "The Cube," *Art in America*, July–August 1966, 47. In 2007, Martin Friedman, longtime director of the Walker Art Center in Minneapolis, wrote: "The process has gone something like this: Take a cube — any cube — and see what happens when one or more of its sides are removed. Or, for that matter, if all sides are removed and only its outline remains. Or, what happens if most of the cube disappears and only a corner is left? What if the cube is repeated in different sizes or sliced at various angles to generate blocky new shapes?" ("Sol LeWitt's Birthday Party," *MoMA Newsletter*, May 2007, 1).

19. Cummings, "Oral History Interview with Sol LeWitt."

20. Quoted in Perl, *New Art City*, 171.

21. Nan Robertson, "Artists Forced to Take Side Jobs," *New York Times*, July 31, 1961.

22. Ibid.

23. Sol LeWitt, interview by Sharon Zane, May 12, 1994, https://www.moma.org /momaorg/shared/pdfs/docs/learn/archives/transcript_lewitt.pdf.

24. Ibid.

25. Ibid.

26. Ibid.

27. Lippard. *Changing*, 48.

28. LeWitt, interview by Zane.

29. Andrew Wilson, "Sol LeWitt Interviewed," *Art Monthly*, March 1993, 152.

30. Cummings, "Oral History Interview with Sol LeWitt."

31. Ibid.

32. Wilson, "Sol LeWitt Interviewed," 153.

33. Cummings, "Oral History Interview with Sol LeWitt."

34. Victor Vasarely, Yakov Agam, and Bridget Riley were among those prominent in the op art movement.

35. Gompertz, *What Are You Looking At?*, 309.

36. Swenson, *Irrational Judgments*, 4.

37. Ibid., 9.

38. Quoted in ibid., 12.

39. Quoted in Roberts, *Converging Lines*, 64.

40. Joyce Purnick, "A Portrait of the Artist: Tortured and Talented," *New York Post*, December 13, 1972. The piece was published as a memorial exhibit of Hesse's work opened at the Solomon R. Guggenheim Museum.

41. Quoted in Roberts, *Converging Lines*, 64

42. Ibid.

43. Quoted in Legg, *Sol LeWitt*, 114.

44. Lippard, *Eva Hesse*, 18.

45. Tom Doyle, interview by author, Roxbury, Connecticut, July 12, 2012.

46. Robert Barry, interview with author, New York City, June 7, 2015.

47. Quoted in ibid.

48. Ibid.

49. Ibid.

50. Grace Wapner, interview by author, Woodstock, New York, July 24, 2013.

51. Ibid.

52. Ethelyn Honig, interview by author, New York City, July 15, 2013.

53. Ibid.

54. Ibid.

55. Ibid.

56. Ibid.

57. Quoted in Lippard, *Eva Hesse*, 23.

58. Ibid.

59. Wapner, interview by author.

60. Ibid.

61. Quoted in Swenson, *Irrational Judgments*, 80.

62. Quoted in ibid.

63. Hesse, *Datebooks, 1964/65*, 49, 56, and 58.

64. Quoted in Lippard, *Eva Hesse*, 28.

65. Quoted in Honig, interview by author.

66. Quoted in ibid.

67. Quoted in Lippard, *Eva Hesse*, 34.

68. Quoted in ibid.

69. Quoted in Roberts, *Converging Lines*, 65.

70. Quoted in ibid., 68.

71. Quoted in ibid.

72. Quoted in Roberts, *Converging Lines*, 17–18. The iconic letter has been published in a variety of places. For two authoritative studies of the artists' influence on each other, see ibid. and Swenson, *Irrational Judgments*.

73. Quoted in Lippard, *Eva Hesse*, 35.

74. The exhibition was organized by Dwan and Robert Smithson.

75. Quoted in Swenson, *Irrational Judgments*, 119.

76. Virginia Dwan, interview by Charles Stuckey, April 18 and May 2, 1984, Archives of American Art, Smithsonian Institution, Washington.

77. To hear Hesse express this point, see Hesse, "Life Doesn't Last."

78. Quoted in Roberts, *Converging Lines*, 64.

79. Quoted in Alastair Sooke, "Eva Hesse: Her Dark Materials," *Telegraph*, August 4, 2009, https://www.telegraph.co.uk/culture/art/art-reviews/5948238/Eva-Hesse-her-dark-materials.html.

80. Begleiter, *Tracing the Rope: Eva Hesse Life + Work*. Of this film, Joe Morgenstern wrote, "It's the film Hesse deserves—lively and concise, though calmly comprehensive; thoughtful and essentially serious, but with a witty appreciation of the oddity, recklessness and absurdity that its subject valued; rich with history, and beautifully made in its own right" ("The Persistence of the Ephemeral," *Wall Street Journal*, May 12, 2016).

81. Lippard, *Eva Hesse*, 79.

82. Roberts, *Converging Lines*, 13.

83. Wapner, interview by author.

7. "WHAT WOULD SOL DO?"

1. Gene Beery, telephone interview by author, May 4, 1012.

2. The quartet played in February 1961, with Thelonious Monk on piano, Charles Rouse on tenor sax, John Ore on bass, and Frank Dunlop on drums.

3. Beery, interview by author.

4. Before World War II, Céline wrote anti-Semitic pamphlets and supported the Axis powers. LeWitt's interest in his work transcended these facts. The question (both then and now) is whether you can separate the artist from the person. The primary argument of this biography is that you cannot, but LeWitt saw things differently.

5. Carol LeWitt, interview by author, Chester, Connecticut, May 29, 2013.

6. Beery, interview by author.

7. Ibid.

8. Robert Mangold, interview by author, Washingtonville, New York, October 27, 2012.

9. Ibid.

10. Ibid.

11. Ibid.

12. Ibid.

13. Marcia Tucker, "Sol LeWitt," *ARTnews*, February 1968, 28.

14. Lawrence Weiner, interview by author, New York, February 1, 2013.

15. Sylvia Plimack Mangold, interview by author, Washingtonville, New York, October 27, 2012.

16. Weiner, interview by author.

17. Andrew Wilson, "Sol LeWitt Interviewed," *Art Monthly*, March 1993, 153.

18. Isaacson, *Leonardo*, chapter 4.

19. Quoted in Roberts, *Converging Lines*, 64.

20. Quoted in Linda Boersma, "Jo Baer Interview," *Bomb*, Fall 1995, 46.

21. John Bernard Myers, "The Cultural Season," *Art and Literature*, Autumn 1964, 77.

22. Lucy Lippard, interview by author, New Haven, Connecticut, April 14, 2015.

23. Ibid.

24. Robert Barry, interview by author, New York City, June 7, 2015.

25. Dorothy and Herb Vogel, interview by author, New York City, January 15, 2008.

26. Sasaki, *Herb and Dorothy*.

27. Vogels, interview by author.

28. Sol LeWitt, undated letter to Megumi Sasaki, director of *Herb and Dorothy*, a copy of which is in the LeWitt Collection. He also wrote in the letter: "Herb & Dorothy came to my studio every week to talk about art. I would tell them about artists whose work I admired such as Bob Mangold, Eva Hesse, Richard Tuttle, Dan Flavin, Mel Bochner, Bob Barry. . . . Their collection is one I have not seen in its totality but it must be one of the most comprehensive of its time, not because of any blockbuster icons it contains but because it gives a depth and shape to the period."

29. Quoted in ibid.

30. Sasaki, *Herb and Dorothy*.

31. Ibid.

32. Vogels, interview by author.

33. LeWitt, undated letter to Sasaki.

34. Vogels, interview by author.

35. Ibid.

36. Ibid.

37. LeWitt, undated letter to Sasaki.

38. Vogels, interview by author.

39. Mary Peacock, interview by author, New York City, February 26, 2013.

40. Marjorie Strider, telephone interview by author, March 14, 2013.

41. Vogels, interview by author.

42. "60 Minutes," January 8, 1995, https://www.cbsnews.com/videos/the-vogels/.

43. Vogels, interview by author.

44. Ibid.

45. Quoted in O'Connor, *From Notes on Patronage*, 162.

46. Ibid.

47. Alberro, *Conceptual Art and the Politics of Publicity*, 9.

48. Naifeh, *Culture Making*, 55.

49. Quoted in Patricia Norvell, "Seth Siegelaub," in Alberro and Norvell, *Recording Conceptual Art*, 31.

50. Tony Candido, telephone interview by author, August 17, 2014.

51. Meyer, *Minimalism*, 151.

52. Veronica Roberts, "Opening LeWitt's Early Boxes," in Roberts, *Converging Lines*, 37.

53. Ibid.

54. Brian Doherty, "Art Avant-Garde Deadpans on the Move," *New York Times*, April 11, 1964.

55. Dan Graham, undated letter to Eva Hesse, Eva Hesse Archive, Allen Memorial Art Museum, Oberlin College, Oberlin, Ohio.

56. Quoted in Sabine Breitwieser, "Interview with Dan Graham, Artist," Museum of Modern Art Oral History Program, November 1, 2011, https://www.moma.org/momaorg/shared/pdfs/docs/learn/archives/transcript_graham.pdf.

57. Quoted in Mike Metz, "Dan Graham," *Bomb*, Winter 1994, 24.

58. Saul Ostrow, "Sol LeWitt," *Bomb*, October 1, 2003, 24.

59. Anne Hoene, "In the Galleries: Sol LeWitt," *Arts*, September–October, 1965, 64.

60. Sol LeWitt, letter to Eva Hesse and Tom Doyle, January 18, 1965, Eva Hesse Archive.

61. Robert Smithson, "Entropy and the New Monuments, *Artforum*, June 1966, https://www.robertsmithson.com/essays/entropy_and.htm.

62. Mel Bochner, eulogy for Sol LeWitt, April 15, 2007. Author has a tape recording of the memorial service eulogies made by Michael LeWitt.

63. Ibid.

64. Dwan, *Dwan Gallery*, 247.

65. Ibid., 248.

66. Ibid.

67. Paul Cummings, "Oral History Interview with Sol LeWitt," July 15, 1974, https://www.aaa.si.edu/collections/interviews/oral-history-interview-sol-lewitt-12701#transcript.

68. Dwan, *Dwan Gallery*, 249.

69. Mel Bochner, "Sol LeWitt," *Arts*, September–October 1966, reprinted in Zevi, *Sol LeWitt Critical Texts*, 147.

70. Quoted in ibid.

71. Peter Schjeldahl, "By Lonely, Difficult Evolutions," *New York Times*, February 18, 1968.

72. Cummings, "Oral History Interview with Sol LeWitt."

73. Ibid.

74. Ibid.

75. Ibid.

76. Larry Bell, telephone interview by author, April 8, 2014.

77. Charles W. Haxthausen, "The Well-Tempered Grid: On Sol LeWitt and Music," in Haxthausen, *The Well-Tempered Grid*, 19.

78. Sol LeWitt, AZ Quotes, https://www.azquotes.com/quote/1435855.

79. Bochner, "Sol LeWitt," 147.

80. Quoted in Lippard, "Homage to the Square," *Art in America*, July–August 1967, 55.

81. LeWitt, "The Cube," *Art in America*, Summer 1966, reprinted in Zevi, *Sol LeWitt Critical Texts*, 72.

82. The show was later considered to be the first major exhibit of minimalism. Of the forty-two artists whose work was on display, only three were women—a typical percentage for the time.

83. Quoted in Meyer, *Minimalism*, 151.

84. Quoted in ibid.

85. Hilton Kramer, "Art: David Von Schlegell at a Happy Standstill; Nonmoving Sculptures at the Royal Marks and Other Current Shows Are Summarized," *New York Times*, May 21, 1966.

86. Mary Peacock, interview by author, New York, February 26, 2013.

87. Lucy R. Lippard, "Sol LeWitt: Non-Visual Structures," *Artforum*, April 1967, 38.

88. Sol LeWitt, postcard to Virginia Dwan, April 28, 1971.

89. Carl Andre, interview by author, New York, April 24, 2012.

90. Ibid.

8. PARAGRAPHS OF ART

1. Paul Cummings, "Oral History Interview with Sol LeWitt," July 15, 1974, https://www.aaa.si.edu/collections/interviews/oral-history-interview-sol-lewitt-12701#transcript.

2. Mary Peacock, interview by author, New York, February 26, 2013.

3. Ibid.

4. Ibid.

5. The exhibit was at the Instituto Torcuato di Tella, in the useo de Artes Visuales. LeWitt took the opportunity to also visit Rio de Janeiro and Lima, Peru.

6. Susana Torre, letter to author, March 5, 2015.

7. Peacock interview by author.

8. Ibid.

9. LeWitt's calendars are stored in unnumbered boxes in the LeWitt Collection.

10. Quoted in Katy Siegel and David Reed, "Making Waves: The Legacy of Lee Lozano," *Artforum*, October 2001, 77. Part of Lozano's rebellion, as expressed in her *Dropout Piece*, was to refuse to speak to other women for six months in the hope that afterward her relationships with them would be better. LeWitt recalled

that waitresses knew that Lozano wouldn't acknowledge their presence (ibid.). In 2014, Carol LeWitt told the writer Jo Applin that whenever she saw Lozano during this period, the artist would cover her eyes and turn away (Jo Applin, "Lee Lozano's Dropouts," *October*, spring 2016, 75–99, https://courtauld.pure.elsevier.com/ws/portalfiles/portal/8335997).

11. Quoted in Siegel and Reed, "Making Waves," 122.

12. Sol LeWitt, "I Find It Difficult to Write a Statement," in Varian, *Art in Process*.

13. "Readymades" was the term used by Duchamp to describe his works that featured manufactured objects.

14. For more on this movement, see Killein and Hendricks, *Fluxus*.

15. Andrea Miller-Keller, "Excerpts from a Correspondence, 1981–1983," in Zevi, *Sol LeWitt Critical Texts*, 102.

16. Andrew Wilson, "Sol LeWitt Interviewed," *Art Monthly*, March 1993, 152.

17. Sol LeWitt, "Paragraphs on Conceptual Art," *Artforum*, April 1967.

18. Quoted in Nika Knight, "Slowly Adapting Art: Moving with the Times: Re-installing Originals," *Oberlin Review*, April 27, 2007, http://www2.oberlin.edu/stupub/ocreview/2007/04/27/arts/Slowly_Adapting_Art_Moving.html.

19. Miller-Keller, "Excerpts from a Correspondence," 102.

20. Nye (1850–1896) was an American humorist. His view on Wagner's music was quoted in Mark Twain, *Tramps Abroad*, 191. However, some historians believe that Nye's comment was about classical music in general.

21. LeWitt made these remarks at MoMA during his retrospective. He was reluctant to speak but was required to as part of his arrangement with the museum.

22. Ibid.

23. Beckett, *Wortward Ho*, 3.

24. Quoted in Rosalind Krauss, "LeWitt in Progress," in Zevi, *Sol LeWitt Critical Texts*, 247.

25. Cummings, "Oral History Interview with Sol LeWitt."

26. LeWitt, "Paragraphs on Conceptual Art," 79.

27. Sol LeWitt, "Serial Project #1," in Zevi, *Sol LeWitt Critical Texts*, 75–77.

28. Sol LeWitt, "Interview by Gary Garrels," *New Art Examiner*, December 2000–January 2001, 15.

29. Robert Rosenblum, "Notes on Sol LeWitt," in Legg, *Sol LeWitt*, 15.

30. Sol LeWitt, "Sentences on Conceptual Art," in Zevi, *Sol LeWitt Critical Texts*.

31. Alexander van Grevenstein, "De Aidebus, Sacris and on Beauty," in Zevi, *Sol LeWitt Critical Texts*, 321.

32. Robert Smithson, *Art International*, March 1968, 33.

33. LeWitt, "Sentences on Conceptual Art," 88.

34. Baldessari, "John Baldessari Sings LeWitt."

35. Martin Friedman, interview by author, New York, July 21, 2013.

36. Quoted in Jane Rainwater, telephone interview by author, October 16, 2012.

37. Robert Barry, interview by author, New York, June 7, 2015.

38. Quoted in ibid.

39. John Baldessari, telephone interview by author, September 18, 2013.

40. Adrian Piper, "Sol: 1928–2007," 2007, http://www.adrianpiper.com/art/sol
.shtml.

41. Adrian Piper letter to author, October 2012.

42. Michael Fried, "Art and Objecthood," *Artforum*, summer 1967, 67.

43. Rosalind Krauss, *Artforum*, April 1968, 57–58.

44. Piper, "Sol: 1928–2007."

45. Adrian Piper, letter to author, October 2012.

46. Ibid.

47. Ibid.

48. The artists in the exhibit included Jasper Johns, Ellsworth Kelly, Jackson Pollack, and Georgia O'Keeffe.

49. Goosen, *The Art of the Real USA*, 11.

50. John Canaday, "The Search for Ultimate Purity," *New York Times*, July 2, 1968.

51. Dorothea Rockburne, email to author, September 14, 2012. In response to the author's request for an interview, Rockburne sent instead the remarks she had prepared following the news of LeWitt's death.

52. Ibid.

53. Ibid.

54. Ibid.

55. Interview of Sol and Carol LeWitt by Adachiara Zevi, 2006, unpublished. This interview, in Chester, Connecticut, was the last that LeWitt gave.

56. Chuck Close, interview by author, New York, June 5, 2012.

57. Ibid.

58. Quoted in Steven Watson, "The Art of Max's," *Max's Kansas City*, 11.

59. Lucy Lippard, interview by author, New Haven, Connecticut, April 14, 2015.

60. Close, interview by author.

61. Ibid.

62. Quoted in Watson, "The Art of Max's," 11.

63. Kosuth. Describing *One and Three Chairs*, a piece he had created in 1965.

64. Ibid.

65. Quoted in "Sol LeWitt," Art Story, 2018, https://www.theartstory.org/artist
-lewitt-sol-artworks.htm.

66. Haden-Guest, *True Colors*.

67. The participants included Andre, Mark Di Suvero, Barnett Newman, Rosemarie Castoro, Dan Graham, Kosuth, Lozano, and dozens of others.

68. Sol LeWitt, "Some Points Bearing on the Relationship of Works of Art to Museums and Collectors," in Zevi, *Sol LeWitt Critical Texts*, 86.

69. Alice Weiner, interview by author, New York, April 12, 2013.

70. Jackie Ferrara, telephone interview by author, August 28, 2012.

71. Janet Passehl, interview by author, Chester, Connecticut, March 6, 2013.

9. UP THE WALLS

1. Quoted in John Slyce, "Hanna Darboven," *Art Monthly*, May 2012, https://www.questia.com/magazine/1G1-289121263/hanne-darboven

2. Quoted in ibid.

3. Daniel Birnbaum, "Art and the Deal" *Artforum*, February 2000, 40.

4. Quoted in ibid.

5. Jan Dibbets, interview by author, Amsterdam August 22, 2015.

6. Ibid.

7. Ibid.

8. Ibid.

9. Quoted in Cherix, *In and Out of Amsterdam*, 100.

10. Rudi Fuchs, interview by author, Amsterdam, August 21, 2015.

11. Dibbets, interview by author.

12. Paul Cummings, "Oral History Interview with Sol LeWitt," July 15, 1974, https://www.aaa.si.edu/collections/interviews/oral-history-interview-sol-lewitt-12701#transcript.

13. Quoted in Jane Rainwater, telephone interview by author, October 16, 2012.

14. Steve Reich, telephone interview by author, September 7, 2014.

15. Ibid.

16. Ibid.

17. Philip Glass, telephone interview by author, March 26, 2015.

18. Glass, *Words without Music*, 226.

19. Quoted by Glass, telephone interview by author.

20. Donald Judd, "Specific Objects," in Seitz, *Contemporary Sculpture*, 74.

21. Andrea Miller-Keller, "Excerpts from a Correspondence, 1981–1983," in Zevi, *Sol LeWitt Critical Texts*, 102.

22. Quoted in Patricia Norvell, in Alberro and Norvell, *Recording Conceptual Art*, 77.

23. Miller-Keller, "Excerpts from a Correspondence," 109.

24. Quoted in Matthew Higgs, "Paula Cooper," *Interview*, August 2, 2012, https://www.interviewmagazine.com/art/paula-cooper.

25. Mel Bochner, eulogy for Sol LeWitt, April 15, 2007. Author has a tape recording of the memorial service eulogies made by Michael LeWitt.

26. Invitation, files of the Paula Cooper Gallery, New York.

27. Quoted in Anna Nosei Weber and Otto Hahn, "Inquiry on the Artistic Situation in the USA and France," reprinted in Zevi, *Sol LeWitt Critical Texts*, 83.

28. Quoted in ibid.

29. Saul Ostrow, "Sol LeWitt," *Bomb*, October 1, 2003, 25.

30. LeWitt quoted in *Metro*, no. 14, June 1968, 14.

31. Lucy R. Lippard, "Dreams, Demands, and Desires: The Black, Antiwar, and Women's Movements," in Campbell, *Tradition and Conflict*, 79–80.

32. Quoted in Grace Glueck, "A Party That Includes You Out," *New York Times*, October 27, 1968.

33. Paula Cooper, interview by author, New York, August 9, 2012. The following quotes from Cooper are also from this interview.

34. Cummings, "Oral History Interview with Sol LeWitt."

35. Cooper, interview by author.

36. LeWitt, "The Draftsman and the Wall," Zevi, *Sol LeWitt Critical Texts*, 93.

37. Robert Barry, interview by author, New York, June 7, 2015.

38. Cooper, interview by author.

39. Sol LeWitt, "Ruth Vollmer: Mathematical Forms," in Zevi, *Sol LeWitt Critical Texts*, 94.

40. Barry, interview by author.

41. Ibid.

42. Ibid.

43. Bernice Rose, "Sol LeWitt and Drawing," in Legg, *Sol LeWitt: The Museum of Modern Art*, 31.

44. Cooper, interview by author.

45. Dwan, *Dwan Gallery*, 34.

46. Rose, "Sol LeWitt and Drawing," 35.

47. Sol LeWitt, in Singer, *Sol LeWitt*, 28.

48. Sol LeWitt, "Wall Drawings," in Zevi, *Sol LeWitt Critical Texts*, 91.

49. Ibid.

50. Interview of Sol and Carol LeWitt by Adachiara Zevi, 2006, unpublished.

51. Sol LeWitt, "Interview by Gary Garrels," *New Art Examiner*, December 2000–January 2001, 46.

52. Ibid.

53. LeWitt, "Wall Drawings," 92.

54. See, for example, *Installation of Sol LeWitt Wall Drawing #50A* and *Sol LeWitt at the Met — Wall Drawing #370 Installation: Days 1–3*.

55. Chris Cobb, "A Perfunctory Affair," December 1, 2008, https://believermag.com/a-perfunctory-affair/.

56. Dibbets, interview by author.

57. Holland Cotter, "Art's Future Meets Its Past: Prada Foundation Remounts a 1969 Exhibition," *New York Times*, August 13, 2013.

58. Barry Barker, "Live in Your Head: When Attitudes Become Form," *Flash Art*, November–December 2010, https://www.flashartonline.com/article/live-in-your-head/.

59. Quoted in Enno Develing, introduction to Develing, *Sol LeWitt*, 9.

60. Quoted in ibid.

61. Quoted in ibid.

62. Quoted in Roberts, *Converging Lines*, 13.

63. Sol LeWitt letter to Sophie LeWitt, April 1, 1970, LeWitt Collection.

64. Quoted in Roberts, *Converging Lines*, 180.

65. Quoted in ibid., 24.

66. Sol LeWitt, notebooks, LeWitt Collection.

67. Ibid.

68. Sol LeWitt, "Artist's Statement," in Develing, *Sol LeWitt*, 5.

10. SEPARATIONS

1. Sol LeWitt curriculum vitae, in Gross, *Sol LeWitt*, 281.

2. Lawrence Weiner, interview by author, New York, February 1, 2013.

3. Alice Weiner, interview by author, New York, February 1, 2013.

4. Ibid.

5. Ibid.

6. Mimi Wheeler, interview by author, New York, December 7, 2013.

7. Ibid.

8. Ibid.

9. Ibid.

10. Susan Ginsburg, interview by author, New York , May 18, 2015.

11. Teerink, *Sol LeWitt*.

12. Carl Andre, interview by author, New York, April 24, 2012.

13. LeWitt postcard to Mimi Wheeler, April 16, 1969, private collection of Wheeler, New York. Wheeler allowed me to read the items in the collection.

14. The quotes are from items in Wheeler's private collection.

15. Wheeler, interview by author.

16. Ibid.

17. Ibid.

18. Ibid.

19. Mimi Wheeler, email to author, October 15, 2015.

20. Petra de Jong, interview by author, The Hague, August 25, 2015.

21. Ibid.

22. The item is in the private collection of Petra de Jong, the Hague.

23. De Jong, interview by author.

24. Ibid.

25. Ibid.

11. CIAO, ITALY

1. Author's conversation with the maître d', Spoleto, October 18, 2005.

2. Bonomo, *But, Where Is Bari?*

3. Marilena Bonomo, interview by author, Bari, Italy, February 22, 2012.

4. Maurizio Calvesi, "L'Arte di Sol LeWitt," *Cartabianca*, May 1968, 51.

5. Bonomo, interview by author.

6. Ibid.

7. Ibid.

8. Interview of Sol and Carol LeWitt by Adachiara Zevi, 2006, unpublished.

9. Ibid.

10. Antonio Carlo Ponti, "Sol LeWitt in Umbria: Traces on a Journey," in Cora and Panzera, *Sol LeWitt in Italia*, 33.

11. Bonomo, interview by author.

12. Ibid.

13. The author, among many others, heard LeWitt say this.

14. Filberto Menna, "Sol LeWitt: A System of Painting," in Zevi, *Sol LeWitt Critical Texts*, 194.

15. Ponti, "Sol LeWitt in Umbria," 33.

16. Interview of Sol and Carol LeWitt by Zevi.

17. Bonomo, interview by author.

18. Interview of Sol and Carol LeWitt by Zevi.

19. Lorenzo Bonomo, interview by author, Bari, Italy, February 22, 2012.

20. Quoted in David Tremlett, "Texts," in Cross and Markonish, *Sol LeWitt, 100 Views*, 117.

21. Quoted in ibid, 120.

22. Quoted in Robin Heidi Kennedy, telephone interview by author, August 14, 2015.

23. Quoted in Michael Brensen, in Singer, *Sol LeWitt Concrete Block Structures*, 13.

24. LeWitt, "Ziggurats," in Zevi, *Sol LeWitt Critical Texts*, 73.

25. Alessandra Bonomo, interview by author, Bari, Italy, February 23, 2012.

26. Beatrice Conrad-Eybesfeld, Skype interview by author, January 28, 2013. The following quotes from Conrad-Eybesfeld are also from this interview.

27. Robert Morris, "Melencolia II," in Gori, *Gori Collection Site Specific Art at the Fattoria di Celle*, 253.

28. Giuliano Gori, interview by author, Pistoia, Italy, November 8, 2013. The following quotes from Gori are also from this interview.

29. Rosemarie Castoro, interview by author, New York, February 4, 2015.

30. John Perreault, "Distillation," *ArtNews*, October 1966, 26.

31. This and the following quoted documents in this paragraph are a part of Andrea Miller-Keller's collection of LeWitt-related material. She let me look through them and make notes.

32. Ibid.

33. Bernice Rose, "Sol LeWitt and Drawing," in Legg, *Sol LeWitt: The Museum of Modern Art*, 36.

34. Quoted in ibid.

35. Lawrence Alloway, *Topics in American Art Since 1945*, 267.

36. The *Flash Art* ad and related material can be found in Gross, *Sol LeWitt*, 230–35.

37. LeWitt's letter to Conrad-Eybesfeld is reprinted in ibid., 235.

38. Sol LeWitt, "Comments on an Advertisement Published in *Flash Art*, April 1973," *Flash Art*, June 1973, 2.

39. Lucio Pozzi letter, Andrea Miller-Keller's collection of LeWitt-related material.

40. Pinchas Cohen Gan letter, ibid.

41. Michael Kirby, "I've Known Sol LeWitt," in Zevi, *Sol LeWitt Critical Texts*, 176.

42. Lawrence Weiner, Miller-Keller's collection of LeWitt-related material

43. Donald B. Kuspit, "The Look of Thought," *Art in America*, September–October, 1975, 76.

44. Joseph Masheck, "Kuspit's LeWitt: Has He Got Style?" in Zevi, *Sol LeWitt Critical Texts*, 226.

45. Ibid.

46. Donald Kuspit, "Letters," *Art in America*, January–February 1977, 5.

47. Joseph Masheck, "Letters," *Art in America*, March–April 1977, 5.

48. Quoted in "Sol LeWitt," *Telegraph*, April 10, 2007.

49. Sol LeWitt letter to James Fitzsimmons, April 22 [no year], LeWitt Collection. The letter may never have been sent.

50. Karen Gunderson, interview by author, New York, January 7, 2014. The following quotes from Gunderson are also from this interview.

12. ART AND TRUST

1. Editorial, "Nomination," *Omaha Herald*, January 26, 1977.

2. Quoted in Dalya Alberge, "It's the Thought That Counts: Sol LeWitt's Involvement with His Art Is So 'Minimalist,' He Leaves Making It to Others," *Independent*, December 22, 1992, https://www.independent.co.uk/arts-entertainment/art-its-the -thought-that-counts-sol-lewitts-involvement-with-his-art-is-so-minimalist-he -leaves-1565005.html.

3. Caroline Tisdall, "Sol LeWitt Exhibition," *Guardian*, June 30, 1971.

4. Quoted in Alberge, "It's the Thought That Counts."

5. Michael Harvey, *South of Houston: Sketches from the Art World in Pen and Youth*, quoted with Harvey's permission.

6. Jo Watanabe, interview by author, New York, June 14, 2014.

7. Ibid.

8. Ibid.

9. Kazuko Miyamoto letter in Andrea Miller-Keller's collection of LeWitt-related material.

10. Anthony Sansotta, telephone interview by author, December 11, 2012. The following quotes from Sansotta are also from this interview.

11. Quoted in Carol Vogel, "Sol LeWitt Throws Curves into a Bastion of the '30s: Christie's Brings a New Mural to Rockefeller Center," *New York Times*, April 22, 1999.

12. Quoted in ibid.

13. Quoted in ibid.

14. Charles W. Haxthausen, "The Well-Tempered Grid: On Sol LeWitt and Music," in Haxthausen, *The Well-Tempered Grid*, 18.

15. Pat Steir, interview by author, New York, August 12, 2012. The following quotes from Steir are also from this interview.

16. Bernice Rose, "A Paragraph on Sol LeWitt," in Cross and Markonish, *Sol LeWitt*, 100.

17. Saatchi, *My Name Is Charles Saatchi and I Am an Artaholic*, 13.

18. Steir, interview by author.

19. Ibid.

20. Ibid.

21. Sol LeWitt, interview by Sharon Zane, May 12, 1994, https://www.moma.org/momaorg/shared/pdfs/docs/learn/archives/transcript_lewitt.pdf.

22. Michael LeWitt, telephone interview by author, July 17, 2012.

23. Grace Glueck, "Jungle Gym for the Mind," *New York Times*, January 29, 1978.

24. Robert Rosenblum, "Notes on Sol LeWitt," in Legg, *Sol LeWitt*, 15.

25. John Russell, "After Cezanne at the Modern," *New York Times*, February 3, 1978.

26. Ibid.

27. Thomas B. Hess, "Sol LeWitt and the Blizzard of Cubes," *New York*, February 27, 1978, 64.

28. Harold C. Richman, letter to Sol LeWitt, March 16, 1978, at the LeWitt Collection.

29. Bernice Rose and Sol LeWitt, "Sol LeWitt," 1978, video recording 78-1B, Museum of Modern Art Archives, New York.

30. Woody Allen and Marshall Brickman, "Manhattan: Screenplay," accessed July 4, 2018, http://yanko.lib.ru/books/cinema/ScreenplayManhattanbyWoodyAllen_sl.htm.

31. Susan Ginsburg, interview by author, New York, May 18, 2015.

32. The author requested interviews with Keaton through her agent and publicist, but neither responded.

33. Julie Ault, "Interview with Lucy R. Lippard on Printed Matter," December 2006, https://www.printedmatter.org/catalog/tables/41.

34. Sol LeWitt, "Sol LeWitt," *Art-Rite*, Winter 1976–77, 10.

35. Ingrid Sischy, telephone interview by author, April 17, 2015. The following quotes from Sischy are also from this interview.

36. Lisa Liebman, telephone interview by author, April 28, 2015.

37. Mike Glier, telephone interview by author, June 3, 2014.

38. Nancy Linn, telephone interview by author, June 27, 2014.

39. Peter Wollen, "Death (and Life) of the Author," *London Review of Books*, February 5, 1998, https://www.lrb.co.uk/v20/no3/peter-wollen/death-and-life-of-the-author.

40. Ibid.

41. Quoted in Peter Wollen, "Kathy Acker," in Scholder, Harryman, and Ronell, *Lust for Life*, 5.

42. Lucinda Childs, interview by author, New York, April 14, 2015.

43. Philip Glass, telephone interview by author, March 26, 2015.

44. Sol LeWitt, letter to Helena Van Dantzig, Lieurac Productions, Paris, August 30, 2005, in a box of memorabilia at the LeWitt Collection.

45. Ibid.

46. Ibid.

47. Judy Padow, telephone interview by author, May 3, 2015.

48. Ibid.

49. Glass, interview by author.

50. Quoted in ibid.

51. Quoted in Childs, interview by author.

52. Glass, interview by author.

53. Philip Glass recalled the incident in a discussion about his memoir, *Words without Music* (interview by Terry Gross, *Fresh Air*, NPR, April 6, 2015).

54. John Rockwell, "Dance: Lucinda Childs and Company," *New York Times*, November 30, 1979.

55. Alan M. Kriegsman, "Dance: Lucinda Childs," *Washington Post*, December 1, 1979.

56. LeWitt, letter to Van Dantzig.

57. Carol Androccio LeWitt, interview by author, Bari, Italy, February 21, 2012.

58. Ibid.

59. Chuck Close, interview by author, New York, June 5, 2012.

60. Carol LeWitt, interview by author.

61. Ibid.

62. Carol Androccio, letter to Sol LeWitt, June 28, 1979, among memorabilia at the LeWitt Collection.

63. Celeste LeWitt, interview by author, Farmington, Connecticut, August 9, 2008.

64. Interview of Sol and Carol LeWitt by Adachiara Zevi, 2006, unpublished.

65. Sol LeWitt, "Interview by Gary Garrels," *New Art Examiner*, December 2000–January 2001.

66. Carol LeWitt, interview by the author, Chester, Connecticut, July 4, 2015.

13. HOMETOWN BLUES

1. Quoted in Andrea Miller-Keller, interview by author, Bloomfield, Connecticut, November 7, 2012.

2. Ibid.

3. Quoted in ibid.

4. Ibid.

5. Ibid.

6. Quoted in "Hartford's Rocks," *Hartford Courant*, November 15, 1997.

7. "Art for the Coliseum," editorial, *Hartford Courant*, July 7, 1980. The editorial also said, "Mr. LeWitt has proposed two dizzying black- and-white striped panels and a three-part mural consisting of a square, a circle and a triangle, on successive backgrounds of red, yellow and blue. His work will do little to humanize an already cold, angular building. The coliseum is no place for intellectual meditation on the nature of art, the response his art is meant to engender."

8. Kathleen Fleming Reed, "The Art of Arrogance," *Hartford Courant*, August 13, 1980.

9. Quoted in Fran Basche, "City Official Consider Changes in Art," *Hartford Courant*, August 13, 1980.

10. Paul Germaine-Brown, letter to the *Hartford Courant*, August 8, 1980.

11. Susanna Singer, letter to the *Hartford Courant*, August 8, 1980.

12. Miller-Keller, interview by author.

13. William Hosley, interview by author, New Britain, Connecticut, January 24, 2013.

14. Ann Barry, "Sol LeWitt Has a Homecoming in Hartford," *New York Times*, September 27, 1981.

15. The three quotes are from letters in Andrea Miller-Keller's collection of LeWitt-related material.

16. Miller-Keller, interview by author.

17. Ibid.

18. Ibid.

19. Albert Speer was one of twenty-three defendants in the first Nuremberg war trial and was sentenced to twenty years in prison.

20. Miller-Keller, interview by author.

21. Mark Rosenthal, telephone interview by author, December 8, 2012.

22. Ibid.

23. Ibid.

24. Quoted in Susanna Singer, interview by author, New York, June 30, 2015.

25. Ibid.

26. Ibid.

27. Ibid.

28. Ibid.

29. Sol LeWitt, "Interview by Gary Garrels," *New Art Examiner*, December 2000–January 2001, 13.

30. Vera Lutter, telephone interview with author, January 29, 2013.

31. Quoted by Marilena Bonomo in a conversation with the author, Bari, Italy, February 21, 2012.

32. Andrea Miller-Keller, "Excerpts from a Correspondence, 1981–1983," in Zevi, *Sol LeWitt Critical Texts*, 102.

33. Ibid.

34. Ibid., 104–5.

35. Ibid., 105.

36. Ann Wood Metelli, interview by author, Spoleto, Italy, November 8, 2014.

37. Ibid.

38. Robin Heidi Kennedy, telephone interview by author, August 14, 2015.

39. Ibid.

40. Lucy Lippard, interview by author, New Haven, Connecticut, April 14, 2015.

41. Ibid.

42. Quoted in Katz, *Naked by the Window*, 12–13.

43. Marilena Bonomo, interview by author, Bari, Italy, February 22, 2012.

44. Katz, *Naked by the Window*, 291.

45. Ibid.

46. Quoted in Carol LeWitt, interview by author, Chester, Connecticut, July 4, 2015.

47. Ibid.

48. The reference was to Restaurant du Village.

49. LeWitt, interview by author.

50. LeWitt, interview by author.

51. Ibid.

52. Ibid.

53. Gabriella de Farrari, interview by author, New York City, August 7, 2015.

54. LeWitt's design efforts on behalf of commercial enterprises included gift boxes for Nina Ricci fragrances.

55. Eva LeWitt comments on parents, circa 1991, LeWitt Collection.

56. Eva LeWitt, interview by author, New York, January 22, 2015.

57. Ibid.

58. Jack Baker, interview by author, Chester, Connecticut, July 10, 2013.

59. Sosse Baker, interview by author, Chester, Connecticut, July 10, 2013.

60. Jack Baker, interview by author.

61. Sosse Baker, interview by author.

62. Ibid.

63. Jack Baker, interview by author.

64. Sosse Baker, interview by author.

65. Patricia Klindienst, interview by author, New Haven, Connecticut, May 9, 2017.

66. Ibid.

67. Peter Good, interview by author, Chester, Connecticut, August 3, 2013.

68. Ibid.

69. Quoted in William L. Schaeffer, interview by author, Chester, Connecticut, May 7, 2015.

70. Ibid.

71. Ibid.

72. Charles van Over and Priscilla Martel, interview by author, Chester, Connecticut, July 14, 2015.

73. Marilyn Buel, interview by author, Essex, Connecticut, September 8, 2014.

74. Ibid.

75. Deb Paulson, interview by author, Chester, Connecticut, August 18, 2013.

76. Morley Safer, "Yes . . . but Is It Art?," *60 Minutes*, September 20, 1993. For more, see Carol Vogel, "Art World Is Not Amused by Critique," *New York Times*, October 4, 1993, and Morley Safer, letter to the *New York Times*, October 5, 1993.

77. Peter Schjeldahl, "The Morley Safer Affair," *Village Voice*, October 26, 1993.

78. Marc Glimsher, Andre Emmerich, and Ellsworth Kelly comments, *60 Minutes*, September 27, 1993.

79. The author witnessed this encounter in the summer of 1997.

14. TOUCHING NERVES

1. Quoted in Barbara Gamarekian, "Show Closing Demanded at Washington Museum," *New York Times*, July 13, 1991.

2. Quoted in ibid.

3. The exhibit was titled *West in America: Reinterpreting Images of the Frontier, 1820–1920*. At the time, Broun had said, "The museum took a major step toward redefining western history, western art and national culture" (quoted in William Deverell, "Fighting Words: The Significance of the American West in the History of the United States," *Western Historical Quarterly* 25, no. 2 [1994]: 187). Andrew Gulliford wrote, "Few Americans were prepared for the blunt and incisive exhibit labels, which sought to reshape the opinions of museum visitors and to jar them out of their traditional assumptions about western art as authentic" ("Review: The West As America: Reinterpreting Images of the Frontier, 1820–1920," *Journal of American History* 79, no. 1 [1993]: 200). In general, the question of government funding came to the fore in cases where exhibits were critical of the actions of the United States.

4. Kim Masters, "Senators Blast Smithsonian for 'Political Agenda'; Appropriations Members Hint at Funding Cuts," *Washington Post*, May 16, 1991.

5. Quoted in Gamarekian, "Show Closing Demanded at Washington Museum."

6. Elizabeth Broun, telephone interview by author, June 18, 2015.

7. Quoted in Gamarekian, "Show Closing Demanded at Washington Museum."

8. Michael Kimmelman, "Peering Into Peepholes and Finding Politics," *New York Times*, July 21, 1991.

9. Jamie James, letter to the editor, *New York Times*, August 11, 1991.

10. Thomasine Bradford, letter to the editor, ibid.

11. Quoted in Barbara Gamarekian, "Museum Restores a Nude to Show," *New York Times*, July 16, 1991.

12. Broun, telephone interview by author.

13. Ibid.

14. Interview of Sol and Carol LeWitt by Adachiara Zevi, 2006, unpublished.

15. Ibid.

16. Ibid.

17. Young, *The Texture of Memory*, 121.

18. Michalski, *Public Monuments*, 173.

19. Peter Friese, "Sol LeWitt: Lost Voices," 2005, http://www.synagoge-stommeln
.de/index.php?n1=2&n2=2&n3=&Direction=130&s=1&lang=engl.

20. Nancy Rosen, telephone interview by author, May 6, 2014.

21. Adorno, *Prisms*, 58.

22. Rosen, telephone interview by author.

23. Godfrey, *Abstraction and the Holocaust*, 227.

24. Ibid.

25. Quoted in ibid., 228.

26. Ibid.

27. Quoted in ibid.

28. Ibid., 229.

29. Witnessed by the author.

30. Stephen Lloyd, speech at the tenth anniversary of the congregation's new
building, Chester, Connecticut, October 21, 2013. Lloyd provided author with a copy.

31. Witnessed by the author.

32. Lloyd speech.

33. Sol LeWitt, dedication, in Gunderson, *Moral Courage during World War II*,
28. Married to the author, Elizabeth Gwillim was one of the congregation's many
Christian members, and she worked passionately on its behalf until her death in
2003. She chose to have her funeral at the synagogue rather than at the Congregational Church in Chester, of which she was also a member.

34. Quoted in Joel Lang, "State Artist Stars in Brazil Exhibit," *Hartford Courant*,
October 8, 1996.

35. Ibid.

36. Quoted in Owen McNally, "LeWitt Mural Distinguishes Atheneum's Spacious New Lobby," *Hartford Courant*, April 13, 1996.

37. Nicholas Baume, telephone interview by author, September 9, 2014. The following quotes from Baume are also from this interview.

38. João Leonardo, Skype interview by author, February 16, 2014.

39. João Leonardo, "Sol LeWitt's Sun," April 2007, http://www.joaoleonardo
.com/texts/sol-lewitt-s-sun."

40. Ibid.

41. Ibid.

42. Leonardo, Skype interview by author.

15. COLLECTING LEWITT

1. Julia Halperin, "How Do You Lose a Work of Conceptual Art? Collector
Sues After Gallery Misplaces Sol LeWitt Certificate," *Blouin Artinfo*, May 29, 2012,

http://www.blouinartinfo.com/news/story/806434/how-do-you-lose-a-work-of
-conceptual-art-collector-sues-after.

2. Daniel Grant, "In 2012's Art World, More Lawsuits Than Art," *HuffPost*, updated February 19, 2013, https://www.huffingtonpost.com/daniel-grant/in-2012s
-art-world-more-1_b_2338534.html.

3. Andrea Miller-Keller, "Excerpts from a Correspondence, 1981–1983," in Zevi, *Sol LeWitt Critical Texts*, 111.

4. Ibid.

5. Rita Reif, "Art of the Mind's Eye Is Part of an Unusual Auction of Conceptual Works," *New York Times*, April 30, 1987. The Gilman Paper Company also sold works by LeWitt contemporaries Dorothea Rockburne, Dan Flavin, and Richard Serra.

6. Marshall Small, "Talk about Lines! A Guy Paid $26,400 for This Drawing—and Then They Demolished It," *People*, May 25, 1987, https://people.com/archive/talk
-about-lines-a-guy-paid-26400-for-this-drawing-and-then-they-demolished-it-vol
-27-no-21/.

7. Quoted in Reif, "Art of the Mind's Eye Is Part of an Unusual Auction of Conceptual Works."

8. Henry McNeil, telephone interview by author, June 11, 2013.

9. Ibid.

10. Susanna Singer, interview by author, New York, June 30, 2015.

11. McNeil, telephone interview by author.

12. Michael Klein, telephone interview by author, July 9, 2014. The following quotes from Klein are also from this interview.

13. Quoted in ibid.

14. Quoted in ibid.

15. Quoted in Carol Vogel, "Sol LeWitt Throws Curves into a Bastion of the '30s: Christie's Brings a New Mural to Rockefeller Center," *New York Times*, April 22, 1999.

16. Quoted in ibid.

17. Quoted in ibid.

18. The account of the party is drawn from the author's own experience that night, referred to the introduction.

19. Andrea Miller-Keller showed a draft of her speech to the author after the event.

20. Martin Friedman, interview by author, New York, July 21, 2013.

21. Martin Friedman, "Sol LeWitt's Birthday Party," Museum of Modern Art newsletter, May 2007, 1.

22. Garrels, "Sol LeWitt, an Introduction," in Garrels, *Sol LeWitt: A Retrospective*, 23.

23. Quoted in ibid., 33.

24. Christopher Knight, "LeWitt Turns the Logical into the Spiritual," *Los Angeles Times*, March 25, 2009.

25. Arthur Lazere, "Sol LeWitt: A Retrospective," Culture Vulture, accessed July 7, 2018, https://culturevulture.net/art-architecture/sol-lewitt-a-retrospective/.

26. Rhona Hoffman, email to the author, August 8, 2015.

27. Ibid.

28. Ibid.

29. Celestine Bohlen, "Step by Step, Sol LeWitt's Work Climbs the Walls at the Whitney," *New York Times*, December 6, 2000.

30. Michael Kimmelman, "Conceptualism, by the Gallon, Covers the Walls," *New York Times*, December 8, 2000.

31. Peter Schjeldahl, "Less Is Beautiful," *New Yorker*, March 13, 2000, 98.

32. Hilton Kramer, "LeWitt's Retrospective: Did He Want to Bore Us?" *Observer*, December 18, 2000.

33. Sol LeWitt, "Paragraphs on Conceptual Art," in Zevi, *Sol LeWitt Critical Texts*, 78.

34. Sol LeWitt, "Sentences on Conceptual Art," in Zevi, *Sol LeWitt Critical Texts*, 88.

35. Sol LeWitt, "Comments on an Advertisement Published in *Flash* Art, April 1973," *Flash Art*, June 1973, 2.

36. Andrew Wilson, "Sol LeWitt Interviewed," *Art Monthly*, March 1993, 152.

37. Tracy Atkinson, untitled entry in Zevi, *Sol LeWitt Critical Texts*, 146.

38. Stolz, *Sol LeWitt Fotografia*, unnumbered page following the book's last photographs.

16. THE WORK OF A LIFETIME

1. Quoted in Jeremy Ziemann, interview by author, Chester, Connecticut, September 14, 2014.

2. Zachary Braiterman, "The Great Wall(s) of Syracuse (Sol LeWitt)," April 18, 2012, features views on the sculpture by Samuel D. Gruber, an art and architecture historian (https://jewishphilosophyplace.com/2012/04/18/the-great-wall-of-syracuse/).

3. Jan Dibbets, interview by author, Amsterdam, August 22, 2015.

4. Dorothy Valakos, "Sol LeWitt," in Prendergast and Prendergast, *Contemporary Artists*, 984.

5. Carol LeWitt, interview by author, Chester, Connecticut, July 4, 2015.

6. Jock Reynolds, interview by author, New Haven, Connecticut, March 19, 2013.

7. Judd, *Complete Writings*, 19.

8. Joseph C. Thompson, interview by author, North Adams, Massachusetts, September 2, 2015.

9. Ibid.

10. Vera Lutter, telephone interview by author, January 29, 2013. The following quotes from Lutter are also from this interview.

11. Gabriella de Farrari, interview by author, New York City, August 7, 2015.

12. Ibid.

13. Carol LeWitt, interview by author.

14. Ibid.

15. Deb Paulson, interview by author, Chester, Connecticut, August 18, 2013.

16. Steve Henry, interview by author, New York, August 9, 2012.

17. Sukey Howard, interview by author, Deep River, Connecticut, August 12, 2014.

18. Marja Bloem, interview by author, Amsterdam, August 20, 2015.

19. Adrian Piper, "Sol: 1928–2007," 2007, http://www.adrianpiper.com/art/sol
.shtml.

20. William Anthony, "William Anthony: Artist," in Cross and Markonish, *Sol Le-
Witt*, 11.

21. William Anastasi, "William Anastasi: Artist," in ibid., 10.

22. Carol LeWitt, interview by author.

23. Quoted in Chuck Close, interview by author, New York, June 5, 2012.

24. Carol LeWitt, interview by author.

25. Close, interview by author.

26. Lutter, telephone interview by author.

27. Susanna Singer, interview by author, New York, June 30, 2015.

28. Quoted in Carol LeWitt, interview by author.

29. Close, interview by author.

EPILOGUE

1. Scott Minner, "Sol LeWitt," April 11, 2007, https://www.legacy.com/obituaries
/name/sol-lewitt-obituary?pid=87165940&page=2.

2. Roger Kimball, "Was Sol LeWitt an Artist?," *New Criterion*, April 10, 2007,
https://www.newcriterion.com/blogs/dispatch/was-sol-lewitt-an-artist.

3. Michael Kimmelman, "Sol LeWitt, Master of Conceptualism, Dies at 78," *New
York Times*, April 8, 2007.

4. Kimball, "Was Sol LeWitt an Artist?"

5. Peter Good, "Remembering Sol Lewitt [*sic*] (1928–2007)," *Design Observer*, July
13, 2007, https://www.designobserver.com/feature/remembering-sol-lewitt-1928
-2007/5547.

6. Carol LeWitt, interview by author, Chester, Connecticut, July 4, 2015.

7. Rabbi Douglas Sagal, eulogy, Chester, Connecticut, April 15, 2007. The following quotes from Segal are also from his eulogy.

8. Chuck Close, eulogy, Chester, Connecticut, April 15, 2007.

9. Mel Bochner, Chester, Connecticut, April 15, 2007.

10. Adrian Piper, "Sol: 1928–2007," 2007, http://www.adrianpiper.com/art/sol
.shtml.

11. Giuliano Gori, interview by author, Pistoia, Italy, November 8, 2013.

12. Nancy Rosen, "Nancy Rosen: Independent Curator and Advisor," in Cross
and Markonish, *Sol LeWitt*, 100.

13. Christopher Knight, "Sol LeWitt's Final Public Wall Drawing," *Los Angeles Times*, March 25, 2009.

14. Quoted by Jasper Nash, email to author, August 14, 2018.

15. Quoted by Joseph C. Thompson, interview by author, North Adams, Massachusetts, September 2, 2015.

BIBLIOGRAPHY

PUBLICATIONS

Adorno, Theodor W. *Prisms*. Cambridge, MA: MIT Press, 1982.

Alberro, Alexander. *Conceptual Art and the Politics of Publicity*. Cambridge, MA: MIT Press, 2003.

——— and Patricia Norvell, eds. *Recording Conceptual Art*. Berkeley: University of California Press, 2001.

Alloway, Lawrence. *Topics in American Art Since 1945*. New York: W. W. Norton, 1980.

Ashbery, John. *Reported Sightings: Art Chronicles, 1957–1987*. Edited by David Bergman. New York: Knopf, 1989.

Beckett, Samuel. *Worstward Ho*. New York: Grove Press, 1983.

Bonomo, Marilena. *But, Where Is Bari? A Journey into Contemporary Art: The Bonomo Gallery since 1971*. Turin, Italy: Umberto Allimondi, 2011.

Burnham, Jack, *Beyond Modern Sculpture; The Effect of Science and Technology on the Sculpture of this Century*, George Braziller, New York, 1968.

Butor, Michel. *Passing Time*. New York: Simon & Schuster, 1960.

Butor, Michel, and Dan Graham. *Conversation*. Edited by Donatien Grau. Berlin: Sternberg Press, 2015.

Campbell, Mary Schmidt, ed. *Tradition and Conflict: Images of a Turbulent Decade, 1963–1973*. New York: Studio Museum in Harlem, 1985.

Cherix, Christopher. *In and Out of Amsterdam: Travels in Conceptual Art, 1960–1976*. New York: Museum of Modern Art, 2009.

Cora, Bruno, and Mauro Panzera, eds. *Sol LeWitt in Italia*. Perugia, Italy: Toro, 1998.

Cross, Susan, and Denise Markonish, eds. *Sol LeWitt: 100 Views*. New Haven, CT: Yale University Press, 2009.

Develing, Enno, ed. *Sol LeWitt*. The Hague, the Netherlands: Haags Gemeentemuseum, 1970.

Dwan, Virginia, *Dwan Gallery: Los Angeles to New York, 1959–1971*. Edited by Judy Metro. Washington: National Gallery of Art, 2016.

Gaddis, Eugene R. *Magician of the Modern: Chick Austin and the Transformation of the Arts in America*. New York: Alfred A. Knopf, 2000.

Garrels, Gary, ed. *Sol LeWitt: A Retrospective*. New Haven, CT: Yale University Press, 2000.

Glass, Philip. *Words without Music*. New York: Liveright, 2015. Kindle.

Godfrey, Mark. *Abstraction and the Holocaust*. New Haven, CT: Yale University Press, 2007.

Gompertz, Will. *What Are You Looking At?: The Surprising, Shocking and Sometimes Strange Story of Modern Art*. New York: Viking, 2012. Kindle.

Goosen, E. C. *The Art of the Real USA, 1948–1968*. New York: Museum of Modern Art, 1968.

Gori, Giuliano. *Gori Collection Site Specific Art at the Fattoria di Celle*. Siena, Italy: Gli Ori, 2009.

Gross, Beatrice, ed. *Sol LeWitt*. Zurich: Editions du Centre Pompidou-Metz, 2012.

Gunderson, Karen. *Moral Courage during World War II: Denmark and Bulgaria*. Edited by Sol LeWitt. Chester, CT: Congregation Beth Shalom Rodfe Zedek.

Haden-Guest, Anthony. *True Colors: The Real Life of the Art World*. New York: Atlantic Monthly Press, 1998.

Haxthausen, Charles W., ed. *Sol LeWitt: The Well-Tempered Grid*. Williamstown, MA: Williams College Museum of Art, 2012.

Hendricks, Gordon. *Eadweard Muybridge: Father of the Motion Picture*. New York: Penguin, 1975.

Hesse, Eva. *Datebooks, 1964/65: A Facsimile Edition*. New Haven, CT: Yale University Press.

Isaacson, Walter. *Leonardo da Vinci*. New York: Simon and Schuster, 2017.

Janson, Horst. *A Basic History of Art*. New York: Harry N. Abrams, 1997.

Judd, Donald. *Complete Writings 1959-1975*. New York: Judd Foundation. 2016.

Kasher, Steven, ed. *Max's Kansas City: Art, Glamour, Rock and Roll*. New York: Abrams Image, 2010.

Katz, Robert. *Naked by the Window: The Fatal Marriage of Carl Andre and Ana Mendieta*. New York: Atlantic Monthly Press, New York, 1990.

Killein, Thomas, and Jon Hendricks. *Fluxus*. London: Thames and Hudson, 1995.

Legg, Alicia, ed. *Sol LeWitt: The Museum of Modern Art*. New York: Museum of Modern Art, 1978.

LeWitt, Sol. *Autobiography*. New York: Multiples, 1980.

———. *Sol Lewitt in Italia*. Perugia, Italy: Gli ori, Maschietto and Musolino, 1998.

Lippard, Lucy R. *Changing: Essays in Art Criticism*. New York: E. P Dutton, 1971.

———. *Eva Hesse*. New York: New York University Press, 1976.

———, ed. *Six Years: The Dematerialization of the Art from 1966 to 1972*. New York: Praeger Publishers, 1973.

McCarthy, Mary. *On the Contrary: Articles of Belief, 1946–1961*. New York: Farrar, Straus, and Cudahy, 1961.

Meyer, James. *Minimalism: Art and Polemics in the Sixties*. New Haven, CT: Yale University Press, 2004.

Michalski, Sergiusz. *Public Monuments: Art and Political Bondage.* London: Reaktion Books, 2013.

Naifeh, Steven W. *Culture Making: Money, Success, and the New York Art World.* Princeton, NJ: Princeton University Press, 1976.

Perl, Jed. *New Art City: Manhattan at Mid-Century.* New York: Vintage Books, 2005.

Prendergast, Sarah, and Tom Prendergast, eds. *Contemporary Artists.* New York: St. James Press, 2002.

Roberts, Veronica. *Converging Lines: Eva Hesse and Sol LeWitt.* New Haven, CT: Yale University Press, 2014.

Saatchi, Charles N. *My Name Is Charles Saatchi and I Am an Artoholic: Everything You Need to Know About Art, Ads, Life, God and Other Mysteries, and Weren't Afraid to Ask.* London: Phaidon, 2009.

Scholder, Amy, Carla Harryman, and Avital Ronnell, eds. *Lust for Life: On the Writings of Kathy Acker.* London: Verso, 2006.

Seitz, William, ed. *Contemporary Sculpture: Arts Yearbook 8.* New York: Arts Digest, 1965.

Singer, Susanna, ed. *Sol LeWitt Concrete Block Structures.* Milan, Italy: Gabrius, 2002.

———, ed. *Sol LeWitt: Wall Drawings, 1984–1992.* Andover (MA): Addison Gallery of American Art, 1992.

Stolz, George. *Sol LeWitt: Fotografia.* Madrid: Fundacion Ico and La Fabrica Editorial, 2003.

Stoppard, Tom. *Travesties.* New York: Grove Press, 1975.

Swenson, Kirsten. *Irrational Judgments: Eva Hesse, Sol LeWitt, and 1960s New York.* New Haven, CT: Yale University Press, 2015.

Thibodeau, Patrick, *New Britain: City of Invention.* Windsor, CT: Windsor Publishing, 1989.

Varian, Elayne H., ed. *Art in Process: The Visual Development of a Structure.* New York: Finch College, 1966.

Young, James E. *The Texture of Memory: Holocaust Memorials and Meaning.* New Haven, CT: Yale University Press, 1993.

Young, La Monte, ed. *An Anthology of Chance Operations.* New York: La Monte Young and Jackson Mac Low, 1963.

Zevi, Adachiara, ed. *Sol LeWitt Critical Texts.* Rome: Incontri Internazionali D'Arte, 1995.

VIDEOGRAPHY

Armstrong, Tim. "Learn to Say F**k You." https://www.youtube.com/watch?v=h2bC-309h4I&t=9s.

Baldessari, John. "John Baldessari Sings LeWitt." 1972. Video Data Bank. http://www.vdb.org/titles/baldessari-sings-lewitt.

Begleiter, Marcie. Eva Hesse, documentary, Zietgiest and Kino Lorber Films, 2016.

Blackwood, Michael. Scene from *Sol LeWitt: 4 Decades*. October 7, 2012. https://www.youtube.com/watch?v=s_4JUZ7Nmog.

Cumberbatch, Benedict. "Sol LeWitt to Eva Hesse." September 26, 2016. https://www.youtube.com/results?search_query=benedict+cumberbatch+sol+lewitt.

Hesse, Eva. "Life Doesn't Last; Art Doesn't Last." April 7, 2016. San Francisco Museum of Art. https://www.youtube.com/watch?v=cpb3xb-yGdY.

Installation of Sol LeWitt Wall Drawing #50A, Modern Art Museum of Fort Worth. July 10, 2013. https://www.youtube.com/watch?v=hys5Jt3PozY.

Sasaki, Megumi, dir. *Herb and Dorothy*. San Francisco, CA: Independent Television Service, 2008.

Sol LeWitt: A Wall Drawing Retrospective. MassMOCA. November 20, 2008. https://www.youtube.com/watch?v=c4cgB4vJ2XY.

Sol LeWitt at the Met — Wall Drawing #370 Installation: Days 1–3. The Met. June 5, 2014. https://www.metmuseum.org/metmedia/video/collections/modern/sol-lewitt-time-lapse-1.

Sol LeWitt at the Met — Wall Drawing 370 Installation: Days 11–14. The Met. June 19, 2014. https://www.youtube.com/watch?v=yGWENojDB6A.

Sol LeWitt Recipes for Art. August 15, 2013. Arts in Context. https://www.youtube.com/watch?v=RIYVHH3LykQ.

Sol LeWitt: Scribble Wall Drawings, September 10–November 30, 2007, Pace Wildenstein Gallery. ConcentrateTV. February 4, 2011. https://www.youtube.com/watch?v=AnKgSWugUWU.

Sol LeWitt: Tate Shots. August 5, 2013. https://www.youtube.com/watch?v=qIHi8FOtWoQ.

Sol LeWitt Wall Drawing #1136. National Galleries. April 27, 2012. https://www.youtube.com/watch?v=QG92R1VRxnI.

Sol LeWitt's Incomplete Open Cubes. San Francisco Museum of Modern Art. September 18, 2013. https://www.youtube.com/watch?v=w9ROCnWMPww&t=37s.

Teerink, Chris, dir. *Sol LeWitt*. Doc.Eye Film. 2012.

Time Lapse of Sol LeWitt's "Wall Drawing # 797." Blanton Museum of Art. July 9, 2014. https://www.youtube.com/watch?v=Gc-c-pYGCrw.

INDEX

207–11; and private collectors,
264–69; reaction to criticism, 127–28,
186–88; scholarship, University of
Illinois, 34–35; and seriality, 65–67,
101–3; 70th birthday celebration,
272–75; and Singer, 225–26; *Sixteen
Americans* exhibition, 63–64; in
Spoleto, 170–90, 226–29; support
of Lutter, 286–88; synagogue
rebuilding, 255–59; Syracuse project,
282; and Syracuse University,
25–33; and Tom Doyle, 73–79; 2000
retrospective, 275–79; and Virginia
Dwan, 104–11; and the Vogels, 95–101;
Wadsworth Atheneum, 218–19,
221–24, 261–62; war experience,
41–47; and Williams College,
284–85. *See also* correspondence;
interviews; wall drawings;
individual works by
LeWitt, Sophie (mother): in
Autobiography, 1–2; life of, 9–12; and
Mimi Wheeler, 163–64; and Nancy
Strider, 59–61; parenting, 15, 18–19;
and Pat Steir, 201–2; as refugee, 6–7
"LeWitt in Progress" (Krauss), 120
"LeWitt's Sistine Chapel." See *Whirls
and Twirls*
Libner, Arnold "Libby," 26, 41–47
Liebman, Lisa, 210
Life (magazine), 100
Linn, Nancy, 210
Lippard, Lucy R.: in *Artforum*, 111;
attitudes toward, 94; on Doyle, 73–
74; *Eva Hesse*, 71; on Hesse, 77; On
Mendieta, 230–31; on *Metronomic
Irregularity II*, 85; MoMa circle,
69–70; on Printed Matter, 207; on
the Vietnam War, 145
Lisson Gallery, London, 191, 269
literalist art. *See* minimalism
lithography, 30–32, 34–35

*Live in Your Head: When Attitudes
Become Form* exhibit, 154–55
Lloyd, Stephen, 257–58
London Review of Books (journal), 211
"The Look of Thought" (Kuspit), 186–87,
203
Los Angeles Times (newspaper), xii, 298
Lost Voices (LeWitt), 252
Louis, Morris, 250
Lozano, Lee, 117, 319–20n10
Lutter, Vera, 59, 227, 286–88, 293

making a living as an artist, 68–69,
139–40
Mangold, Robert, 89–90, 91
Mangold, Sylvia Plimack, 91
Manhattan (film), 205–7
manifesto. *See* "Paragraphs on
Conceptual Art" (LeWitt)
maritime images, 17
marketing, 117, 132–33, 226, 265–66
marketplace. *See* art market
Marmon, Stefan, 256
Marsh, Joanna, xiii
Martel, Priscilla, 240
Martin, Agnes, 183–84
Masheck, Joseph, 187
Massachusetts Museum of
Contemporary Art (MASSMoCA),
153, 285, 297, 299
mathematics, xiv, 58, 125, 186
MATRIX Gallery, 218, 223
Matter, Mercedes, 55
Matthew of Bristol, Spanish warship, 17
Max's Kansas City, 116, 130–32
MCA (Museum of Contemporary Art),
276–77
McCarthy, Mary, 52
McConathy, Dale, 113
McCusker, Danny, 214
McKee, David, 267
McNeil, Henry, 267–69

Garnet Books

Titles with asterisks (*) are also in the Driftless Connecticut Series

*Garnet Poems: An Anthology of
Connecticut Poetry Since 1776**
Dennis Barone, editor

*The Connecticut Prison Association and
the Search for Reformative Justice**
Gordon Bates

*Food for the Dead: On the Trail of
New England's Vampires*
Michael E. Bell

*The Long Journeys Home: The
Repatriations of Henry 'Ōpūkaha 'ia
and Albert Afraid of Hawk**
Nick Bellantoni

*Sol LeWitt: A Life of Ideas**
Lary Bloom

*The Case of the Piglet's Paternity:
Trials from the New Haven Colony,
1639–1663**
Jon C. Blue

Early Connecticut Silver, 1700–1840
Peter Bohan and Philip
Hammerslough

*The Connecticut River:
A Photographic Journey through
the Heart of New England*
Al Braden

*Tempest-Tossed: The Spirit of
Isabella Beecher Hooker*
Susan Campbell

*Connecticut's Fife & Drum Tradition**
James Clark

Sunken Garden Poetry, 1992–2011
Brad Davis, editor

*Rare Light: J. Alden Weir in Windham,
Connecticut, 1882–1919**
Anne E. Dawson, editor

*The Old Leather Man: Historical
Accounts of a Connecticut and
New York Legend*
Dan W. DeLuca, editor

*Post Roads & Iron Horses:
Transportation in Connecticut from
Colonial Times to the Age of Steam**
Richard DeLuca

*The Log Books: Connecticut's Slave
Trade and Human Memory**
Anne Farrow

*Birding in Connecticut**
Frank Gallo

Dr. Mel's Connecticut Climate Book
Dr. Mel Goldstein

*Hidden in Plain Sight:
A Deep Traveler Explores
Connecticut*
David K. Leff

*Maple Sugaring: Keeping It Real
in New England*
David K. Leff

*Becoming Tom Thumb: Charles
Stratton, P. T. Barnum, and the
Dawn of American Celebrity**
Eric D. Lehman

*Homegrown Terror: Benedict Arnold
and the Burning of New London**
Eric D. Lehman

*The Traprock Landscapes of
New England**
Peter M. LeTourneau and
Robert Pagini

*Westover School: Giving Girls
a Place of Their Own*
Laurie Lisle

ABOUT THE DRIFTLESS CONNECTICUT SERIES

The Driftless Connecticut Series is a publication award program established in 2010 to recognize excellent books with a Connecticut focus or written by a Connecticut author. To be eligible, the book must have a Connecticut topic or setting or an author must have been born in Connecticut or have been a legal resident of Connecticut for at least three years.

The Driftless Connecticut Series is funded by the
Beatrice Fox Auerbach Foundation Fund
at the Hartford Foundation for Public Giving.
For more information and a complete list
of books in the Driftless Connecticut Series,
please visit us online at
http://www.wesleyan.edu/wespress/driftless.